THE COLLECTED WORKS OF
SAMUEL TAYLOR COLERIDGE . 13

LOGIC

General Editor: KATHLEEN COBURN
Associate Editor: BART WINER

THE COLLECTED WORKS

Memento III.

We commenced ~~our present inquiry~~ by adopting the old division of Knowledge into the Theoretic, or intellective; and the Practical, or that which respects the acts of the will, the judgments of Conscience, the Rules of Conduct, and the ~~~~ of the practical reason: and ~~~~ settled, that as far as the present inquiry was concerned our attention was to be given exclusively to the former i.e. the Theoretic.

It was next determined that we should confine our inquisition, to the data presented to us by Reflection, and as they appear to us in the act of reflecting; and to the immediate inferences from these, made necessary by the laws of ~~the~~ Reflection. ~~~~ What those laws are, is a subject ~~~~ for future enquiry; but be they what they ~~~~ it is easy to imagine some Superior Being, ~~~~ of contemplating ~~~~ the individual minds and ~~~~ objects ~~~~ of ~~~~ how far and in what manner the ~~~~ are modified ~~~~ the human mind by its own mechanism; and lastly of looking at the Objects independent of such modification. Now he, who disclaims all pretensions to ~~answer,~~ such as we have ~~~~ imagined ~~in the~~ ~~~~ prerogative of this kind, or who, tho' believing that a substitute, or a something analogous to it, subsists even for the human intelligence, ~~~~ from it and ~~~~ to reason without reference ~~~~ in the same way as he would ~~~~ intelligence, nevertheless abstracts (i.e. voluntarily withdraws his attention) from it and agrees to reason as tho' no such power existed, is said to ~~~~ or reason of things stand on the point of Reflection. And here we agreed to take our position – i.e. to ~~~~ take things as they appeared from the point of reflection, and to assume nothing

1. A draft of a section of the *Logic* in Coleridge's hand.
See p 245, below.

THE COLLECTED WORKS OF

Samuel Taylor Coleridge

Logic

EDITED BY

J. R. de J. Jackson

ROUTLEDGE & KEGAN PAUL

✤ BOLLINGEN SERIES LXXV

PRINCETON UNIVERSITY PRESS

The Collected Works, sponsored by Bollingen Foundation,
is published in Great Britain
by Routledge & Kegan Paul Ltd
39 Store Street, London WC1E 7DD and Broadway House,
Newtown Road, Henley-on-Thames, Oxon RG9 1EN
ISBN 0 7100 0254 8
and in the United States of America
by Princeton University Press, Princeton, New Jersey
ISBN 0-691-09880-8
LCC 68-10201
The Collected Works constitutes
the seventy-fifth publication in Bollingen Series

The present work is number 13 of the Collected Works

Designed by Richard Garnett
Printed in the United States of America
by Princeton University Press

THIS EDITION
OF THE WORKS OF
SAMUEL TAYLOR COLERIDGE
IS DEDICATED
IN GRATITUDE TO
THE FAMILY EDITORS
IN EACH GENERATION

CONTENTS

LIST OF ILLUSTRATIONS

ACKNOWLEDGMENTS

EDITORS have good reason to be aware of their debts to their predecessors. In my own case I owe a great deal to the preliminary investigations of Alice D. Snyder. Had it not been for the existence of her *Coleridge on Logic and Learning*, I doubt that I should have ventured to tackle Coleridge's *Logic*. In building on her foundations I have been assisted by many others. The recent completion of Earl Leslie Griggs's edition of the *Collected Letters of Samuel Taylor Coleridge* seems in retrospect to have been indispensable; and advance access first to Volume III of Kathleen Coburn's edition of *The Notebooks of Samuel Taylor Coleridge* and, more recently, to some of the information in the forthcoming Volume IV has been a most important privilege. I have benefited from earlier volumes of *The Collected Works of Samuel Taylor Coleridge*, and editorial colleagues have been able to give me advice based on some of the volumes that have yet to appear. Two books were published late enough in my preparation for me to realise how very much I had needed them: G. N. Orsini's *Coleridge and German Idealism* and Thomas McFarland's *Coleridge and the Pantheist Tradition*. Wherever possible I have revised in the light of their discussions.

Colleagues and friends have contributed willingly and sometimes unawares. It is a pleasure to record their names here, although the list can only be an imperfect one: Merton Christensen, E. G. Clarke, Thomas McFarland, Eric Rothstein, G. N. Orsini, C. A. Silber, D. W. Smith, George Whalley, and Ian Willison. My greatest personal debts are four: to Kathleen Coburn for first having invited me to edit the *Logic*, and for her patient and steadying advice and close reading over the years; to Bart Winer for his unfailingly alert eye for inconsistencies and mistakes and for his tact in drawing them to my attention; to Lorna Arnold for trying to repair the inadequacies of my Greek and Latin (such flaws as may remain must be attributed to my failures to understand good advice); and finally to H. J. Jackson, who has shared the presence of this edition in the family, reading and proofreading it with me and adding good things to its notes.

The following people kindly replied to letters of enquiry: F. A. Reeve, the Manager of Bowes and Bowes (Cambridge); H. R. Creswick, the Librarian of the University Library, Cambridge; L. M. White, from the Headmaster's office, Merchant Taylors' School; H. M. Colvin, the Librarian, St John's College, Oxford; and the Librarian of the Postgraduate Medical Library, the Radcliffe Infirmary, Oxford. Helpful information was provided by the Archivist of the Vintners' Company and by Bernard Stutfield. These kindnesses to a complete stranger were much appreciated.

I have enjoyed the use of the following libraries and have been helped by their staff: The British Library—its Department of Manuscripts, its Newspaper Library at Colindale, and, especially, its Department of Printed Books; the Middlesex County Archive; the Library of the Ontario Legislature; the State Library of Austria; Somerset House; the University of Toronto Library; the Library of the University of Vienna; the Library of the Victoria and Albert Museum; Victoria College Library; and Dr Williams's Library. Microfilms have been helpfully provided by the Henry E. Huntington Library and by the Widener Library of Harvard University.

I am indebted to the Canada Council for supporting a year's leave of absence and for several grants in aid of summer research. The work has also been supported by the University of Toronto, Bollingen Foundation, and Princeton University Press.

Victoria College   J. R. DE J. JACKSON
University of Toronto
24 February 1978

EDITORIAL PRACTICE, SYMBOLS, AND ABBREVIATIONS

J. H. MUIRHEAD said of the manuscript of Coleridge's *Logic* that it is "manifestly incomplete, and bears the marks of illiteracy on every page".[1] In fact the manuscript is in very much the state that one would expect of an uncorrected transcription of a text originally taken down from dictation. It lacks essential punctuation; its sentences are frequently not separated from one another or are separated at the wrong point; its paragraphing is erratic and sometimes contrary to the sense of what is being said; it abounds in misspellings, words misheard, foreign words mistranscribed (in the case of Greek phrases, often left out with only a blank space to indicate the author's intentions). Uncorrected, the manuscript makes slow reading.

To have recorded all the corrections would have eased the editor's mind, but it would have required massive and obtrusive textual annotation. In the event, obvious misspellings have been corrected silently; corrections of other obvious mistakes are recorded in the textual notes. Henry Nelson Coleridge's tale of the shorthand writer who was asked to take down Coleridge's lectures on Shakespeare reminds one of the dangers: "with regard to every other speaker whom he had ever heard, however rapid or involved, he could almost always, by long experience in his art, guess the form of the latter part, or apodosis, of the sentence by the form of the beginning; but...the conclusion of every one of Coleridge's sentences was a *surprise* upon him. He was obliged to listen to the last word."[2] An editor's tendency, when he comes to correct a text, is like the shorthand writer's; he expects what is normal. For Coleridge the normal is often not good enough. Although an effort has been made to keep textual annota-

[1] John H. Muirhead *Coleridge as Philosopher* (1930) 268. For details of the manuscript, see "Description", below. Here and throughout this edition, the title *Logic* will refer only to British Museum MS Egerton 2825 and 2826, and not to other writings planned, begun, or completed by Coleridge on the general subject of logic. Related manuscript fragments are presented in Appendixes B–E, two of them from what Alice D. Snyder called the "Bristol Notebook", which is now referred to as VCL MS BT 16. This manuscript is described in *L&L* (pp

52–3) and its various parts are printed there in full (pp 53–4, 54–66, and 139–52). One of these, entitled "Outlines of the History of Logic: Chapter I. Of Philosophy in General" (*L&L* 54–66) is arguably a trial run for Chapter I of the "Introductory Parts" of the *Logic*, but its mode is partly allegorical, and, as its subtitle suggests, its subject matter is considerably wider; it has therefore been reserved for separate presentation in *Shorter Works and Fragments*.

[2] *C Talker* 145.

tion to a minimum, emendations that altered the sense or could in any way be regarded as doubtful have therefore been recorded.

Coleridge's footnotes are indicated by symbols (*, †, etc) and are printed full measure. Editor's footnotes are numbered and (when not too brief) printed in double columns. The order of the editor's footnotes follows (perhaps Coleridgian) logic: i.e. it is assumed that when the text contains an asterisk or a dagger the reader then turns from text to note and then goes back again. The editor's footnotes, which are sometimes notes on Coleridge's footnotes, follow that order. Thus the footnote indicators within the text may leap from 1 to 5, notes 2–4 being notes on Coleridge's footnotes. Textual notes ($^{a-b}$, etc) appear at the foot of the page, preceding the editor's notes. The spelling and punctuation, which reflect the habits of the unknown transcribers and amanuenses and not Coleridge's practice, have been standardised.[1] The foliation numbers of the manuscript are recorded in square brackets—[1 4]—at the beginning of each chapter. Paragraphs have been numbered to make them easier to refer to in the editor's analytical outline (Appendix G),[2] and the editor's subdivisions of paragraphs are indicated by a letter in parentheses—2(a), 2(b), etc. Greek breathings have been added where necessary, but Greek accents, which Coleridge, like many of his contemporaries, frequently did not use, have not been. Greek words have been inserted by the editor only when blank spaces were left for them in the manuscript. Passages presented explicitly as quotations have been placed within quotation marks when these were lacking. Quotation marks have also been placed around long quotations in languages other than English. The editions referred to in the editor's foot-notes are the ones that Coleridge used, when these are known, but cross references to standard texts or to section numbers of works conveniently subdivided are also provided. The following symbols are used (with "logic" as an example):

[logic]   A reading supplied by the editor
[?logic]   An uncertain reading
[. . .]   An illegible word or phrase
⟨logic⟩   A later interpolation

---

[1] In Appendixes B–F manuscripts in Coleridge's hand are reproduced literatim, including his cancellations, with the exception that "it's" (possessive) has been normalised to "its", for the light they may throw on his processes of composition. Cancelled passages that cannot be deciphered have been omitted.

[2] Coleridge seems to have felt that the numbering of paragraphs, so common in philosophical works, could be an advantage. He wrote to J. H. Green on 30 Sept 1818 about memoranda of their recent conversations, "the numbering of §§s, and the references to numbered §§s, we shall find very convenient, preventing repetitions and yet increasing the sense of connection and continuity". *CL* IV 873.

ABBREVIATIONS

(In the works listed, place of publication is London unless otherwise noted)

AR (1825)	S. T. Coleridge *Aids to Reflection* (1825).
BL (1907)	S. T. Coleridge *Biographia Literaria* ed John Shawcross (2 vols Oxford 1907).
BM	British Library, formerly British Museum
B Works	*The Works of George Berkeley* ed A. A. Luce and T. E. Jessop (9 vols 1948–57).
C	Samuel Taylor Coleridge
C&S (*CC*)	S. T. Coleridge *On the Constitution of the Church and State* ed John Colmer (London and Princeton, N.J. 1976). *The Collected Works of Samuel Taylor Coleridge* x.
C at H	Lucy E. Watson *Coleridge at Highgate* (1925).
CC	*The Collected Works of Samuel Taylor Coleridge* (London and Princeton, N.J. 1969–).
C d r V	Immanuel Kant *Critik der reinen Vernunft* (2nd ed Riga 1787). The corresponding page numbers of Norman Kemp Smith tr *Immanuel Kant's Critique of Pure Reason* (London and New York 1933) are given in parentheses after each reference.
CL	*Collected Letters of Samuel Taylor Coleridge* ed Earl Leslie Griggs (6 vols Oxford and New York 1956–71).
C Life (G)	James Gillman *The Life of Samuel Taylor Coleridge* (1838).
CN	*The Notebooks of Samuel Taylor Coleridge* ed Kathleen Coburn (New York, Princeton, N.J., and London 1957–).
CRB	*Henry Crabb Robinson on Books and Their Writers* ed Edith J. Morley (3 vols 1938).
C 17ʰ C	*Coleridge on the Seventeenth Century* ed Roberta F. Brinkley (Durham, N.C. 1955).
C Talker	R. W. Armour and R. F. Howes *Coleridge the Talker* (1949).
DC	Derwent Coleridge
De Q	Thomas De Quincey
De Q Works	*The Collected Writings of Thomas De Quincey* ed David Masson (14 vols 1896–7).
DNB	*Dictionary of National Biography* (1885–).

DW	Dorothy Wordsworth
D Works	_The Philosophical Works of Descartes_ ed E. S. Haldane and G. R. T. Ross (2 vols Cambridge 1911).
_EB_	_The Encyclopaedia Britannica_ (11th ed 29 vols Cambridge 1910–11).
Ed Rev	_Edinburgh Review_ (Edinburgh [1802]–1929).
EHC	Ernest Hartley Coleridge
Friend (CC)	Samuel Taylor Coleridge _The Friend_ ed Barbara E. Rooke (2 vols London and Princeton, N.J. 1969). _The Collected Works of Samuel Taylor Coleridge_ IV.
Gillman SC	_Catalogue of a Valuable Collection of Books_ Henry Southgate & Co (No. 805 Thursday 30 March 1843).
Green SC	_Catalogue of the Library of Joseph Henry Green...sold by auction_ (Sotheby Jul 1880). Marked copy: BM S-C S 805 (1).
HC	Hartley Coleridge
HEHL	Henry E. Huntington Library
HNC	Henry Nelson Coleridge
Kant in England	René Wellek _Immanuel Kant in England_ (Princeton and London 1931).
Kneale	William Kneale and Martha Kneale _The Development of Logic_ (Oxford 1964).
_L&L_	_Coleridge on Logic and Learning_ ed Alice D. Snyder (New Haven and London 1929).
LCL	Loeb Classical Library
Lects 1795 (CC)	S. T. Coleridge _Lectures 1795: on Politics and Religion_ ed Lewis Patton and Peter Mann (London and Princeton, N.J. 1971). _The Collected Works of Samuel Taylor Coleridge_ I.
Logic	BM MSS Egerton 2825 and 2826.
Logik	Immanuel Kant _Logik: ein Handbuch zu Vorlesungen_ ed Gottlob Benjamin Jäsche (Königsberg 1800). The corresponding page numbers of Thomas Kingsmill Abbott tr _Kant's Introduction to Logic_ ... (1885) are given in parentheses after each reference.
_LR_	_The Literary Remains of Samuel Taylor Coleridge_ ed H. N. Coleridge (4 vols 1836–9).
_LS (CC)_	S. T. Coleridge _A Lay Sermon_ ed R. J. White (London and Princeton, N.J. 1972). In _Lay Sermons: The Collected Works of Samuel Taylor Coleridge_ VI.
L Works	_The Works of Charles and Mary Lamb_ ed E. V. Lucas (7 vols 1912).
M Chron	_The Morning Chronicle_ (1769–1862).

MLN	*Modern Language Notes* (1886–).
MPL	S. T. Coleridge *A Moral and Political Lecture* (Bristol [1795]).
M Post	*The Morning Post* (1772–1937).
N	Notebook (numbered or lettered) of S. T. Coleridge
N&Q	*Notes and Queries* (1849–).
NYPL	New York Public Library
OED	*Oxford English Dictionary* (13 vols Oxford 1933).
Omniana	*Omniana, or Horae Otiosiores* ed Robert Southey with articles by S. T. Coleridge (2 vols 1812).
Orsini	Gian N. G. Orsini *Coleridge and German Idealism* (Carbondale and Edwardsville, London and Amsterdam 1969).
Phil Trans	*Philosophical Transactions of the Royal Society* (1665–1886).
P Lects (1949)	*The Philosophical Lectures of Samuel Taylor Coleridge* ed Kathleen Coburn (London and New York 1949).
Prelude (1959)	William Wordsworth *The Prelude* ed Ernest de Selincourt rev Helen Darbishire (1959).
Prolegomena	Immanuel Kant *Prolegomena zu einer jeden künftigen Metaphysik . . .* (Riga 1783).
PW (EHC)	*The Complete Poetical Works of Samuel Taylor Coleridge* ed Ernest Hartley Coleridge (2 vols Oxford 1912)
RS	Robert Southey
RSL	Royal Society of Literature
RSL Trans	*Transactions of the Royal Society of Literature* (Second Series 37 vols 1843–1919).
SC	Sara Coleridge
SH	Sara Hutchinson
Sh C	*Coleridge's Shakespearean Criticism* ed Thomas Middleton Raysor (2 vols 1960).
SH Letters	*The Letters of Sara Hutchinson from 1800 to 1835* ed Kathleen Coburn (Toronto 1954).
SM (CC)	S. T. Coleridge *The Statesman's Manual* ed R. J. White (London and Princeton, N.J. 1972). In *Lay Sermons: The Collected Works of Samuel Taylor Coleridge* VI.
Stanley	Thomas Stanley *The History of Philosophy* (3rd ed 1701).

Tennemann	Wilhelm Gottlieb Tennemann *Geschichte der Philosophie* (11 vols Leipzig 1798–1819).
TL (1848)	S. T. Coleridge *Hints Towards the Formation of a More Comprehensive Theory of Life* ed Seth B. Watson (1848).
TT	*Specimens of the Table Talk of the Late Samuel Taylor Coleridge* ed Henry Nelson Coleridge (1835).
VCL	Victoria College Library, University of Toronto.
VS	Immanuel Kant *Vermischte Schriften* (4 vols Halle and Königsberg 1799–1807).
Watchman (*CC*)	S. T. Coleridge *The Watchman* ed Lewis Patton (London and Princeton, N.J. 1970). *The Collected Works of Samuel Taylor Coleridge* II.
WL (*M* rev)	*The Letters of William and Dorothy Wordsworth: the Middle Years* ed Ernest de Selincourt, rev Mary Moorman and Alan G. Hill (2 vols Oxford 1969–71).
WPW	*The Poetical Works of William Wordsworth* ed Ernest de Selincourt and Helen Darbishire (5 vols Oxford 1940–9).
WW	William Wordsworth

CHRONOLOGICAL TABLE

1772–1834

1772	(21 Oct) C b at Ottery St Mary, Devonshire, to the Rev John and Ann (Bowdon) Coleridge, youngest of their 10 children	George III king (1760–1820) Wordsworth 2 years old Scott 1 year old *M Post* began
1774		RS b
1775		American War of Independence C. Lamb b
1776		Adam Smith *Wealth of Nations* Gibbon *Decline and Fall* (–1788)
1778		Hazlitt b Rousseau and Voltaire d
1780		(Jun) Gordon Riots
1781	(Oct) Death of C's father	Kant *Critik der reinen Vernunft* Schiller *Die Räuber*
1782	(Jul) Enrolled at Christ's Hospital preparatory school for girls and boys, Hertford (Sept) Christ's Hospital School, London, with C. Lamb, G. Dyer, T. F. Middleton, Robert Allen, J. M. Gutch, Le Grice brothers; met Evans family	Priestley *Corruptions of Christianity* Rousseau *Confessions*
1783		Pitt's first ministry (–1801) Kant *Prolegomena*
1784		Samuel Johnson d
1785		De Quincey b Paley *Principles of Moral and Political Philosophy*
1789		(14 Jul) French Revolution Blake *Songs of Innocence* Bowles *Sonnets* Mendelssohn *Morgenstunden*
1790		Burke *Reflections on the Revolution in France*

1791	(Sept) Jesus College, Cambridge, Exhibitioner, Sizar, Rustat Scholar; met S. Butler, Frend, Porson, C. Wordsworth, Wrangham	(Mar) John Wesley d Paine *Rights of Man* pt I (pt II 1792) Boswell *Life of Johnson* Anti-Jacobin riots at Birmingham
1792	(3 Jul) Encaenia, C's prize-winning Greek Sapphic *Ode on the Slave-Trade*	Pitt's attack on the slave-trade Fox's Libel Bill
1793	(May) Attended Cambridge trial of Frend (7 Nov) First poem in *Morning Chronicle* (2 Dec) Enlisted in 15th Light Dragoons as Silas Tomkyn Comberbache	(21 Jan) Louis XVI executed (1 Feb) France declared war on England and Holland (Mar–Dec) Revolt of La Vendée (16 Oct) Marie Antoinette executed (16 Oct) John Hunter d Irish Act to admit RC's to commissions up to rank of colonel Godwin *Political Justice* Wordsworth *An Evening Walk* and *Descriptive Sketches*
1794	(7–10 Apr) Back at Cambridge (Jun) Poems in *Cambridge Intelligencer*; set out with Joseph Hucks to Oxford (met RS); planned pantisocracy with RS; Welsh tour (Aug–Sept) Met Thomas Poole; engaged to Sara Fricker (Sept) With RS published *The Fall of Robespierre* (Cambridge); *Monody on Chatterton* published with *Rowley Poems* (Cambridge) (Dec) Left Cambridge; sonnets in *M Chron* (24 Dec) Began *Religious Musings*	(23 May) Suspension of Habeas Corpus (28 Jul) Robespierre executed; end of the Terror (Oct–Dec) State Trials: Hardy, Tooke, and Thelwall acquitted of charge of treason Paine *Age of Reason* (–1795) Paley *Evidences of Christianity*
1795	(Jan) Bristol lodgings with George Burnett, RS (Feb) Political lectures (late Feb/early May) *MPL* published (May–Jun) Lectures on Revealed Religion (16 Jun) Lecture on the Slave-Trade (Aug–Sept) Quarrel with RS; pantisocracy abandoned (4 Oct) Married Sara Fricker (26 Nov) Lecture on the Two Bills (3 Dec) *Conciones ad Populum* published (c 10–18 Dec) *An Answer to "A Letter to Edward Long Fox"* and *Plot Discovered* published; *Watchman* planned	(Jun–Jul) Quiberon expedition (26 Sept) WW and DW at Racedown (Nov) Directory began (3 Nov) Treason and Convention Bills introduced (18 Dec) Two Acts put into effect Lewis *Ambrosio, or the Monk*
1796	(9 Jan–13 Feb) Tour to Midlands to	(Jul) Robert Burns d

sell *The Watchman*; met Erasmus Darwin, Wright of Derby
(1 Mar–13 May) *The Watchman* in ten numbers
(16 Apr) *Poems on Various Subjects*
(19 Sept) Hartley b; reconciliation with RS
(31 Dec) *Ode on the Departing Year* in *Cambridge Intelligencer*; move to Nether Stowey

(Sept) Mary Lamb's violent illness
(Nov) Catherine of Russia d
England treating for peace with France
Threats of invasion of England
Jenner performs first smallpox vaccination

1797 (Mar) WW at Stowey
(5 Jun) At Racedown
(Jul) DW, WW, and Lamb at Stowey; DW and WW in Alfoxden House
(16 Oct) *Osorio* finished; *Poems, to Which Are Now Added, Poems by Charles Lamb and Charles Lloyd*
(13–16 Nov) C's and WW's walk to Lynton and *Ancient Mariner* begun

(Feb) Bank of England suspended cash payments
(Apr–Jun) Mutinies in the British Navy
(9 Jul) Burke d
(17 Oct) France and Austria sign peace treaty
(Nov) Frederick William II of Prussia d
(Nov) *Anti-Jacobin* (to 8 Jul 1798)

1798 (Jan) C's Unitarian sermons at Shrewsbury; Hazlitt heard C preach on Church and State; Wedgwood annuity £150 accepted
(Mar) *Ancient Mariner* completed
(Apr) *Fears in Solitude*
(18 Sept) *Lyrical Ballads* published; WW, DW, and C to Hamburg; met Klopstock
(Oct) C to Ratzeburg

(Feb–Oct) Irish rebellion
(Apr) Helvetic Republic
(12 Jun) Malta taken by French
(Jul) Bonaparte invaded Egypt
(1–2 Aug) Nelson's victory in Battle of the Nile
Horne Tooke *Diversions of Purley* vol I (vol II 1805)
Lloyd *Edmund Oliver*
Bell introduced Madras system of education in England

1799 (Apr) C had news of death of Berkeley C; C at University of Göttingen
(May) Ascent of Brocken
(29 Jul) In Stowey again
(Sept–Oct) Devon walking tour with RS; met Humphry Davy in Bristol; experiments with nitrous oxide
(Oct–Nov) First Lakes tour, with WW
(26 Oct) Met Sara Hutchinson
(27 Nov) Arrived in London to accept *M Post* offer
(Dec) DW and WW at Town End (later Dove Cottage)

(Nov) Directory overthrown
(Dec) Constitution of Year VIII; Bonaparte First Consul
Schiller *Die Piccolomini* and *Wallensteins Tod* published
Royal Institution founded

1800 (Jan–27 Mar) *M Post* reporter and leader-writer; wrote (13, 15, 27 Jan) on union with Ireland and on Catholic Question; translating *Wallenstein* at Lamb's

Kant *Logik*
Schelling *System des transcendentalen Idealismus*
(Mar–Apr) Pius VII Pope
(25 Apr) Cowper d

	(Apr) To Grasmere and WW	(14 Jun) Battle of Marengo
	(May–Jun) In Stowey and Bristol	Burns *Works* ed Currie
	(24 Jul) Move to Greta Hall, Keswick	(Aug) Union of Great Britain and Ireland
	(Sept–Oct) Superintended printing of *Lyrical Ballads* (2nd ed)	(5 Sept) Malta after long siege fell to Engllsh
1801	(Jan) *Lyrical Ballads* (1800) published; prolonged illnesses	(Mar) Pitt resigned over Emancipation
	(Jul–Aug) With SH at Stockton	Addington ministry (–1804)
	(15 Nov) In London writing for *M Post*	(Jul) Bonaparte signed Concordat with Pope
	Christmas at Stowey	Davy lecturer at Royal Institution
		RS *Thalaba*
1802	(Jan) In London: attended Davy's lectures at Royal Institution; writing for *M Post*	(25 Mar) Peace of Amiens
		(18 Apr) Erasmus Darwin d
		(8 May) Bonaparte Consul for Life
	(Mar–Nov) In Lakes, severe domestic discord	(2 Oct) WW married Mary Hutchinson
	(Apr) *Dejection*	(Oct) French army entered Switzerland
	(Aug) Scafell climb; visit of the Lambs	*Edinburgh Review* founded
	(Sept–Oct) Writing for *M Post*	Cobbett's *Weekly Political Register* founded
	(Nov) Tour of S Wales with Tom and Sally Wedgwood	Paley *Natural Theology*
	(23 Dec) Sara C b	Spinoza *Opera* ed Paulus (1802–3)
1803	(Jan–Feb) In Somerset with Wedgwoods, Poole; with Lamb in London; made his will	(Feb) Act of Mediation in Switzerland
	(Jun) *Poems* (1803)	(30 Apr) Louisiana bought by U.S. from France
	(summer) Visits by Hazlitt, Beaumonts, and S. Rogers to Lakes; Hazlitt's portrait of C	(18 May) England declared war on France
	(15–29 Aug) Scottish tour with DW and WW	(25 May) Emerson b
		(Sept) Emmet's execution in Ireland
	(30 Aug–15 Sept) Continued tour alone	Cobbett *Parliamentary Debates* (later Hansard)
		Hayley *Life and Posthumous Writings of Cowper*
		Chatterton *Works* ed RS and Cottle
		Malthus *Principles of Population* (2nd ed)
1804	(Jan) Ill at Grasmere, then to London; portrait by Northcote	(12 Feb) Kant d
		(Mar) Code Napoléon
	(9 Apr) In convoy to Malta	(Apr) 2nd Pitt ministry (–1806)
	(Aug–Nov) Sicily, two ascents of Etna; stayed with G. F. Leckie; private secretary to Alexander Ball, British High Commissioner at Malta	(18 May) Napoleon made Emperor
		(12 Dec) Spain declared war on Britain
		Blake *Jerusalem*
1805	(Jan) Appointed Acting Public Secretary in Malta; news of loss of John Wordsworth on *Abergavenny*	(Apr) Third Coalition against France
		(9 May) Schiller d
	(Sept–Dec) In Sicily	(26 May) Napoleon King of Italy

(Dec) To Naples and Rome

(17 Oct) Napoleon's victory at Ulm
(21 Oct) Nelson's victory at Trafalgar
(2 Dec) Austerlitz
Horne Tooke *Diversions of Purley* vol II (vol I 1798)
Hazlitt *Principles of Human Action*
Knight *Principles of Taste*
Scott *Lay of the Last Minstrel*
RS *Madoc*

1806 (Jan) In Rome, met Washington Allston, the Humboldts, L. Tieck, and Schlegel; to Florence, Pisa
(23 Jun) Sailed from Leghorn
(17 Aug) Landed in England; London, job-hunting, Parndon with the Clarksons and to Cambridge
(26 Oct) In Kendal
(Nov) Keswick, determined on separation from Mrs C
(Dec) At Coleorton with WW and SH, crisis of jealous disillusionment with them

(Jan) Pitt d, "Ministry of all the Talents" under Grenville, who resigned (Mar 1807) after rejection of Bill to open all commissions to RC's
(6 Aug) Holy Roman Empire ended
(26 Aug) Palm executed
(13 Sept) Fox d
British blockade
(Oct) Jena
(Nov) Berlin Decree and Continental System
Arndt *Geist der Zeit* (–1818)

1807 Coleorton; heard WW read *Prelude* and wrote *Lines to William Wordsworth*
(Jun) With C family at Stowey
(Aug) Met De Quincey; in Bristol
(Nov) In London

(Mar) Portland ministry (–1809)
(25 Mar) Abolition of slave-trade
(Jul) Peace of Tilsit
(2 Sept) Bombardment of Copenhagen by British fleet
(Dec) Peninsular War began
Davy and oxymuriatic acid
WW *Poems in Two Volumes*
RS *Letters from England by Don Espriella; Specimens of the Later English Poets*
C. and M. Lamb *Tales from Shakespeare*
Letters of Peter Plymley
Parnell *An Historical Apology for the Irish Catholics*

1808 (15 Jan–Jun) In rooms at *Courier* office, Strand; lectures at Royal Institution on Poetry and Principles of Taste; illnesses, Bury St Edmunds
(Jun) Miniature painted by M. Betham
(Jun–Aug) Bristol, Leeds, Keswick
(Jul) Review of Clarkson's *History of the Abolition of the Slave-Trade*
(1 Sept) Arrived Allan Bank, Grasmere
(Nov) First Prospectus of *The Friend*; Kendal

Bell–Lancaster controversy
Sir Arthur Wellesley to Portugal
Crabb Robinson *Times* correspondent in Peninsula
(1 May) Hazlitt married Sarah Stoddart
(30 Aug) Convention of Cintra signed
(Dec) Dr T. Beddoes d
Dalton *New System of Chemical Philosophy* and pub of atomic theory
Lamb *Specimens of English Dramatic Poets*

		Scott *Marmion*
		John and Leigh Hunt's *Examiner* began
		Goethe *Faust* pt I
		Croker *A Sketch of the State of Ireland*
1809	(1 Jun–15 Mar 1810) *The Friend*, 27 numbers plus supernumerary (7 Dec–20 Jan 1810) "Letters on the Spaniards" in *Courier*	(Feb) *Quarterly Review* founded (9 Mar) Byron *English Bards and Scotch Reviewers* (May) Napoleon's capture of Vienna and his excommunication; Pius VII imprisoned WW *Convention of Cintra* pamphlet (21 Sept) Canning–Castlereagh duel Perceval ministry (–1812)
1810	(Mar) SH left for Wales; last number of *Friend* (Oct) To London; Montagu precipitated WW–C quarrel; with Morgans in Hammersmith (Nov) Personal association with HCR began	(Mar) Battle over admission of press to House of Commons (May) First Reform Bill since 1797 introduced (Jul) Napoleon annexed Holland George III recognised as insane WW *Guide to the Lakes* Mme de Staël *De l'Allemagne* Scott *Lady of the Lake* RS *Curse of Kehama*
1811	(Mar) Met Grattan (20 Apr) First table-talk recorded by John Taylor Coleridge (Apr–Sept) Contributions to *Courier*, including 3 letters on the Catholic Petition; J. Payne Collier met C (18 Nov–27 Jan 1811) Lectures on Shakespeare and Milton at Scot's Corporation Hall, Collier, Byron, Rogers, HCR attending (Dec) George Dawe bust of C	(5 Feb) Prince of Wales made Regent Scheme to set up representative assembly in Dublin (Nov to 1815) Luddite uprisings Shelley *Necessity of Atheism*
1812	(Feb–Mar) Last journey to the Lakes to collect copies of *Friend* (Apr) With the Morgans, Berners Street, Soho (May–Aug) Lectures on drama in Willis's Rooms; portrait by Dawe (May) Lamb and HCR patch WW quarrel (Jun) Catherine Wordsworth d (Jun) *The Friend* reissued (3 Nov–26 Jan 1813) Shakespeare lectures in Surrey Institution (Nov) Half Wedgwood annuity withdrawn; RS and C *Omniana* (Dec) Thomas Wordsworth d	(11 May) Perceval shot; Liverpool PM, resigned but resumed after Canning (pro-Catholic) declined to serve with Wellesley (18 Jun) U.S. declared war on Great Britain (22 Jun) Napoleon opened war on Russia (Oct–Dec) The retreat from Moscow Combe *Tour of Dr Syntax in Search of the Picturesque*
1813	(23 Jan) *Remorse* opened at Drury Lane	(May) Grattan's Bill for Relief of Roman Catholics abandoned

(2 Sept) Met Mme de Staël
(Oct–Nov) Bristol lectures on Shakespeare and education; with Morgans at Ashley

(Jul–Aug) Peace Congress at Prague failure
(10 Aug) Austria declared war on Napoleon
(Sept) RS Poet Laureate
(Autumn) Wellington successful in Peninsula; Switzerland, Holland, Italy, Rhineland, Spain, Trieste, Dalmatia freed of French rule
RS *Life of Nelson*
Northcote *Memoirs of Reynolds*
Leigh Hunt imprisoned for libel (1813–15)

1814   (5 Apr) Lectures at Bristol on Milton, Cervantes, Taste; lecture on French Revolution and Napoleon; under medical care of Dr Daniel for addiction and suicidal depression
(3 May) Charles Danvers d
(1 Aug) *Remorse* performed in Bristol
(Aug–Sept) Allston portrait of C; Allston's exhibition of paintings; essays "On the Principles of Genial Criticism" published in *Felix Farley's Bristol Journal*
(Sept) At Ashley with the Morgans
(20 Sept–10 Dec) "Letters to Mr. Justice Fletcher" in *Courier* anticipate arguments in *Church and State*

(Jan) Invasion of France by Allies
(Mar) Castlereagh's treaty with Austria, Prussia, and Russia against Napoleon
(6 Apr) Napoleon's abdication
(May) First Treaty of Paris; Napoleon exiled to Elba; Restoration of the Bourbons
(8–9 Jun) Cochrane perjury trial
(Sept–Jun 1815) Congress of Vienna
(24 Dec) Peace of Ghent signed by Britain and U.S.
Inquisition re-established in Spain
WW *Excursion*
Scott *Waverley*
Cary's *Dante* completed

1815   (Mar) At Calne with the Morgans
(Jun) *Remorse* performed at Calne
(Jul–Sept) Dictating *Biographia Literaria*
(Aug–Sept) *Sibylline Leaves* and *Biographia Literaria* sent for publication in Bristol

(Mar–Jun) The Hundred Days: Napoleon escaped Elba, returned to France
(6 Apr) Allies mobilise vs Napoleon
(18 Jun) Waterloo
Restoration of Louis XVIII
Napoleon from Plymouth to St Helena
(20 Nov) Second Treaty of Paris
WW *Poems* of 1815; *The White Doe of Rylstone*
Scott *Guy Mannering*

1816   (Feb) Grant from Literary Fund, also from Byron
(Mar) London: illness
(10 Apr) Sent *Zapolya* to Byron
(15 Apr) Accepted as patient and house-mate by Dr Gillman, Moreton House, Highgate
(May–Jun) *Christabel* published (three editions); renewed acquain-

(24 Apr) Byron's departure from England
(21 Jun) Motion for relief of Roman Catholics rejected in the Lords
(7 Jul) Sheridan d
Parliamentary Committee on Education of the Poor
(Nov) *Cobbett's Political Register* reduced price to 2d

tance with Hookham Frere; offered Stuart tract or essays on Catholic Question
(Dec) *Statesman's Manual* published
Hazlitt's antagonistic reviews in *Examiner* (Jun, Sept, Dec) and *Edinburgh Review* (Dec)

(2 Dec) Spa Fields Riot
Shelley *Alastor and Other Poems*
Peacock *Headlong Hall*
Maturin *Bertram*
J. H. Frere ms tr of Aristophanes

1817 (Apr) Second *Lay Sermon* published
(14 Apr) *Remorse* revived
(Jul) *Biographia Literaria, Sibylline Leaves* published
(summer) Met J. H. Green
(Sept) Met Henry Cary
(Nov) *Zapolya* published; C's tr of Hurwitz's *Hebrew Dirge* for Princess Charlotte; Tieck visited C

(13 Feb) RS *Wat Tyler*
(4 Mar) Habeas Corpus suspended
(27 Mar) Sidmouth Circular on libels
(Apr) *Blackwood's Magazine* founded as *Edinburgh Monthly Magazine*
(May) Motion for relief of Roman Catholics rejected in the Lords
(6 Nov) Death of Princess Charlotte
Elgin Marbles purchased by government and put in BM
Keats *Poems*
Hazlitt *The Characters of Shakespeare's Plays*
Moore *Lalla Rookh*
Ricardo *Principles of Political Economy*
Cuvier *Le Règne animal*

1818 (Jan) "Treatise on Method" in *Encyclopaedia Metropolitana* published
(Jan–Mar) Lectures on poetry and drama
(Jan) Met T. Allsop
Annotated 1817 Catholic Emancipation Debate in copy of Hansard
(Apr) Two pamphlets supporting Peel's Bill against exploitation of child-labour
(Nov) *The Friend* (3-vol edition)
(Dec) Lectures on the History of Philosophy (–Mar 1819); literary lectures (–Mar 1819)

(28 Jan) Habeas Corpus restored and never again suspended
(1 Jun) Parliamentary motion for universal suffrage and annual parliaments defeated
(Jun) Westmorland election
Keats *Endymion*
(Aug) *Blackwood's* and *Quarterly* attacks on Keats
Hallam *Middle Ages*
Hazlitt *Lectures on the English Poets*
Lamb *Collected Works* (dedicated to C)
Peacock *Nightmare Abbey*

1819 (Mar) Financial losses in bankruptcy of publisher Rest Fenner
(29 Mar) Lectures end
(11 Apr) Met Keats in Millfield Lane; HC elected Fellow of Oriel; revived interest in chemistry; occasional contributions to *Blackwood's* (to 1822)

(May) Grattan's Motion for Relief of Roman Catholics defeated
(Jun) Grey's Bill to abolish Declaration against Transubstantiation defeated

1820 (May) HC deprived of Oriel Fellowship

(29 Jan) George III d
Accession of George IV

(Aug) Green began to act as weekly amanuensis to record C's work on Books of O and N Testament
(Oct) DC to St John's, Cambridge
(Dec) Recommended writings of friend Hyman Hurwitz

Cato Street Conspiracy
(Feb) Parliament dissolved
(Jun) Grattan d. Plunkett became main Irish spokesman
Revolution in Spain and Portugal
(Aug–Nov) Trial of Queen Caroline
Crawfurd *History of the Indian Archipelago*
Godwin *Of Population, in Answer to Mr Malthus*
Keats *Lamia and Other Poems*
Lamb *Essays of Elia*
Shelley *Prometheus Unbound*
RS *Life of Wesley*
WW *The River Duddon*

1821 (Apr) Ms notes on Grenville's speech supporting anti-vetoists
(Apr–May) Projected 3 Letters to C. A. Tulk, MP, on Catholic Question
(Jul) Reunion with brother George
(autumn) Invitation to lecture in Dublin refused

(Feb) Plunkett's Motion for Relief of Roman Catholics with 2 Securities (ban on foreign correspondence and veto on appointments) passed by majority of 6 in Commons, rejected by 39 in Lords after intervention of Grenville (Apr)
(Feb) Keats d
(Aug–Sept) King visited Ireland
Napoleon d
Greek War of Liberation
De Quincey *Confessions of an English Opium Eater*
Hazlitt *Lectures on Elizabethan Drama*
Mill *Elements of Political Economy*
RS *Vision of Judgment*

1822 (spring) C's "Thursday-evening class" began; SC's tr of Martin Dobrizhoffer *An Account of the Abipones, an Equestrian People of Paraguay*
(Nov) Meeting with Liverpool and Canning at Ramsgate
(Nov–Feb 1823) Wife and daughter visit C at Highgate
(29 Dec) HNC began recording his *Table Talk*

(30 Apr) Canning's Catholic Peers Bill carried by 5 in Commons, rejected by 42 in Lords
(Jul) Shelley d
(Aug) Castlereagh d and Canning became Foreign Secretary
(Nov–Dec) Faction-fights between Orangemen and Catholics in Ireland
Byron *Vision of Judgment*
Grattan *Speeches*
Shelley *Hellas*
Blanco White *Letters from Spain* [Doblado]
WW *Ecclesiastical Sketches*

1823 (Jun) Asked J. T. Coleridge to read Ms "Logic"
(Jun–Jul) Heard Edward Irving preach

Foundation of Catholic Association by O'Connell and R. L. Sheil
(Apr) Plunkett's Motion for Relief of Roman Catholics abandoned for lack of support

(Aug) Consulted Taylor and Hessey about MS "Logic"
(Sept) *Youth and Age* begun
(Sept) Sought admission to BM through Sir Humphry Davy
(Dec) Gillmans and C moved to 3, the Grove

(May) First meeting of Catholic Association in Dublin
(Jun) First meeting of Catholic Association in London
War between France and Spain
(Aug) Death of Pius VII
Hazlitt *Liber Amoris*
RS *History of the Peninsular War*

1824 (Mar) Elected FRSL, annuity of £100

(Apr) Byron d
(May) Lansdowne's Bills to allow English Catholics the vote and to act as JP's defeated

(May) Taylor and Hessey advertised the "Elements of Discourse"
(Jun) Carlyle and Gabriele Rossetti called at Highgate
DC B.A. Cambridge
J. T. Coleridge became Editor of *Quarterly*

Foundation of London Mechanics' Institution
Cary tr *The Birds* of Aristophanes
Godwin *History of the Commonwealth of England*
RS *The Book of the Church*

1825 (10 May) *Aids to Reflection* published
(18 May) Royal Society of Literature essay "On the *Prometheus* of Aeschylus"
(May) 6 essays, including 1 on Church and State, promised to publisher (J. A. Hessey)
(Jun) Partnership of C's publishers (Hessey & Taylor) dissolved
(Jul) Blanco White visited C at Highgate; C received copy of *Evidences*, informed White he was about to put to the press "a small work on the Church"
(Nov) Corrected proofs of Hurwitz's *Hebrew Tales*; proposed three lectures on projected London University
(Dec) Received Blanco White's *Letters from Spain* and *Poor Man's Preservative*
Marginal notes on subject of Church and State in Hooker and other 17th century writers; DC ordained

(Feb–May) Burdett's Motion for the Relief of Roman Catholics, with 2 "wings" for Veto and State payment of Clergy passed in Commons, but defeated in Lords after intervention of Dukes of York and Liverpool
(May) Liverpool's speech on Coronation Oath; quoted with approval by Canning
(Aug) Frere arrived in England
Brougham *Practical Observations upon the Education of the People*
Butler *The Book of the Roman Catholic Church*
Hazlitt *Spirit of the Age*
Lawless *An Address to the Catholics of Ireland*
Mill *Essays on Government*
Blanco White *Practical and Internal Evidences against Catholicism*

1826 (spring) Intensive work on Daniel and the Apocalypse
(summer) Frere spent long periods with C
(Jul) Letter to Edward Coleridge on mysticism, later incorporated in *Church and State*
(Sept) Frere obtained promise of sinecure of £200 from Liverpool for C; never carried out

General Election with Corn Laws and Catholic Emancipation as main issues
England sends troops to Portugal
Whately *Elements of Logic*
HNC *Six Months in the West Indies*
Irving *Babylon and Infidelity Foredoomed of God*
Turner *History of Henry VIII*
RS *Vindiciae Ecclesiae Anglicanae*

Blanco White *A Letter to Charles
Butler*

1827 (Feb) Lord Dudley Ward intended
to speak to Liverpool on C's
behalf
(10 May) Thomas Chalmers called
at Highgate; C's serious illness
DC married Mary Pridham
Sir George Beaumont d, leaving
£100 to Mrs C
Poole visited C at Highgate

(Feb) Liverpool seized with paraly-
tic stroke
(Mar) Burdett's Bill, which dis-
pensed with 2 "wings", rejected
in Commons by 4 votes
(Mar) Canning PM
(8 Aug) Canning d
(Aug) Goderich Ministry
University of London founded
Blake d
Hallam *Constitutional History*
Hare *Guesses at Truth*
Irving tr of *The Coming of Messiah*
Keble *Christian Year*
Phillpotts *Letter to Canning on the
Bill of 1825*
Tennyson *Poems by Two Brothers*

1828 (Feb) Marginal notes on Brougham
A Speech (Land as a Trust)
(22 Apr) Fenimore Cooper met C
(21 Jun–7 Aug) Netherlands and
Rhine Tour with Dora and WW
(Aug) *Poetical Works* (3 vols); John
Sterling called at Highgate

(Jan) Wellington Ministry
(Feb) Brougham's speech on Law of
the Country
(Apr) Repeal of Test and Corpora-
tion Acts
(May) Burdett's Bill for Relief of
Roman Catholics passed in Com-
mons, rejected in Lords (Jun)
(Jul) O'Connell elected at Clare
(Aug) Peel and Wellington in
correspondence over the Catholic
Question
(Dec) Lord Liverpool d
Russia goes to war with Turkey
The Greek Question
Brougham *A Speech on the Present
State of the Law of the Country*
Hazlitt *Life of Napoleon* vols I, II
Phillpotts *A Letter on the Coronation
Oath*

1829 (Jan) Consulted Thomas Hurst
about the MS "Logic"
(Jan–Feb) Refused to sign Petition
against Catholic Emancipation
(spring) Illness delayed writing on
Church and State
Poetical Works (2nd ed)
*Poetical Works of Coleridge, Shelley,
and Keats* (Galignani, Paris)
(Sept) SC married cousin HNC;
Lady Beaumont left C £50; Poole
visited Highgate
(Sept) Working on proofs of *On the*

Meetings held throughout the coun-
try to petition against Catholic
Emancipation
(Jan) King agrees to discussion of
Catholic Emancipation in Cabinet
(Feb–Mar) Bill passed to suppress
Catholic Association
Act passed to raise franchise in
Ireland from 40s to £10
(10 Mar) 1st Reading in the Com-
mons of Catholic Relief Bill
(30 Mar) 3rd Reading passed by 178
votes

	Constitution of the Church and State (Dec) *Church and State* published	(31 Mar) 1st Reading in Lords (10 Apr) 3rd Reading passed by 104 (13 Apr) George IV gave reluctant assent (May) Sir Humphry Davy d Arnold *Sermons* Hurwitz *The Elements of the Hebrew Language* RS *Sir Thomas More* [Isaac Taylor] *Natural History of Enthusiasm*
1830	(Jan) Revision of *C&S* into chapters *On the Constitution of the Church and State* (2nd ed) (Jun) HNC and SC settled in High-gate (Jul) C made his will Republication of *The Devil's Walk* "by Professor Porson" (Sept) Detailed marginal notes in Blomfield's *Charge*	Reform Agitation (Jun) Death of George IV (Jun) Accession of William IV (Nov) Grey Ministry Greece independent Bishop Blomfield *Charge* to Clergy of London Diocese Comte *Cours de philosophie positive* Lyell *Principles of Geology* Miller *Sermons* Tennyson *Poems Chiefly Lyrical*
1831	Royal Society of Literature grant withdrawn; refused personal grant from Grey; Frere made up loss Last meeting with WW; *Aids to Reflection* (2nd ed) Active interest in Parliamentary Reform, reflected in *Table Talk* and marginalia	(Mar) Lord John Russell introduced Reform Bill in Commons Dissolution of Parliament Second Reform Bill rejected by Lords Final Reform Bill introduced British Association founded Hegel d J. S. Mill *The Spirit of the Age* in *Examiner* Peacock *Crotchet Castle* Review of *C&S* in *Eclectic Review* (Jul) Walsh *Popular Opinions on Parliamentary Reform*
1832	Legacy of £300 from Steinmetz	Grey resigned; Wellington failed to form Ministry; Grey recalled (May) Reform Bill passed Scott d Green *Address Delivered in King's College* Martineau *Illustrations of Political Economy* Park *The Dogmas of the Constitution* RS *Essays, Moral and Political*
1833	HC's *Poems* dedicated to C (24–9 Jun) To Cambridge for meetings of British Association (Jul) Harriet Martineau visited C (5 Aug) Emerson called at Highgate HC's *Biographia Borealis* published	Arnold *Principles of Church Reform* Carlyle *Sartor Resartus* Keble Sermon on "National Apostacy" begins Oxford Movement Lamb *Last Essays of Elia*

Mill "Corporation and Church Property"

Smith *Seven Letters on National Religion*

Tracts for the Times (Newman et al)

1834 (Apr) Instructed Hurst to dispose of his share in the editions of *AR* and *C&S*

(Jul) Proofs of *Poetical Works* (3rd ed)

(25 July) Death at Highgate

New Poor Law

Augustus Hare d (Feb)

Malthus d (Dec)

Lamb d (Dec)

Bentham *Deontology*

EDITOR'S INTRODUCTION

PROVENANCE

WHEN Coleridge died in 1834, his papers and most of his books passed into the hands of his friend and literary executor, the surgeon Joseph Henry Green.[1] Although Green died in 1863, his library was not finally dispersed until 1880, when it was auctioned off by Messrs Sotheby, Wilkinson and Hodge. The manuscript of the *Logic* appeared as Item 554 in the sale catalogue for 28 July and was described as follows:

Logic. Introductory Chapters and Elements of Logic in MANUSCRIPT *of several hundred pages, presumed to be in the autograph of the late J. H. Green, Esq., half morocco. &c. 2 vol.*

The copy of the sale catalogue in the British Museum, which is annotated by the auctioneer, gives the purchaser's name as Riggall and the price as eighteen shillings.[2]

The buyer was the surgeon Edward Riggall, and he bought a number of other items at the same time, most of them books of philosophy, theology, and medicine, together with three copies of an engraving of Coleridge's study.

Riggall's library was sold by auction in 1892 by Messrs Sotheby, Wilkinson and Hodge. The manuscript of the *Logic* appeared as Item 885 in the sale catalogue for 24 March 1892 and was described as follows:

GREEN (JOHN HENRY, F. R. S.) Introduction to the History of Logic— Elements of Logic, ORIGINAL MSS. 4*to.* (2).

The auctioneer's note in the British Museum copy of the sale catalogue listed the buyer as Macmillan and the price as seven shillings.[3]

The new owners were the Cambridge booksellers Macmillan and Bowes. According to a note written by Charles A. Ward on the fly-leaf of the manuscript of the *Logic*, the two volumes were included in

---

[1] See *C at H* 88.

[2] BM copy: S.–C.S. 805. (1).

[3] BM copy: S.–C.S. 1026. (2).

the November book catalogue of Macmillan and Bowes in 1892, and he bought them before the end of the year for eighteen shillings. Unfortunately no copy of this catalogue has yet come to light, but a note pencilled onto the flyleaf (II 1), which reads "Elements of Logic/ Introduction to the History of Logic/ 2 Vols. 18/–", was presumably written by a member of the firm of Macmillan and Bowes.

During Ward's period of ownership the manuscript was entrusted to others on at least two occasions: first, when he sent it to Oxford to see whether he could interest members of the faculty there in it, and later when he sent it to Lucy E. Watson to have the handwriting identified.[1] On 12 December 1899 the British Museum bought the manuscript from Ward for the sum of ten pounds.[2] It appears listed in the published catalogue of Egerton MSS for that year.

Although the line of descent is reasonably clear, the failure of the Green and Riggall sale catalogues to identify the manuscript as Coleridge's is puzzling. The table of contents in Green's hand is clearly headed "Coleridge's Logic"; as the manuscript was not in Coleridge's hand and was part of Green's library, the inference may have seemed less obvious then than it does now. On the other hand, it may be that Green's table of contents, which is written on paper different from that used in the rest of the manuscript, was attached later.[3]

DESCRIPTION

The manuscript is heavily bound in two volumes of very unequal size. The first (Egerton 2825) consists of 90 folios and the second (Egerton 2826) of 467. The folios of the *Logic* are of heavy laid paper varying in colour from cream to pale grey, but a number of folios have been added to the manuscript at different stages of its history either as endpapers or by being tipped in. The leaves measure approximately 26 by 21 centimetres. The *Logic* is in the hands of two transcribers, but it contains numerous annotations, insertions,

---

[1] Ff 173 and 196 of the ms (Egerton 2826) preserve her comments tipped in. See "Description", p xxxv, below.

[2] Information kindly provided by the Keeper of Manuscripts, BM.

[3] See the letter to *N&Q* ser 8 III (28 Jan 1893) 64–5, in which Ward quotes two passages from the *Logic* and asks his readers to identify their source: "I attribute it to the pen of Coleridge simply because I believe nobody else in England to be capable of writing it." Ward's appeal seems to make sense only if he had acquired the manuscript without Green's table of contents. Could it have been given to him subsequently by one of his correspondents?

and additions by others. In the descriptions that follow, all materials are in ink unless otherwise noted.

Analysis of the *Logic*:

Volume I

ff 4–9—Hand A.

ff 10–89—Hand B.

Volume II

ff 3–172—Hand B.

ff 174–195—Hand A.

ff 197–277—Hand A.

f 278—blank.

ff 279–460—Hand B.

Analysis of the remaining ff:

Volume I

f 1—notes in the hands of C. A. Ward and (?) E. Riggall.

f 2—notes in the hand of C. A. Ward.

f 3—table of contents in the hand of J. H. Green.

f 90—note in pencil in the hand of C. A. Ward.

f 91—blank leaf with pasted-on label initialled by the British Museum inspector, and dated January 1901.

Volume II

f 1—notes in the hands of C. A. Ward and (?) Edward Riggall, and notes in pencil by a member of the firm of Macmillan and Bowes.

f 2—notes in the hand of C. A. Ward.

f 173—a card tipped into the manuscript, in the hand of Lucy E. Watson.

f 196—a card tipped into the manuscript in the hand of Lucy E. Watson.

f 461—note in pencil in the hand of C. A. Ward.

ff 462–5—tipped-in transcription in an unidentified hand of a letter from Coleridge.

ff 466–7—note in J. H. Green's hand.

f 468—endpaper initialled by the British Museum inspector, and dated January 1901.

Although the manuscript is a reasonably clean copy, it contains a number of fairly obvious errors and a few blank spaces to indicate omissions. Some of the corrections are by J. H. Green; some could be his but are so cramped by being inserted into narrow spaces or are so brief that one cannot be sure. C. A. Ward has annotated the manuscript copiously in pencil, generally confining himself to meditative comments on the verso blank pages, but occasionally allowing himself to suggest a reading where the manuscript is obscure. At one point there is a pencilled note that refers to a note by Ward (II 321). Wherever these corrections or insertions have been used in the text, there is a note to alert the reader.

Transcriber A seems to have been untroubled by Coleridge's Greek quotations, but Transcriber B, although he occasionally attempts them in an obviously unpractised hand, generally leaves blank spaces for them. Some of these have been filled by Greek hands that do not resemble that of Transcriber A. Green seems the most likely person to have made these corrections, but they are not all alike and have not been identified.

PUBLIC NOTICE

Public interest in Coleridge's manuscript remains was stimulated by the appearance in 1836 of Thomas Allsop's *Letters, Conversations and Recollections of Samuel Taylor Coleridge*, in which Coleridge was revealed as claiming to have written several works that had not come to light. Coleridge's own friends were familiar with his optimistic weakness for referring to things he was about to write in terms that suggested that he had already finished them, but strangers were piqued by the thought that important philosophical works, the "Opus Maximum", or the "Logosophia" perhaps, might be lying neglected among his papers.

Discussion began innocently enough with an enquiry inserted in *Notes and Queries*.[1] The correspondent, who used the pseudonym "Theophylact", asked: "Are we ever likely to receive from any member of Coleridge's family, or from his friend Mr. J. H. Green, the fragments, if not the entire work, of his *Logosophia*?" He added, "We can ill afford to lose a work the conception of which engrossed much of his thoughts, if I am rightly informed, towards the close of his life."

Two years later, Clement Mansfield Ingleby, who had already asked after the whereabouts of a manuscript on "the subject of ideas" to which Sara Coleridge had referred in her preface to *Biographia Literaria* (1847),[2] announced in the same journal the results of a conversation he had had with Coleridge's literary executor, Joseph Henry Green. On this occasion Green had revealed that he had the following items in his possession:

[1] *N&Q* ser 1 IV (1851) 411.   [2] Ibid ser 1 VI (1852) 533.

(1.) A complete section of a work on *The Philosophy of Nature*, which he took down from the mouth of Coleridge, filling a large volume; (2.) A complete treatise on *Logic*; and (3.) If I did not mistake, a fragment on *Ideas*.[1]

Ingleby added:

The reason Dr. Green assigns for their not having been published, is, that they contain nothing but what has already seen the light in the *Aids to Reflection, The Theory of Life*, and the *Treatise on Method*. This appears to me a very inadequate reason for withholding them from the press.

A year later, Ingleby, who had read Allsop in the interim, returned to the subject with a touch of the asperity that was to mark his Shakespearean criticism. After quoting passages that refer to Green's work as an amanuensis for Coleridge, Ingleby made the following complaint:

How has Mr. Green discharged the duties of this solemn trust? Has he made any attempt to give publicity to the *Logic*, the "great work" on *Philosophy*, the work on the Old and New Testaments, to be called *The Assertion of Religion*, or the *History of Philosophy*, all of which are in his custody, and of which the first is, on the testimony of Coleridge himself, a finished work? We know from the *Letters*, vol. ii. pp. 11. 150., that the *Logic* is an essay in three parts, viz. the "Canon", the "Criterion", and the "Organon"; of these the last only can be in any respect identical with the *Treatise on Method*. There are other works of Coleridge missing; to these I will call attention in a future Note. For the four enumerated above Mr. Green is responsible. He has lately received the homage of the University of Oxford in the shape of a D.C.L.; he can surely afford a fraction of the few years that may still be allotted to him in re-creating the fame of, and in discharging his duty to, his great master. If, however, he cannot afford the time, trouble, and cost of the undertaking, I make him this public offer; I will, myself, take the responsibility of the publication of the above-mentioned four works, if he will entrust me with the MSS.[2]

Knowing, as we now do, the complicatedly incomplete state of the manuscripts, and remembering that Green was trying to do his duty to Coleridge's memory by working at his own *Spiritual Philosophy*, it is easy to understand his vexation at the rhadamanthine tone of this article. Referring to it as "an inconsiderate, not to say a coarse attack", he replied by describing the manuscripts in his care, explaining why he felt that they ought not to be offered to the public. Of the *Logic* he had this to say:

... I apprehend it may be proved by reference to Mr. Stutfield's notes, the gentleman to whom it is ... said they were dictated, and who possesses

[1] Ibid ser 1 VIII (1853) 43.   [2] Ibid ser 1 IX (1854) 497.

the original copy, that the work never was finished. Of the three parts mentioned as the components of the work, the *Criterion* and *Organon* do not to my knowledge exist; and with regard to the other parts of the manuscript, including the *Canon*, I believe I have exercised a sound discretion in not publishing them in their present form and *unfinished* state.[1]

He ended his letter by referring to the work "in which I hope to present the philosophic views of my 'great master' in a systematic form of unity—in a form which may best concentrate to a focus and principle of unity the light diffused in his writings, and which may again reflect it on all departments of human knowledge, so that truths may become intelligible in the one light of Divine truth". Ingleby replied respectfully, but urged the expediency of publishing the *Logic*, the *Cosmogony*, and the *History of Philosophy*.[2]

In 1867, after Green's death, Ingleby gave an account of Coleridge's manuscripts as far as he had been able to deduce where and what they were, by way of encouraging the Coleridge family to publish them.[3]

Following this publication there seems to have been a lapse of over twenty years before the *Logic* was mentioned in print again. In 1893, however, spurred on by an article celebrating the commemoration in Nether Stowey of Coleridge's birthday, Charles A. Ward announced that he had acquired the work. "There have drifted to me by accident (though at each step in the descent traceable historically) two volumes, quarto, of MSS., bound, entitled respectively 'The History of Logic' and 'Elements of Logic'".[4] Two years later Ward wrote again to the *Athenaeum* to complain of the lack of public response: "To my astonishment there was not a reply of any sort, from reader, student, or publisher." He mentioned that James Dykes Campbell had expressed interest, and also that the manuscript had been sent to Dr Murray of Oxford, at Murray's request, "when all the bigwigs were in residence", that it was shown to them and returned after about three months "without one single word of comment from anybody, either combative or appreciative".[5]

There was a reply from Lucy E. Watson, the granddaughter of Coleridge's friend Dr Gillman, in which she assured Ward that some

[1] Ibid ser 1 ix (1854) 543–4.

[2] Ibid ser 1 ix (1854) 591.

[3] "On the Unpublished Manuscripts of Samuel Taylor Coleridge" *RSL Trans* ser 2 ix (1870) 102–34; read to the RSL in 1867.

[4] "Coleridge's 'Logic'" *Athenaeum* (1 Jul 1893) 35. Ward had previously announced his enthusiasm for C as "saint, seer and sage" in a long note to the Preface of his *Oracles of Nostradamus* (1891).

[5] "Coleridge" *Athenaeum* (26 Oct 1895) 571.

people were interested. She was subsequently shown the manu-script.[1] Nothing more seems to have come of Ward's efforts, how-ever, and in 1899 he fulfilled his responsibility to the manuscript by selling it to the British Museum.[2]

WHEN THE *LOGIC* WAS WRITTEN

Dating the *Logic* is largely a matter of educated guesswork. As early as 1803 Coleridge outlined a treatise that resembles it in some respects,[3] and less than a month before he died he was still talking about it enthusiastically as work in progress when the respectful but uncomprehending Earl of Dunraven visited his bedside.[4] During the intervening years he often mentioned plans and problems that are related to one aspect of philosophy or another, but it is usually difficult to be sure how far they overlap with the *Logic* and often impossible to tell whether they are actual or projected. The water-marks in the manuscript reveal nothing about the date of composi-tion. Even topical references within the *Logic* tell us no more than that Coleridge seems to refer at one point to material in *Aids to Reflection* (1825), and the reference might well have been made before *Aids to Reflection* was published. On three occasions, however, Coleridge seems to have offered to publishers manuscripts that can probably be identified with the *Logic*: in 1823, again in 1826, and finally in 1829.

On 5 June 1823, he wrote to his nephew, John Taylor Coleridge, to ask him whether he would be willing to look over what sounds like a rough draft of the *Logic*. He described it as follows:

"The Elements of Discourse, with the Criteria of true and false Reasoning, as the ground-work and preparation for Public Speaking and Debate—addressed to the Students and Candidates for the Pulpit, the Bar or Senate"—this Product of how many Years' Labor is now in such a state that I am most anxious that it should be, not indeed read but, sufficiently looked over and into by some man of good sense and academic education, as to enable him to form a satisfactory general notion of the Plan, principal Contents, and Style of Execution.[5]

---

[1] Ibid (23 Nov 1895) 719.
[2] In 1929 Alice D. Snyder included twenty-three pages of selections from the *Logic* in *L&L* and gave a detailed account of the ms. Since that time it has been customary to include the work in discussions of C's thought. See particularly: J. H. Muirhead *Coleridge as Philosopher* (1930); *Kant*

in England; Georg Gerdt *Coleridge's Verhältnis zur Logik* (Berlin 1935); Elio Chinol *Il Pensiero di S. T. Coleridge* (Venice 1953); and Orsini.
[3] Letter to Godwin 4 Jun 1803: *CL* II 947–8.
[4] *C Talker* 206–7.
[5] *CL* V 275.

Coleridge probably appealed to his nephew because he thought him, quite rightly, a practical man of letters,[1] because his manuscript was still in an unfinished state, and perhaps because he needed ammunition against the scepticism of the publishers towards his productions.[2] His response to his nephew's polite refusal describes it further:

> my MSS is legible enough for the demands of the London Press—that is, it will occasion no more trouble to the Compositors than they are in the habit of submitting to. But what would be no Drawback to a man, who has only to look at word after word, and line after line, and who unconcerned with the sense and argument is not at all confused or bewildered by the crossings out, the side Slips to be substituted, the directory marks of transposition, &c—all which are sad interruptions and annoyances to a Reader—even tho' it were a Novel or Pindaric Ode instead of an Elementary Treatise.—[3]

The subject matter of this work as he outlined it very briefly in his first letter is even more limited than the *Logic*: "It is . . . a Work of Logic for those purposes to which Lord Bacon in his Novum Organum very wisely confines the science of Logic—namely, *forensic* purposes, denying it's applicability, as a positive Organ, to all subjects . . . in which the absolute Truth is sought for . . .".[4] The audience aimed at was the same as that aimed at by the *Logic*,[5] the contents were slightly more restricted, and the manuscript was evidently made up of materials "already written out" (to use one of his own distinctions). J. T. Coleridge advised him to submit it directly to the publisher John Murray.

The manuscript Coleridge had offered to his nephew was the culmination of several years of work on different projects. He had spoken of a practical book on logic for the use of those entering the professions as being a part of his "Logosophia" in 1815; it was to be one of six treatises:

> The second Treatise is (Λόγος κοινός)[6] on the science of connected reasoning, containing a system of Logic purified from all pedantry & sophistication, & applied practically to the purposes of ordinary life, the Senate, Pulpit, Bar, &c . . .[7]

---

[1] J. T. Coleridge (1790–1876) briefly succeeded Gifford as editor of Murray's *Quarterly Review* a year later; in 1835, he was appointed Judge of the King's Bench. "His fairness of temper often caused him to be selected as an arbitrator". *DNB*.

[2] See his letter to Wrangham 5 Jun 1817: *CL* iv 736–7.

[3] *CL* v 277–8.
[4] *CL* v 275.
[5] See "Aims", below, pp lix–lxi.
[6] I.e. common logic.
[7] To John May 27 Sept 1815: *CL* iv 589. For earlier plans in 1803, see *CL* ii 947–8, 952.

Here the audience and the practical and introductory nature of the *Logic* are anticipated, but Coleridge goes on to say that the treatise will include a discussion of various forms of sophism (in the manner, presumably, of Aristotle's *Sophistici Elenchi*), and the *Logic* does not include it.[1] The third treatise too, "(Logos Architectonicus)[2] on the Dynamic or Constructive Philosophy . . .",[3] sounds like a germ of what was to become Part Three of the *Logic*. The plan of the "Logosophia" is outlined again a few days later in roughly similar terms for another friend:

The second—The science of connected [reasoning] (with the History of Logic from Aristotle to Condilliac) freed from [sophistication &] pedantry, and applied to the purposes of real Life—the Bar, the [Pul]pit, the Senate, & rational Conversation.—The third, the Science of Premises, or transcendental Philosophy—i.e. the examination of the Premises, which in ordinary & practical reasoning are taken for granted.[4]

Apart from its overemphasis on a history of logic, the outline would be a pretty fair description of the *Logic*.

The plan appears again in a letter written on 25 September 1816, this time as five treatises on the Logos. Two of them anticipate the *Logic*: "1. Λόγος προπαιδευτικός or Organum verè organum. 2 Λόγος ἀρχιτεκτονικός, or the principles of the Dynamic or Constructive Philosophy as opposed to the Mechanic."[5] References to the "Logosophia" increase in frequency for the next few years. It is mentioned several times in *Biographia Literaria* (at one point as being ready to go to press), and recurs in a number of his letters thereafter.[6] The "Logosophia" was never finished, but parts of Coleridge's great plan did find their way into print in one form or another, and others were left in substantial, if unfinished, form in manuscript.

The *Logic* was one of these, and that it was brought so close to completion may, I think, be attributed to Coleridge's having thought of it as an introductory and practical book. It is first mentioned in this light as an independent work in a letter to John M. Gutch written early in 1817. Coleridge was listing a number of items the copyrights of which he had given up to Gale and Fenner; one of them was "a volume, on the method of forming first and detecting fallacious Arguments, or on the practical Logic for the use of the Student, for

---

[1] For an example of C's preliminary work on a discussion of sophisms, see App E, below.
[2] Constructive Logic.
[3] *CL* IV 589.

[4] To Daniel Stuart 7 Oct 1815: *CL* IV 592.
[5] To Hugh J. Rose: *CL* IV 687.
[6] *BL* chs 8, 12 (1907) I 92, 179, II 230; e.g. *CL* IV 736, 806–9.

the Pulpit, the Bar . . .".[1] He was obviously referring to the second treatise of his "Logosophia", and his mention of it as a separate work suggests that he regarded it as a saleable commodity and, perhaps, one he could produce with relatively little effort. It was not the only work of a saleable kind that he hoped to present to the public; his public lectures of 1818 and 1819, and later his *Aids to Reflection*, were similar in intention. But the writing of the *Logic* was probably encouraged by two developments, only one of which was directly connected to it—the bankruptcy of his publishers and the commencement of his private classes in philosophy.

In March 1819 Coleridge discovered that his publishers, Rest Fenner, had gone bankrupt. He described the nature of his own loss in vivid terms in letters to Francis Wrangham and Thomas Allsop in September. The essence of it was that he had been obliged to write off his profits from the 1818 edition of *The Friend* and to use the remaining profits from his lectures to buy up copies that would otherwise have been remaindered. He was forced, therefore, to look about him for those parts of his literary and philosophical plans which it seemed most practical to turn into books; the *Logic* and, later, *Aids to Reflection*, both designed for young men about to enter the professions, were the most appropriate.

Coleridge's philosophical classes were crucial to the preparation of the *Logic*, partly because they provided him with the momentum he habitually derived from willing amanuenses, and partly because they gave him an opportunity to try out his practical and introductory works on real young men. On 23 May 1818 he described the sort of class he would like to teach:

In one form only would Lecturing meet my own judgement and inclination, namely, with from 20 to 30 young men of ingenuous birth and education from 18 or 19 to six or seven and twenty years old, to *go thro'* a steady course of Philosophy on a plan which I am now trying with two medical friends.[2]

The plan that follows is more elaborate than the *Logic*, but the hypothetical audience is the same. One of the two medical friends he referred to was Joseph Henry Green, the other was probably Gillman's assistant, J. H. B. Williams,[3] and the subject matter of their "conversations", of which Green evidently took memoranda, seems in 1818 at least to have ranged quite as widely as the "Logo-

---

[1] *CL* iv 701.
[2] To Hugh J. Rose: *CL* iv 862–3.
[3] See e.g. C's letter to him of 12 Dec 1817: *CL* iv 789–91.

sophia" ever promised to.[1] On 31 January 1819 he was able to write to Southey of his progress first in having had his philosophical lectures taken down in shorthand, and second in dictating his *magnum opus* to Green: "I give 4 and oftener five hours twice a week, and Mr Green . . . writes down what I say—so that we have already compassed a good handsome Volume . . .".[2]

Reports of progress with the *Logic* do not begin to appear until 1820. On 26 November, however, he wrote to Thomas Allsop of the urgency with which he was now working on the *Logic* and on his "Assertion of Religion".[3] Work was a refuge from the disappointment and despondency he felt at his son Hartley's expulsion from Oriel. As he wrote apologetically to J. G. Lockhart in December:

you will no longer wonder, that as often as possible I have hid myself in old books, & in the forwarding my "Logic", and "Assertion of Religion as implying Revelation, & of Christianity as the only Revelation of universal Validity"—or that I have not even looked into a new book, and that the Publications of my intimate Friends remain uncut on my shelves.—[4]

Gratifying though it is to find these references to the *Logic*, they must be regarded with some caution. A letter written to H. F. Cary in January of 1821 may be taken as a case in point. Once again progress is described, this time in some detail:

I am. . .getting regularly on with my LOGIC—in 3 parts—1. The Canons (Syllogy) 2. the Criterions (Dialectic) 3. Organic or Heuristic (εὑριστικόν) with a sketch of the History of the science from Aristotle to Bacon, & a disciplinary Analysis of Condillac's ψευδο-Logic prefixed, & concluding with a Glossary of philosophical Terms arranged *methodically* in the order & connection of the Thoughts; but with an Alphabetical Index—and every Sunday I devote with Mr Green, my Fellow-student & Amanuensis, to my (Anti-Paleyo-grotian) Assertion of Religion . . .[5]

The three parts are to be found in the *Logic*, as, arguably, is the history of logic, but the analysis of Condillac, the glossary, and the alphabetical index have not come to light. We cannot be sure, therefore, how far the work had been carried. By the autumn of 1821, Coleridge wrote cheerfully to Allsop:

I entertain some hope . . . that my Logic, which I could begin printing immediately if I could find a Publisher willing to undertake it on equitable terms, might prove an exception to the general fate of my publications. It is a long Lane that has no turning . . .[6]

1 See *CL* IV 863, 869–70, 873–6.   4 *CL* V 127.
2 *CL* IV 917.   5 *CL* V 133–4.
3 *CL* V 119–20.   6 *CL* V 177.

And that winter he went so far as to decline an invitation to give lectures in Dublin, on the grounds that he would have to interrupt his work on the *Logic* and the "Assertion".[1]

At the beginning of 1822 Coleridge found himself provided with two new amanuenses, both of them students of his and of the age for which his *Logic* was intended. On 25 January he wrote to Allsop with the following news:

with Mr Stutfield and Mr Watson I have already proceeded on two successive Thursdays, and compleated the Introduction, and the first Chapter, amounting to somewhat more than a closely printed Octavo Sheet, requiring no such revision as would require Transcription—and that three or four young men at the Table will make no addition, or rather no change.[2]

It is not clear whether the dictation to Stutfield and Watson was from the previous copies or whether he was dictating a new work. At any rate he was able to write to Allsop on 9 February that "The Logic goes on briskly . . .".[3]

It was at this point that Coleridge's plan to add some other students began to be put into effect. On 25 February 1822 the following advertisement appeared in the *Courier*:

Mr. COLERIDGE proposes to devote a determinate portion of each week to a small and select number of gentlemen, not younger than 19 or 20, for the purposes of assisting them in the formation of their minds, and the regulation of their studies. The plan, which is divided between direct instruction and conversation, the place, and other particulars, may be learnt by personal application to Mr COLERIDGE, at Highgate.[4]

The details of the class were communicated to Daniel Stuart, the proprietor of the *Courier*, who had presumably provided the advertisement as a favour to Coleridge, in a letter on 15 March 1822.[5] The course resembles the *Logic* in its main outlines, but goes beyond it; it was planned to take two years to complete. The only account we have of the way in which the course was actually conducted appeared in *Fraser's Magazine*, a year or so after Coleridge's death.[6] The author of the report declared that it was Coleridge's intention "to put his pupils in possession of such a volume of logic, though in manuscript, and taken down from his own lips".[7] But the

[1] To Allsop 3 Dec 1821: *CL* v 189.
[2] *CL* v 204.
[3] *CL* v 210.
[4] A photograph of it appears in *L&L* facing p 71.
[5] See below, p lix.

[6] *Fraser's Magazine* xii (Nov, Dec 1835) 493, 619–29. *The Wellesley Index to Victorian Periodicals* attributes the article to J. C. Hare, but on unverifiable authority.
[7] *Fraser's Magazine* xii 493.

lecture he recorded, although it is of a philosophical nature, does not resemble the *Logic*.

Although it has been claimed that the *Logic* was a result of Coleridge's philosophical class of 1822–3, it seems, therefore, more likely that the sequence was the other way round.[1] We know that Coleridge had already conceived the outlines of his *Logic* before he announced the class; he claimed in quite specific terms that he was already dictating a manuscript that sounds like the *Logic*; and the only account we have of the class does not correspond with the *Logic*. Perhaps the most that we can conclude is that the momentum that produced the *Logic* was shared with the philosophical class and that the class provided him with samples of the kind of audience he was aiming at in the *Logic*, of young men preparing for the professions.

A most interesting letter of 16 May 1822 describes one of these young men, John Watson, to Southey:

He has been for the last 18 months a House-mate of mine, as a sort of temporary Partner of Mr Gillman's rather than as an ordinary Assistant—and his remaining so long I have some reason to think owing in great measure to the advantages, which he believes himself to receive from his daily intercourse with me, and from the weekly attendance on my Lectures on the principles of Reasoning, or Logic as a Canon, a Criterion, and lastly an Organ of the mind.[2]

Evidently the young amanuensis attended the philosophic class as well as the daily sessions of conversation and dictation. Coleridge went so far as to describe his progress with the *Logic* to Southey in these terms:

I expect to have my introductory Work, on the art and Science of Conclusive Discourse, or the Laws of Thinking & Inquiring, with the rules of Acquiring, *testing*, arranging and applying Knowlege, ready for the Press by August, with the History of Logic prefixed and a Glossary of Philosophical Terms in the order of the Thoughts but with an alphabetical Index, as the Appendix.[3]

The outline had not changed much since Coleridge's description of it in January 1821, although the analysis of Condillac seems to have been removed. The glossary and appendix were retained. The optimism expressed to Southey, then, seems to have embraced the completion of a plan on which work was already under way.

More than six months later Coleridge thought himself close to

[1] *L&L* 71.   [3] *CL* v 227.
[2] *CL* v 226–7.

finishing the *Logic*. In a letter written to Allsop on 26 December 1822 he described the work:

in all it's three main Divisions, as the Canon, or that which prescribes the rule and form of all *conclusion* or conclusive reasoning: 2. as the Criterion, or that which teaches to distinguish Truth from Falsehood—containing all the possible sorts, forms, and sources of Error, and means of deceiving or being deceived—3. as the Organ, or positive instrument for discovering Truth—together with the general Introduction to the whole.—1

Here we are much closer to the *Logic* itself, the plan having been simplified. It seems likely that, as a result of actually writing the work, Coleridge began to find not only that he had enough material on his hands if he stuck to essentials, but that some of the parts he had originally hoped to include were really extraneous and separable. In his letter he proceeded to discuss the practicalities of his progress:

with regard to the former [the *Logic*] we are in sight of Land—... Mr Stutfield will try to give 3 days in the week for the next fortnight, and ... I have no doubt, notwithstanding Mrs Coleridge & little Sara's expected arrival on Friday next, that by the end of January the whole work will not [only] have been finished—for that I expect will be the case, next Sunday Fortnight, but ready for the Press.—In reality, I have *now* little else but to transcribe—and even this would in part only be necessary, but that I must of course dictate the sentences to Mr Stutfield & Mr Watson, & shall therefore avail myself of the opportunity of occasional correction & improvement.2

He added that he proposed to offer the work to Murray, and that by that time:

... I shall have the Logical Exercises—or the Logic exemplified and applied in a Critique on 1. Condillac, 2. Paley. 3. the French Chemistry & Philosophy—with other miscellaneous matters, from the present Fashions of the age, moral & political, ready to go to the Press with, by the time the other is printed off ...3

Part of the original plan, then, had finally been given an independent status. Coleridge did not give it up; he merely discovered that he had the makings of a complete and coherent work without it.

The visit of Mrs Coleridge turned out to be more of an interruption than he had expected. In April 1823 the *Logic* was still unfinished. In a letter to his son Derwent, Coleridge used it as an excuse for not writing a letter:

... I will myself write, as soon as ever I can put the last hand to my

1 *CL* v 263–4.　　　　　　　　　3 *CL* v 265.
2 *CL* v 264.

Elements of Discourse—which is grown from a mere Pistolette into an adult Blunderbuss—without any pun on the *Canons* of Logic—[1]

His appeal to J. T. Coleridge was made a month and a half later.

If our initial conjecture that Coleridge had completed a rough draft of the *Logic* by June 1823 is correct, his reluctance to approach a publisher directly can readily be understood. His own publications had never been successful, and such reputation as he had certainly was not for writing practical introductory works.[2] His appeal to his nephew implies that he anticipated the doubts that might occur to a publisher confronted with the *Logic*. If so, he was justified in doing so. Following J. T. Coleridge's advice, he approached Murray—who had already published *Christabel, Kubla Khan, and the Pains of Sleep* in 1816. On 7 July he wrote despondently to Charlotte Brent:

... I have been always at the West End of the Town—and mostly dancing attendance on a proud Bookseller, & I fear, to little purpose—weary enough of my existence, God knows! and yet not a tittle the more disposed to better it at the price of Apostasy or Suppression of the Truth.—If I could but once get off the two Works, on which I rely for the Proof that I have not lived in vain, and had these off my mind, I could then maintain myself well enough by writing for the purpose of what I got by it—but it is an anguish, I cannot look in the face, to abandon just as it is completed the work of such intense & long continued labor—& if I cannot make an agreement with Murray, I must try Colbourn—& if with neither, owing to the loud Calumny of the Edingburgh & the silent but more injurious detraction of the Quarterly Review, I must try to get them published by Subscription.[3]

Coleridge's fears were realised. Murray remained unco-operative. We do not know whether Coleridge approached Colburn, presumably Henry Colburn the proprietor of the *New Monthly Magazine*, but in August 1823 he took the *Logic* to the publishers of his forthcoming *Aids to Reflection*, Taylor and Hessey, and a new phase had begun.

On 16 August 1823 Coleridge wrote to Taylor and Hessey as follows:

There are two or three other things of more Moment to me at least, on which I should be glad to consult you—particularly, on two Works, one of which is finished and perfectly ready for the Press, and the other nearly so—works that have occupied the best hours of the last twenty years of my Life ...[4]

[1] *CL* v 273.
[2] Cf *CL* iv 737 (5 Jun 1817): "'Your works, Sir! have *never* covered the expences'—& to this I have no reply to make".
[3] *CL* v 280–1.
[4] *CL* v 294.

The two works must have been the *Logic* and the "Assertion of Religion" (to which he often refers during this period).[1] But *Aids to Reflection* continued to occupy his time and attention. In order to prepare it for publication Coleridge was forced to lay the *Logic* aside temporarily. He did not forget it, and he evidently expected that it would go to press as soon as the *Aids to Reflection* had been published.

On 18 February 1824, for instance, he wrote to John Anster, "As soon as this little Pioneer [*Aids*] is out of hand, I go to the Press with the Elements of Discourse, or the Criteria of true & false Reasoning . . .".[2] We find Coleridge reminding Hessey of it, in a cheerful letter about the proofs of *Aids to Reflection*:

In the next work (the Elements of Discourse) I must make a bargain with the Printers or Compositors, that the Initial Letters shall be printed as in the MS.—When Adjectives are used substantively, as the Beautiful, the Good; or Substantives are used that in other places are participles, as the Being, a capital is necessary.[3]

On 24 February 1824 Coleridge wrote to his friend George Skinner explaining the need for such a work:

Heretical as it will sound from & to a Cambridge Man, yet I confidently anticipate a convert in you to my Creed respecting the importance of Logic as the one of the two Organa of Philosophy and physical Science—Mathematics taken as the other and the imperfection of either without the other. Shall I take a step further and plunge over head and ears? Yes! to you I will whisper my belief, that hitherto neither Logic nor dialectic has been presented to the English Reader or even to the University Students otherwise than in a dress at once tattered and repulsive, and that on the strength of this belief I devoted so many laborious months, I might say Years to my "Elements of Discourse".[4]

The remark that follows suggests that he may have been preparing to revise the *Logic*:

A recent perusal of Aristotle's Analytics & Topics with a superficial looking thro' his Metaphysics convinces me likewise, that we have not even a philosophic statement either of the value or the defects of his logical Works or of what parts possessed only a temporary and accidental Value and what possess a permanent worth.[5]

In May 1824 Taylor and Hessey advertised the "Elements of Discourse" as forthcoming.[6]

[1] See e.g. *CL* v 227, 265, 281, 337, and 354.
[2] *CL* v 337.
[3] 19 Jan 1824: *CL* v 323–4.
[4] *CL* v 340–1.
[5] *CL* v 341.
[6] See *CL* v 337n, referring to Edmund Blunden *Keats's Publisher: A Memoir of John Taylor (1781–1864)* (1936) 154n.

During this year, reports of progress with *Aids to Reflection* were sometimes accompanied with comments on the need to get on with the *Logic*. On 12 April 1824 he wrote to Wordsworth: "I must now set to work with *all* my powers and thoughts to my Leighton, and then to my logic, and then to my *opus maximum!*"[1]

On 6 October, he referred in the course of a letter to Gillman to "that little Box . . . in which Watson's Copy of the Logic is contained".[2] On 26 April 1825 Coleridge wrote in rather definite terms to Richard Cattermole that "The second, or the Elements of Discourse, is finished: and in preparation for the Press."[3] But Cattermole was secretary of the Royal Society of Literature, and Coleridge may have wanted to impress him with an air of confidence appropriate to a recently appointed Royal Associate of the Royal Society.

More important or reliable evidence is a letter Coleridge sent to John Hookham Frere in January 1826 along with a presentation copy of *Aids to Reflection*. Frere was attempting to secure some form of pension from the government for Coleridge, and Coleridge in his letter outlined the state of his unpublished works. He mentioned three: the *Logic*, which he says is "finished and transcribed for the press": his "Opus Maximum", "of which the MSS *materials* are complete"; and finally, a volume entitled "Travels in Body and Mind, or the Sceptic's Pilgrimage to the Temple of Truth", which he declared that he expected to have ready for the printer by the end of October.[4] His remarks about the contents of the *Logic* made it plain that even at this late date we are not being told about the final version. The one described to Frere is evidently aimed partly at the detection of sophisms; Coleridge mentions "a reduction of all the modes of deceptive argument to a few distinct classes, with examples of each, commencing with some Bull, or broad & palpable Absurdity . . .".[5] One can only conjecture that Taylor and Hessey, whose partnership was in any case dissolved in 1825,[6] must have declined to publish the *Logic* in roughly its present form, or that

---

[1] *CL* v 354.

[2] *CL* v 375. This passage suggests either that Watson had made a copy of the whole, and perhaps Stutfield too, or that each had made partial copies. For Green's comment on the existence of Stutfield's transcript see above, pp xxxvii–xxxviii.

[3] *CL* v 428.

[4] *CL* vi 539–40.

[5] *CL* vi 540. For mss related to the *Logic*, see Appendixes B–F. Cf also N 29 f 99ᵛ for a proposed chapter on noumena and phenomena; f 95, for a discussion of practical instances of false logic, and, for an outline of part of the *Logic* leading into discussion of the syllogism, ff 39–42ᵛ. This material will appear in *CN* IV along with various other entries pertinent to the *Logic*.

[6] Blunden *Keats's Publisher* 177.

Coleridge did not present it to them because it was unfinished, and that having turned aside from the work in order to complete *Aids to Reflection*, he was left with the necessity of returning to it after it had been allowed to cool for three years.

Coleridge did not abandon the *Logic*. At some stage, probably in the latter half of 1827, either he or J. H. Green seems to have started having it and some of his other manuscripts "transcribed" for the press. This procedure should probably be distinguished from his customary dictation to an amanuensis, which was useful to him when he was composing. It is likely that the transcription was made from the manuscript or manuscripts dictated to Watson (and possibly Stutfield) during the 1822–3 period. The effect would be to make a more attractive manuscript, but it would also have given Coleridge an opportunity both to make corrections and to add materials, probably by attaching manuscripts to the *Logic* that had not previously been part of it. We get hints of this activity from his letters. One to Blanco White, written on 28 November 1827, mentions it as being in progress.[1] In August of the following year he wrote to H. N. Coleridge, "... I am now employed in making out for the Press the first in the series of my Works, that on the Power and Use of Words ...".[2]

In November, he wrote to his friend Hyman Hurwitz:

it is my purpose immediately on my return to put to the Press, if I can secure a fair Publisher on fair terms, my long-announced Work on the power and use of *words*—in short, an Organum verè organum, or Logic in it's living uses, for the Senate, the Pulpit, the Bar ...[3]

He added the request that Hurwitz enquire of Taylor whether he was interested in it. Little seems to be known about Coleridge's relations with Taylor at this stage. His improving reputation and the relative success of *Aids to Reflection* (which Taylor was proposing to bring out in a second edition) may well have made the publisher look more favourably on the *Logic*. Early in 1829, Coleridge forwarded a set of terms for Taylor's consideration along with a letter to Thomas Hurst, who evidently was to act as an intermediary. Three works are mentioned in it, and the third is

one large Volume of the Power and Use of Words, including a full exposition of the Constitution & Limits of the Human Understanding, &c with a compleat System of Logic in it's three functions, as Canon, or the Logic of *conclusion*; as Criterion, or Logic applied to the *Premises*; and as

[1] *CL* vi 714.
[3] *CL* vi 773.
[2] *CL* vi 750.

Organ, or Logic as an instrument of discovering the Truth of Things in themselves . . .[1]

The description for the first time entirely corresponds to the *Logic*. Taylor, however, must have declined the offer, and the second edition of *Aids to Reflection* when it appeared in 1831 did so over the imprint of Hurst, Chance and Co.

This failure to interest Taylor seems to mark the end of Coleridge's efforts to prepare the *Logic* for publication. A year before his death he turned to it again as being properly introductory to the more advanced parts of his philosophy. He wrote to J. H. Green on 26 July 1833:

I went to Ramsgate, in the intention of reviewing our Logic, your transcripts of which I had taken with me, and in the hope of rendering the Chapters already written a fit preparation for, & foundation of, the more important third Part—on the IDEAS . . .[2]

The reference is puzzling. The *Logic* as we now have it is not transcribed by Green (other manuscripts were, e.g. the "Opus Maximum"), although it might well have been transcribed under Green's supervision and at his expense. Second, if Coleridge did take it to Ramsgate with him it seems inconceivable that he could have resisted the temptation to annotate it. The last allusion to the *Logic* appears in a letter to John Sterling written on 29 October 1833, in which Coleridge wishes that he could prepare his whole system for the press with Sterling's and Green's help—"as far as it exists in writing, in any *systematic* form—that is beginning with the Propyleum, On the Power and Use of Words—comprizing Logic, as the Canons of Conclusion; as the criterion of Premises . . .".[3] As he proceeds, it becomes clear that the work once intended as a practical introduction for young men entering the professions has once again been absorbed into the more ambitious "Logosophia".

AMANUENSES AND TRANSCRIBERS

The evidence suggests that Coleridge dictated the *Logic*, probably to two amanuenses, then annotated it, and that it was finally written out in a fair copy without his being present to give advice. Before the 1820's his habit of dictating his works had become fixed; it seems to have helped him to commit himself to paper and it took advantage

[1] *CL* VI 781n.
[2] *CL* VI 946–7.
[3] *CL* VI 967.

of his remarkable gift for extempore discourse. His relationship with his amanuenses was generally one that lent the dictation some of the dimensions of a conversation.

The earliest account we have of this method appears in a letter Dorothy Wordsworth wrote to Lady Beaumont in 1810 about his progress with *The Friend*:

The fact is that he either does a great deal or nothing at all; and that he composes with a rapidity truly astonishing, if one did not reflect upon the large stores of thought which he has laid up, and the quantity of knowledge which he is continually gaining from books—add to this his habit of expressing his ideas in conversation in elegant language. He has written a whole *Friend* more than once in two days. They are never re-transcribed, and he generally has dictated to Miss Hutchinson, who takes the words down from his mouth.[1]

One result of Sara Hutchinson's co-operation was that Coleridge kept *The Friend* going for considerably longer than his closest friends had expected; when it stopped at the twenty-seventh number it was only after ill health had obliged her to leave him.[2]

By the time Coleridge went to live with Dr and Mrs Gillman in Highgate in 1816, his reliance on dictation for his public writings had become a necessity. He mentioned it in a letter to Gillman:

I presume, there will be no Objection to Mr Morgan coming to me, as my literary Counsellor and Amanuensis at $\frac{1}{2}$ past 11 every morning & staying with me till $\frac{1}{2}$ past 3. I have been for so many years accustomed to dicta[te] while he writes that I now cannot compose without him—.[3]

Before the end of the year the Gillmans themselves had been pressed into service.[4]

The term "literary Counsellor" that Coleridge applied to his friend John Morgan is a reminder that his amanuenses were not expected to be mere mechanical drudges. Sara Hutchinson's presence and sympathy must have helped to sustain him during the difficult months when *The Friend* was getting under way. We are given a hint that he paid attention to her opinions when he says of an alteration he had made: "the WHOLE passage was inserted, and intertruded, after the rest was written, reluctante Amanuensi meâ, in order to *unrealize* it even at the risk of *dis*naturalizing it . . . ".[5] Gillman too was ready to sympathise and admire:

---

[1] *WL* (*M* rev) I 391.
[2] For DW's opinion that C could not have gone on much longer in any case, see *WL* (*M* rev) I 398.
[3] *CL* IV 630.
[4] See *CL* IV 683, 692.
[5] To RS c 24 Dec 1809: *CL* III 266·

Mr Gillman . . . observed a few days ago, that till the time that he had been occasionally my Amanuensis he had not the remotest conception of what, how great, and (almost) how endless the difficulties are of composing where the Writer understands, and binds himself down to attend to, the three-fold Ordonnance of Sound, of Image, and of Logic.[1]

In a way, the amanuenses provided Coleridge with an advance glimpse of the reactions of the reading public. Meeting them regularly helped him to keep up the momentum of composition and gave him a chance to try out the effects of what he had to say.

The identity of the amanuenses and transcribers of the *Logic* is obscured by the problems involved in dating the work. Part of it at least seems to have been dictated to two young men, John Watson and Charles Bradshaw Stutfield.[2] In the letter to Thomas Allsop of 25 January 1822, Coleridge reported that

with Mr Stutfield and Mr Watson I have already proceeded on two successive Thursdays, and compleated the Introduction, and the first Chapter, amounting to somewhat more than a closely printed Octavo Sheet, requiring no such revision as would require Transcription . . .[3]

Another letter to Allsop in December of the same year claims that the end of the work is in sight:

In reality, I have *now* little else but to transcribe—and even this would in part only be necessary, but that I must of course dictate the sentences to Mr Stutfield & Mr Watson, & shall therefore avail myself of the opportunity of occasional correction & improvement.[4]

At this point Coleridge's philosophical class intrudes. He had advertised it in the *Courier* on 25 February 1822, and he outlined the intention of it in a letter to Daniel Stuart on 15 March:

from 12 to 2 or $\frac{1}{2}$ past 2 I meant to *dictate*, each of my Auditors being his own & [my ama]nuensis—the remaining hour & a half t[o be spent in] conversation, questions, discussions &c . . .[5]

Stutfield and Watson, as we have seen, had already begun to take dictation, and there is no way of telling to what extent their sessions coincided with the meetings of the class once it had begun. One curious piece of evidence is the pencilled note scrawled on an end-paper of Coleridge's copy of Kant's *Logik*: "After I have ceased

---

[1] To R. H. Brabant 5 Dec 1816: *CL* IV 692.

[2] Both were in their middle twenties in 1822. Watson was a sort of assistant to Dr Gillman and had been a member of the household for over a year (*CL* V 226–7); Stutfield was the son of an old Bristol friend of Thomas Poole's, and a vintner like his father.

[3] *CL* V 204.

[4] *CL* V 264.

[5] *CL* V 220.

dictating, I would be left with Watson and St".[1] The inference that he had the book in his hand while dictating is borne out by the substantial sections of Kant's *Logik* that appear in the *Logic*, but the purpose of the note is baffling. Did Coleridge want to be left alone with Watson and Stutfield after the other members of the class had left, or was he afraid that he might be? And was the note written to himself or to some diplomatic third party—perhaps his fellow-thinker J. H. Green? Whether the *Logic* was dictated to the philosophical class or not, it seems plain that it was intended to provide an educational experience for the amanuenses.

The description of Coleridge's class informs us that he was in the habit of dictating deliberately to his pupils, "whether from memory or immediate impulse, his sublime lessons, permitting them to take his words down in writing".[2] The composition of the *Logic* itself makes it seem likely that he sometimes dictated translations to them, Kant's *Logik* being a case in point. Manuscript remains that seem to be rough drafts of the *Logic* written in Coleridge's own hand suggest that these too were probably made use of.[3] However fluent the dictation may have been, it seems certain that Coleridge had ready access to his books and papers.

When he broke off his dictation in 1823, Watson and Stutfield had probably both completed copies of it. Coleridge evidently retained Watson's copy, for, as we have noticed above, he refers to it in the letter to Gillman written in October 1824: "that little Box ... in which Watson's Copy of the Logic is contained".[4] Stutfield's copy is referred to in the correspondence between J. H. Green and C. M. Ingleby, but nothing further is known of it.[5] The manuscript of the *Logic*, however, is neither of these. It is watermarked variously 1824 and 1827; it seems to be all of a piece and cannot therefore have been written out before 1827. The two hands in which it is written do not appear elsewhere in Coleridge's manuscript remains, and it seems likely that the two volumes of which the manuscript is made up are the transcripts referred to as Green's in the letter Coleridge wrote to him in 1833.[6] In November of 1827 Coleridge mentioned to Blanco

---

[1] BM copy.

[2] *Fraser's Magazine* xii (1835) 493.

[3] E.g. BM Egerton MS 2801 ff 74, 85–7, and 139; N 29 ff 39ᵛ–44, 46ᵛ–47ᵛ; and two pages of ms in the Beinecke Rare Book and Manuscript Library, Yale University, one of which is reproduced as the frontispiece.

[4] *CL* v 375.

[5] See above, pp xxxvii–xxxviiii.

[6] See above, p li. The possibility that Stutfield and Watson were themselves the transcribers, or that they took dictation at a later date, has to be ruled out on the following grounds: (*a*) comparison of samples of Watson's

White that one of his books was "now transcribing for the Press . . .".[1] The transcription was probably taken care of by Green's amanuenses.

While Coleridge's amanuenses undoubtedly helped him, they occasionally made mistakes. He complained of Morgan's errors in the preparation of *Biographia Literaria* in 1815 and used them as an excuse for delay in sending copy to the printer.[2] His notebooks contain amusing examples of the kinds of errors that could creep in when an amanuensis nodded:

"The abominations of Tiberius at Capreae".—These were the words, I dictated. My Amanuensis wrote them down exactly thus—"The burning Nations of Tibby Harris and Cap. Ray".[3]

and again:

"*Officious for Equivalents*" (I was speaking of the small German Potentates) This my Amanuensis wrote—"*Fishing for Elephants*"—which as I at the time observed, was a sort of *Noah's* angling, that could hardly have occurred except at the commencement of the Deluge . . .[4]

Coleridge may have embroidered these blunders a little for the sake of a good story, and the *Logic* shows no sign of error on such a scale. Nevertheless, because it is manifestly an uncorrected transcription of a dictated work, some mistakes and ellipses are to be found in it. The rendering of "Novum Arcanum" for "Novum Organum" would have amused Coleridge, as would "Equinus" for "Aquinas". The manuscript is underpunctuated throughout, and the transcribers' inability to cope with Greek phrases and their uncertainty about where sentences begin and end make one wish that Coleridge had fulfilled his intention of reviewing the *Logic* in 1833. He recorded sadly, "day has followed day, without any work . . .".[5]

---

handwriting (the transcript of the "Essay on Faith" in NYPL Berg Collection, which C identified as in Watson's hand, and the presentation copy of Milton *Poems* in the Widener Library, Harvard University) shows it to be quite unlike; further, Watson died of consumption in Jul 1827, and C lamented that he had seen so little of him for many months (*CL* VI 693); (*b*) Stutfield's hand has been harder to find samples of and only signatures have been traced (eight signatures on his will at Somerset House, dated 1853, and another in the Middlesex County

Archive, dated 1823, on his being sworn in as a justice of the peace); they are quite similar to Hand B in the ms but in the absence of further evidence the similarity of hand is inconclusive. However, Stutfield was in touch with C (who stood godfather to Mary Coleridge Stutfield in 1831) during the period from 1827 to 1833 (*CL* VI 676–7, 841, 869–70, and 961).

[1] *CL* VI 714.
[2] To Gutch 17 Sept 1815: *CL* IV 586.
[3] *CN* III 4240.
[4] *CN* III 4239.
[5] To Green 26 Jul 1833: *CL* VI 947.

SOURCES

Coleridge's use of sources in the *Logic* can be looked at from two points of view. It provides us with a most interesting glimpse of his methods of composition, and at the same time it raises the issue of plagiarism. Substantial parts of the *Logic* are translations or quotations from works by other writers—Kant, Moses Mendelssohn, and Schelling in particular—and although Coleridge makes generous general acknowledgments and some specific ones, there is a danger that readers unfamiliar with his sources may mistake vintage Kant for vintage Coleridge.[1]

A letter that Coleridge wrote in 1819 in response to an invitation to give a series of lectures outlines the way in which he usually prepared himself for them. He made the following declaration:

> ... I would not lecture on any subject for which I had to *acquire* the main knowledge, even though a month's or three months' previous time were allowed me; on no subject that had not employed my thoughts for a large portion of my life since earliest manhood, free of all outward and particular purpose ...[2]

He added:

> during a course of lectures, I faithfully employ *all* the intervening days in collecting and digesting the materials. ... The day of the lecture, till the hour of commencement, I devote to the consideration, what of the mass before me is best fitted to answer the purposes of a lecture ...[3]

It was Coleridge's practice to confine himself, in his lectures and his writing, to topics that were familiar to him, and to prepare himself for particular occasions by dipping back into books and his own papers for materials that would best illustrate or explain what he wanted to say. Just as conversation brought out his flow of thought by providing him with an appreciative listener, and the presence of amanuenses with a stimulus to compose, his books permitted him to indulge in mental dialogues with the authors and to record his part in them in marginalia. The *Logic* seems to have been written while Coleridge was in the midst of his books and manuscripts, moving

---

[1] The general problem of C's use of his sources is treated fully and subtly in Thomas McFarland *Coleridge and the Pantheist Tradition* (Oxford 1969). For useful summaries of modern discussions of the topic, see René Wellek "Coleridge's Philosophy and Criticism" in *The English Romantic Poets: A Review of Research and Criticism* ed Frank Jordan Jr (New York 1972) 209–58.

[2] To J. Britton 28 Feb 1819: *CL* iv 923.

[3] *CL* iv 924.

from one to another with a sure recollection of passages that seemed to him to put the case he was making with the force and clarity it deserved. In some instances he must have dictated translations with the books in his hand; English texts—his own writings among them —were probably placed in front of the amanuensis to be copied out; occasionally he must have used his own manuscript copies of passages that he had singled out from books earlier.

Coleridge used his sources in three ways. He drew examples from them; he borrowed explanations of difficult points; and he drew much of the inspiration for the *Logic* as a whole from one of them. The examples are the simplest to deal with. Two pages are quoted from Kirby and Spence's *Introduction to Entomology*—the passage in question being a description of phosphorescent ephemerae—and applied to a description of the way in which we imagine the points and lines of plane geometry. Several pages of discussion of kinds of questions that may be asked are taken from the notes at the back of Moses Mendelssohn's *Morgenstunden* and slightly rearranged. In the case of Kirby and Spence Coleridge probably thought that a scientific account of the ephemerae would interest the reader (he had commented on similar phenomena himself years before their book was published); in the case of Mendelssohn he had found an explanation of a point that was needed in the *Logic* and that was aimed at readers in Germany of the level he was hoping for in England.

Most of Coleridge's borrowings from his own books—from *The Statesman's Manual, Biographia Literaria*, and the second *Lay Sermon*—appear in his footnotes, as though at some stage he had felt that they would provide helpful glosses on what he was saying, and perhaps from a very human wish to remind readers of their existence. Two of the major borrowings from *Biographia Literaria* were of passages from other authors. One of these, a Latin quotation from Kant's *De mundi sensibilis atque intelligibilis forma et principiis*, he never tired of recommending to young men who asked him what they ought to read; the other, the theses derived from Schelling, expressed in succinct form the various implications of looking at the relationship of subject and object.[1]

Borrowings from Kant, however, are much the most important. Coleridge's discussion of the syllogism is largely quotation from "Die falsche Spitzfindigkeit der vier syllogistischen Figuren"; one gets the impression that, like Kant, he was not much interested in the topic but felt obliged to deal with it as a traditional part of formal

[1] For a discussion of C's contribution to the theses, see *CN* III 4265n.

logic. Shorter passages are taken from Kant's *Logik*—a book put together by G. B. Jäsche from lecture notes—from *Principiorum primorum cognitionis metaphysicae nova elucidatio*—an early work that Coleridge valued because it seemed to him to illustrate the bent of mind that was to lead to the philosophical achievements of Kant's maturity—and from the *Prolegomena zu einer jeden künftigen Metaphysik*. These works interested Coleridge because of their relationship to the *Critique of Pure Reason*.

In *Biographia Literaria* Coleridge acknowledged the effect that Kant's philosophy had had on him:

> The writings of the illustrious sage of Königsberg, the founder of the Critical Philosophy, more than any other work, at once invigorated and disciplined my understanding. The originality, the depth, and the compression of the thoughts; the novelty and subtlety, yet solidity and importance of the distinctions; the adamantine chain of the logic; and I will venture to add (paradox as it will appear to those who have taken their notion of IMMANUEL KANT from Reviewers and Frenchmen) the *clearness* and *evidence*, of the "CRITIQUE OF THE PURE REASON;" of the "JUDGEMENT;" of the "METAPHYSICAL ELEMENTS OF NATURAL PHILOSOPHY;" and of his "RELIGION WITHIN THE BOUNDS OF PURE REASON," took possession of me as with a giant's hand. After fifteen years' familiarity with them, I still read these and all his other productions with undiminished delight and increasing admiration.[1]

Coleridge's enthusiasm did not find much of an echo among his English contemporaries.[2] In the *Logic* he tried to introduce the sections of the *Critique of Pure Reason* that had so struck him when he was young. Parts he paraphrased, but for much of the material he borrowed he was content to translate into an idiomatic English that is a credit to the original.

It should be added that the conception of the *Logic* as a whole—Coleridge's reason for feeling that he had something new to say—is derived from the *Critique of Pure Reason*. This was the part of Kant that he felt was of greatest value. He tried to present it in an introductory and educational garb, not as a tribute to Kant but as a contribution to the cause of better thinking and of truth.

---

[1] *BL* ch 9 (1907) i 99.   [2] See *Kant in England* 3–62.

COLERIDGE'S AIMS

At one point in the *Logic*, Coleridge mentions that he is writing for those "filling or destined to fill the higher and middle stations of society . . . though with especial reference to those who are forming themselves for public and professional life, the pulpit, the bar, the senate, the professor's chair, or for that which belongs to all and includes the qualities of all, the public press . . .".[1] His audience then was very much the same as the one he had had in mind when writing his Lay Sermons (to the upper and middle classes of society). Like the roughly contemporaneous *Aids to Reflection*, which he subtitled "in the formation of a manly character", it was directed to the young. The nature of his audience is best described in the letter he wrote to Daniel Stuart on 15 March 1822 apropos of his philosophical class:

it was suggested, that . . . I might form a Class of five or six men, who are educating themselves for the Pulpit, the Bar, the Senate, or any of those walks of Life, in which the possession and the display of intellect are of especial importance.—That sort of *Knowlege* which is best calculated to re-appear as Power—all that a Gentleman ought to possess, and most of what it is most desirable that every gentleman should possess—the Root, and Trunk of the Tree, as the Antecedent common to all the different Branches . . .[2]

Whereas *Aids to Reflection* was to further the moral development of young men, the *Logic* and the philosophical class were to contribute to the development of their ability to think for themselves.

Quite early in his life Coleridge had thought of earning a living as a teacher of young men, and his letters contain some of his theories about the course education should take. In one of them, written to Charles Lloyd, Sr, whose son was about to domesticate with Mr and Mrs Coleridge in Nether Stowey, an ambitious curriculum is outlined:

While your Son remains with me, he will, of course, be acquiring that knowledge and those powers of Intellect which are necessary as the *foundation* of excellence in all professions, rather than the immediate science of *any*. *Languages* will engross one or two hours in every day: the *elements* of Chemistry, Geometry, Mechanics, and Optics the remaining hours of study. After tolerable proficiency in these, we shall proceed to the study of *Man* and of *Men*—I mean, Metaphysics and History—and finally, to a thorough examination of the Jewish and Christian Dispensations, their doctrines and evidences . . .[3]

[1] Below, p 144.
[2] *CL* v 220.
[3] 14 Nov 1796: *CL* I 256. Cf *CL* I 209.

The range of subject matter is what first strikes one here, but Coleridge's emphasis on "elements" and "powers of Intellect" is really more significant. He had a great respect for facts and for applied learning, and he possessed a daunting command of both, but as he grew older he came to feel that his own special contribution as a teacher had more to do with what he called "Method" and "Principles".

Nevertheless, he was aware that method was only a part of education. One of his marginalia describes the way in which he thought a scholar contemplating metaphysical research should be prepared:

i.e. 1. by common logic. 2. by the elements of Geometry and universal Arithmetic. 3. by psychology empiric—4. by philosophical Grammar—5. by Dialectic, or transcendental Logic—that which determines on the legitimacy of the major or premise of every Syllogism by that such discrimination of the faculties, which as gives to each its due, & precludes false predicates, (ex. gr. accidents of time and space of νοουμενα, the ideas of the pure Reason) & (6.) lastly, by a subdued and loving habit of Soul.[1]

In another he provides a guide to the ages at which he felt that these subjects should be studied:

From one year to 7 Language, with writing. From 7 to 12, Languages with Cyphering.—12 to 15. Language, Composition, Oratory, Mathematics—15 to 18—These, adding History and Logic, the latter in the two lower forms, the Canonic and the Criterional—For the Universities I would reserve the Organic & the transcendental.[2]

His own *Logic* was designed to bridge the last two periods, introducing readers to the "Canonic and the Criterional" logic and to the "Organic & the transcendental". Only the canon and criterion were completed. The *Logic* should be looked upon as an elementary and introductory work intended for the equivalent of modern undergraduates. It is not meant to be a contribution to the development of philosophy or an argument against philosophical antagonists. At points Coleridge actually achieves the sort of simplicity that one expects from introductions, but for the most part the *Logic* shifts abruptly from level to level in a manner reminiscent of *Biographia Literaria*. One of Coleridge's rueful notes sums up the likely reaction of the students for whom the book was meant:

[1] Note on the flyleaf of Proclus *The Philosophical and Mathematical Commentaries on the First Book of Euclid* tr Thomas Taylor (1792) I (BM copy).

[2] Heinrich Steffens *Die gegenwärtige Zeit* ... (Berlin 1817) II 748–9 (BM copy).

Readers of my Logic, or the method of legitimate Thinking and Discoursing, who yet expect to find short and easy ~~instruction~~ Receipts on how to think without thinking at all—how to think without thought—how many! *Alas*! S. T. C—.[1]

Logic has been the starting point for aspiring philosophers since classical times, and Coleridge was no exception,[2] but his interest in it deepened and increased. In a note dated 3 January 1810 he makes a distinction between thought and attention and says that "in the new light afforded by it to my mind I see more plainly why Mathematics cannot be a substitute for Logic . . . and why therefore Cambridge has produced so few men of genius & original power since the time of Newton . . .".[3] As a Cambridge man himself, and a loyal one, albeit neither a mathematician nor a graduate, he took wry comfort in the conviction that the logic that Oxford insisted upon and Cambridge neglected was a travesty of the real thing.[4]

He was not alone in believing that logic was important and that the standard textbooks were inadequate and misleading. John Stuart Mill tells in his *Autobiography* how at about the same time he and his friends were looking for books on logic:

Our first text-book was Aldrich, but being disgusted with its superficiality, we reprinted one of the most finished among the many manuals of the school logic, which my father, a great collector of such books, possessed, the Manuductio ad Logicam of the Jesuit Du Trieu. After finishing this, we took up Whately's Logic, then first republished from the Encyclopaedia Metropolitana, and finally the "Computatio sive Logica" of Hobbes.[5]

Coleridge shared Mill's dissatisfaction with the traditional presentation of logic, a dissatisfaction that Sir William Hamilton, Augustus de Morgan, and Mill were to try to meet by looking at the problems of logic in a new way. Coleridge, however, was dissatisfied for different reasons and seems to have been unaware of the exciting developments that were beginning to take place.[6] When he spoke in his letter

[1] On the endpaper of F. H. Jacobi *Ueber die Lehre des Spinoza* . . . (Breslau 1789) (BM copy).
[2] See e.g. *CL* I 625 (to Godwin 22 Sept 1800).
[3] *CN* III 3670. Cf an earlier note (?Dec 1803): "Of Logic & its neglect, & the consequent strange Illogicality of many even of our principal writers—hence our Crumbly friable Stile/ each Author a mere Hour-Glass/—& if we go on in this way, we shall soon have undone all that Aristotle did for the human Race, & come back to Proverbs & Apologues—". *CN* I 1759.
[4] See the letter to Skinner quoted above, p xlviii, *CL* v 340–1. For a detailed and critical contemporary view of the state of Oxford logic, see William Hamilton's anonymous review article "Recent Publications on Logical Science" *Ed Rev* LVII (1833) 194–238.
[5] *Autobiography* (1873) 122.
[6] For C's failure to appreciate Hegel's contribution, see Orsini 242–3.

to Skinner about logic and dialectic not having been presented to the English reader in a satisfactory form, the nationality of the reader is significant. What Coleridge meant was that the logic of Kant had not yet been made available. Kant has been criticised for paying lip service to the importance of logic while really presenting a "curious mixture of metaphysics and epistemology".[1] Coleridge, who in the matter of logic relied upon Kant's authority, followed suit.

In a letter to his nephew, J. T. Coleridge, in 1825, he explained what it was about Kant's philosophy that counted with him:

> ... Immanuel Kant I assuredly do value most highly; not, however, as a Metaphysician but as a Logician, who has completed and systematized what Lord Bacon had boldly designed and loosely sketched out in the miscellany of Aphorisms, his Novum Organum—in Kant's Critique of the Pure Reason there is more than one fundamental error; but the main fault lies in the Title-page, which to the manifold advantage of the Work might be exchanged for—An Inquisition respecting the constitution and limits of the Human Understanding.[2]

It was this part of Kant's philosophy that Coleridge offered to his readers; the *Logic*, from a philosophical point of view at least, is essentially a popularisation of the *Critique of Pure Reason*.

The philosophical arguments of the *Logic* are often complex and subtle; the complexity and the subtlety are Kant's. Coleridge is a faithful interpreter of his master in the field of logic, and he does not at any point attempt to revise, refute, or refine. He comments and explains, and he paraphrases and selects, but he does not offer new arguments. His reticence may be explained in part by the admission, which he would have been the first to make, that it is very difficult to improve on Kant. There is no evidence to suggest that Coleridge was capable of this sort of sustained thinking or that he ever attempted it. The other part of the explanation is that Coleridge was not really interested in the technical difficulties solved by Kant; what he cared about was the consequence of Kant's solutions. A remark recorded in the *Table Talk* is representative of his attitude:

> There are two kinds of logic: 1. Syllogistic. 2. Criterional. How any one can by any spinning make out more than ten or a dozen pages about the first, is inconceivable to me; all those absurd forms of syllogisms are one half pure sophisms, and the other half mere forms of rhetoric.[3]

This underestimate of the syllogism may be derived from Kant, but the impatience with what might be called philosophy for philosophy's

---

[1] Kneale p 355.   [3] *TT* 23 Sept 1830.
[2] *CL* v 421.

sake is Coleridge's own. He was perfectly able to appreciate the most advanced philosophy of his time, and he took great pains to keep abreast of it, but he did not contribute to it. The technical aspects of philosophy (and formal logic in particular), like chemistry, geology, archaeology, anthropology, and medicine, and all the other elaborate sciences that he tried to weld into a unified way of understanding his world, found an important place in his mind. For the most part he was content to dabble in them, to read the latest authorities and talk to the experts; only when their conclusions seemed to have unpalatable implications did he concentrate on the details and seek alternative explanations. He is often an acute critic in fields remote from his own, but he was unlikely to be a discoverer.

The interest of the *Logic*, therefore, does not lie in its bearing on the development of philosophy, but in the light it sheds on Coleridge's opinions in the 1820's. His declared aim of training the minds of young professional men is perfectly genuine, and there can be no doubt that most readers of the *Logic* will find that they are indulging in intellectual exercise. But the student of the literary Coleridge is likely to be seeking different game.

Coleridge's analysis of his own intellectual development in *Biographia Literaria* provides an excellent introduction to the *Logic*. In the *Biographia* we are told that as a young man he passed through three philosophical phases: first materialism, represented by David Hartley; then idealism, represented by Berkeley; and finally, the critical philosophy as it is found in Kant and Schelling. His account of these phases is offered as both an explanation and a warning: an explanation of the reasons for his beliefs, but also a warning to others in the hope that they may benefit from his experience. The *Logic* is another of Coleridge's attempts to do for others what he felt he had managed to do for himself. It is ostensibly a less personal document than the *Biographia*, but his conviction that its implications were of vital importance, even if the philosophy involved was elementary and derivative, is based on their close relationship to the growth of his own mind.

The *Logic*, like the *Critique of Pure Reason*, restricts its discussion to the limits and procedures of the understanding. It does not deal directly either with sense experience or with the pure reason. And yet Coleridge's account carries an undertone of digression that bears purposefully upon our conceptions of sense experience and the pure reason. He seems unable to resist recurrent discussions of the way in which we see things and the way in which God may be supposed to see things. This undertone may not be wholly deliberate, but it provides a hint of aims in the *Logic* that have not been openly declared.

One of the most striking of these aims has to do with the discussion of our concepts of space and time. In 1801, when he was twenty-eight, Coleridge wrote a letter to Thomas Poole that was to become famous; it contains the following statement:

The interval since my last Letter has been filled up by me in the most intense Study. If I do not greatly delude myself, I have not only completely extricated the notions of Time, and Space; but have overthrown the doctrine of Association, as taught by Hartley, and with it all the irreligious metaphysics of modern Infidels—especially, the doctrine of Necessity.[1]

As the "extrication" of space and time is central to Part Two of the *Logic*, the religious consequences attached to it at such an early date are of considerable interest to us here. An even earlier letter, written in 1798, picks up another major theme of Part Two of the *Logic*—the problem of cause and effect. Coleridge refers to "Hume's system of Causation—or rather of non-causation":

This is the pillar, & confessedly, the *sole* pillar, of modern Atheism—if we could clearly & manifestly detect the sophisms of *this* system, I think, that Butler's Analogy *aided* by well-placed notes would answer irresistably all the objections to Christianity founded on a priori reasonings—& these are the only reasonings that infidels use even with plausibility.[2]

These statements bring us very close to Coleridge's attitude to philosophy, and consequently to his attitude to logic. The arguments are sought with partisan intensity because the conclusions they support run counter to the claims of the enemies of Christianity.

To put the matter in its starkest terms, Coleridge was a Christian who tried to confront the arguments philosophers had used against the beliefs of Christianity by meeting the philosophers on their own ground. The topics of necessity and cause and effect could be discussed in a cool and disinterested way as merely philosophical problems, but their consequences made them matters of urgent interest to the believer. If our actions are determined by external stimuli we cannot be held morally responsible for them—the unappetising consequence of eighteenth-century materialism. If the relationship of cause and effect is merely a habit of mind and not a necessary reality, we have no reason to assume that there must have

---

[1] *CL* II 706.   [2] To J. P. Estlin 13 Feb 1798: *CL* I 385-6.

been a first cause, or God—a consequence of Hume's reasoning. The extrication of space and time provided a philosophical lever to use against both of these unacceptable consequences. Kant's discussion of space and time in the *Critique of Pure Reason* lacks Coleridge's religious motive (although Coleridge thought that he must merely have concealed it), but it provides Coleridge with the very weapon he needed.

Coleridge's presentation of space and time exemplifies one sort of concealed aim that we should be on the lookout for in the *Logic*— central arguments with direct theological implications. His discussion of the verb substantive, the verb "to be", is an example of what seems to be a recurrent digression but is in fact more in the nature of a revealing major theme. The discussion of language that takes up so much of the "Introductory Chapters" should not be passed over as a merely decorative opening intended to beguile the reader. Coleridge raises two issues: the nature of the verb substantive and the relationship of verbs to nouns. Both of these issues had important philosophical implications in the early nineteenth century, and although Coleridge could scarcely have expected his young readers to notice them, they help to explain why in talking of language in a general way these issues should have occurred to him.

The question as to whether language began with verbs or with nouns dominated discussions during the eighteenth century. The *locus classicus* of the controversy is Locke's assertion in the *Essay on Human Understanding* that "if we could trace them to their sources, we should find, in all languages, the names which stand for things that fall not under our senses to have had their first rise from sensible ideas".[1] This view fitted the materialist philosophy very well, and Lockeans among Coleridge's contemporaries like Horne Tooke used it as a basis for etymological hypotheses.[2] The idealist alternative was to propose the verb as the original form of language, and in particular the verb "to be" or, as they termed it, the "verb substantive". William Vincent is representative of this school. According to him:

[the old grammarians] call Εἰμι, the verb substantive, because, as they say, it can stand alone, and all other verbs they call adjectives, because, in their opinion, they all comprehend the verb Εἰμι, or depend upon it for support. . . . What then is the sense of Εἰμι? it is the verb that represents *existenc[e]*,

[1] Bk III ch 1.
[2] In Ἔπεα πτεροεντα. *Or, The*   *Diversions of Purley* (2 vols 1798, 1805).

and this so preeminently, that it is applied with peculiar energy and propriety to the Deity as Self-existent.[1]

The appeal of this view to Coleridge must have been considerable to judge by the space devoted to the principle "Sum or I am" as a first principle in Thesis VI of Chapter 12 of *Biographia Literaria*. By the time of the *Logic*, however, he had begun to show signs of dissatisfaction with it. A note on the endpapers of one of his books reveals the grounds:

Yes! the more I sink in to my Soul, the clearer becomes my conviction, that the πρωτον και κοινον ψευδος of Schelling, Solger, Hegel, & the Germans since Fichte, consists in deducing the whole Grammar of Philosophy and Religion from the Verb Substantive, Esse, *alone*: excluding (t its co-ordinate) the auxiliary Verb, *Habere*. Our Father, that *art—thine* is the Kingdom and the Power and the Glory![2]

The danger of the idealist position was that while it affirmed existence it neglected reality.

Coleridge's solution was entirely in keeping with the spirit of the *Logic*, which is to reject the extremes of materialism or idealism either by Kant's method of showing that the matter on which they disagree is not capable of being decided by human beings or by trying to reconcile the positions. In this case he used a diagrammatic description to show that the verb substantive is a mid-point between the extremes of verb and noun, expressing the "indifference of being and action, of substantive and verb . . .".[3] From time to time in later parts of the *Logic* he strays to the theological implications of his introductory discussion. He refers explicitly to the divine "I am", and states that "a fact of all human language is . . . a fact of all human consciousness".[4] He relates universal grammar to universal logic. These references and assertions have little to do with the steps essential to his exposition of logic, but, because they reflect upon the

---

[1] *The Origination of the Greek Verb. An Hypothesis* (1794) 9–10.

[2] K. W. F. Solger *Philosophische Gespräche* (Berlin 1817) (BM copy). For a longer discussion of the verb substantive in its grammatical context, see N 29 ff 26–28.

[3] Below, p 17. A similar line of thought appears in a note on the endpapers of Kant *Metaphysische Anfangsgründe der Natur-Wissenschaft* (Riga 1787) (BM copy): "we might . . . treat Nature as a language the parts of speech of which are all Verbs, the infinitive moods however becoming Substantives, or at least capable of being construed as such—and then we should have

Body = verb substantive = subsistit

Material = Verb transitive. mediae vocis = existit, se manifestat

Matter = Verb impersonal = videtur . . .".

[4] Below, p 82. Cf p 120.

similarities between the human mind and God's mind, they bear directly upon the religious tenets that in turn made him feel that an elementary logic was needed.

Different ways of understanding the *Logic* will occur to readers who come to Coleridge from different points of view. But it is the concealed aims rather than the declared ones that make the book much more than a derivative introduction to Kant.

LOGIC

INTRODUCTORY CHAPTERS

CHAPTER I

Sketch of the History of Logic

1   One of the latest[a] speculative discoveries at which the civilised man arrives is the high expedience of drawing as sharp and distinct a line as possible around each several science[1] (the word "science" being here taken in its highest sense, as any kind or quantum of knowledge that has been reduced to rules).[b]

2(a)   The naturalists have in modern times at least set the example and furnish us with an illustration.[2] It is not indeed improbable that Aristotle himself, who in his logical and metaphysical works has devoted so large a space to the principles of definition, distinction, and distribution, was led to the subject by the experience required in his *physical* researches.[3] Impressed with the necessity of method to the successful cultivation of *natural philosophy*, and sensible that a method, which should be suited to all understandings, must be drawn from the laws and constitution of the understanding itself, he invented *logic* as a supplement to mathematics and the other organ (ὄργανον δεύτερον)[4] of the *real* sciences. To this view of the art, compared with which its uses as a groundwork of rhetoric and a training for forensic debate are but accessory and of equivocal worth, we may, I repeat, not improbably attribute the noticeable fact that in

---

a ms: latent   *b* Parentheses inserted

---

[1] A characteristic theme. In *Friend* (*CC*) I 94, C stresses the need to distinguish between what is science and what is not; here he refers to the importance of distinguishing between one science and another; as the *Logic* proceeds he turns to distinctions between the different branches of philosophy. In this paragraph and the next, C seems to be expanding on material in N 29 f 46ᵛ, which is in turn based on Kant "Ueber den Gebrauch teleologischer Principien in der Philosophie" *VS* III 107, C himself providing the reference. Ff 33ᵛ and 47–47ᵛ also

anticipate the *Logic*; see below, pp 21–3.

[2] In N 29 f 46ᵛ, C uses botanists as his example. For his views on the contribution of botanists in the eighteenth century, see *Friend* (*CC*) I 466–9.

[3] C is probably drawing on Tennemann here (III 31). Cf *P Lects* Lect 5 (1949) 184, where Aristotle's progress through the stages of observation, discrimination, and abstraction is referred to.

[4] I.e. the "second instrument" or "other organ" of the sciences concerned with physical reality.

one and the same great mind we venerate the inventor of logic and the father of natural philosophy. Equally singular, though calculated to excite very different emotions, is the fact, for fact it is, that the defect for the prevention of which logic was invented is perhaps nowhere more strikingly exemplified than in the most popular modern books, French and English, professing to *teach* logic and having its name as their title. In some of these (as in Dr. Watts' *Logic*,[1] for instance) the essentials of common logic, which have remained without change from their first promulgation by Aristotle and which are indeed as little susceptible of change as the rules of common arithmetic, are to be found, but so blended with metaphysics, theology, psychology, grammar, and in short what not, that had it been the professed object of these writers to teach the art of comparison instead of the science of method they could scarcely have adopted a more successful plan.[2] In the far-famed *Logic* of Condillac, on the other hand, the student may find the whole theory of materialism (borrowed without acknowledgment from David Hartley) only not one syllable concerning logic itself.[3] How different has been the course pursued by the great naturalists of this and the preceding century,[4] who, rather than hazard confusion by co-ordinating heterogeneous subjects, have chosen to create a new class —genus or species as the occasion appeared to warrant—and who at all times have preferred the inconvenience of a newly minted or obsolete term to the evil of a loose and equivocal designation, how-

[1] Isaac Watts *Logick: or, the Right Use of Reason in the Enquiry after Truth . . .* (1725). This Lockean book passed through seven editions by 1740 and was still being reprinted in 1822. In Nov 1799, C was reading selections from it in Vicesimus Knox *Elegant Extracts; or, Useful and Entertaining Passages in Prose* (1784) (*CN* I 531), and he quoted one of them in *The Friend* in 1818 (*Friend—CC*—I 484). For a detailed account of the nature and significance of Watts's *Logick*, see Wilbur Samuel Howell *Eighteenth-Century British Logic and Rhetoric* (Princeton 1971) 331–45.

[2] On the adequacy of Aristotle's logic and the wrongheaded interpolation of other materials into it by the moderns, see Kant *C d r V* pp viii–ix (17–18).

[3] Étienne Bonnot de Condillac (1715–80) *La Logique, ou les premiers developpemens de l'art de penser, ouvrage élémentaire* (Paris 1781). C claimed an acquaintance with Condillac's book as early as 13 Feb 1801 (*CL* II 675); he seems to have intended to take it to Malta with him in 1804 (*CL* II 1139) and may have done so; he proposed to attack Condillac's "Ψευδο-Logic" as late as 8 Jan 1821 (*CL* V 133). C's charge that Condillac plagiarised from David Hartley (1705–57) appears in a letter to William Godwin on 4 Jun 1803 (*CL* II 947); it is repeated in the posthumously published *Theory of Life* (*TL*—1848—61n).

[4] See above, p 5 n 2.

ever the latter had been familiarised by usage or sanctioned by authority.[a] [1]

2(b) If this insight into the distinct[b] import of terms as well as into the necessity of new or newly defined terms for the expression of different objects be of high importance in science, the extension of the process to words in general as the exponents of all our thoughts and notices is no less fruitful and expedient in our practical concerns and in the intercourse of ordinary life. We may even assert[c] that it is this power and habit which above all others marks and constitutes the intellectual superiority of one man over another. It need scarcely be observed that this approximate use of words cannot exist without a proportionably indistinct[d] knowledge of things.[2] The rules, however, by the knowledge of which the process is facilitated, and by the acquirement of which the mind is led to the perception of its necessity, belong to logic.

2(c) But here arises a question of no mean importance. In what state do we suppose or require the mind of the individual to be to whom these rules are to be presented? The scheme of arranging the communication of knowledge scientifically, so as to begin with that knowledge which requires or supposes no other previous knowledge in order to its intelligibility, and much more the notion of teaching the sciences in a predetermined series on the same principle, such a scheme, I say, were it even feasible in itself (which in relation to the human intellect is more than doubtful)[e] must at all events be impracticable in that state of society in which alone the sciences can be imagined to exist.

3 In the infancy and childhood of individuals (and something

---

[a] A mark here and another in the margin of the ms may indicate either that a new paragraph should begin at this point or that the material that follows should be relegated to a footnote
  [b] ms: distant   [c] ms: assent   [d] ms: distinct   [e] Parentheses inserted

[1] Cf *P Lects* Lect 5 (1949) 173–4 on the minting of new terms. C wrote the following note on the flyleaf of his copy of Kant's *Logik* (BM copy): "An advantage great beyond what a regular Scholar unacquainted with the English World as it now is & has been for the last century can easily appreciate, did the old Logicians, Philologists and Philosophers possess—in that they had either to *ground* the pupil's mind in the appropriate import & use of terms, or might safely presume on readers so grounded by others. The self-conceit of well-cloathed Sciol-ism and the consequent only not universal abuse & laxity of words they had not to struggle with."

[2] A conventional theme: cf Bacon *Novum Organum* "Aphorismi" bk I 43: *Works* (1740) I 367; Hobbes *Leviathan* pt I ch 4; Locke *Essay on Human Understanding* bk III ch 10; Berkeley *A Treatise Concerning the Principles of Human Knowledge* (*B Works* II 39–40); Leibniz *Nouveaux essais* bk III ch 10; and, in jest, Sterne *The Life and Opinions of Tristram Shandy* vol III ch 31.

analogous may be traced in the history of communities) the first knowledges are acquired promiscuously.—Say rather that the plan is not formed by the selection of the objects presented to the notice of the pupils, but by the impulses and dispositions suited to their age, by the limits of their comprehension, by the volatile and desultory activity of their attention, and by the relative predominance or the earlier development of one or more faculties over the rest. This is the happy delirium, the healthful fever, of the physical, moral, and intellectual being, Nature's kind and providential gift to childhood.[1]

4   In the best good sense of the words, it is the light-headedness and light-heartedness of human life! There is indeed "method in't",[2] but it is the method of Nature, which thus stores the mind with all the materials for after use, promiscuously indeed, and as it might seem without purpose, while she supplies a gay and motley chaos of facts, and forms, and thousandfold experiences, the origin of which lies beyond memory, traceless as life itself and finally passing into a part of our life more rapidly[a] than[b] would have been compatible with distinct consciousness and with a security beyond the power of choice! Or shall we call this genial impulse a will *within* the will,[3] that forms the basis of choice and the succedaneum of instinct, which the conscious choice will perfect into knowledge? Promiscuously we have said, and seemingly without design, and yet by this seeming confusion alone could Nature (by which we would be always understood to mean the Divine Providence in the creation) have effected her wise purposes, without encroachment on the native freedom of the soul and without either precluding, superseding, or overlaying, the inventive, the experimentative, combinatory, and judicial powers.[4]

5   But not alone this storing of the mind with the common notices of things, together with those expressions for the same which we acquire by imitation as our mother-tongue, not this alone is necessarily antecedent to all systematic study. The same holds good with regard to the rules and the habits of orderliness or arrangement, regulated by purposes of use and expedience relatively to time and

---

a ms: rapid   *b* Transcriber B takes over

[1] C objected to what he regarded as underestimates of the importance of what children learn, in works such as Kant's *Anthropologie* and Eschenmayer's *Psychologie*. Cf *Destiny of Nations* lines 18ff: *PW* (EHC) I 132.

[2] Shakespeare *Hamlet* II ii 204.

[3] I.e. the conscience.

[4] Paragraphs 2(c), 3, and 4 are almost identical with N 29 f 43ᵛ.

place, to the object and the individuals immediately concerned. And for these likewise ample provision has been made by the necessities that continue the human animal for so long a time under care and governance; in short by the domestic state, and by the social, which is the extension of the domestic; both which, conjointly, are as truly the *natural* state of man, as the wilderness is that of the tiger, and the sea that of the solitary shark.

6   As far as concerns facts, or the knowledge of things derived immediately from the individual's own observation, enough and even more than the child has distinct places for in its memory, or powers of perception to distinguish, come of their own accord. Man's first effort in his behoof is to render him a *social* being; capable of communication, and consequently capable of understanding and being understood.

7   The Latin word from which our "educate" is taken is itself a derivative.[1] *Educare ab educere*: "educate" from "educe", that is, "draw forth", "bring out". In its primary sense it is applied to plants, and expresses the process by which man imitates, carries on, and adapts to a determined human purpose, the work of *education* (evolution, development) performed by Nature.[2] What Nature has *educed*, man *educates* or trains up. In the next step, by an obvious extension of the meaning, the term is made to include all the preparatory and auxiliary labours and contrivances by which the eductive powers and tendencies of Nature are protected, invigorated, or even called into act by adjustment of circumstances ($=$ *surrounding* influences *quotquot* STANT[a] CIRCUM).[3] Hence the vernal shower, as standing in a similar relation to the educible and eductive nature in the seed or plantule, and bringing to it at once excitement and nurture, is happily said by the Roman poet[4] to *educate* the flower: and in the response, that follows, by a still bolder metaphor he applies the word to the eductive or educing Nature itself, poetically

[a] ms: STANTO

[1] Cf the account in the *Bristol Gazette* of C's lecture of 18 Nov 1813 on "The New System of Education" (reprinted *Athenaeum* 13 Mar 1909 pp 316–17). For C's association of "educing" with Dr Bell's "eliciting the faculties of the human mind", see *Friend* (*CC*) I 540n and *SM* (*CC*) 40–1. C described James Boyer—his own teacher at Christ's Hospital—as "an admirable educer no less than Educator of the Intellect ...". *PW* (EHC) I 3n.

[2] Cf *AR* (1825) 6n: "there are few modes of instruction more useful or more amusing than that of accustoming young people to seek for the etymology, or primary meaning, of the words they use". In the *Logic*, C often makes a point by considering the derivation of a term. Cf *C&S* (*CC*) 13n.

[3] "As many as stand about".

[4] Catullus.

contemplated as an *active* power distinct from the *educibility* and from the product *educed*.

> Ut flos in saeptis secretus nascitur hortis,
> Ignotus pecori, nullo convulsus aratro,
> Quem mulcent aurae, firmat sol, *educat* imber,—
> .   .   .   .
> Ut vidua in nudo vitis quae nascitur arvo
> Numquam se extollit, numquam mitem *educat* uvam ...

Catulli LX. 40–50[1]

8   Lastly, the word in its most comprehensive acceptation was applied to the householder man in relation to the young of his own species, and made to express the collective process in which the educator is himself (instead of) the dews and showers, the sun and the breeze, to the congenerous plant; and the home and its indwelling pieties are the protecting, warming and predisposing soil natal to both, which yet the trainer, like the enriching olive-tree, *forms* by continuing to *fill*, and by having gives to that which, as he helps and bends it to grow up beneath and around him, he at once *trains* and *supports*. It could not be otherwise therefore than that the simple and the metaphorical uses should at length change places, and the secondary or applied sense become the proper and ordinary acceptation of the term. Still, however, its correspondence to the primary import remains unaltered, and the analogy is kept up throughout. The process of *educing* from without is correlative to the *evolving* nature from within, to the intensity of the *power* and the *quid, quale et quantum*[2] of the possible *product*. In other words, the process of *eduction*, or bringing out, is determined by the forms and faculties developing or seeking to develop themselves from within. Still, likewise, education consists of *two* parts, the process of *educing*, and that of *training*: and in the *human* education as in the education of plants, the educing must come first: and as this must be conducted with a constant view to the natural evolution, which it is to accompany and assist, so must the *training* likewise be regulated in part by its office as carrying on, and of course adapting itself to, the process of education, and in part by the particular purposes intended in each particular case.

[1] *Poems* 62.39–49. In C's ed, *Catulli Tibulli Propertii Opera* (1774), numbered 60. Tr. F. W. Cornish (LCL 1962) 89: "As a flower springs up secretly in a fenced garden, unknown to the cattle, torn up by no plough, which the winds caress, the sun strengthens, the shower draws forth....As an unwedded vine which grows up in a bare field never raises itself aloft, never brings forth a mellow grape...".

[2] Mediaeval Scholastic terms: "the what, what sort of, how much".

9   If then eduction be the first stage of education, what is the first step in the eduction? In what way do we first draw or bring out the faculties of the nascent mind? We may reply without hesitation that *in substance* this is found in the question—"What is the *word* for such or such a thing?" Though *formally*, and as a direct *question*, it takes place more frequently in the teaching of a *foreign* language.[1] And what is the form or law in the mind to which this first act of education corresponds? Evidently, that by which we remember things in consequence of their co-presence. The word "table" is sounded at the same time that the eye and the touch are directed to the thing, table. We begin δεικτικως, that is, *demonstrando.*[2]

10   This, however, would barely lead us beyond the precincts of the powers common to men and the higher animals. Not only memory, but even perception, beyond a very limited extent, is impossible otherwise than by the sense of likeness. And here again, we see the beneficent effects of that promiscuous presentation of objects, of which we have before spoken, and which, like a puzzle invented for the purpose of evoking the faculties, at once sustains and relieves the attention by the charms of novelty and continual change, and at the same time by a gentle compulsion[3] solicits the mind to make for itself from the *like* effects of different objects on its own sensibility the links which it *then* seems to *find*, unconscious that both the form, and the light by which it is beheld, are of its own eradiation and but *reflected* from external nature. We may confidently affirm that this catenary curve of likeness is the line in which all the senses evolve themselves and commence their communion with the world, and their *purveyorship* for the understanding.

11   It cannot, indeed, be denied that in all *likeness* a *difference* is involved (*nil simile est idem*);[4] but it needs little observation of children to be convinced that they are attracted by the one without any conscious attention to the other. The child will select the harebell, the violet, the sweet-briar, the crocus, or the myrtle, because they are all alike *sweet*; or fill his lap with the gaudier flowers of summer, because they are all alike gaily *coloured*, long before he

[1] Cf C's own way of learning German in Ratzeburg in 1798. *BL* ch 10 (1907) I 137–8n.

[2] I.e. we begin demonstratively, by pointing things out. On the part played by touch in our "first education", cf *P Lects* Lect 3 (1949) 115.

[3] Cf *BL* ch 14 (1907) II 12: "gentle and unnoticed, controul" of the will and understanding.

[4] One of C's favourite tags— "nothing like is the same", or, in another version, "no likeness goes on all fours". See below, e.g., pp 132 and 143.

has adverted even to the most obvious differences. And even when he has begun to *distinguish*, it is by comparative intensity of impression, by difference of *degree* in the same *sort*, rather than by differences in the sorts themselves, that the child makes its earliest distinctions. "I *like* this, better than that", or "The violet is far sweeter than the primrose", are forms of comparison that precede the remark that the smell of the rose is a much sweeter sort than the smell of the jonquil. The latter comparison not only follows the former, but follows it with an interval, being indeed subsequent to the perception of difference by contrast. To illustrate this by a familiar instance—the perception, white, will awaken the recollection of black, and vice versa, before either of the two will be found to recall its own different *shades*.

12   It is a truth of no mean interest or pregnancy, and which requires only to be reflected on to be found such, though to many minds from want of reflection it will, at the first hearing, sound like a paradox, that of all the *material* elements of knowledge, all that external Nature can furnish as the *stuff* of which our knowledge is composed, the far greater part has been furnished by the time that the child passes into the the boy or even at a yet earlier period.[*] Nature has done her part. The needful notices (*notitiae rerum*)[1] have been given; the *tracing* is finished, and she but goes on to refresh and deepen the etching.

13(a)   Here then the process of artificial education, that is, relative to the *intellectual* powers (and in this relation only it is here spoken of), may be said to commence: so far at least, that at this point the agency of *man*, the scheme of *human schooling*, may be singly and severally contemplated. What it *should* be, and what in the main it *is* and ever has been, among the cultivated portions of mankind, may be easily known from its aim and object: which can be no other than to render the mind of the scholar a fit organ for the continued reception and reproduction, for the elaboration, and finally for the application, of these *notices* supplied by sensation and perception, gradually superinducing those which the mind obtains, or may be taught and occasioned to obtain, by reflection on its own acts, and which, when formed and matured into distinct thoughts, constitute

[*] Though if we regarded the subject from a higher point of view, it would perhaps be more *philosophical* to describe the various impressions or influxes from without as *the stuff*, *which* our *knowledge composes*, *informs*, and makes *objects* of. But of this hereafter.

1 Literally, "the notices of things".

(and in distinction from the former may be *called*) the mind's "notions"—the word being taken in its best and most proper sense. We take for granted that in order to a full and distinct attention the object to be attended to must be distinctly presented. The contrary position would indeed involve a contradiction in terms.

13(b) If then we have rightly stated the *aim* of human education, in its main divisions; and if the latter and that which is more especially the *end* or *final* aim, be the formation of right *notions*, or the mind's knowledge of its own constitution and constituent faculties as far as it is obtained by *reflection*; it is obvious that in order to its realisation[a] the several faculties of the mind should be specially disciplined, and as (if I may be allowed the illustration) the muscles of the leg and thigh are brought out and made prominent in the exercises of the riding school,[1] that *so* should the intellectual powers be called forth from *their* dormant state, so as to become the possible and probable objects of conscious reflection in and for themselves, apart from the particular and contingent *subject matters*, on which they are successively exerted—but, again, in order to this (at least as the best way of securing and facilitating this result) that the *subjects* themselves, on which the faculties are employed, should be in the first instance and as much as is possible the work and (if I may so say) the *reflection* of these faculties, such as owe their own existence to the functions of the human intelligence, and to the laws by which the exercise and application of these functions are governed and determined. But a subject perfectly answering this character is provided for us in the privilege and high instinct of language.[2]

13(c) Now the law that first discloses itself is, as we have seen, the law of *connection* or *association* of different objects by perception of likeness—a process that will be found to involve the exercise of an *abstracting* power. For the likeness of A. B. C. (say, a rose, a peony, and a *camelia japonica*) consists of one or more marks *common* to all three: and the perception of the likeness supposes the act of attending

---

[a] ms: realization that

[1] The analogy between mental and physical exercise was a favourite one. See *CL* III 253, 253–4, 255, and *Sh C* II 35–6.

[2] C's ideas about the way in which children should be taught are exemplified in a fragmentary ms dialogue in which a teacher discusses the peculiarities of Greek, Latin, and English by catechising a child of ten. BM MS Egerton 2800 ff 175–7. The paper is watermarked 1825, and the dialogue is probably a by-product of C's tutoring of the young Henry Gillman in the winter of 1825–6. Cf *CL* VI 535. There is another similar ms dialogue in the BM: MS Egerton 2800 ff 179–80ᵛ.

to this common mark apart from the qualities and appearances with which in the *real* objects it is inseparably united. But though even the child on the lap both professes and exercises the power of abstraction, it does not follow that he abstracts *consciously*. In order to this, the act itself must be made an object of *reflection*.[1] The boy must not only abstract, but must be induced to *reflect* on what he is doing. This therefore is the second power that is to be exercised (dating from the supposed commencement of artificial and systematic education): it is to [be] called forth at the same time and in union with the law of likeness, and the simplest and more especially *human* products of that law, considered in its influences on the intellectual faculties of man.

14   It is clear that abstraction is an imaginary process;[2] that no form can really be presented, separated from some particular thing or reality, or that any law or rule can be made known, but by means of a something which acts or is acted upon, under that law or according to those rules. Even the rule or ruler itself (to take a trivial instance) must be of some particular wood or metal, though when we are employing or considering it, merely as a *rule*, this becomes indifferent and we abstract from the particular concrete, that is, we draw away our attention (*abstrahimus*) from the accidental fact that the ruler is of wood, or of iron, of oak, or of mahogany.

15   Everything in nature, in the inanimate no less than in the animate world, takes place according to *rules*; though we may not in all cases know them. These rules, again, must be all reducible to certain laws, though we may not hitherto have discovered them. The water falls according to law, to the law of gravity; and this law, modified in its application by the nature of the subject, gives the rules by which the water moves under all conceivable circumstances. The fish in the water, the bird in the air, move each according to pre-established rules; and the discovery and communication of these rules are the object of comparative anatomy and physiology. In short, universal nature is nothing more than a connected aggregate or chain of phenomena according to rules; and only in relation to human purposes can any appearance or natural incident be said to have taken place irregularly.[3]

[1] Fichte makes the same remark. Johann Gottlieb Fichte *Ueber den Begriff der Wissenschaftslehre oder der sogenannten Philosophie* (Jena & Leipzig 1798) 46. C's annotated copy is in the BM.

[2] Cf Berkeley *Alciphron: B Works* III 293.

[3] This paragraph is a free translation of the opening paragraph of the Introduction of Kant *Logik* (1800) 1.

16   To recall then and bring together the result of the preceding paragraphs, in order to call forth, to strengthen, and discipline the powers of the intellect, we have found it necessary to consider them apart from all particular occasions and subjects. Common sense would condemn the teacher of geometry who should present his circles, triangles, etc to the scholar in gaudy and variegated colours.[1] From this error, however, the child is preserved by Nature in that first period of his education which Nature herself begins as schoolmistress and continues as guide. Here the choice of the subject has been made for us and the vehicle provided, as we have already observed. Words "were from the beginning",[2] nor would it have been possible, had the matter been[a] left to our own invention, to have discovered or invented a medium possessed of advantages so many, so peculiar, and so appropriate, to all its various and numerous purposes.

17(a)   But as words are, themselves, the earliest products of the abstracting power, so do they naturally become the first subject matter of abstraction; and consequently the commencement of human education. Hence it is that civilisation, and the conditions under which a people have become progressive and historical, commences with an alphabet, or with some equivalent discovery imperfectly answering the same purpose.[3]

17(b)   Amid all the variety of sounds, of which any given language avails itself, those that most resemble each other will be the first noticed, the most easily imitated, and the longest retained. The fondness of children for rhymes will have struck every observer. In a following stage, the difference between likeness and sameness will have been noticed, and the first effort of art will consist in directing the attention to the mental elements or *factors* of likeness (viz. the same and the different)[b] to effect which, one of the two must be

---

a ms: have been
b Parentheses inserted; in ms the passage is set off by a comma and a colon

[1] J. P. Collier's diary transcript of the second of C's 1811–12 series of lectures records that "Coleridge in the strongest manner censured the practice of teaching mathematics by making the illustrations obvious to the senses. We should think and not feel". R. A. Foakes, ed *Coleridge on Shakespeare* (1971) 58. C may have had in mind the suggestions of his friend Thomas Beddoes *Observations on the Nature of Demonstrative Evidence; with an Ex-* *planation of Certain Difficulties Occurring in the Elements of Geometry: and Reflections on Language* (1793) viiff, 63–5. Cf also the passing reference to "[*tangible*] geometry" in *P Lects* Lect 9 (1949) 281. Cf *CN* III 3455n.

[2] John 1.1 (var).

[3] Cf C's notion that "The whole of the progress of society might be expressed in a dictionary . . .". *P Lects* Lect 5 (1949) 173–4.

presented to the attention separately, and this will of course be the one first mentioned (the *same*), as being the *radical* element, as it were, or the *positive* factor of the *conception* "likeness", "like", and that too which corresponds to the faculty earliest developed in the mind, namely, the sense of a like that differs from the same only by a difference of *degree*, or even (in the first instances) only numerically.

18 Consistently with this the first implements of artificial education are an alphabet and an accidence; that is, first, a catalogue of the letters, or articulate sounds, in which all the *differences* of language are comprised, and which of course, therefore, are the *positive* elements of the likeness of any two series of words, that contains each the whole number. They are that in respect to which the two series or sentences are the *same*, the relative *positions* of the letters constituting the difference, and supplying the negative element of likeness.

19 And secondly, a catalogue of the significant syllables, or that portion of language by which a *same* meaning is found in combination with a *different* meaning in any number of different words—a combination possible only under one condition, that the difference is in the object, the sameness in the *relation*. Thus in the alphabet, under which I include the process of reading and spelling, the letters themselves give the positive element of the like = the same; and the relative *positions* of the letters form the negative element = the different: while in the accidence, as the process of parsing and construing, the *radical* portions of the words import the difference, and the positions in respect of space (cases[a]) or of time (the tenses) or of subjective relations (the moods) express the sameness. [b]Hence in [the] respect [that] their abstract and universal characters are concerned (and of these alone we are now speaking) [this community and intersimilitude of the parts of speech] is a necessary consequence of their common derivation or rather *production* from the verb substantive.[c] For all words express either being or action, or the predominance of the one over the other. In philosophical grammar, they are either substantives, or verbs, or as adnouns and adverbs express the modification of the one by the other. But the verb substantive ("am", *sum*, εἰμι) expresses the identity or coinherence

---

[a]   ms: *cases*

[b-c] ms: Hence in respect their abstract and universal characters are concerned (and of these alone we are now speaking) is a necessary consequence of their common derivation or rather *production* from the Verb Substantive. [The facing page bears an attempt to make sense of the passage by drawing from a sentence on I 35: ~~Hence, considered as *Parts of Speech*, or in respect of their abstract Characters, according to which they are severally classed as Verbs or Nouns, Ad~~. The editor has combined from this and from another on I 34 passages where C repeats parts of the sentence in the same words, to make the present text]

of being and act. It is the act of being.[1] All other words therefore may be considered as tending from this point, or more truly from the mid-point of the line, the *punctum indifferentiae* representing the *punctum identitatis*,[2] even as the whole line represents the same point as produced or polarised.

20   In this simple diagram *A* (= the point of identity)[a] is supposed to generate by perpetual eradiation the line *BC*, the pole *B* representing being in its greatest predominance, and the pole *C* action in like manner: while the point *a*, expressing the indifference of being and action, of substantive and verb, is the more especial representative or analogon of the *point A, as* a point. *A*, the point of identity, is verb and substantive in one and as one; *a*, the point of indifference, is *either* verb *or* substantive, or even both at the same time, but *not* in the same *relation*. Such in grammar is the *infinitive*: and though instances of its functions as indifferently verb or substantive are far more frequent and idiomatic in the Greek, Italian, French, and German languages, they are not wanting in our own. Take, for example, the two following lines from Spenser:

> For not to dip the hero in the lake
> Could save the son of Thetis from *to die*.[3]

Here the infinitive, "to dip", is a substantive as the nominative case of the verb, "could save"; and at the *same* time but in a different relation, it is a verb active, governing "the hero" as its accusative case or object. So too the verb neuter is governed as a substantive in "from to die"; and in Greek the preceding article would have been declined in the case required by the preposition.

21   Before I proceed, however, I must request the reader to bear in mind that I am not speaking of language *historically* or pretending

---

[a] Parentheses inserted

[1] See Editor's Introduction, above, pp lxv–lxvii.

[2] "Point of indifference", "point of identity".

[3] *The Ruins of Time* lines 428–9 (var). The quotation and the application of it are taken from James Harris *Hermes: or a Philosophical Inquiry Concerning Universal Grammar* (1751): *The Works* ed Earl of Malmesbury (1801) I 305n; the variation is C's own. He uses the same example in N 29 f 28 and in annotations to Edward Irving *Sermons* (3 vols 1828) and *The Quarterly Journal of Foreign Medicine and Surgery* I (1818–19) 331.

to narrate etymological *facts*. There have been men and of no mean rank in the republic of letters who have strenuously contended for the *bona fide* derivation of the whole Greek language from ἐω as the oldest form of the Greek verb substantive: and if this could be *proved* true of any one language, it would be irrational not to concede the high probability of a similar orgination in all.[1] But with this theory I am in no wise concerned, as opponent or advocate. Indeed, with *any* scheme of etymology the present subject is as little connected, as the doctrine of determinate proportions in the science of chemistry, or an enquiry into the generation or evolution of numbers according to Pythagoras, with the question whether the cyphers in use were originally Arabic, or Indian, or mere corruptions and gradual transformations of the Greek letters, used for the same purpose. It is to the elements of grammar that we are now directing our attention; and of grammar as a purely abstract and *formal* science, that therefore takes the lead in the scheme of artificial[*] education because it reflects the forms of the human mind, and gradually familiarises the half-conscious boy with the frame and constitution of his own intellect, as the polished glass does the unconscious infant with the features of its own countenance.

22(a)   *Grammatically* considered then, I say, that all words may be classed under one or other, or (to take up my former metaphor) they may be described as tending to one or other of the two poles

---

[*] The sense in which this epithet is used cannot be more happily or adequately explained than in the exquisite passage of the *Winter's Tale* (Act IV. Scene 3[a]) ending with

This is an Art
Which does mend Nature: change it rather: but
The Art itself is Nature.[2]

[a] ms: 2.

[1] C seems to have been thinking of the theory that the "duads" "ἀω, ἐω, ἰω, οω, υω", are the "roots of the [Greek] language...": Jame Burnet, Lord Monboddo *Of the Origin and Progress of Language* (6 vols Edinburgh 1773–92) II 193 and 522. Thomas Beddoes misrepresents this theory slightly as implying "that the verb is the parent word of the whole Greek language...". *Observations* 156. William Vincent (1739–1815), the headmaster of Westminster, was prominent among the men who argued that the verb "to be" was the original Greek verb. See his anonymous *The Origination of the Greek Verb. An Hypothesis* (1794) and *The Greek Verb Analysed. An Hypothesis. In Which the Source and Structure of the Greek Language, and of Language in General, Is Considered* (1795), esp pp 1–26. (C's annotated copy is in VCL.) C referred to Vincent's work in a disparaging tone in a letter to George Coleridge in 1802 (*CL* II 803). Vincent's views were given a spirited trouncing by the associationist Thomas Gunter Browne: *Hermes Unmasked...* (1795).

[2] Shakespeare *Winter's Tale* IV iii or iv 95–7.

of the verb substantive, and as represented by the points between the mid-point and the two extremes of the line. But as they are all *like* to the verb substantive, they are for that reason at once like and yet opposite to (contradistinguished from) each other, every substantive a verb, and every verb a substantive, in order to its own significance (the two sexes, their derivation from the *homo androgynus*, and the retiring of the latter from the world of the senses into the invisible world of self-consciousness, in the fable of Plato and of the rabbinical writers, may furnish an amusing illustration of the preceding ideas.[1] It is not indeed impossible that this mythic tale may have been originally intended as a grammatical allegory.)

22(b)   It is sufficient, however, if I have succeeded in unfolding the true character of the education sanctioned by the experience of ages, and its perfect correspondence to the provisions and designs of Nature; if I have shown in what manner its first lessons come in aid of that power of abstraction by which, as the condition and the means of self-knowledge, the reasoning intellect of man is distinguished in *kind* from the mechanical understanding of the dog, the elephant, the bee, the ant, and whatever other animals display an intelligence that we cannot satisfactorily reduce to mere instinct; if, in short, against the caprice of fashion and the pretexts of its pandars and flatterers I have vindicated the old schooling as a scheme eminently entitled to the name of education, inasmuch as by means admirably adapted to the present faculties and the future purposes of the scholar it gradually raises into acts and objects of distinct consciousness what Nature and the alone true *natural* state of man had previously called forth as *instincts* of humanity.[2]

23   The charters and other records of our oldest schools, both of those exclusively intended for the instruction of the more numerous class in and for their own rank (e.g. Sir Roger Cholmley's[a] school at Highgate, founded in Elizabeth's reign)[3] and those of a mixed

a ms: Cholmondely's

[1] See Plato *Symposium* 189–93 and *Midrash Rabbah* ed H. Freedman and Maurice Simon (1939) I 54. See also Philo *De opificio mundi* 151. The allusion was commonplace. See, e.g., Isaac D'Israeli *Curiosities of Literature* 4th ed (1795) I 217–18. For C's interest in rabbinical materials, see *CL* IV 558–9 (?24 Mar 1815), *CL* IV 656–7 (16 Jul 1816), *CL* IV 681 (22 Sept 1816). He had included some "Specimens of Rabbinical Wisdom" in *The Friend,* derived from J. J. Engel *Schriften* (Berlin 1801) vol I. See *Friend* (*CC*) I 370–3 and II 170–1, 308–9.

[2] For C's low opinion of the new schools, see *BL* ch 1 (1907) I 7–8.

[3] The Highgate free grammar school was founded in 1562 and incorporated by letters patent in 1565 by Sir Roger Cholmley. For C's interest in the school see E. L. Griggs *CL* v 171–3n; it was

character, in which provisions were made for raising a certain
number of the more promising scholars into a higher rank, and
qualifying them for the learned professions (among which Christ's
Hospital, never by me to be named without reverence, stands
prominent),[1] furnish striking proofs, how highly our great ancestors,
the fathers of our Church and the lights and pillars of Protestantism
throughout the world, appreciated the advantages of learning, *in
conjunction with common arithmetic, the A B C, and the rudiments
of grammar,* independent of any further progress in the learned
languages and without the remotest view to the study of the books
therein written, or to what we now call *classical* scholarship.[*] If
our own experience on English ground permitted a doubt to remain
as to the truth and justice of their conclusion, a moment's compari-
son of the Scottish with the Irish peasantry would remove it
forever.[3]

24(a)   Greatly then do those persons mistake the purpose, and
[?unjustly][a] do they detract from the merit, of the invention, who
suppose that the accidence (syntax included) was exclusively con-
trived for *the looking out for words* in a dictionary, that was itself
contrived with a view to the accidence. Were this all, the object
might be obtained in a much easier and more efficacious way by the
use of a dictionary, which contains[b] the significant, though indetach-
able, syllables; hence considered as *parts of speech*, or in respect of
their abstract characters, according to which they are severally
classed as verbs or nouns, adverbs or adnouns, etc, all words have a
ground of *likeness* to each other: the most different are akin.
(Abstractly[c] considered, I mean: and of *abstracts* alone we are now
speaking. The act and faculty of *abstraction* it is which through the
medium of its earliest and most universal *proceeds* we are now en-
deavouring to elucidate.)

24(b)   This community and intersimilitude of the parts of speech
is a necessary consequence of their common derivation, or rather

[*] See the concluding paragraph of this chapter.[2]

---

a Blank space left in ms   *b* ms: containing   *c* ms: Abstractedly

---

particularly on his mind in the summer
of 1822 and again in 1830 (*CL* v 235,
237, 241, 242–3, and vi 833–5).

[1] For accounts of C's connection
with Christ's Hospital, see *BL* ch 1
(1907) i 4–11; Charles Lamb "Recol-
lections of Christ's Hospital" and

"Christ's Hospital Five and Thirty
Years Ago" *L Works* i 139–49 and
ii 12–22.

[2] The reference seems to be to the
last paragraph but one.

[3] Cf the similar comparison in *AR*
(1825) 7–8n.

production, from the verb substantive. For all words express either being or act, or the predominance of the one or the other.[1] We cannot conceive even the merest *thing*, a stone for instance, as simply and exclusively *being*, as absolutely passive and *actionless*. Were it but the act of reflecting the light by which it is seen, or as the sum of the acts of attraction by which its particles cohere, and the stone *is*. And as little, on the other hand, can we conceive or imagine the purest act, a flash of lightning for instance, as *merely* an act, or without an abiding or continuing somewhat, as the inseparable ground, subject, and substance of the action.

25   As soon as the pupil has been sufficiently familiarised with words and their import,[*] to possess a somewhat to which the rules

[*] Memorandum. In the preface to assign the reason for so often repeating a position in Latin. First the dog-Latin[a] is easy in proportion as it is barbarous so that a mere knowledge of the Latin accidence will enable the reader to construe it, and it certainly assists not only in fixing the meaning on the mind but in seeing it for itself independent of the words.

"To put" (a corruption or abbreviation of *posit*, still retained in the verb "to deposit" from the Latin *pono, posui, positum*) is the *verb*, answering to "position" as the noun, in the same way as "to build" and a "building", "fix" and "fixture", etc. "To put" is in logic the same as "to affirm", the former being the *technical* word, and one of those that have passed from the schools into common usage; the latter, perhaps, the more elegant, and with the additional advantage of being less equivocal[b] inasmuch as "put" is likewise used technically for "propose" or "assume", as in the phrase so frequent among lawyers, "to put a case".

"To determine" = "to put" (or "affirm") a predicate with exclusion of its opposite, subject and predicate in logic answering to the substantive and its characterising adjective in grammar. (N.B. Hence as the adjective belongs to the substantive, and enters into the conception of the latter as a constituent part, both alike are entitled to the prefix "noun", that is, name.)

That which determines a subject in reference to any one predicate, and of course by means of that predicate, is called *the reason* and in laxer and less guarded language *the cause*. (To be avoided therefore when our object is to discipline the mind by attention to a rigid propriety of speaking when we have agreed *to play the strict game*.)

The determining reason (*ratio determinans*) may be of two kinds—that which determines a subject antecedently, and that which determines it by a consequent. It is antecedent when its notion precedes the subject determined—that is, when it must be supposed in order to the intelligibility of the thing determined. ("Antecedenter determinans est, cujus notio praecedit determinatum: hoc est, qua non supposita, determinatum non est intelligibile.")[2] It is consequent, when

a ms: Log-Latin   *b* ms: equivously

[1] C repeats the botched passage of p 16, above.

[2] This paragraph and the preceding one are expansions of the opening sentences of Kant "Principiorum primorum cognitionis metaphysicae nova elucidatio" sect II prop iv *VS* IV 131. The Latin sentence is quotation. On the endpapers of one of the copies of volume IV now in the BM (C.43.a.9), C has written of the "Principiorum . . . elucidatio": "This *Degree* Essay, 1755,

could apply; from thence to the doctrine of arranging words and sentences perspicuously; an art which has hitherto had no appropriate title, having been confounded with one or all of the others, and which I therefore propose*ᵃ* to distinguish by the term "rhematic",[6] for reasons the importance of which will be seen in another place when we have to speak on the syllogistic figures.[7]

26   Thence rhetoric, or the art of declaiming persuasively; and lastly logic, as the art and science of discoursing conclusively. In the

the determining reason presupposes the notion of that which is determined by it. ("Consequenter determinans est, quae non poneretur nisi jam aliunde posita esset notio, quae ab ipso determinatur.")[1] The first is by some logicians[2] technically called (*ratio* CUR) the reason "how" or "wherefore", or (*ratio* ESSENDI *vel* FIENDI) the reason of the "being" or "becoming" of the thing determined, the latter the *ratio quod*, which I do not know how to English better than the reason "for"—that is, *ratio* COGNOSCENDI, or that which enables us to know that the thing is determinately so or so. Example: I affirm of myself that I am. If a reason were required of me, in the latter sense (*ratio consequenter determinans*),[3] I could only answer—"I am because I am"—*sum quia sum*—for "*I* am", in the first person, *implies* self-consciousness. The only reason I can assign for my being conscious of myself is that I am a self-conscious being. This is the *ratio cognoscendi*, but if the question were put in the former sense, and the RATIO ESSENDI *vel* FIENDI demanded, I should then answer—*Sum quia Deus est et ita voluit.* "I am, because God is, and hath willed me to be". Example: The eclipses of Jupiter's satellites give the reason *for* (*rationem* CONSEQUENTER *determinatum*) the motion of light *in time*. But for these I should not have *known* that the appulse was not coinstantaneous with its emission. But if the reason "why?" be asked, a Cartesian would assign the elasticity of the globules of the air and the intermundane ether;[4] while you and I perhaps might content ourselves with a humble *Nescio, nisi quod Deo sic placitum est.*[5]

ᵃ ms: proposed

for admission as Member of the Philosophical Faculty, is a worthy *Dawn* of the Kantean Day. Nothing but the Insight into the *equal* necessity of the supposed *Contrary*, & the consequent conversion of contraries into Opposites, was wanting to have made the young Immanuel the founder of The System of the *Prothetic*, as the antecedent Identity of the Thetic & Antithetic—or rather of the + and minus *Antithetic*."

[1] The sentence is from the "Principiorum . . . elucidatio" sect II prop iv. See *VS* IV 131. C continues to quote and paraphrase Kant throughout his note.

[2] Notably Kant.

[3] "The consequent determining reason".

[4] The whole passage, "Example: The eclipses . . . the intermundane ether", is a selective translation of Kant "Principiorum . . . elucidatio" sect II prop iv *VS* IV 132–3.

[5] "I do not know, unless it is because God is pleased that it should be so". Cf marginal comment on Schelling's "Ich bin, weil Ich bin! das ergreift jeden plötzlich" ("I am, because I am! That strikes everyone right away"): "jeden? [I] doubt i[t.] Many w[ill] say, I a[m] becaus[e] God ma[de] me." *Philosophische Schriften* (Landshut 1809) I 9 (BM copy).

[6] C's use of the word (*TT* 23 Sept 1830) is the first instance recorded in *OED*.

[7] See below, pp 53ff.

following table the reader will find these four with their several definitions.

27   A table of the formal sciences, or systematised arts, of which words are the subject and medium.

1   *Grammatice*—Συναρτησις γραμματων
2   *Rhematice*—Συνταξις ῥηματων
[3]   *Rhetorice*—Συνθεσις πεισματων
[4]   *Logice*—[?Συνδησις] λογισμων[1]

28   How valuable, how desirable in all cases, and how indispensable, the formal sciences of figure, number, and motion are, and fully disposed as I am to prefix over the portal of schools of higher philosophy οὐδεις [ἀγεωμετρητος εἰσιτω],[2] still the four presented in this table assuredly contain all the preparation for the study of realities, scientific, historic, or technical, and are adapted to awaken and discipline all the powers to be exerted in the acquirement and exercise of them, which the concerns of life and society require, whether for the bar, the pulpit, or the senate.[3]

29   These, however, in substance at least, are indispensable for all men whose object supposes knowledge and the development of the intellect.

[1] "Grammar—fitting together of letters/ Rhematic—Arrangement of words/ Rhetoric—Putting together of persuasions/ Logic—[?Binding together] of reasonings". The missing word is supplied from a similar table in N 29 ff 46ᵛ–47ᵛ.

[2] The motto said to have been placed above the door of Plato's Academy: "Let no man enter . . . who has not previously disciplined his mind by Geometry" (C's paraphrase in *LS—CC*—173). He continues: "He considered this science as the first purification of the soul, by abstracting the attention from the accidents of the senses". C used the quotation in *Watchman* (*CC*) 34 and in a marginal note to Jakob Böhme *Works* (4 vols 1764–81) cited in *CN* II 2894n.

[3] An indication of the audience C had in mind. Cf the outline in BM MS Egerton 2801 f 197, addressed to "Individuals . . . not younger than eighteen or nineteen . . ." who are preparing themselves for "the Bar, the Pulpit or the Senate . . .".

CHAPTER I[I]

1   Logic from the Greek λεγω.[1] The absolute etymon of this word, by which I mean the particular visual image, or other sensuous impression, which is at the root of its proper constituent syllable, is far beyond historic research, though an equivalent of the particular root, if not the root itself, may perhaps be discovered by speculative combinations and analogy of roots certainly known.

2   The old Greek grammarians, or rather philologists, or men of letters (for either of these would be a more appropriate translation of the *grammatici*),[*] assign to the initial λ the sense of additional force, whether in consequence of a single energy or of the same energy repeated.[3] The objections of Ruhnkenius are weak, and the very words on which he founds his own whimsical hypothesis, that the initial λ expresses ugliness or hatefulness, may readily be explained in conformity with the more simple and natural belief of the ancients themselves.[4] The feelings of disgust and hatred, we know by experience, either find or make some sound significant of additional effort, as the means of expressing their own intensity. It is probable that offences to the taste, as connected with food, form the first objects of hate, in other words, that hate was primarily *disgust*: (*disgustas*) thus—"eat", "ate", and "hate"; *essen* and *hassen*; while in the Latin, the same addition of strength is expressed by the change of the lower to a higher vowel and this probably in the earlier ages of the Latin language— aspirated—*edi–odi—*.[5]

3   I have said that the words given by him in proof of his hypothesis might be brought under the rule to which he opposes them; but it would be far more consistent, both with analogy and probability, to consider them as purely accidental, and, by way of proof,

[*] *Veteres Graii^a grammatici*—verbatim the literati among the elder Greeks, from [?γραμματα][2]—literally.

[1] "I speak".
[2] "Letters".
[3] I.e. the lexicographers Hesychius and Suidas, quoted by Ruhnken; see next note, below.
[4] David Ruhnken "Epistola critica

I" in *Homeri hymnus in Cererem* ... *accedunt duae epistolae criticae* (Leyden 1782) 86–9.
[5] Cf *CN* I 1293 (Dec 1802): "eat–hate–essen–hassen odi–edi".

to select an equal or greater number of words equally or more associated with dislike and aversion under any one of half a dozen other initials.

4   Assuredly the sound of this liquid,[1] as it is now sounded, and doubtless was so by the Greeks, from the first periods of their literary history, must appear a strange choice for the expression of effort of any kind, painful or pleasurable. If it expressed any one act or image more than another, it would seem to be—continuity and the absence of resistance,[*] as in the word "liquid"; thence, easy motion, and in this way, it might easily [?come to mean] motion rendered easy by repetition, as that of [a] pendulum or the motion in rocking;[2] and thus would maintain or justify its affinity, as well as its neighbour-hood, to the μ. But the λ as well as the soft σ, the *b*,[3] and the *v*—the *h* and the modern[a] *w*—are frequently the softer, and more easily pronounced, representatives and substitutes of those harsh and difficult sounds that occur in the first and ruder states of all nations and of all languages spoken by a rude and imperfectly civilised people. Such doubtless was the digamma of the Pelasgic Greeks,[†]4 for had it originally marked a sound similar to our *v* or *w*, I know not what reason could be assigned, or what cause imagined, for its having become obsolete and lost out of the alphabet; but if we suppose it to have resembled the Hebrew "ngain",[5] or the sound which, by the vowel prefixed, is still preserved in the double *g* as in ἀγγελος[6] and in the Latin *angor*,[7] we need only attempt to pro-

---

[*] or diminished degree of resistance   [†] Greek Pelasgi rather.

a ms: Modlin

[1] I.e. the letter λ.

[2] Cf Plato *Cratylus* 427B.

[3] Cf *CN* I 4 for C's early theorising about labials. N 29 ff 28ᵛ–29 contains a discussion parallel to the *Logic*.

[4] On whom see e.g. the long note in Lord Monboddo *Of the Origin and Progress of Language* I 414–16n.

[5] In C's time, a current spelling of "ayin"—e.g. "the sixteenth letter of the Hebrew alphabet, Oin, as it is called by some, and Ain or Gnain by others …". *The Classical Journal* VIII (1813) 97. A parallel passage in N 29 f 43 has "Naing". For the difficult pronunciation of the letter, see *Gesenius' Hebrew Grammar* ed F. Kautzsch and A. E. Cowley (Oxford 1910) 32–3. In Wilhelm Gesenius *Ausführliches grammatisch-kritisches Lehrgebäude der hebräischen Sprache …* (Leipzig 1817) 12, "ayin" is used as an example of a Hebrew sound that is almost impossible for Western Europeans to imitate. C had access to Gesenius in J. H. Green's library (see *Green SC* item 214), and the topic is one he could have talked over with his learned friend Hyman Hurwitz.

[6] Pronounced "angelos"; tr "messenger". Cf below, p 92.

[7] "Anguish" or "torment".

nounce it as an initial to convince ourselves that it requires organs of pronunciation which travellers have so often found occasion to wonder at in the language of barbarous tribes but which they have in vain attempted to imitate.

5   The gradual diminution of the effort and consequent gradual softening of the sound into others less distinct but more vocal will be an unfailing accompaniment of civilisation. Nor unfortunately does this process always stop at the desirable mean. A nation may rebarbarise into the opposite extreme of effeminacy, or mere paucity of conception and combinations, from the loss of ancient literature; may produce the same effect, even where positive feebleness cannot be justly asserted. Thus the modern Italians have gradually dropped the aspirate and indeed as many other of the stronger and deeper sounds as the necessity of retaining the distinct meaning of their words would permit. A similar loss of all the gutturals and of most of the diphthongs is noticeable in the modern Greek; though an Italian effeminacy will be the last censure cast on the present natives of the Peloponnesus and its adjacent islands.[1]

6   I am far, however, from contending that this representation of a harsh by a softer sound is generally or even frequently instanced by the initial λ, though the transition of the Latin *clamare* into the Spanish *llamare*[2] might lead us to infer that the philologists who wrote while the Greek was yet a living tongue might have found reasons for supposing such a pronunciation of the initial λ in so large a number of words (in many perhaps the relics of the former sound)[3] as, taken in conjunction with the import of the words, appeared to sanction the supposition that the letter was characteristic of power, or what is called, technically, corroboration, generally in connection with motion in its easiest form—that of recurrency.

7   The original sense of the word λεγω appears to have been that of picking up, a taking up a something that had been sought after; hence a choosing, a determining; all in connection with the discursion, deliberation, or the going backward and forward, or the balancing of the mind, antecedent to, or accompanying, the act of picking up or selecting; hence by natural association, it became associated with the balance and signified to ponder, to weigh, which is found in the

---

[1] C acknowledges the reputation popularised by Lord Byron's stirring characterisation of them in *Childe Harold's Pilgrimage* Canto II (1812), and confirmed by the outbreak of the Greek war of independence in 1821.

[2] "To call". The verso of the preceding page of MS Logic has the word "diphthong" at this point.

[3] The verso of the preceding page of the manuscript of the *Logic* has the word "stronger" at this point.

classical λογιζεσθαι:[1] thence lastly, that which is the result of weighing or considering, λογοι.[2]

8   In the early periods of the human race and at present, wherever a scanty population is spread over a large and uncultivated domain, whether in the pastoral or the hunting states, man is comparatively a silent animal.[3] Conversation is almost confined to affairs of moment. The conversations themselves are entitled "words", or some equivalent term, as for instance the "palavers" or "palabras" of the Africans: we might therefore expect that the particular speeches, the harangues of the individual, should be distinguished from light or ordinary talk by some appropriate name. At all events, we may expect to find it so, whenever, as was the case in Greece, the race, climate, geographical circumstances, and above all the confluence of kindred tribes,[*] were favourable to the formation of a copious language; thus it was that select, considerate, well-weighed, deliberate words were named λογοι in distinction from ρηματα, that is, fluents, *vocabula fluentia*: λογο[ι λογιζομενοι].[4]

9   That fables are likewise entitled λογοι, as λογοι [?Αἰσωπικοι],[5] will surprise those only who, misled by the unwise custom of putting books of fables in the hands of children, have forgotten that the original and, at all times, the most pertinent use of apologues was in speeches on delicate and hazardous subjects, addressed to kings or unruly popular assemblies. The fable of Jotham [is] the earliest on record;[6] that of Menippus[7] might be cited in proof, if indeed the subjects and purposes of all the ancient fables (those of Phaedrus are undoubtedly modern)[†] did not suffice of themselves to convince an

[*] congenerous   [†] Perotti[a] 1590[8]

[a] ms: Pirotto

1 "To calculate".

2 "Words", "language".

3 C would have found a long exposition of this view in Monboddo *Of the Origin . . .* I bk 2. For C's awareness of a much discussed contemporary instance of man in a savage state, see *CN* I 1348.

4 Sentence ends with λόγος (no full stop): "Flowing utterances [in distinction from] [considerate] word[s]". Cf below, pp 89, 96, and 120. Cf also the more elaborate discussion in N 29 f 60 of the distinction between λόγος and ρῆμα, which is based on Georg Friedrich Creuzer *Symbolik und*

Mythologie der alten Völker (2nd ed 4 vols Leipzig & Darmstadt 1819–21) I 45–7.

5 "[Aesopian] fables". Cf "Μυθοι Αισωπικοι" in the parallel discussion in N 29 f 60.

6 Judges 9.7–15.

7 Menippus seems to have been substituted by mistake for the more obviously apt Menenius Agrippa with his fable of the belly and the members —see *Coriolanus* I i 101–61.

8 Some scholars, notably J. F. Christ (1700–56), thought that Niccolò Perotti (1430–80) was the author of the fables attributed to Phaedrus. Their genuine-

intelligent reader. At a somewhat later period, those who collected the speeches or "words of weight", and with these (as was natural) the momentary events that were the occasion or result, were entitled λογιοι, and the writings themselves λογοι. [a]As these were supposed to be the faithful reports of the speeches, they of course could not be metrical; this is the most probable origin of prose writing.

10   Thus λογοι acquired the sense of histories, which at first, like our oldest chronicles, included natural, as well as political, events, incidents, and phenomena—*voces natura[e] et mortalia verba*;[1] and hence the earliest Greek historians were the first prose writers.

11   A chronicle can of course have no closer connection than what the circumstances of time, place, and the identity of the agent, in a series of acts or fortunes, may supply; what is more than this must be given by the skill or the passion of the narrator: thus the meaning of the word λογοι as histories was limited by ἐπος,[2] from ἐπειν[b]—ἐπειν in the sense still preserved in ἐπεσθαι, *sequi*, "to follow"—"to follow in close order".[3]

12   A skilful arrangement of events and harangues to an artful and harmonious whole was an ἐπος, an epic poem; the poet, ἐποποιος,[4] or simply ποιητης, the maker, to distinguish him from the historian, who received the form and sequency of his narration, no less than the contents, from the actual occurrences. He alone can be appropriately styled a poet who, whencesoever he may have derived the materials of his work, supplies the form, connection, and unity from his own mind, or, as both the piety and humility of the early poet dictated, from his genius, his muse, or special ἀγαθ[οδαιμων].[5] That such works among the Greeks were all metrical follows from the process above given, and indeed flows out of the nature of the language itself.

13   It is, however, the ἐπος, the ποιησις, the contexture, the original infusion of the poet's own shapings, that constitute the

---

[a] New paragraph in ms   [b] ms: ειπειν

---

ness was demonstrated in *Codex Perottinus* ed Cataldo Jannelli (Naples 1809 [1811]) and Cataldo Jannelli *Ad Perottinum Codicem* (Naples 1811), but C, in N 29 ff 60–60ᵛ, nevertheless draws a parallel between Perotti's relationship to Phaedrus and James Macpherson's to Ossian. The first printed edition of Phaedrus was that edited by Pithou (Troyes 1596); the ms date may be a transcriber's error.

[1] "Voices of nature and human words".

[2] "Word, speech, tale, saying" etc, and, in the plural, "epic poetry".

[3] A false etymology from Creuzer *Symbolik* I 46. According to him, ἐπειν means "to fasten together".

[4] "Epic poet"; by derivation, "word-maker".

[5] "Good spirit".

essential qualities, ἐποποιια, and distinguish the *Waverley* or *Guy Mannering*, with no less propriety, than the *Marmion* and *Lady of the Lake*, from the[a] λογος or λογ[ι]οι of the chronicles.[1]

14 Soon, however, the happy genius of Greece inspired a portion of the same power into the works of her prose narrators, but working by different means. Intelligent research came in the stead of invention; thought and reflection supplied the links of causation and formed while they explained the connection of events and their common relation as parts of one comprehensive scheme; either general, or what we now call the ways of Providence, or for the manifestation and evidence of some particular purpose or moral as in Thucydides. [b]Thus the λογογραφια, or record of weighty matters, or memorabilia, was elevated into history (ἱστορια, ἱστορησις, from ἱστορειν, to search into, to make a diligent enquiry concerning) and the logograph into the historian.[c] But in how extensive a sense the term "history" was received we learn from the invaluable treatise of Hippocrates on Air, Water, and Situation; which he himself entitles ἱστ[ορικη] ἀποδειξις,[d] i.e. an experiential representation, a demonstration founded on enquiry, literally inquisitive demonstration, in the sense in which the word demonstration is still used, by the teachers of anatomy.[2]

15 Thus, the poet and the historian having obtained each a proper name, the derivatives from λογος are now appropriated to men of superior knowledge, the highly informed, the men of understanding, e.g. the [λογιοι των Περσεων και Αἰγυπτιων][3] in Herodotus, i.e. the intelligent class among the Persians or Egyptians, not the

---

[a] ms: a

[b-c] Ms shows signs of recasting; it reads: "Thus the Λογογραφια was elevated into from   to make search into.

    "The Λογογραφια, or record of weighty matters, or Memorabilia, was elevated into history (ιστορια ιστορησις from ιστορειν to search into, to make a diligent enquiry concerning) and the Logograph into the historian." The facing page bears the following note: "The λογογραφια or record of weighty matters of Memorabilia was elevated into history historia ιστορησις from"

[d] ms: Ισταρι Αποδειξις

[1] Sir Walter Scott *Waverley; or, 'Tis Sixty Years Since* (1814), *Guy Mannering* (1815)—which C thought of going to see in the theatre (*CL* IV 625) in 1816—*Marmion; a Tale of Flodden Field* (1808), and *The Lady of the Lake; a Poem* (1810). Although Scott did not acknowledge his authorship of the Waverley novels until 1827 (in *Chronicles of the Canongate*—Edinburgh—I xxi–xxviii), C had guessed it in Mar 1820 (*C Life*—G—

227; cf *CL* VI 602).

[2] Περὶ ἀέρων ὑδάτων τόπων. The passage that C attributes to Hippocrates does not appear in the course of the work. Is C thinking of the opening of Herodotus: "'Ηροδότου 'Αλικαρνησσέος ἱστορίης ἀπόδεξις ἥδε ..."? ("What Herodotus the Halicarnassian has learnt by inquiry is here set forth ...". Tr A. D. Godley—LCL 1960.)

[3] Herodotus 1.1.

learned, which, as an honorary epithet, was not introduced till a later stage of the process. In the earlier time, yet still later than the Homeric period, the great men were entitled σοφοι and σοφισται,[1] but in the sense of wise men—the wise. The latter term was afterwards appropriated by Plato and Aristotle to those adventurers who pretended to teach wisdom as an art or trade.[*] But in Herodotus the two words σοφοι[b] and [σοφισται] occur as perfect synonyms, signifying men distinguished as the lights and ornaments of society, whether as legislators, poets, or men of research. The name, however, as I have already hinted, is later than the epic period. The word σοφον first occurs in the hymns falsely attributed to the author or authors of the *Iliad*,[3] and of a later date even than the *Odyssey*, but still proceeding from the Homeric school.[4] Yet from the time of Lycurgus to that of Pindar, poets, philosophers, and lawgivers were comprised indifferently under this term as friends and familiars of the gods, the inspired, the enlightened from above, the formers and benefactors of mankind! What they knew, was regarded by their countrymen as a kind of loftier property, a power that belonged to the possessor by an especial gift or infusion, which no diligence could acquire, which no rules could teach, which no effort of volition could produce, but as an immediate presence of which it was not lawful to enquire whence it sprang, as if it were a thing subject to place and motion, nor to pursue it with a view of detecting its secret source; but they—the wise—watched quietly till it suddenly shone upon them, preparing themselves for the same, as the eye waits patiently for the rising sun. Such was the conception which the Greeks, soon after their formation into constitutional states, had of all honourable eminence in intellect, of all genuine intellectual greatness; as Apollo, the god of conscious intelligence, manifested future

[*] Vide *Friend* vol. 3 p. 112–127—the wisdom-mongers—sophists.[a]2

[a] In ms the note is given in the text and is punctuated as part of the following sentence, separated from it by a semicolon and a dash

[b] ms: σοφος

[1] E.g. the Seven Wise Men are called σοφισται. Herodotus 1.29. C is perhaps using the discussion of the early meanings of σοφός in Christoph Meiners *Geschichte des Ursprungs, Fortgangs und Verfalls der Wissenschaften* ... (2 vols Lemgo 1781–2) I 112–17. Tennemann (I 345n) would have drawn his attention to it.

[2] *Friend* (CC) I 436–43. C refers to the 1818 ed.

[3] C seems to have substituted the *Hymns* for the *Margites*. See the fragment preserved in Aristotle's discussion of σοφία in *Nicomachean Ethics* VI (1141a).

[4] For C's views on the multiple authorship of Homer's works, see *P Lects* Lects 2, 3 (1949) 87–8, 120. Cf *TT* 12 May 1830 (HNC's note) and *CRB* I 320–1.

events through the mouth of the Pythoness,[1] so, through the mouth of Pindar, he revealed the powers of song, and through Pythagoras he brought forth the hidden principles into light:—these were all alike inspired—all alike had a genius ([δαιμων]) and the influences and illapses of the god or genius were diffused through the whole man, his moral impulses no less than his intellectual perceptions.

16   Hence on the one hand it was supposed a contradiction to be vicious and yet a man of genius and on the other what was learnt or could be learnt was but little in extent, still less in value, and least of all in worth.

17   Learning was a servile attainment as opposed to the ingenuous or the distinctions suitable to free men or citizens, which in this point of view we might not inaptly render—gentlemen. We may refer to the well-known passage of Pindar: "He alone is the wise man who understandeth much out of himself—but they who have learnt—the learned—pour forth empty words as the crows clamour against the godlike bird of Jove."[2]

18   This state of feeling, as associated with learning and the learned, could not be permanent; though the substantial part of the distinction, that which discriminates immediate knowledge from such attainments as were communicable by words or other mere passive impressions, will forever retain its worth and full value. Pythagoras himself, who modestly substituted the title [φιλοσοφος] for the [σοφος],[3] had[a] already prepared for this change by giving the name of [μαθησις], that is, the learning, and [μαθηματα], things to be learnt, to the study and contents of the mathematics, in which he included music and rhythm as a preparatory discipline or προπαιδεια, through which the pupils were to pass on their road to wisdom or the knowledge of the immediate.[4] The original sense of the term was still so far present that the [μαθησις] and the [μαθηματα], the acquisition and the acquirements, were still subordinate: but they acquired a reputability by being employed in the service of that which was excellent on its own account. A still greater influence was exerted by the writings of Herodotus and of Hippocrates, or rather of the accumulation of knowledges derived from experience, the fruits of research ([ἰστορια]). It became evident that the man who depended wholly on

a ms: has

1 The priestess of Apollo at Delphi.
2 *Olympian Odes* 2.85–8: "they who have learnt" is μαθόντες. Cf μαθησις, μαθημα, below.

3 Cf *Friend* (*CC*) 1 436. This tradition is recorded in Stanley 352.
4 Cf Stanley 377.

his experience was poor and unprovided for the contingencies of life compared with those in whose memory, as in a storehouse, the fruits of many men's experiences were preserved; that with the same degree of natural understanding or mother wit, the man who had appropriated to himself the judgments, the ends proposed, the means adopted, the results confirmatory or dissuasive, of all those who from tradition, whether fixed or still oral, were known to have distinguished themselves in any given office or exigence, would enter on such an office better qualified for the performance of its functions, would meet with that or other equivalent exigence with less probability of being taken by surprise, than any merely self-taught man at the conclusion of his career. Henceforward learning could not but dignify the possessor, and the communication of the same advantage to others, by collecting records and by comments and verbal interpretation, removing or lessening the difficulties which the collector and communicator had himself struggled with, could not but become merit, increasing with the progression and increase of human experience.

19   Still, however, so numerous were the passages in the ancient poets and philosophers, *a*in which*b* what we should now entitle book-knowledge was held in contempt for its emptiness and even reprobated for its tendency to inflate the mind and thus unfit it for communion with immediate truths, that a certain macula lives still adhered to the term.[1] The [σοφος] was a title that never appears to have been chosen, even by those men whose chief claim rested on their learning. They went back again to the earliest period, and resumed the term derived.[2] The period at present in our view must have its commencement dated from the formation of the Platonic and Aristotelian schools, under the immediate successors of Alexander and principally in Egypt, if we speak of the full formation of the terminology to which the historic etymology of λεγω and its derivatives now leads us. But the aim, the philosophic anticipation which lies at the ground of this terminology, had a much earlier date and appears more or less distinctly, even from the introduction of the term νους into the speculative researches of Greece by Anaxagoras.[3] But as far as the term now under consideration is concerned, it is displayed with*c* particular force and is of noticeable

a–b ms: that   *c* ms: by

[1] E.g. Plato *Phaedrus* 274E–278A.
[2] I.e. "philosopher".
[3] On Anaxagoras and νους (mind) cf *CN* I 208, quoting Aristotle *Meta-*

physics 1.4 (985a) and *P Lects* Lect 4 (1949) 146, alluding to Plato *Phaedo* 97B–98B.

recurrence in the small number of genuine and unsuspected fragments of Heraclitus.[1] The doctrine of Aristotle differed indeed materially from the principle of the Platonist,[a] such as the latter is proved to have been, under the second master of the Academus, by an invaluable fragment of Speusippus,[b] Plato's nephew and successor.[2] That Aristotle, however, did not differ from his great master and rival as to the existence of the distinction which I am now about to notice is evident from his own words: "there must be something transcending the λογος",[3] that is, logical faculty, viz. that which is the principle of this faculty, to which numerous other passages of the same import might be added from his logical and metaphysical works. As in the present stage of the enquiry we are not concerned with the truth or philosophical validity of the conceptions, nor the right with which the terms were appropriated to them, nor discussing the rightfulness with which the terms in question were selected for their expression, but solely with the historical fact that such conceptions were entertained and that certain words acquired such and such meanings, and underwent such and such changes of sense in consequence; the reader will perceive that these prefatory notices are neither out of place nor[c] without a pertinent end. We will therefore proceed, having first premised that we shall name this

, this 　　　[d] the νους or pure reason, but without any reference to the divers opinions concerning its nature.

20　At this time the substantive λογος, we have said, acquired a new sense, and was employed to express the intelligential faculty itself and this in a threefold relation: first it signified the logical

---

[a] ms: Platonix　　[b] ms: Spenciphus　　[c] ms: not　　[d] Blank spaces left in ms

[1] For C's interpretation of Heraclitus on λογος see *SM* (*CC*) 95 and 97, where C is using Friedrich Daniel Schleiermacher "Herakleitos der dunkel . . ." *Museum der Alterthums-Wissenschaft* ed F. A. Wolf and P. Buttman (2 vols Berlin 1807, 1810) I 313–533. Schleiermacher (I 316) distinguishes between the modest number of genuine fragments and the reports and mentions of ancient writers. W. K. C. Guthrie *A History of Greek Philosophy* (1962–) I 419–34 discusses the Logos in Heraclitus.

[2] C refers to the fragment in *P Lects* Lect 5 (1949) 175. It is quoted in Tennemann III 9n from Stobaeus *Eclog. Physic.* I c 3 p 38: "the Nous is not the same as the One or the Good, but has a nature of its own". C's version in *P Lects* runs as follows: "I refer to the passage in which we are told that the intelligential powers, by the Pythagoreans and Anaxagoras called the *Nous*, (the *Logos* or the *Word* of Philo and St. John) is indeed indivisibly united with, but yet not the same as the absolute principle of causation, THE PATERNAL One, the super-essential Will . . .".

[3] C gives the gist of Aristotle's distinction in *De anima* 3.5; Scholastic philosophers had pointed out its significance—e.g. Aquinas *Summa theologica* Ia.79, 4.

faculty, the reasoning power, in short the understanding including the judgment, in distinction from the νοῦς or reason. Secondly it signified the understanding, as the discursive faculty, or that which employed itself on the conceptions of the mind and the general terms representing them, in distinction from the intuition, or intuitive power of the mind, as employed on the forms of perception in time and space, that is, number and figure; but in both instances, with abstraction of all that is furnished from without, of all that does not belong to the mind of its own right. Here the λόγος is distinguished from θεωρια, as the understanding from the sense, and of course distinguished as from its equal and collateral. Thirdly the λόγος was used in a somewhat larger sense, as the mind or intellective power abstractedly from the νοῦς, or pure reason, as the supposed identity of the *intellectio* and the *intelligibile*;[1] from the reason, I say, as at once the light of the mind and its highest object, and no less in abstraction from the sensations and impressions, as far as the conditions, causes, and materials of these were found in the body or through its medium. The knowledge derived from the latter sources, as far as it was derived from them exclusively, was considered as fluctuating and below the formal sciences; in our present use of words, it was merely empirical (that word used *in sensu inferiori*,[2] though exclusively of all moral defect), but which, when reduced under the forms or inherent rules of the understanding, was capable of being elevated into experience and of becoming the substitute, and often the indispensable substitute, of the permanent truths of the pure reason, that is, in all those numberless cases of which the larger portion of our active life consists, where we must accept the probable in all its degrees, in lieu of the certain. In this third distinctive use of the term, the λόγος may be rendered the understanding, considered not so much as either excluding or including the sense as without any conscious reference to it. Or perhaps I should[a] be better understood, if I said it was the understanding including the faculty of the *pure sense* without reference to its peculiar objects. The last sense is in immediate connection with the former, or rather an application of it to a particular and correspondent science—that of logic; of which no other definition need be given than that it contains the rules or forms of the understanding, on whatever objects they are employed, in exclusive reference to the correspondence of these objects to its own forms; in other words, it is the science which affirms or denies

---

a ms: shall

1 "The intellect", "the intelligible".   2 "In a lower sense".

the formal truth of our conceptions or of positions the value of which is derived from their dependence the one on the other.

21   It is probable, however, that the following diagram may assist in the impression, if not the comprehension, both of what logic properly means and likewise of the sense in which the terms "above" and "below" have been used in the preceding paragraph.

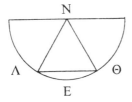

22   We will suppose that NΛΘ[a] is the section of a circle, of which N is the centre: from which the radii NΛ and NΘ are drawn and which, in conjunction with the extracircumferential E, we may conceive as determining the chord connecting Λ and Θ; and we will also suppose that the eye is directed upward, from the chord to the centre.

23(a)   Thus regarded, we should be allowed to speak of Λ as below N, = to Θ, and above E; or of N as above, and E as below, Λ. But it is equally evident that by imagining the figure in a different relation to the eye, instead of above we might with the same propriety use the word inward or more inward, central or deeper, and this commutation of terms exists in all cultivated languages; more especially when the subject spoken of [is] in reference to the mind or the feelings of man. Instances repeatedly occur in which the same truth may be indifferently extolled as sublime or profound: a high sense of honour, or a deep feeling of the right, etc. Now let the N signify the νοῦς, or the reason, as the something transcendent of the understanding; the Λ and the Θ, the λογος and the θεωρια, represent the understanding and the sense[b] as the two constituents of the mind; while the extracircumferential E, the power acting on or from without, and the chord ΛΘ,[c] [serve] at once as the common boundary and medium of communication. Thus we have a view of the powers from which the sciences derive their name or character. To obtain a view of the latter we have only to consider the N as representing the indemonstrable, because the ground of all demonstration, or the absolute, that is, irrelative, because the ground of all relation (the consideration of which, as the primary truths—*aeternae veritates*[1]—independent of all time and place and in which the reason itself consists, gives rise to the science once called the first philosophy, then ontology, by others—but more laxly *et improprie*[2]— metaphysics, but for which the term "noetic", or the science corresponding to the νοῦς, would be the most unpresuming and most appropriate exponent).[a] The Λ would represent the science of the permanent relations in conceptions, as inferior to the absolute, but superior to the variably relative, or facts, which we find, but do not understand or conceive in and of themselves. And the Θ is[b] the mathematics, as the science of number and measure,[c] arithemetic and geometry, or the forms of perception inherent in the faculty itself, and which may be considered in itself as a collateral science with logic; which[3] in its use is fitly recommended by Plato as introductory to the other sciences in its elements and then their assiduous companion and ally, but which in no sense of the word can be admitted as a mode of logic or a substitute for it.[4]

23(b)   These three sciences, [the] noetic, the logic, and the mathematic, are comprised in the term "metaphysics", as being all above, or transcendental to, the physics ([μετα φυσικα]), as having a higher evidence than that which the senses can afford, or which can belong to objects of the bodily sense considered as matters of fact, a phrase,[5] like many others which we shall have occasion to notice in the progress of the work, that has been vulgarised by its vulgar use, but [which,] in its origin and literal import, is strictly and beautifully expressive. Thus by the mathematic we have the immediate truth in all things numerable and mensurable; or the permanent relations of space and time. In the noetic, we have the immediate truth in all objects or subjects that are above space and time; and, by the logic, we determine the mediate truths by conception and conclusion, and by the application of all to the world of the senses, we form facts and maxims of experience [d]which is[e] one of the two provinces in and on which the formal sciences are to be employed and realised.

23(c)   The reader is once more reminded that the truth and reality of the positions assumed in these distinctions is not here asserted; they would be wholly out of their place in this division of our work.

[a] Parentheses inserted   [b] ms: as   [c] Full stop in ms
[d-e] ms: ~~which as one of the two provinces in and on~~ *which* as

[1] Literally, "eternal truths".
[2] "And improperly".
[3] I.e. "the mathematics".
[4] *Republic* 7.525–6; *Laws* 5.747 and 7.818–19.
[5] I.e. "matters of fact".

24   It is only necessary that such is the meaning of the words, and that such and no other are the appropriate objects of the sciences so called; for aught that we are here concerned with, thought may be the mere result of organisation; the brain may be an organ for the secretion of mind, according to the recent assertion of a medical philosopher;[1] or the aggregate of ideas, conceptions, and images may be founded in vibrations, either of strings, or of a tremulous fluid, permeating on strings.[2] With all this the logician has as little to do as common sense has; sufficient for him that thoughts are thoughts and that the laws by which they act are the laws of thought, for to these laws, and to these only as far as they contain the rules of reasoning conclusively, is his science confined. Finally, all truth, and consequently all true knowledge, rests on the coincidence of the object with the subject. Even what is called fact merely expresses the result of this coincidence. On the other hand, the operations of the mind and the contemplation of nature, the act and power of contemplation itself, could not escape attention, and yet there was no evidence [that] *that* implied or [was] necessarily contained in the former.

25   This writing desk, for instance, would, it seems to us, exist though there were no subject, or sentient being, to look at it: nor should we expect any sentiency to arise out of it, or any power of contemplating itself to reside *within* it actually or potentially.[*] As, then, the sum of the objective was entitled nature, as comprising all the phenomena by which other existence than our own is made known to us, *so was the sum of all the subjective comprehended in the name of mind* or intelligence. Both conceptions are in necessary antithesis. Intelligence is conceived as exclusively representative, nature

[*] It is true that these facts in relation to their groundwork or origin are referred to somewhat without us, which we think of as that which supplies (or rather that which consists of) the passive materials for this coincidence. But these materials should be called the matter of fact rather than the fact, as though as uppermost in the attention of the beholder, they (the materials) soon became confounded with reality, were spoken of as the only real objects, as substantial things, in opposition to mere thoughts: and the sum of such objects (or the objective, taken collectively) was entitled nature.

[1] C ascribes this statement elsewhere to "Dr Elliotson, the great standard-bearer of Materialism, the Ali of the physiological Mahomet [?Mesmer]...". (BM MS Egerton 2801 f 69ᵛ—water-mark 1821). The reference is to a note in John Elliotson (1791–1868) tr of J. F. Blumenbach *The Institutions of* *Physiology*...(2nd ed 1817) 130. C mentioned the book in *Friend* (*CC*) I 154–5n and in a letter to Thomas Curtis in Dec 1818 (*CL* IV 886).

[2] Cf the account of Hartley's theory in *BL* ch 6 (1907) I 74ff. See below, pp 265–6n.

as represented; the one as conscious, the other as without consciousness. From this state, there necessarily arise[a] three distinct theories, each having its own value in its own proper province. In the act of perception, the object and subject are so instantly united that we cannot determine to which of the two the priority belongs.[1] In the tune produced on an Aeolian harp, it is perfectly indifferent whether we take[b] the organic harp or the breeze as the first of its two efficient causes;[2] the quotient stands in the same relation to both the factors. There is here no first and no second, both are coinstantaneous, and the common product is indivisibly one. If then we would explain the one out of the other, we must of necessity begin by giving an arbitrary or hypothetical antecedence to one of the two. Take the following as an illustration. A person believing himself to be fully awake beholds the form of a well-known individual at the bedfoot. The figure remains the same in relation to the percipient whether we attribute the antecedence in its causation to a cause working outwardly or to the percipient himself. In the first instance we should explain the subjective, that is, the state of the percipient, at that moment, out of the objective. We should conceive an object originating the production, and the subject as merely receiving the same, as the wax receives and retains the impression of the seal. In the latter case, we should begin with the state of the subjective, and from this explain the supposed object. And this object would in truth be no more unsubstantial in this instance than the subject is in the former, on the present supposition in which object and subject are taken separately for the purpose of explaining the one by the other. For what can the recipient or the subject be if it be not an object, after the object has been presumed as its efficient cause? In the thing all reality has been comprised, and there remains nothing for the subject but to be nothing, or a power or property of the former, or a result not separable from it, even as the cutting is a result not separable from the edge of the knife. In assuming the object as the antecedent of the subject, I make the subject objective; as when the beholder says, "it was a real man that I saw"; and, in like manner, the object becomes wholly subjective when we assume the subject as the proper antecedent of the object. "Nay", would the physician answer, "what you saw was a mere thought or fancy of your own."

26   Which then of these shall we choose, or by what means shall

---

[a] ms: arises   [b] ms: state

[1] Cf *BL* ch 12 (1907) i 174ff.   [2] Cf below, p 142.

we evade the necessity of choosing between either, and what theory would result from this last division? We have asserted, however, that each of the three views has a value of its own, in its own province and for its own purposes. We will begin then as the philosopher of Greece began, with nature—here then the objective is taken as the first and we have to account for the subjective: it is evident then that we must jealously exclude whatever is confessedly subjective from our views, *our terms must be the pure exponents of the phenomena*, or, by generalisations, capable of being reduced to such phenomena, and, if this be impossible without presuming some power, this power must derive all its attributes from the phenomena in which it is manifested, and be assumed strictly commensurate with its effects; a power thus taken is an empirical law in reality, and in severe accuracy of language, it is a fiction invented for the *generalisation of history*, and for the purpose of enabling the observer to reflect on the sum total of a successive series, collectively and abstracted from the succession. All interference of spirits, as existences, entities existing separately from the object, and of all final causes, in any way distinguished from the efficient cause and lastly of all cause, of cause itself, that can in any way be otherwise than verbally distinguished from the effect, is an inconsistency which, by removing all the force of the reasoning, not merely invalidates the conclusion, but by its inevitable action on the observer himself, and on the character of the images which he abstracts by means of his senses, renders the observations themselves insecure and places them in the list of things like garments mistaken in the dark for a person, or meteoric lights mistaken as battling angels, or half fancies, the detection of the real portion in which is itself a task better suited to the fancy than to the philosophic judgment.

27   Yet a purity so austere, so stern and coercive a discipline of the mind, was not to be expected in the first and youthful period of philosophy; and there was a craving withal which even the most strenuous exercise of the judgment could neither have explained nor gratified. The objects of sense are in continual flux, and the notices of them by the senses must, as far as they are true notices, change with them. The senses themselves are but particulars, subject to the same flux, and capable of communicating their own character to the notices of which they are the media; nay, the very understanding itself, even independent of the causes that always in each individual possessor render it more or less turbid or uneven, does in the language of our immortal Verulam "ipsa sua natura radios ex figura et

sectione propria immutat".[1] Our understanding not only reflects the objects subjectively; that is, substitutes the relations which the objects bear to its (the understanding's) own particular constitution for the inherent laws and properties of the objects themselves; but all its presentations and reflexes; in other words, the understanding itself, as far as it expresses the aggregate of these, is itself but a phenomenon of the inner sense, and requires therefore the same corrections as the phenomena transmitted by the outward sense. Whence then arise the necessary, the permanent, the universal, or the truths having these attributes, and whence, if not from these, are we to derive the rules and principles by which our observations and reflections are to be corrected? The necessity therefore of a something prior to the objective, in the order of information, at least prior in order to a true knowledge of the objective itself, is strikingly exemplified in the fact that of all the observations or facts of nature collected in this first period, either in Greece or Egypt, nothing has survived but dreams and fancies, the hypotheses of children (see Stanley's history of philosophy before Anaxagoras),[a2] and from which if our gratitude in other and higher respects did not influence our judgment, as far as natural history (physics) is[b] concerned, Pythagoras himself is but an uncertain exception. Happy therefore was it for mankind when it occurred to try the alternative.

28   The subjective was assumed as the first, and previously to the attempt of directly explaining the objective out of it, it occurred to, might I not almost say it was inspired into, the greatest of philosophers,[3] if not the first who merited, as well as assumed, that name, to try first, by effectuating that rigid exclusion of the opposite, which ought to have been, but was not and indeed could not have been, persistently even attempted in the former case. The perception of a truth, permanent, necessary, raised above all accident and all change, had flashed upon him in a geometrical contemplation.[c] He perceived at once that this truth had no respect either to the magnitude, the figure, or the tactual properties; to nothing, in short, into which phenomenal nature must be analysed, as into its ultimate elements;

---

a Ms closes sentence after "children" and has no parentheses or comma
b ms: are   *c* Comma in ms

[1] Bacon *Distributio operis: Works* (1740) I 15 (var). Tr: [as an uneven mirror] "by its very nature distorts the rays according to its own figure and section". C quotes the same passage in *Friend* (*CC*) I 491.

[2] The discussion of Anaxagoras in Stanley begins at p 63, following the account of the Seven Wise Men and Anaximander and Anaximenes.

[3] Pythagoras. Cf *P Lects* Lect 2 (1949) 97ff and *SM* (*CC*) 50 and n.

it was true, absolutely in and for the mind only; its proper being was in the mind, and, in contemplating it, the intelligence was contemplating its own acts and their products, as realised in its own imagination. Henceforward, then, it was to be inquired what the subjective could effect by its own powers, by reflection on its own acts and the products of those acts, for and within its own sphere. The mind was now considered as an island, unapproachable from without, or whatever importations were thrown on its shores from the unknown region were carefully distinguished from the indigenous growth. The result of this grand experiment was formal knowledge—or science considered in its purity and prior to its application. Science then refracted itself, if I may use so bold a metaphor, into the sciences, as the pure light into its various rays, and these of two kinds, in accordance with the two different faculties of the mind. First the sciences that refer to the acts of sense, either to the sense which employs itself on ideal space or the sense which has time as the material of its contemplation. These are the sciences or, rather, twofold science of number and measure: arithmetic and geometry. The other division had for its subject the forms of thought, in their necessary dependencies, one on the other, and this, as we have before shown at large, is the science of logic. The third question which gives priority neither to the objective nor subjective, but subjects both, as co-ordinates, to a third, higher than either, belongs not to the present work. As the assumption in all natural enquiries (physics) is that of negative materialism, however remote the naturalist himself may be from a materialist, even so in the formal sciences there is no other assumption but that of negative idealism, however little faith may be attached to the latter as a system of philosophy. The logician, and in like manner the geometrician, will say, "I am no Berkeleyan, but while I am engaged in the science of logic, I must reason as if I were." This is what is meant by the epithet "negative", that, namely, which abstracts from, without asserting the nonentity of, its opposite.[1] The logician, as far as he is treating of the forms of logic, abstracts his attention from the outward world without denying either its reality or the reality of its connection with the mind.

---

[1] Cf "*negative* faith": *BL* ch 22 (1907) ii 107.

A synopsis of the main points contained in the preceding chapters, for the purpose of aiding a self-examination into the sum of our acquirements

29   There are two questions which every student should put to himself, the one at each stage of his progress, the other at the end of the course. The former, "*Have I learnt, that is, made myself master of, that which has been taught, whether by oral or written instruction, and what are the main particulars?*" The second, "*Have I reason to believe that my faculties are improved and my means enlarged?*" For that alone is truly knowledge in relation to the individual acquirer which reappears as power,[1] and the improvement of the faculties, the only sure measure and criterion of the attainments.

30   In aid of the former question, I have thought it convenient to annex the following repetition. Let us suppose that on our ascent we have attained a convenient resting place, have agreed to pause, to turn round toward the road over which we had been passing, and employing ourselves in pointing out the principal objects and turns of the road, or, if I may be allowed the phrase, the several reaches which we had examined close at hand, and endeavoured to impress on our memory, as at once the landmarks of the road and the fruits of our journey. First, then, it has been required of me that I should consider the mind in and for itself, separately from the objects of the senses and sensations. All that belongs to the former we have for our present purposes agreed to comprise under the name of "subjective", or intelligence, and all the latter under the term "objective" or nature. By this, however, we are not bound, nor understood, to deny the existence of either the one or the other, nor to establish any real chasm or interspace between the two, any more than (to take a rude and sufficient illustration) we do in having the boundaries that divide Prussia from Saxony for the purpose of confining our attention to the former. We may indeed assert the exclusive reality of either, and we know, from the history of philosophy, that the assertion has been made seriously and in good faith in both instances. But this belongs to philosophy and constitutes a philosophic system: in the one case the system of idealism, more commonly known to the English reader under the name of Berkeleyanism, and in the other the system of materialism. These, I say, belong to philosophy, and we are engaged in the consideration of science, and moreover in relation to a particular science, that of logic. Next in importance is the distinction which

[1] Cf *SM* (*CC*) 24 and n 2.

I have been called upon to observe and make between real and formal knowledges, and the real and formal sciences in consequence. I need only ask myself, what are the matters treated of the will, the soul, the conscience,[*] to see at once that, although I acquire my convictions otherwise than[a] by my senses, and even without relation to the forms of sense, such as extension, motion, partibility, and the like, yet I attribute as much reality to the former class as to the latter. Whether I speak of a man's soul or his body, I speak of a something which I suppose to subsist of itself and not contained in the act of my contemplation. But when I say that what is true of all must be true of each, or *quae de generica notione statuuntur omnibus inferioribus sub eadem complexis competere*[†], or simply affirm that *omnis[b] cujuslibet notio est[c] vel generalis vel individualis,*[2] I am not speaking of any thing, but of the acts of my own mind and the law or form according to which it acts or ought to act. Now the sciences which teach these forms are hence contradistinguished as formal sciences, and, in this acceptation of the word, logic, geometry, and arithmetic are all alike formal sciences.[‡] Thirdly, as we proceeded, we were led to consider the mind in the threefold relation. First in reference to those permanent and universal truths which in the peculiar sense are entitled truths of reason, and mind contemplated

[*] Which we know to exist, or believe at least that we know to exist, by the light of reason.

[†] Whatever is affirmed of a *generic* conception applies to all subordinates (or particulars) comprehended in that conception.[1]

[‡] That this does not contradict the application of the term "objective" to the truths of geometry, and wherein the distinction lies between objective and real, when the former term is thus applied, will be found fully explained in the second part of this work and in the glossary.[3] Sufficient at present that in this connection and use of the words, "objective" is opposed to "subjective" as "universal" to "individual", and not as "real" to "formal". James sees that as yellow which to men in general appears as red, and this we say is subjective: that is, results from that individual subject. But no mind can confound the properties of a circle with those of a square. These are truths which subsist in all beings possessing the faculties of sense and intelligence, independent of all will and without relation to individuality. They are in all minds as though they were but in one mind, and being in one mind are the same as in all. Hence they are called universal truths, while those which being equally universal are at the same time transcendent to sense, and irrelative to space and time, are entitled *eternal* truths.

[a] ms: then   [b] ms: ante   [c] ms: ut

[1] C's translation. A rendering of the *dictum de omni et nullo*, which is believed to be derived from Aristotle *Prior Analytics* bk I sec 1 (24[b] 26). See Kneale p 79n.

[2] "Every notion, of whatever it may be, [is] either general or particular".

[3] See below, pp 72–6. The planned glossary, mentioned again on pp 267–8, has not come to light. See, however, N 29 ff 128[v]ff for a complicated sample entry.

as the source of these is*a* designated the reason, or, using the Greek term for the after-convenience of its derivation, the νοῦς. These we characterised neither as object nor as subject exclusively, but as the identity of both as at once formal and real; or in other words, forms that implied their own reality. We will take mind itself; not this man's mind, nor yours, individually, nor even the human mind generally, but *mind* absolutely. Now of this we assert that the form or act of contemplating, which it will be found convenient to call the "position" of it, implies the reality. *Ponitur mens: ergo est,*b *nam mentem ponere ipsa mens est.*[1] These truths (conceived as a system) form the science of noetics, more frequently, but less appropriately, entitled metaphysics. In subordination to these, and as more properly constituting the mind in its specific sense as the *human* mind, we found the λογος (the understanding) and the [θεωρια], the sense. Below these we have to add the senses which we may consider as the common boundaries of intelligence and nature: and the following table will place the whole before us in one view.[2]

31   The sciences pure and mixed and in the order of their senses.

Μετα Φυσικα

A—Noetics = the evidence of reason[*]
B—Logic = the evidence of the understanding
C—Mathematics =*c* the evidence of sense

Φυσικα

D—Empiric = evidence of the senses†
Scholium. The senses = sense + sensation + impressions.

[*] Noetics or truths of reason applied
First. To being absolutely considered = ontology.
Second. To the will as absolute and one with the supreme reason = theology.
Third. To the finite will = ethics.
Therefore we cannot in noetics as we may *in logicis* require a reason for a truth; for it is reason.
† The empiric D, brought under the rules of the understanding B, and the forms of sense (= *intuitus puri*)[3] C, becomes experience.
a—Experience in application to figure, number, position, and motion succes-

a ms: are   *b* ms: *ergo, est*   *c* ms: = to

[1] "The mind is posited: therefore it is, for the positing of mind is mind itself."

[2] The table is given in a slightly garbled version in ms—C's marks, indicating footnotes, having been misread. It has been corrected by the editor from another ms in C's hand, which must have been the direct or indirect source of it and of paragraphs 32 and 33: BM MS Egerton 2801 ff 85–6 (for which see Appendix D, below).

[3] "Pure intuitions". The phrase appears in Kant *De mundi sensibilis atque intelligibilis forma et principiis* (Königsberg 1770) § 14.3 and § 15c: *VS* ii 457, 462.

32   Now with none of these have we at present any immediate concern, B only excepted. We are now exclusively seeking that evidence which arises from the perfect coincidence of a conception or proposition (that is, words intended to express conception) with the laws of the understanding, or the rules that result from the constitution of the understanding itself considered abstractedly from its objects, even as the mechanist would examine an engine previously to its use, or an astronomer a quadrant or telescope.

33   It is the same whether we say the constitution of the understanding or the constituent forms of the understanding, the understanding being considered as the band or copula of these. Thus a steam engine, of course, comprises all the component parts; but these parts, considered in themselves as individual things, do not involve or constitute the idea of the steam engine: it is the steam engine = the parts + the copula of the parts.

34   We have learnt that the proper subject of logic, in the strict and simple sense of the term, is not *what* we understand nor *how much*, but simply *how* we understand. Not *quid* nor *quantum*; but

---

sive and coexistent = physiography, that is, description of nature as the aggregate of objects (*natura naturata*).[1]

b—Experience in application to acts, that is, manifestations of a will; acts simultaneous or successive of men, or of nature considered as an agent (*natura naturans*)[2] = history.

We have therefore physiography, a description of nature; 2, physiology, the relations of nature; and physiogony, the history or genesis of nature. Experience, in application to the laws and principles of a and b, acquires, according to the matters so treated, the names of phenomenology,[3] physiology, including somatology and psychology, and lastly anthropology.

---

[1] C defines *natura naturata* and *natura naturans* in *P Lects* Lect 13 (1949) 370: "in speaking of the world without us as distinguished from ourselves, the aggregate of phenomena ponderable and imponderable, is called nature in the passive sense,—in the language of the old schools, *natura* NATURATA—WHILE THE SUM OR AGGREGATE OF THE POWERS INFERRED AS THE SUfficient causes of THE former (which by Aristotle and his followers were called the SUBSTANTIAL FORMS) is nature in the active sense, or *natura natur*ANS". See also *C 17th C* 651: "*natura naturata*—an effect, a product, not a *power*"; and *AR* (1825) 244n: "that is, the sum

total of the Facts and Phenomena of the Senses". In BM MS Egerton 2801 f 1, C refers to Spinoza's use of these Scholastic terms, thinking perhaps of *Ethics* pt I prop xxix scholium.

[2] See n 1, above.

[3] C remarks elsewhere that "The doctrine concerning material nature would . . . (the word Physiology being both ambiguous in itself, and already otherwise appropriated) be more properly entitled Phaenomenology, distinguished into its two grand divisions, Somatology and Psychology". *Friend* (*CC*) I 467. Cf Appendix D, below. The Kantian origin of the term is noticed by Orsini (p 72).

quomodo. This therefore is equivalent to the form or mode in which we understand: and a moment's reflection will convince us that a mode or form or scheme implies certain relations; either the relation A to the relation B to[a] the same subject, e.g., the relation of the length to the breadth in the same table: or of one subject to another subject having the same or different relations. But this, again, by pursuing the act of reflection we shall find to imply a plurality, or alterity,[1] in some sense or other; though it be a plurality which involves no breach of unity, that is, does not prevent us from asserting the unity of the same subject, in some other point of view. Try to represent space without inclosing the same in some figure, here you would have a subject perfectly arid of plurality and alterity, and in the same moment you will experience the impossibility of attaching any form thereto: in other words, you will see that to say the form of any subject, or the mode, supposes at least certain distinctions in that subject, or, as in the present instance, certain distinct acts of the mind called forth in the treatment thereof.

35   Let not the student be either surprised or offended by these technical terms. If he have been previously a student in anatomy, in botany, or in chemistry, he must have learnt from his own experience that the feeling of uncouthness in technical terms will diminish as the sense of their convenience increases, and as the meaning expressed by each becomes more familiar both in itself and in its association with the given terms. At least, it would be difficult to discover why "identity", "unity", "plurality", or even "haecceity"[b][2] and "alterity" (*haec et altera sive res sive forma*)[3] as abstract terms, expressing certain acts of the mind, should stand a worse chance than "hydrogenation" and "oxygenation", or "protoxides", "deut-oxides", "tritoxides", and "peroxides" in chemistry, as generic terms for sundry acts of nature or for the forms and phenomena resulting. In both cases the words are employed as marks for recollection or marks of security—means by which we bring a train of equivalent or similar particulars into one group before the memory, or by which we refer to a past ascertainment with a conviction that we have ascertained the same, and have it in our power to renew our

---

[a] For "in"?   [b] ms: *haeneity*

[1] The state of being other; otherness.
[2] Individuality;   thisness.   Duns Scotus' term; cf *P Lects* (1949) 438–9, quoting a marginal note in Tennemann VIII 765.

[3] "This and the other whether thing or form". The same phrase appears in BM MS Egerton 2801 f 88ᵛ.

distinct insight into the grounds and process whenever we please. In another division of the present treatise, the student will find this subject treated of more at large, under the heads of abstraction and generalisation, and wherein they differ.[1] The bracketed sentences[2] therefore must be regarded as *anticipations*, the entire rejection of which we have already shown to be impracticable (see chapter first)[3] and, were it not so, yet obstructive and occasioning unnecessary difficulties in the acquisition of knowledge.

[1] See below, pp 62–4.
[2] Presumably the four preceding paragraphs. The brackets have not survived transcription.
[3] See above, pp 7 ff.

[PART ONE]

Logic may be conceived of either as perfectly abstracted from the objects, or imperfectly in which latter sense it would rather belong to Logic applied or Logic sensu improprio. In the former sense it may be said to consist wholly in the form of the syllogism that is in conclusion or the mode in which we conclude whether we have concluded truly or erroneously in fact Still as long as we have concluded according to a certain legitimate form the conclusion is logically legitimate. From this alone the student will perceive that Logic properly so called is neither capable of being a primary and direct instrument of discovering truths nor could have been intended as such but if not of discovering, so neither can it be of itself and unaided the means of distinguishing the truth from falsehood otherwise than formally. Since in the discrimination of truth no less than in the discovery a consideration of the objects is supposed. But it is part of the definition of Logic that it abstracts from the object. Yet on the other hand it is evident that without such consideration and unaccompanied by those other faculties which are called into act during our attention to such objects, Logic would be an hollow science, our conclusions as worthless as our premises are empty, and that in fact it

[PREFACE]

1   Logic may be conceived of either as perfectly abstracted from the objects or imperfectly, in which latter sense it would rather belong to logic applied, or logic *sensu improprio*.[1] In the former sense it may be said to consist wholly in the form of the syllogism, that is, in conclusion or the mode in which we conclude, whether we have concluded truly or erroneously in fact, still, as long as we have concluded according to a certain legitimate form, the conclusion is logically legitimate. From this alone the student will perceive that logic properly so called is neither capable of being a primary and direct instrument of discovering truth nor could have been intended as such; but, if not of discovering, so neither can it be of itself and unaided the means of distinguishing the truth from falsehood otherwise than formally,[a] since in the discrimination of truth, no less than in the discovery, a consideration of the object is supposed. But it is part of the definition of logic that it abstracts from the object. Yet on the other hand it is evident that without such consideration and unaccompanied by those other faculties which are called into act during our attention to such objects, logic would be an hollow science, our conclusions as worthless as our premises are empty, and that in fact it would be the assertion of a form in which, however we may vary the names of the terms, we assert nothing more than the form itself; and a thousand syllogisms would amount to nine hundred and ninety-nine superfluous illustrations of the syllogism itself, that is, of what a syllogism is.

2   If then this pure and simple logic be neither an organ for the discovery (ὄργανον),[2] nor a test for the distinguishing of truth (κριτήριον),[3] what may it be affirmed to be? The answer is that it is a canon or form to which all legitimate constructions of the understanding must correspond. In the same sense as the celebrated canon of Polycletus[b] [4] in relation to the human form in statuary, and as the

---

[a] Ms begins new sentence here   [b] ms: Policletes

[1] "In a loose sense".
[2] "Instrument".
[3] "Criterion".

[4] The Greek sculptor (second half of the 5th century B.C.) whose statue of a youth carrying a spear was said

term has been used in the present subject and known by the ancients *ex graecis logice canonica Epicuri*.[1]

3 In the widest and most comprehensive sense of the term "logic", the science may be divided into or reduced under three several heads. The organon or *logice organica, heuristica* (εὑριστικη),[2] the criterion or *logice dialectica*,[3] and the canon or *logice simplex et^a syllogistica*.[4] In strict accuracy indeed, as we have already shown, the term "logic" belongs exclusively to the third science. But as the larger and more comprehensive sense is in almost universal use, instead of wasting our time in repeating cautions respecting it, or having on each recurrence of the word in this its laxer application to add *sensu improprio* or the like, it will be wiser to succumb to the general practice at once; we will, therefore, henceforward consider the canonic [as one of the parts of logic].

4 Whether we regard [the] canonic, the dialectic, and the organic as three sciences and logic as the common term comprising all three, [considering] the comparative priority, simplicity, or ease of acquirement of these three, we shall adopt natural as well as expedient order by commencing with logic as the canon; then proceeding to dialectic as the criterion; and ending with the heuristic or organon.

---

a ms: *ad*

---

to have embodied his theories of rhythm and proportion. Pliny the Elder *Naturalis historia* 34.55.

[1] "From the Greeks, the logical canon of Epicurus". Cf Kant *Logik* Einleitung: "a *universal Art of Reason* (*Canonica Epicuri*), the Art of making any branch of knowledge accord with the form of the understanding". *Logik* p 5 (p 3).

[2] "Organic or heuristic logic".

[3] "Dialectical logic".

[4] "Simple and syllogistic logic".

[CHAPTER I]

Pure Logic or the Canon

1   There are few who cannot recollect or place themselves in that state of mind in which their eye has rested either on a cloudless sky or the general aspect of the starry heavens or on a wide common bounded only by the horizon without consciously attending to any particular object or portion of the scene. There will be many too, I doubt not, [not] unwilling to confess that they have been sometimes in that state of mind which they could perhaps describe by no other term than that of thinking, and yet if questioned of what they were thinking about must answer nothing. Nay, this is a state which not seldom takes place when the mind is preparing itself for the highest efforts of thought, and even during such efforts the energy continuing during the momentary occultations of the past objects of the consciousness, as we continue the act of gazing in the brief intervals of the flashes at night in a storm of thunder and lightning.

2(a)   Well, we will suppose our eye to have rested on a waste common with that absence of attention to any particular object or portion of the same to which we have referred. Some accident or other, some sudden recollection that has started up and been particularised in the mind itself or a sudden gleam of sunshine which has formed a sort of brighter island on the waste, has directed our conscious attention to some one portion.[1] We describe the outline and so distinguish it and set it apart as it were abstractedly from the rest. Previously to this it was evident that there was no conscious attention existing, consequently none that we could draw away from any one object to another; but now we have two objects present to our consciousness and, as it were, candidates for our voluntary attention: that contained within the outline and that which it excludes and, relatively to the mind contemplating it, separates itself from. In order to avoid the image of interspace which is apt to intrude on the fancy in connection with the word "separate"

[1] Cf *CN* II 2370 and Orsini pp 88–90.

we might expediently hazard the more [un]usual phrase "severalise itself".

2(b)   As far as the process of conclusion is alone concerned, it is indifferent whether I suppose a common bounded only by the horizon or any portion of this common, a cultivated part, for instance, surrounded by a ring fence.[1] The latter indeed would be accompanied with an exertion of the comparative power not found in the other; for we cannot distinguish or set apart one thing from[a] another of the same kind without some degree of conscious attention to that from which we separate as well as to the thing so separated (the logical terms corresponding to this distinction will be found in a following paragraph[2] as constituting the difference between universal and particular propositions),[b] and the difference of the mental act I have proposed to express, the former by the word "clusion" (*vide* Introd[uction])[3] and the latter [by the word] "seclusion". The succeeding ratiocination, however, is, as I have already said, the same in both cases.

2(c)   We will suppose then that at some after time the conversation turned on some part of this common to which the horizon was the boundary, or of that more consciously contradistinguished from the surrounding objects by the ring fence. We will suppose too that we distinctly recollected this as a part of the common, and that we had known that the subsoil of the whole space was calcareous.[4] We could not hesitate in concluding that in this supposition the subsoil of the portion included must be so likewise. Now in syllogistic logic the larger or including space is named the major or superior position of the syllogism, and this again [is] divided into the subject which would correspond to its boundary, which in universal propositions we have compared to the horizon, and in particular propositions to

---

[a] ms: for   [b] Parentheses inserted

[1] C had earlier used this illustration in a letter on elementary logic to his son DC (then aged eighteen). *CL* IV 885: late Nov 1818.

[2] See below, pp. 60–1.

[3] The passage in parentheses evidently baffled the transcriber, who seems merely to have copied the shapes of the indecipherable letters in front of him; the reading given here is a hypothetical reconstruction of what they probably meant. Did C intend to refer his reader to the justification of technical terms on pp 46–7?

[4] In early Oct 1822, C wrote to James Gillman from Walmer, where he was holidaying: "It seems to me the healthiest Spot, I ever sojourned on— the Clay here covering the calcareous Subsoil with a thin coat . . .". *CL* v 253. He added: "Hitherto, I have not attempted any Brain-work. On the contrary, I have tried to keep my mind as composed and vacant, as possible. . . . On Thursday, however, I propose to begin work in good earnest—my Logic, to wit." *CL* v 254.

the ring fence. On the other hand the field or plot which from some cause or other had attracted our attention so that we had a distinct and secure recollection of its having been a part of the area above mentioned, only contained or included within it, corresponds to the minor of the syllogism. The field or plot being the minor subject, but the predicate of this subject is simply that of its having been contained, and inasfar as what is said of all must be true of each one,[a] we may therefore, without any deviation from ordinary language, affirm that the subject of the major is the predicate of the minor, "all that common land is calcareous: but such a field is common land". But if the subject of the minor in this sense is one with the subject of the major, the predicate of the major is of course in the same sense the predicate of the minor, and the expression of this as a necessary consequence we name the "conclusion": accordingly we add, therefore, "the field is calcareous", and the syllogism is completed.

3   As superfluity is better hazarded than[b] obscurity and as the repetition of the same truth in a different form or in an additional example is useful at least in familiarising the memory to the technical terms of the science, with which it is well to be acquainted even when they might with advantage be superseded by simpler language, we will now take the old example found in all the elementary works of logic since the time that the letters of the alphabet used by the great founder of logic[1] were to the no small ease of the memory exchanged for the names of men.[2] "All men are mortal. Socrates is a man, therefore he is mortal."

4(a)   "All men are mortal." This is entitled the major and represents what we have called the primary act of seclusion. "Caius is a man." This is termed the minor and represents what we have called the act of inclusion; "Caius" is included in the term "all mankind". It is evident, therefore, that "Caius", or the subject in the minor, can have no distinctive predicate of its own, for that would be to reverse the object in view, or to speak more accurately, it is precluded in the very nature of the process which corresponds to the rule (κανων) abstracted from the forms of the understanding itself. For the intention is that of referring "Caius" to "mankind". The minor subject to the major, the *sub*ordinate to the *super*ordinate, and not to

---

[a] ms, redundantly: each one with the subject of the major   [b] ms: then

[1] Aristotle.
[2] C seems to mean the substitution of examples such as "All men are mortal, Socrates is a man ..." for "All A is B, C is B ...".

distinguish the minor subject from others of its own rank, nor[a] that of distinguishing the *sub*ordinate from its *co*-ordinates. Again, if we repeated the predicate of the major subject, we should have two independent assertions without connection or interdependence; nothing therefore could follow from a juxtaposition in which the precedence of the one or of the other would be arbitrary or accidental. "All men are mortal. Caius is mortal" is either two independent unconnected positions, or, secondly, the term "Caius" is merely equivalent to "a man", and this again of the same meaning as "all men", it being indifferent whether we say "man is mortal" or "all men are mortal"; or lastly it is what is called "enthymeme", that is, a mere abridgment in the verbal stating of a syllogism, the mental process being taken as understood. The mind passes through the same process more or less rapidly. The omission is in the words only by which the mental process is conveyed.

4(b)   If then the minor subject can have no predicate of its own, that being the reverse of the intention, nor yet the predicate of the major subject, as that would be either tautologic or destructive of the required connection, there remains only the major subject itself for the predicate of the minor, substituting only the distinction of minor for major, the included for the including.

5   "Caius is a man", and thus in consequence of his[b] being thus identified with the major subject asserts his[c] equal claim to the predicate of that subject. Therefore "Caius is mortal".

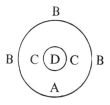

6(a)   *A* is the major subject[1] comprehending the whole space within the circumference *B*, which represents the predicate of the major subject. The space *D* represents the minor subject and it is asserted that the space which is secluded by *B* includes the space *D*, which is included by *C*, and that therefore *A* and *D* are concluded by *B*. This is the form of the syllogism[d] in the common books of logic

---

[a] ms: not   [b] ms: this   [c] ms: its   [d] Ms begins new sentence here

[1] The diagram is derived, probably indirectly, from Leonhard Euler (1707–83). C would have found a version of it in Kant *Logik* 160 ("Allgemeine Elementarlehre" pt 2 § 21).

entitled the first figure, but in truth it is the only figure which is strictly and exclusively logical, the other[s] deriving their concluding altogether from the[ir] convertibility into this the first figure, that is, they are logically conclusive only as far as it can be shown that they imply the same mental process and differ only in the verbal connection or in the objects or matter of the reasoning as contradistinguished from the form, with which alone the science of logic is concerned.[1]

6(b) To seclude, to include, and thus to conclude constitutes syllogism, but it must be evident that this once seen, the whole force of the intellect must be exerted on the primary act, on the justification of the terms by which we seclude and of the fact implied in the predicate by which we include.[2] Both these, however, imply knowledges that are more than logical, that are real and not merely formal. "All stones think, all men are stones, therefore all men think", is absurd in reason and common sense. But we have only to prefix an "if" to both the major and minor to make it a perfectly legitimate syllogism. For if all stones thought and if all men were stones it would necessarily follow that on this account men must think; but all syllogisms must be considered as hypothetical until the major position and the lack of the minor have[a] been ascertained by reason or experience. But the application of this truth belongs to the following division.[3]

7 Whenever, and this will be most often the case, the subjects of the reasoning are thoughts not things, or conceptions and facts and not the passive objects of the sight, it is evident that an act of reflection is required of which, at least in the latter cases, we are scarcely conscious from the immediateness of the evidence. We may therefore establish it as a rule that all legitimate syllogisms are grounded on a just analysis of conceptions.[4] In this point of view the total sum of human knowledge may be represented under the image of a tree[5] so as to convey in a just and lively manner the principle on which all formal logic rests. The outward points meet in sprays; these under in

a ms: has

[1] Cf *CN* III 4230: "the other 3 [forms] found in all books of Logic are either Sophisms, or true only in consequence of their convertibility into the first—& belong therefore to Rhetoric . . .".

[2] Parallel passages may be found in *CL* IV 885 (late Nov 1818), *CN* III 4228, and *TT* 23 Sept 1830.

[3] I.e. the organon of the planned Part Three.

[4] "All legitimate . . . of conceptions", translated from Moses Mendelssohn *Morgenstunden oder Vorlesungen über das Daseyn Gottes* (Frankfurt & Leipzig 1790) 7. C's copy is in the BM.

[5] "the total sum . . . a tree": ibid 7.

twigs; the twigs in boughs; the boughs in branches; and the branches in one common trunk. We will suppose that the fibres of the trunk or stem run through all the branches, boughs, twigs, and sprays, and, in like manner, the fibres of the branches through all the remaining subdivisions.[1] And to make the likeness perfect we must further assume that at every minor ramification they take certain fibres which they had not received from the higher division,[2] fibres of their own growth, or, what would answer equally well, modifications[a] of the material received from below. We shall thus have a striking image of the relations in which our conceptions stand to each other. All individual things, [which] would answer to the extreme points of the tree, meet in different species; the species in kinds or *genera*; the kinds or *genera* in class[es], and finally the classes unite in some most general conception answering to the trunk or stem[3] in this genealogy of logic. The only change necessary to be made in the application of the metaphor is that what in the tree, considered as rising skyward, would be the higher must in logic be expressed as the lower, that is, the minor or less comprehensive, and vice versa, and what in the natural tree we should call the lower, in the logical tree we name the higher or superior. What is affirmed of any superior conception must be likewise attributable to all the lower or minor conceptions, but what is asserted of the lower as peculiar to them can only be affirmed of the divisions still lower. Whatever is true of all men must be true of Socrates, but many things may be true of Socrates which are far enough from being applicable to all or even to a majority of the human race. On this principle depends the force of all conclusion: the fibres represent the marks, characteristics, or, in technical logic, the predicate of the subject; the marks predicable of the trunk belong to all the branches, the marks of the branches to all the boughs and twigs that spring out of them, and so [?on][b] to the extreme points or individual things, while the reverse of this would produce a false conclusion. If, however, it should be asked how are we to determine what fibres are attributable to the trunk, what to the branches, etc, or by what rule we are to determine the proper appurtenance of the predicate to the subject, this would lead us into the

a ms: in adifications [cf p 126, below, at n 2]
b ms: are

1 "The outward points … remaining subdivisions": ibid 7–8.
2 "at every minor … higher division": ibid 8.

3 "We shall thus … trunk or stem": ibid 8 (loosely translated).

distinction between real and not real on the one side, and of the conceivable and inconceivable on the other. Strictly speaking, logic is concerned with the latter only, or where, as in the self-evident truths of reason, the difference between real and conceivable ceases. For even in the premises, the assertions, whenever they refer to facts, may be regarded as hypothetical, or with an "if" understood.

[CHAPTER II]

On the Logical Acts

1   If we reflect on the operations of our own minds while we were employed in the foregoing process, we shall discover first the act of attention, in which the mind exercises the power of directing itself to one or more objects with a particular force. The same is doubtless exercised by the brute creation, but we have no sufficient ground for assuming that this takes place in them by any energy of the percipient power itself, taken separately from the stimulus applied to it by external impressions. We hesitate, therefore, in naming it an act of attention, the word "act" being here contradistinguished from the results of any mere passive sensation or impress[ion]. Still less are we entitled to *conclude*, however much in the case of certain animals we may be inclined to *conjecture*, that this attention exists in connection with any process of thought. Consequently we cannot name it an act of the understanding. This remains exclusively appropriate to the human faculty.

2   But if we attend exclusively or at least more expressly to one subject there will arise two possible cases. This object may either be really separable from the others which are near it, that is, it may be a concrete, or not really separable.*a* And again we may either attend to it, being at the same time conscious likewise of the objects from which we have separated it; or our whole attention, and with it, therefore, our whole consciousness, [may] have been concentred towards it. In the last case it would be a simple act of attention, in the former it would necessarily be accompanied by an act of comparison. This we have before shown, though in different terms, in the distinction between universal and particular propositions, and on it we have grounded our proposal to name the act exerted in the major of the syllogism, the act of *clusion* where the proposition is universal, and of *seclusion* where it is particular.[1] The latter, it is evident,

---

a Ms unpunctuated

[1] "All men are mortal" and "some men are mortal" are examples of universal and particular propositions respectively.

implies a comparison of the object *secluded* with the object or objects FROM which it is secluded, and this comparison will be implied, though not always expressed, in the predicate by which the major subject of the particular proposition is defined. It does not follow indeed that this comparison shall be carried on distinctly through all the objects from which the predicate separates the subject of the proposition. When, for instance, we determine a certain class of animals by the epithet "quadruped", we certainly imply a consciousness that there are other animals which are not so, though it may be indifferent whether the comparison be distinctly made of quadrupeds with birds, or with insects, or with the footless reptiles, or with them all in rapid succession.

3   In the second case, viz. where no real separation is possible, where the attention is particularly directed to an accident, property, or inseparable part of a concrete, and this attention is continued for the purpose of reflecting on this accident exclusively, we herein exercise a power which is called the power of abstraction; and both in etymological and logical propriety we ought not to say that we abstract something (*abstrahere aliquid*),[1] but that we abstract from something. When on looking at this scarlet cloth on our table we confine our thoughts to the colour, we abstract from the cloth. The accusative case understood being the attentient. It would be absurd to say that we abstracted the colour itself, unless indeed we were speaking, not as logicians, but as chemists or dyers, when of course we should not mean the colour but the colouring matter. But I possess the power, having thus once abstracted my *ᵃattention from the scarlet cloth, [of abstracting it] from*ᵇ all other concretes having the same colour; but in doing this, I exert another power—that of substantiation, on which is grounded the conversion of the adjective into the substantive. We speak of the green leaves, but in abstracting from leaves, grass, etc, etc, we can reflect on the green in nature; and whether in the latter case we say green or greenness is logically indifferent and determinable only by the idiom of the language in which we speak, when it is not, as in many languages it is, grammatically as well as logically indifferent. Observe likewise that the act of substantiation here spoken of is logical or an act of the understanding, and not an act of the fancy[2] which may or may not accompany

ᵃ⁻ᵇ ms: attention, not only from the scarlet cloth, but from

1 C is translating Kant freely throughout this paragraph. See *De mundi sensibilis* sect II § 6: *VS* II 449, and the "Allgemeine Elementarlehre" pt 1 § 2 *Logik* 146–7.

2 As distinguished from the imagination?

the former. It is not necessary that I should bring up any image in my mind, unless, indeed, the *word* itself can be called such, and the presence of this as an image is common to accident and to substance. The unity of conception, to which we are now about to proceed, is of itself sufficient to constitute this logical, abstract, and merely logical substantiality. In the strict propriety of language we should, perhaps, instead of abstract conceptions (*conceptus abstracti*), use the participle active (*conceptus abstrahentes*),[1] acts of conceiving, in which we abstract from such and such concretes. The most frequent mistake, however, is that of confounding abstraction with generalisation.[2] In the term "sheep", so far from withdrawing my attention from the animal, I am bringing a succession of these animals into comparison with each other and in consequence of certain essential likenesses, without abstracting from the differences, but on the contrary with a full insight into the compatibility of these differences with the points of essential likeness (or logical identity) I form the general conception "sheep"; now the most abstract conception is that which has nothing [in] common with anything at all different from it. This is the conception expressed in the word "something", for the only conception or term that is different from it is "nothing", and between these of course there is no point in common.

4   Nevertheless, in the process of thinking there is found to be a transition from the abstract into the general, and this we shall perhaps explain most intelligibly by a declaration of the proprieties of the three terms which in ordinary life are most frequently confounded: I mean, "idea", "abstraction", and "generalisation".

5   N.B. It would perhaps be the more proper expression to say that an abstraction is capable of being reduced to a generic conception by its reduction,[a] that is, its being brought back again to the objects from which it had been abstracted, in order to determine whether or no it was universally applicable or its compatibility with all the differences contained in the concretes. Thus an abstraction followed by an act of comparison of the common conception which by means of this abstraction we had formed, with the differences, constitutes a proper generic conception. Thus an abstraction is in all

[a] ms: reductive

[1] "Abstracting conceptions".
[2] Abstraction and generalisation are compared in a marginal note to Heinrich Steffens "Ueber die Vegeta-
tion" in *Jahrbücher der Medicin* ... (Tübingen 1808) III ii [127]ᵛ (BM copy); they are distinguished from one another in *P Lects* Lect 5 (1949) 184–5.

cases a common conception but not in all cases a generic conception. In other words, the abstract in the most comprehensive sense contains the generic, but in another is contradistinguished from it when we wish to express that it is merely an abstract. An idea, on the contrary, is opposed equally to the abstract and to the generic.[1] We have seen that an abstract conception may be matured by following acts of the mind into a generic.

6   We shall hereafter show in what manner an abstraction at the time that it passes into a generalisation becomes connected or rather coincides with an imperfect image or impression of a whole without distinction of the component parts (which image might not inappropriately be termed an abstraction of the sense in the same [way] as the corresponding conception to this image is[a] an abstraction of the understanding).[b] But an idea must be conceived of as anterior to all image and is that which is presupposed in all form and in every concrete as far as the same is reducible to any determinate law. It has therefore no common point with abstraction and, as generalisation is an abstraction, therefore none with generalisation. But what have no point in common are diverse in kind and therefore insusceptible of all comparison, even that of opposition, by a law the importance of which we shall have ample occasion of learning in a more advanced stage of the work—*opposita*[c] *semper unigena*, or there is no opposition between heterogeneous subjects.

7   Some of the ablest foreign logicians (and even the greatest logician since the time of Aristotle [d]and the founder of the critical philosophy[2] forms no exception) have incurred or sanctioned this error by their assumption that in the formation of a pure idea we abstract from image, etc, etc.[3] But this is true only in a lax and impermissible sense of the term "abstract", that act of simply excluding or rather precluding whatever would tend to disturb the mind as impertinent and heterogeneous. It would sound strange, were a man to say that in constructing a watch or describing a diagram he abstracted from the pictures in the room or abstracted from the noise of the children playing under his window; and if, instead of impressions made on the senses, we put images and thoughts equally impertinent to and diverse from the immediate object of our

---

[a] ms: in   [b] Parentheses inserted   [c] ms: *oppositer*
[d] Redundant opening parenthesis in ms

[1] For a similar distinction between "idea" and "abstract conception", see *C&S* (*CC*) 168.

[2] Kant.

[3] E.g. *C d r V* 34–5 (66).

attention, we should be as little justified in this application of the term. "An idea", says Kant, "contains in it all its subordinates".[1] An abstraction has all its subordinates under it, but so that each subordinate contains more than its superordinate, and the first abstraction contains the least of all. Now there is, to say the least, an ambiguity in the word "contain". We will suppose the first abstraction to be "thing". Its subordinates secondly "organisation", thirdly "animal". Though I confess that any order at all which can justify the use of the words "subordinate" and "superordinate" is merely arbitrary. But waiving this, surely the second is no less an abstraction than the first, and the third is as much as either; and how can one abstraction contain more than another when abstraction is contradistinguished from idea in consequence of its not containing any reality at all? In fact the word "contain" or "comprehend" means no more than that such a term is predicable, without contradiction or incongruity, of a quarter or less number of things, and in this sense rather has been, than may be, said to comprehend them.

8   We have seen what the nature of the syllogism is, considered exclusively as the logical canon or the rule according to which the understanding proceeds in conclusive reasoning. What is affirmed [of any thing is true] of every other contained in the same. Divested of technical terms we may give this rule and at the same time explain it by compressing what has been before said. When an act of conscious attention is directed towards an object by means of some mark applying to the same throughout, and we afterwards think of any part or content of this object as a thing of itself, but with the recollection of its having been included in the former, the mark by which we distinguished the first belongs of necessity to the second likewise, inasmuch as the mark was universal, or applicable to the object throughout, to all its parts and consequently to each. *Quicquid de o[mni] positum est, ponitur de unoquoque.*[2] For object, substitute the conception of an object or its presentation in the mind, and the process becomes logical, that is, subjective in reference to the understanding, aloof from the question of its reality independent of the

1   "Was von einem Begriff allgemein bejahet wird, wird auch von einem jeden bejahet, der unter ihm enthalten ist" (". . . Whatever is universally affirmed of a concept is also affirmed of everything contained under it"), the *dictum de omni et nullo*, as Kant says. "Die falsche Spitzfindigkeit der vier syllogistischen Figuren" § 2 in *VS* i 591 (tr Abbott *Kant's Introduction to Logic* pp 81–2). Cf *C d r V* 337 (289).

2   "Whatever is affirmed of the whole is affirmed of every single [part]". Another rendering of the *dictum de omni et nullo.*

understanding. On this account what we have before called "object" we now entitle the "subject", and the mark by which it is distinguished and fixed in the consciousness we name the "predicate". It is evident therefore that the value of the syllogism in relation to the purposes of truth and actual knowledge must consist in the legitimacy of the first position, technically called the major of the syllogism, and this again must consist either in the propriety of the mark or predicate of the subject or in the fact of an existence correspondent to a subject so characterised. It is the former, however (the subjective legitimacy, I mean), in which the logical canon is properly concerned. Supposing a syllogism to commence with the assertion of a falsehood, but in other respects without fault, the answer would consist, not in a detection of[a] any error in the form of reasoning. The logic, we should reply, is just, and convert it into an hypothetical syllogism by pre-fixing an "if" or other equivalent condition, it would be as true in logic as it is false in fact. In a former page we have given a syllogism of this kind which commences and concludes in an absurdity, and yet as far as the logical process alone is in question is undeniably correct.[1] To use a trivial and somewhat ludicrous illustration, chalk is returned from the [mill][b] instead of flour, but there is no fault in the mill or the grinding.

9 Let us not, however, think too meanly of the process, whatever the asserted facts may be correspondent to the logical subjects. The combination of the one with the other by the common mark, and the absolute necessity of this combination, are not only true but real; not only real, but, for the mind, the condition of all other reality. If A = C, and B be contained in A, THEN B is [c]contained in[d] C.[2] This proposition thus stated is a truth of mind: a somewhat that in the mind actually exists, as any object recognised by the senses exists without us. Strictly speaking, indeed, the former may be said to occupy a higher rank, for its evidence is immediate, whereas, that the latter exists *out of us* or *without us* would, if examined exclusively on speculative grounds, derive its evidence from a truth formed

---

[a] ms: in   [b] Blank space left in ms   [c–d] ms: equal to

1 See above, p 57.
2 Two syllogisms seem to have been confused here. One is given as a correction in the text here; the other may be found in Leibniz: "if A is the same as B, and if C is the same as B, then A and C must be the same as each other". Of the latter, Leibniz adds,

"this principle is a direct consequence of that of contradiction, and forms the basis of all logic; and if it ceases, we can no longer reason with certainty". *Theodicée* Preliminary Dissertation § 22 (tr E. M. Huggard *Theodicy . . .*—1951—87).

within us, and we may appropriately say with us. The proof will have been anticipated by every man who has attempted to return a speculative reply to the well-known position [of] Bishop Berkeley,[1] or who, without this occasion, has endeavoured to satisfy his own mind as to the difference between his sight of an object taken as an impression on the mind through the medium of the senses, and the outward cause and correspondent of this impression. The permanence, the regular recurrence under the same conditions, the absence of all conscious activity in himself, the unconnectedness of the impression with the trains of thought immediately preceding it, the marked character of contingency; these and other grounds of conviction will suggest themselves to his understanding, or whatever else may have occurred to him in reflection and experience as the contra-distinctions of our waking perceptions from our dreams or our trains of thought. He seeks reasons on which to ground his assertion of the outward *a*reality and *derives* the evidence of that reality from those reasons.*b* He does so, I mean, as an intellectual being, though he may not perhaps derive his faith in it as a man. For the former, the truth and real existence of the conclusive act in the mind, he brings no reason, for it is itself reason and as such having its evidence in itself and immediate.

10(a)   This, therefore, is well worthy to be the first position of the dialectic or the sifting or discriminating office of the mind, the criterion or test of the reason and of the understanding. By marks distinguishing the one from the other, thus enabling us to assign to each its proper realm and functions in the acquirement and establishment of truth either directly or indirectly by the detection and removal of error and falsehood, [it] must of course take place of all other criteria, both as being their foundation and as supplying the principle of insight into their nature and value.

10(b)   We may commence this inquisition by defining the reason (I mean solely in reference to the logical process) as the source of principles, the understanding as the faculty of rules. The reason is all *end, summa finium*. The understanding all *means, summa mediorum*.[2] Thus, rules are in all cases means to some end. A truth the oversight of which is exemplified and may be profitably illustrated by the false

---

a–b ms: reality from those reasons and *derives* the evidence of that reality. [The transcriber's eye skipping from one "reality" to another?]

[1] I.e. "the *esse* is *percipi*". *A Treatise Concerning the Principles of Human Knowledge: B Works* ii 42ff.

[2] Cf *C&S* (*CC*) 58–9.

conclusions of certain French critics, who, having borrowed the rules of tragedy which Aristotle had abstracted and generalised from the composition[s] of Aeschylus, Sophocles, and other Greek poets, treated them as ends to which all the parts of every tragedy were to be adapted as means. A conclusion which was of necessity false as often as the end[s] proposed by the Greek dramatists or imposed on them by local and accidental circumstances, e.g. the magnitude and construction of the Athenian theatre, the historical origin *ᵃof the Greekᵇ* tragedy, and in consequence of this, the necessity and essential character, adding the minor circumstances which grew out of the preceding and derived their propriety from them, the buskin (*cothurnus*), the tragic mask (*persona*), and the music with the musical recitation of the words throughout, were different from the ends proposed by the modern poets or imposed on them by their local and accidental circumstances. The science of criticism dates its restoration from the time when it was seen that an examination and appreciation of the end was necessarily antecedent to the formation of the rules, supplying at once the principle of the rules themselves and of their application to the given subject. From this time we have heard little (among intelligent persons, I mean) of the wildness and irregularity of our Shakespeare. Nay, when once the end which our myriad-minded bard had in view and the local accidents that favoured or obstructed or in any way modified its manifestation are once thoroughly comprehended, the doubt will arise whether the judgment or the genius of the man has the stronger claim to our wonder, or rather it will be felt that the judgment was the birth and living offspring of his genius, even as the symmetry of a body results from the sanity and vigour of the life as the organising power.[1] This subject on the one hand requires so particular and heedful an inquisition and on the other hand is of an importance and fruitfulness so well calculated to remunerate the pains and patience requisite for its investigation that I need not apologise for having introduced it by an instance of its application that at first sight would seem remote and almost alien from the dry pursuits and unattractive interests of a formal science.

11   We have proposed to distinguish the reason from the understanding, and from these distinctions to derive a determinate notion

ᵃ⁻ᵇ ms: or the Greeks

[1] For similar passages, see *CL* IV 620   *Sh C* I 194–8, and *CN* III 4384 f 158ᵛ. (to William Sotheby, 31 Jan 1816),

of each as far as the purposes of logic make requisite or expedient. In a science which derives its name and character from the *logos* or understanding, as distinguished from the intuitive faculty, or the sense, and from the *nous* or the reason, there would be some propriety in beginning with the understanding, were it not expedient on many more substantial grounds (and here again permit me to repeat the request, that the student should bear in mind that we are examining neither in any universal application but both alike as far only as the purposes of logic are concerned).[a]

12(a)   On the same ground that we have defined reason as the source of principles and the understanding as the faculty of rules, the reason being the *finis finium* or sum of ends, while the understanding is the faculty of means and the sense the faculty of materials, we may proceed further to define the reason as the power of ideas, the understanding the faculty of conceptions, and the sense the source and faculty of intuitions and perceptions. What then, as we are at present treating more immediately of the understanding, what, I say, are conceptions or thoughts? Wherein does the discursive act of the mind consist? In other words, what is that act or effort which declares and manifests itself in any conception, and on which the possibility of conception itself as a species of knowing rests? What is the act that must be presupposed in the conception as the product of that act in order for it to become intelligible to us?

12(b)   This act is no other than that by which a multiplicity of given presentations are comprehended in some one representation. By this means the several original presentations acquire a unity, and in this function[*] of unity the act of the understanding or the

[*] N.B. A power acting in and by its product or representative to[b1] a predetermined purpose is a function—the vital functions are consequences of the VIS VITAE or *principium vitale*,[2] and presuppose the organs as the functionaries.

There is a unit contained in every conception of the understanding and constituted by the act itself, as indeed the very term CON*cipere*[3] implies. Hence this act is named in the higher logic the function of unity. The product, however, is merely an ENS *logicum*,[4] and many of the worst errors and bewilderments in

a Parentheses inserted   *b* ms: of

[1] The amendment accords with the form of the sentence in C's hand in BM MS Egerton 2801 f 139. C's entire footnote seems to have been based on one of his own manuscripts, BM MS Egerton 2801 ff 139, 139ᵛ.

[2] "Vital force", "vital principle".

[3] "To conceive". Cf *C&S (CC)* 13 and n 2.

[4] "Logical entity". Defined below, pp 176, 231, 234, 239–40. Cf C's note to Schelling *System des Transcendentalen Idealismus* (Tübingen 1800) 486 (BM copy): "a mere ens logicum, like Motion, Form, Color, &c".

discursive act consists. But here I must recall to you a former remark, that provided we are aware of the unindividual and transcendent character of the reason as a presence to the human mind, not a particular faculty or component part of the mind, provided, I say, we keep this master truth steadily in view, it is (philosophically) indifferent whether we take the term "understanding" as a perfect

the history of physiology have arisen and still rise from mistaking this *ens logicum* for an *ens* REALE,[1] a somewhat existing out of the mind. Let this be borne in mind in perusing the following definition of a *power*. By generalising a continuous act or a series of acts essentially the same and then contemplating this generality as a unity, we form the notion of A POWER. A power has no scientific sense, no philosophic genesis or derivation, where it is not coincident and commutable with a law, or introduced confessedly as the surrogate or substitute of a law not yet discovered and as a means and part of the process of the discovery—an *ens logicum* to be reasoned WITH, not to be reasoned *from*.

If you wish to know still further and more particularly what I mean by a law, I borrow my reply from the judicious Hooker. "That by which we assign to each thing the kind, that by which we determine the force and power, that by which we point out the form[a] and measure of working—that same we term a law."[2] By way of illustration: long after Sir Isaac Newton, astronomers were perplexed by certain anomalies in the moon's motion. It was questioned whether [they] would be considered as objective to gravitation, taken as an universal law of bodies,[3] or whether, being in contradiction to this law, they might not be illusions of the senses arising from the position and other partial relations of the observers. The former supposition was too extravagant to obtain a moment's faith with men conversant with the application of the law to the phenomena of body. The latter only would be retained, viz. that of the appearances being illusive or unreal, but for the anticipation of some extension of our knowledge which a law once clearly seen into cannot fail to inspire and which in the present instance was speedily realised. La Place succeeded in reducing these to the common law of gravitation and of deducing them out of the same,[4] and the phenomena were by one and the same act understood and substantiated.

[a] ms: force

1 "A real thing".

2 Richard Hooker (1594–1662) *Of the Laws of Ecclesiastical Politie* bk I § 2 (var): *Works* (1682) 70. The amendment of ms "force" to "form" is in accordance with Hooker and with C's variant rendering of the same passage in *Friend* (CC) I 493. The marginal note in C's copy in the BM objects to the definition as "a self-destroying Absurdity".

3 Cf BM Add MSS 36532 f 8, in which Newton's law appears, in the hand of an amanuensis: "that all bodies tender to their centres in the direct proportion of their relative masses".

4 C mentions the "recent" solution of Pierre Simon, Marquis de Laplace (1749–1827) in a marginal note to Heinrich Steffens *Geognostisch-geologische Aufsätze, als Vorbereitung zu einer innern Naturgeschichte der Erde* (Hamburg 1810) 123 (BM copy). According to A. Wolf *A History of Science, Technology, & Philosophy in the 18th Century* (2nd ed 1961 rev D. McKie) I 99: "Laplace devoted a whole Book of the *Mécanique Céleste* [5 vols Paris 1799–1825] to a detailed study of the lunar inequalities, which he deduced as consequences of the single law of gravity". Cf *P Lects* Lect 12 (1949) 360.

synonym of "mind" and then consider the understanding in a twofold application, that is, now exercised discursively and now through the intuitive power, or whether we take the term of "the mind" exclusively as the common term or genus and "the understanding" and "the sense" as its two component faculties or species. Philosophically it is indifferent, but practically we have found and shall continue to find many and important grounds of expedience for preferring the latter as the avowed and declared terminology adopted throughout the present work, and, let me be permitted to add, in all my other philosophical writings. Were there indeed no other motive than the universally admitted and understood diversity of metaphysic [(μετα φυσικα)], logic and mathematics, and the convenience and exact correspondence of these to the three sources of the reason (νους), the understanding (λογος), and the sense ([?θεωρια]),[a] even this would suffice to incline the scales in favour of the scheme which has been already presented in a synoptic form in a preceding page.[1]

13   In consistency, therefore, with our own nomenclature, we must take the function of unity as twofold; original, namely, or the unity of primary perception, and derived. The latter of which alone is logical and properly belonging to the understanding in our confined and appropriated sense of that word. It is implied in the designations that the derivative unity presupposes the original, the object being common to both.[*] The representation[b] which rises out of the logical function of unity is[c] called a common conception (*conceptus communis*) and depends upon our power of combining a multiplicity of presentations in one and the same act of consciousness.[2] Instead of common conceptions some writers have employed the phrase of "complex ideas" and the innovation has obtained no small currency; but unhappily we think, the first word being indefinite and leaving it doubtful whether it refers to the process and antecedent materials, or to the consciousness, or to the conceptions abstractedly. Applied

[*] To understand a thing is to refer it to a law containing the principle of its explanation; and the rules inherent in the mind itself, according to which the mind proceeds in this reduction, constitute logic as the science appropriate to the understanding (λογος) as one of the two faculties of the mind, the sense or intuitive faculty ([θεωρια])[a] being the other, [and] the reason (νους) as the universal power presiding over both.

a ms: (μαθησις)   *b* ms: representative   *c* ms: and is

1 Above, pp 44–5.
2 Paragraph 13 to this point is translated freely from Tieftrunk's

introduction to Kant "Die falsche Spitzfindigkeit . . ." *VS* I 577.

to the consciousness, the very essence of which is unity, it is absurd, and applied to the conception it is false and a falsity that never fails to arise when we are speaking of one thing with the image of another and a different thing before our imagination: when, for instance, we propose to speak of a thought but in reality are under the influence of some confused image derived from the mixture or combination of bodies, that is, we speak of the constituents or constitution of a thought as if we had been talking of the components of an olio or a pudding. A common conception is as indivisibly one as an individual perception, but if the first term be at best vague and inappropriate, the second, which confounds conception with idea, is altogether a misnomer, as we have already shown. For a common conception is that by which I present to myself the identity of the consciousness in a manifold and different presentation, as in the instance of a house. In the same act of consciousness I comprise the presentations of the roof, the chimney, the wall, etc, etc.[1] But this is evidently impossible if these manifold images were not comprisable in one and the same act, though in order to this act there have been many antecedent acts, each including a narrower and narrower sphere and directed towards a less and yet less complex object. I could not, it is evident, make myself conscious that swans are white unless the sense of whiteness had been previously combined with sundry other impressions in the one impression "swan": nor even so if I had [not] previously combined it with different sets of images or presentations in other total impressions [such] as lilies, cliffs, snow, summer clouds, and the like. For to make myself conscious of anything I must reflect on it. Or rather to make myself conscious of a thing and to reflect on it are but different expressions of the same act. But that on which I reflect (*reflecto* = turn back or turn inwardly upon) must have been taken up into my mind (*apprehensio*) antecedently and in order to the reflection. This apprehension or primary combination of A (we will say) with b, c, d, in the act of *perceiving* the given object corresponding to the impression A, b, c, d, has by some logicians been called the synthetic function of the understanding,[2] and the reflection on the same or the reflex consciousness of this combination *as* a combination, by attending to A distinctly and with the recollection of its existing in combination with E, F, G: H, L, M, etc, etc, as well as with B, C, D—in other words, that A is common to many and different objects or complex impressions. In consequence

---

[1] The three last sentences are also based on Tieftrunk, *VS* I 578.

[2] The Critical philosophers. E.g. Kant *VS* I 578.

of which, all these several impressions may be classed together under A as the common mark or character of the class. This reflex or secondary consciousness, I say, the writers above mentioned have named the analytic function of the understanding.[1]

14   Where the meaning is determined and thoroughly understood, there, as far as the containing sentence or period is alone considered, the names may be of slight importance, though even here I could not regard them as altogether indifferent. But where instruction is to result from a connected whole, the parts of which are various yet interdependent, distinctness in the first appropriation of the terms and strict consistency in the use of them are such mighty assistants of the truth, so eminently conducive to the first apprehension of the meaning and to its connection with other truths whether by likeness or by contrast, each point of distinction serving as hook or eye for that from which it distinguishes as well as the thread for the holding together for all the particulars comprehended in the same distinction, that we need make no apology for preferring any given nomenclature or scheme of terms on the mere ground of its permitting a more perfect consistency in the use of each severally (a recurrence with less sensible variation of purport than in any former nomenclature, but in fact this consistency must[a] commonly, if not always, be itself the result of other and higher advantages, as for instance an exacter correspondence to the differences of the things and objects themselves or at least to our conceptions of the same).[b] Hence no man in the habit of connected thinking, no man for whom distinct conception[s] have become a necessity of his intellectual being, can use a lax and as it were staggering terminology, in which the meaning must in each instance be collected from the context and dilated or compressed according to the demand, without inward dissatisfaction as well knowing that such flexible terms are neither signs nor causes of wisdom on any occasion. And, vice versa, an exact and manageable terminology is at once a secure test of an exact and original thinker, and one of the most important benefits that he can confer on mankind.[2]

15   For these reasons I should not hesitate in substituting the term "mind" for "the understanding" in speaking of the synthetic function and should justify the change by the great conveniencies that result both for the teacher and the learner in using "the mind"

[a] ms: most   [b] Parentheses inserted

[1] Ibid.   [2] Cf above, p 7 n 2.

as the common term while "the understanding" and "the sense" are reserved for the designation of its two constituent faculties. Let it not, however, be thought that by referring the synthetic function to the sense and the analytic to the understanding, I[a] mean the unity in the former instance to be a mere simultaneity of passive impressions without distinguishable interspaces, as for instance a landscape [in] a small concave mirror[1] or the image of a lake on the retina of the eye, which is an act of agents external to the mind, if it be an act at all. No! I speak of a function which, as I have before explained, supposes a power of conferring unity in the mind itself, which power in the very introduction of the work we have learnt to recognise as mental forms or primary moulds. In the production of a single line, the first and simplest manifestable form in nature, or in a simple surface as a production of the line in all directions equally, as in the most complex figure that can result from surfaces as bounded by lines, there is a unity presupposed in the mind of the geometrician necessary as predetermining the figure which is to be the product of the act of the indefinite number of points that may be supposed to constitute a circle, or, in more scientific terms, of all the simple acts of position which the geometrician performs in the description of the circumference; the unity of the whole, or the contemplation (θεωρημα) as indivisibly one, must have been present to the mind previously to any or all of the acts exerted, in order to its production. I am well aware that the unprepared imagination will at first find a difficulty in mastering the conception of forms as acts, in distinguishing the act of length from the product which is at the same time the image or representation[b] of that act, and this again from the line on the slate or paper which is but the picture of this image—three stages which some of the later Greek philosophers designated by the terms ἐνεργεια θεωρητικη, εἶδος, and εἰδωλον.[2] For the removal of this difficulty there is but one way—that of placing yourself in such situations, or as it were positions, of mind as would be likely to call up that act in our intellectual being and then to attend to it [c]as its necessary[d] transient and subtle nature will permit. I have secured to myself to have experienced it often when connecting two bright stars, the one directly above the other as the extremities of the same line. I

[a] ms: that I [b] ms: representative
[c-d] C. A. Ward corrects to "so far as its necessarily"

[1] Cf *CL* I 154 (10 Mar 1795) for the image of "a Landscape on a Convex Mirror".

[2] "Perceiving energy, image", and "picture".

seemed, if I may so express it, to have a something between a sense and a sensation of length more perfect than any actual[a] filling up of the interval by a succession of points in contact could have given me. I seemed to find myself acting as it were in the construction of that length undisturbed by any accompanying perception of breadth or inequality which must needs accompany all pictures of a line. It was length without any necessity of abstracting from breadth or depth; in other words, it was a self-conscious act snatched away as it were from the product of that act. But the happiest illustration of the act of the intuitive imagination and its close connection with its product in the mental diagram, I believe, the most exact but assuredly the most amusing mode of conveying what I mean, I have seen in the ephemerae and other minute and half-transparent insects who by the exceeding velocity of motion actually present to our eyes a symbol of what Plotinus meant when, speaking of the geometricians and then of Nature as acting geometrically, he says θεωρουσα θεωρηματα ποιει, her contemplative act is creative and is one with the product of the contemplation.[1]

16   Réaumur[2] describes with great eloquence the emergence of a world of ephemerae from a river as seen by torchlight: he represents the moving transparency as composed of ephemerae in jointed and articulated triangles of silver light, and these things the great naturalist appears actually to have mistaken for real and produced by the contact of the flies. "The light of the flambeau exhibited a spectacle which enchanted every one that beheld it.[. . .] Never had an[y] armillary sphere so many zones, as there are here circles, having the light for their centre. There was an infinity of them crossing each other in all directions, and of every imaginable inclination, all of which were more or less eccentric. Each zone was composed of an unbroken string of Ephemerae, resembling a luminous strip of silver lace, formed into a circle deeply notched, and consisting of equal triangles placed end to end (so that one of the angles of each triangle touched the middle of the base of the triangle preceding), and all moving with astonishing rapidity. The wings of the flies (says Réaumur) [. . .] formed this appearance".[3] I can, however, add my

a ms: actually

[1] *Ennead* 3.8.4 (var); referred to again on p 245, below. Quoted at greater length in *BL* ch 12 (1907) I 173.
[2] This report of the French scientist R. A. F. de Réaumur (1683–1757) is taken from William Kirby and William Spence *An Introduction to Entomology* . . . (4 vols 1815–26) II 370. (Vol II is dated 1817.) C refers to the work in *AR* (1825) 210, and acknowledges his source briefly here (pp 74–5).
[3] Kirby and Spence II 370 (var).

own testimony to that of Messrs Kirby and Spence in their delightful introduction to entomology,[*] who consider, or I venture to say have ascertained, that this was a visual deception of Réaumur, well as he deserves the praise of the most accurate observers. "[. . .] Walking in the day-time with a friend, [. . .] our attention was caught by myriads of small flies, which were dancing under every tree; viewed in a certain light they appeared (as the Ephemerae did to Réaumur) a concatenated series of insects moving in a spiral direction upwards, but each series, upon close examination, [. . .] was produced by the astonishingly rapid movement of a single fly".[1] So far Spence, but I can add that I have twice seen the ascent of the ephemerae in a strong moonlight, the beams passing through an opening in a branching tree that overhung the water on which the moonlight formed a small island in deepest shade, and here by intensely watching the phenomenon I satisfied myself that the different spiral figures were each produced by the image [of] motion which the single insect left on the eye; each of which overtook the preceding before the impression had ceased, on the same principle as boys produce the circle of light by a piece of kindled charcoal whirled rapidly round.[2]

17 I shall not regret the space or time which this apparent digression has cost me, if it should be found to have assisted in forming the right conception of mathematical lines, points, and surfaces, as acts of the imagination that are one with the products of those acts. For this is of especial importance to our present pursuit, in which we must evermore bear in mind that we are throughout treating of mental processes wholly abstracted from all outward realities, and consequently that we must learn to consider the sense itself, or the faculty of original and constructive imagination, aloof from all sensation and without reference to any supposed passive impression from objects extrinsic to the percipient; but if so, if the passive be wholly separated, what can remain but acts and the immediate results of the same in the subject or agent himself; for this is the very principle from which we commence, that we confine

[*] The only defect which I have to complain of in this most interesting work is the prevalence of the anxious spirit of minute teleology, which [is] unphilosophical in itself, and sure to injure ultimately the amiable and pious purposes for which it was intended.

1 Ibid II 371 (var).
2 C recorded a number of examples of this phenomenon. See, e.g., *CN* I 549, for what seemed to be "Vortices of flies"; "whirling round a live Coal" (*CL* II 974).

ourselves to the mind, and that the mind is distinguished from other things as a subject that is its own object, an eye, as it were, that is its own mirror, beholding and self-beheld. This once understood, we are no longer startled by the definitions of Euclid and understand the definition of the point as having no magnitude, the line without breadth, and the surface without depth, as mere[a] popular ways of guarding the boyish geometrician against the supposition that things are the subject matter of the science at the threshold of which he is preparing to place his foot. Perhaps, however, it would have been more expedient even in point of intelligibility to have conveyed the same meaning by the simple declaration that the points, lines, and surfaces of geometry are not bodies nor parts of bodies, but acts of the mind and figures which are the offspring of what the great founder of logic[1] has called intellectual notions[b][2] having their proper canons or mirror in the imagination of the geometrician, even as the luminous zones and triangles of the ephemerae had their receptive and retaining table in the eye of the observer.

18　　The analogy which the processes of outward perception have to these purely intellectual constructions is a subject of deepest interest and highest importance, but the contemplation belongs to the third and concluding portion of my work,[3] in which logic in its most comprehensive sense, as the formal science of the rational understanding, is employed as an organ for the discovery and advancement of real knowledge, whether it consist of realities in the world of the senses or the higher realities of the intelligible world. This primary mental act, which we have called the synthetic unity or the unity of apperception, is presupposed in, and in order to, all consciousness. It is its condition (*conditio sine qua non*) or that which constitutes the possibility of consciousness *a priori*, or, if we borrow our metaphor from space instead of from time, *ab intra*.[4] Both metaphors mean one and the same, viz. an act or product of the mind itself considered as distinct from the impressions from external objects. We may illustrate the sense of this so frequent and so frequently misused term "*a priori*" by likening it to the stains in the old cathedral glass which predetermine[c] the character of the rays which it transmits and which it reflects. But above all, and leading us at once to our present disquisition, it is this synthetic unity which first gives

---

[a] ms: were　　　[b] ms: motions　　　[c] ms: predetermines

[1] Kant.
[2] Amended in accordance with *C d r V* 377 (314).

[3] The unforthcoming "organon", mentioned again on p 100, below.
[4] " From within".

meaning and determinate import to the word "is" in all affirmations. The repetition of this synthetic act in the understanding, or, what amounts to the same, the reflection on this act, completes the consciousness.

19 In the first act we have seen that a principle of unity is contributed by the mind itself. But if there be a uniting power, there must be that which is to be the subject or matter of the union, and by what name shall we designate this latter? At present we know no more of it than that it is opposite to unity: for how else should unity have been superinduced on it? But the opposite to one is the many, and by this name or its synonyms have philosophers in all ages and languages agreed in designating the same; but observe, only in relation to the mind and that which the mind can discover of what is not contained in its own consciousness by a light of its own. But such knowledge, it is plain, can only be negative, and when the external, the immediately sensuous, the supposed impressions from external agents are comprised under the common term of "the many", "the manifold", or "multeity", or "the indistinguishable" (to which we may add the phrases adopted by symbolical writers or mystics,*a* viz. "chaos", "the waters", etc, etc[)]. In all these there is or there ought not at least to be any pretence of determining the nature and character of the external agents considered as powers separate from the mind and having like the mind a principle of subsistence in themselves. For logically, that is, as far as the acts and conclusions of the understanding or the sense are alone concerned, the mind has acquired no right of affirming even the external existence of such agents otherwise than as an affirmation is implied in the act of distinguishing these impressions, or, in more appropriate language, these stimulations and excitements from itself as not belonging to its own self-consciousness. On the point at which we are at present standing, it is altogether indifferent whether it be the matter of a waking perception, as a perception of*b* a rainbow, or the matter of a waking intuition, as in the imaginative formation of a diagram in geometrical contemplations, or lastly the matter of a phantasm, "the stuff that dreams are made of".[1] The matter is that unknown [?το μη ὸv][2] on which the mind is to act and which is of necessity supposed in consequence of that act. We may therefore safely entitle

---

a Ms has closing parenthesis here   *b* ms: in

[1] Shakespeare *Tempest* IV i 156–7 (var).   [2] Cf *CL* II 1197: "the absolutely inanimate is called by the Platonists, τὰ μὴ ὄντα . . .".

the assumption of its existence a logical postulate. On this ground the existence of A is such as implies the existence of B as its opposite, inasmuch as the form under which we find A existing is no absolute form but that of an opposite, as much (by way of illustration) as the existence of a North implies that of the South: but the opposite found in the act of making one, the characteristic of the opposite to this, must be that of receiving a unity which did not belong to it in its own nature.

20   Without the primary act or unity of apperception we could have nothing to be conscious of. Without the repetition or representation of this act in the understanding [that] completes the consciousness we should be conscious of nothing. It will appear, however, on a moment's self-examination that a mere repetition of this act, a mere representation of the product of the act, could in no respect differ from the former in kind, at least more than the second echo from the former, or a secondary rainbow from the principal arch; something more must take place in order to constitute it a repetition by the understanding, and this something is the act of reflection. Experience has shown us that numerous acts of perception, or, to use our own logical terms, that the function of synthetic unity has been long at work and the products multiplied previously to the dawning of a distinct consciousness or reflection on the same.[1] How indeed could it be otherwise? Then, when the mind has many and different forms as the products of its percipient energies, will it have an interest awakened of distinguishing the one from the other. But in order to this the mind must have acquired a consciousness of that which all have in common: for absolute and total heterogenes there is no need of distinguishing. But that which all have in common is the coexistence of the many in the one, the many being the characteristic of the subject in its supposed anterior state ere the one had been communicated thereto and the one or unity as the gift of the mind itself being the object. But for this latter the subject would for us have no existence whatever: or, omitting the words "for us", we need not hesitate to affirm that *the* subject *that* in this case is spoken of would not exist at all.

21   Now this resolution of any given representation into the object and subject and the coexistence of both as one we call a judgment, at least it is the first and most generalised definition of the term, judgment, which is most happily expressed in the Teutonic

[1] Cf *AR* (1825) 68–9. C commits himself here to a position over which he had once felt obliged to equivocate. See *BL* ch 12 (1907) i 174.

languages by *Urteil*, and the judgment itself or the judicial faculty *Urteil*[s]-*kraft*, that is, the power of resolving a thing into its primary and original constituent parts.[1]

22(a)   This then is common to all positions; and having discovered this we are now enabled to proceed in the search of the marks by which one may be distinguished from another and one class from another.

22(b)   It has been affirmed and it will shortly be more fully explained and proved that neither the subject nor its predicate do either singly or placed in mere juxtaposition contain the principle, or what is here perfectly equivalent, the mental affirmation, of their reality or objective being. This is accomplished when the mind bears witness to its own unity in the subject represented to it, and this act with this consciousness of the same is conveyed or expressed in the connective "is". "The house is white".[2] Now it is evident that this reflection could not have [taken] place, that this resolution of a manifold into its constituent parts, the house as representing the subject, and the white as representing its predicate or distinctive attribute, if these constituents had not been previously united by the mind, and not, likewise, unless the same predicate had been found united with other subjects and the same subject united with other predicates, as a "white rose", a "red house".[3] Now the act of reflection[*] in all instances [?is subsequent] to this—to this product, I say, of the mind's own synthetic power. It may well be that the subject has no existence but in the mind. For instance, let the position be, "Cerberus is three-headed", or, "the Chimera is triform". The act by which the mind combines the three heads or the three forms with all the manifold which is again united in these into a one-formed shape beheld in one act, that is and must be real, and this reality it is, and not those so-called principles of identity and contradiction, which logicians without exception have hitherto talked [of] as the foundations of logical evidence,[4] which supplies us with the Archimedian standing-room[5] from which we may apply the lever of all our other

[*] That which enables us to reduce particulars to classes.

[1] False etymology. C offers this theory elsewhere; see *CN* III 4228 and N 29 f 106.

[2] The last two sentences are from "Die falsche Spitzfindigkeit . . ." *VS* I 583.

[3] Cf *C d r V* 69–70n (89). Cf below, p 82.

[4] C had referred to them earlier as the "Axioms of Logic" (*CN* III 4230), and discusses them at length on pp 87–91, below.

[5] A reference to the remark attributed to Archimedes: "Give me a place to stand and I will move the earth". C mentions it elsewhere (e.g. *CN* I 1166, II 2811, and III 3592).

intelligent functions. The mind affirms firstly its own reality. Secondly, that this reality is an unity. Thirdly, that it has the power of communicating this unity, and lastly, that all reality for the mind is derived from its own reality, and in proportion to the unity which is its form and communication, that is, its own form and thence the form of the subject to which it has been transferred. The whole collectively is comprised in the Latin sentence "mens est forma formans", the mind is, and it is a form, and it is formative.

23   Here then arises an apparent contradiction. We have found object and subject the common constituents of all representations of which reality is affirmed, that is, which are connected by the verb "is", and we have here an object which is said to contain the principle of reality in itself exclusively, nay, in contradistinction from whatever is not mind. This contradiction admits but of one solution. There must be some object which is in one and the same indivisible act or moment a subject likewise and, vice versa, a subject that in one and the same moment is an object likewise; it must be both in one. Now does there exist such an object-subject and subject-object? We reply, "yes! and it is found in the reality of self-consciousness". I contemplate myself. Myself the object is one and the same with the I or subject, and the first rule of logic[a] is in accordance with the first rule of grammatical syntax—that the case which follows the verb substantive, and as such stands for the objective, is the same with the case that precedes, that is, the subjective case. There may be many SUBJECTS (the living principle, for instance, in plants) which we may call powers, lives, principles, active FORMS, that which manifests itself and without which there is no conceivable *objectivity*; but *that* subject alone is a mind which is its own object; and an object which includes without confounding the subject is the definition of mind, and in the same moment we have the first ground of classific distinction, and we subdivide subjects into those which are in themselves their own object, that is, minds, and those which are not, that is, simply subjects.

24   We have stated that the objectivity or reality which is asserted in every judgment, as the major in all logical syllogism, is expressed in the term "is". We have seen too that this term expresses in the first instance the reality of the act itself by which certain positions were combined or seen as one; for instance, "the house is white". Now the question is, what is the agent expressed in this act? If it be an act of the mind it would seem to follow that when we affirm that

[a] ms: logical

a spirit is a simple substance, or any other so-called judgment, we can mean no more than this, "as sure as I am, so surely this is". Now the truth implied in the position "I am" is the ground and condition of all truth: whatever therefore is as true as this must necessarily be true in the highest degree.[1] Such was the reasoning on which the sect of the Dogmatists, Descartes and his followers among the moderns and the Stoics among the ancients, grounded their metaphysical and theological systems; but how erroneously the following distinctions will readily exhibit.[2]

25 It is undeniable that the origin and fundamental knowledge must be somewhat which being thought of must therefore *be*, and which *being* must necessarily be *thought* of. It is no less evident that if we take this somewhat as the first, and which, being presupposed in all other knowledges is so far anterior to them, there is no other assumed which is then to think of it, it must therefore be thought of by itself; and this primary and preconditional truth may therefore be characterised as that which, thinking, must be, and which, being, must think. It must exhibit the perfect coincidence or (to use a term at once more vital and more accurate) coinherence of reality and conception. Now this character is found in the *sum* and *cogito*,[3] in either and in both; for *sum* implies *sum cogitans*:[4] for it is not merely self, but a self-assertion of a self, and in like manner *cogito* involves *cogitans*;[5] for what indeed, even etymologically considered, is *cogitans* but the blending of the two terms *cogito* and *ens*, a being that asserts itself.[6] This then is self-consciousness, and the Dogmatist therefore affirms that the primary underived truth commences in self-consciousness. But to prepare for the detection of the sophism which will be found to lurk in this position we have established the distinction between the synthetic and the analytic function of unity. If the question were: "what is the origin of our knowledge of all truths?", if the enquiry were confined to the *principium sciendi*, the *quomodo scimus nos scire?*,[7] the answer must doubtless be self-consciousness, inasmuch as the terms are identical. But we have

[1] Cf Editor's Introduction, above pp lxv–lxvii.

[2] For C's view of the dogmatists, see his note to p 206, below.

[3] "I am", "I think".

[4] "I am, thinking". See below, pp 84–5.

[5] C appears to be drawing on *C d r V* here, but, untypically, on the 1st ed of 1781 p 355 (337). Cf p 85 n 1, below.

[6] *Ens* ("being"); cf C's comments on the verb substantive, above, pp 16–19 and below, p 120. For his interest in the correlation of knowing and being, see *CN* III 4265.

[7] "The principle of knowing", the "how we know that we know".

enquired for something more and higher than this self-consciousness which supposes reflection, and reflection an act antecedent thereto. It were therefore a contradiction in terms to call that a primary truth which is admitted to be secondary or derivative, and we must first secure an absoluteness, an independency, to the position "I am" before we can communicate certainty to other positions on the ground of their being one with it or a part of the self-consciousness. But to affirm of any finite being that it is absolute is a contradiction in terms: in order to absoluteness there must be an "is" (*est*) which necessarily involves the "I am", and again an "I am" without which no "is" would be conceivable. This therefore and this alone can be the *principium essendi et sciendi*[1] or the perfect identity of being and knowing and therefore the ground and source of both. Without any present reference to any religious or superhuman authority the title "I Am" attributed to the Supreme Being by the Hebrew legislator[2] must excite our admiration for its philosophic depth, and the verb substantive or first form in the science of grammar brings us the highest possible external evidence of its truth. For what is a fact of all human language is of course a fact of all human consciousness. The verb (*verbum*), the word is of all possible terms the most expressive of that which it is meant to express, an act, a going forth, a manifestation, a something which is distinguishable from the mind which goes forth in the word, and yet inseparable therefrom; for the mind goes forth in it, and without the mind the word would cease to be a word, it would be a sound, a noise. If we ask ourselves how we know anything—that rose, for example, or the nightingale hidden in yonder tree—the reply will be that the rose (*rosa subjecta*)[3] manifests itself, that it renders itself objective, or the object of our perceptions, by its colour and its odour, and so in the nightingale by its sound. And what are these but the goings from the subject, its words, its verb? The rose blushes, the nightingale sings. (And here again we have an instance of the difference between the *principium sciendi* and the *principium essendi*. If we considered the[a] point relatively to our knowledge, the conception of our going forth or production would be the more general form of the manifestation, the word or the verb: so far at least that we might venture to use this term in cases to which we should hesitate in applying the term "act"

---

[a] ms: to

[1] Literally, "the principle of being and knowing".

[2] Moses, Exod 3.14.

[3] "The rose as a subject", or "the underlying rose"—a play on the derivation of *subjecta*.

in its highest sense, that namely in which the agent originates the act. On the other hand, in relation to the *principium essendi*, all going forth, all manifestation, must of necessity have had their origin in an act, and all that lives and moves derives whatever agency and whatever semblance of agency there be therein in consequence of that act and its continuation.)

26   The sum of the preceding argument may be thus recapitulated.

27   We have been seeking for the principle of our certainty and we have found it necessary to distinguish between the *principium sciendi* and the *principium essendi*. Now such a principle cannot be any *thing* or any *particular object*. For its very purpose is to constitute the objectivity in all objects as far as they are objects of our consciousness (*principium realitatis non potest ipsa*[a] *esse res*).[1] Each thing is what it is in consequence of some other thing. The water could not be that particular water were it not for the air, the banks, etc, etc. An infinite and independent thing is no less a contradiction than an infinite circle or a sideless triangle. Besides, a thing is that which is an object of which itself is not the sole percipient, but an object is inconceivable without a subject as its antithesis. *Omne perceptum percipientem supponit*[2] (understand that [?otherwise] the words would have no meaning for us, they would possess no logical import). "Tall" and "short" express a relation the seat of which is in the understanding, ἐν τῷ λόγῳ, and neither of these would have any meaning but as being the correspondent opposite of the other.

28   But neither can the principle be found in all subjects in contradistinction from an object: for *omnis perceptio*, that is, *omnis percipiens in actu perceptionis supponit perceptum*.[3] We may borrow an illustration from physics. It is impossible that negative electricity should be assumed as the principle of positive electricity, for it presupposes it, and equally impossible that positive electricity should be assumed as the principle of the negative, for it presupposes the negative, that is, they mutually suppose each the other. But whatever can be thought of must be either an object or a subject or some third

---

[a] ms: *ipsam*

[1] "The principle of reality (thingness) cannot itself be a thing".

[2] "Everything perceived implies a perceiver". The passage, from "Each thing is what it is ...", is from "Thesis v" *BL* ch 12 (1907) I 182 (var). The material borrowed from *BL* in paragraphs 27–33 is derived ultimately from Schelling *System des Transcendentalen Idealismus*.

[3] "Every perception, that is, everyone perceiving, posits a thing perceived". C's Latin makes the point more deftly.

which is neither separately because it is the root and identity of both. If the principle is to be found, as we have demonstrated that it is not to be found either in any possible object or any possible subject taken separately, [as no other third is conceivable],[a] the principle must be found in that which is neither subject nor object exclusively, but which is the identity of both.[1]

29   The principle thus characterised manifests itself as in the εἰμι, *sum*, or "I am", which we shall hereafter express indiscriminately by the words "mind", "self", or "self-consciousness", the preference being at once determined and explained by the context. In this, and in this alone, object and subject, being and knowing, are identical, each involving and supposing the other; it is a subject which becomes a subject in and by the very act of making itself its own object, or to familiarise ourselves gradually with the technical language of our science, it is a subject which becomes subjective by the act of constructing itself objectively to and for itself; but which never is nor can be an object except for itself, and only so far an object as by the very same act and in the same indivisible moment it becomes a subject.[2]

30   So much for the principle generally; the distinction between it as a principle of knowing (*principium sciendi*) and a principle of being (*principium essendi*) will require still less attention to be understood. If a man be asked, "How do you know that you are?", he can only reply, "Sum quia sum", "I am because I am", that is, "I know myself to be, because I know myself to be".[3] But if the absoluteness, the primary underived and independent character of this certainty having been admitted, he were again asked, not how he KNOWS that he is, but how he, that individual person, *came* to be, then in relation to the ground of his existence, not to the ground of his *knowledge* of that existence, he might, rather must, reply, if he reply at all, "Sum quia Deus est",[4] or, still more philosophically, "Sum quia in Deo sum".[5] I know that I am because I am and am self-known; but that I am and know myself to be, there is but one

---

[a] Space left in ms; missing passage supplied from *BL*

[1] The paragraph is a variant of the second paragraph of "Thesis V" *BL* ch 12 (1907) I 182.

[2] The paragraph is a variant of the first paragraph of "Thesis VI" ibid I 183.

[3] The sentence is a variant on the final sentence of "Thesis VI" ibid.

[4] "I am because God is".

[5] "I am because I am, in God". Variant on the final paragraph of the Scholium to "Thesis VI" ibid. Cf C's formulation in a letter to C. A. Tulk on 12 Jan 1818 (*CL* IV 807).

assignable reason—that Being and Will which we express by the word "God".

31 If then we elevate our conception to the absolute Self, Spirit, or Mind, the underived and eternal "I Am", then and herein we find the ^aprinciple of being, and^b of knowledge, of idea, and of reality: the ground of existence, and the ground of the knowledge of that existence, absolutely one and identical; both are alike adequately expressed in the term "sum quia sum",[*] "I am because I affirm myself to be".[11]

32 All truth is either mediate, that is, derived from other truth, or immediate. The latter, of which we have been treating under the name of truth absolute or principle of truth, may be designated by the formula A = A, [a] formula which, however, must be here taken to signify not only self-evidence but self-originated as excluding the conception of any truth previous to it. On the other hand, the former,

---

* There is an objection to the celebrated first position of the Cartesian school, *cogito, ergo sum*, as being tautological, the term *cogito* being implied in the *sum* and adding nothing thereto.[1] For *cogito* is *sum cogitans*, but the *cogitans* is anticipated in the *sum*,[2] as we may see by turning it into the third person and by the want of evidence in the converse. *Cogitat ergo est*[3] is true, it being a mere application^c of the logical rule *quidquid in genere est, est in specie. Est cogitans ergo est.*[4] It is a cherry-tree, therefore it is a tree. But *est ergo cogitat*[5] is illogical. For *quod est in specie non necessario in genere est.*[6] It is a tree, therefore a cherry-tree, would make but a poor syllogism. The whole we can say is that it may be true. We cannot too early familiarise the mind to the distinction between the conditional finite "I", which knows itself less in distinct consciousness by occasion of experience, which is so far not improperly named by the followers of Kant the empirical "I" (*das empirische Ich*), and the absolute "I am", and likewise the inherence of the former in the latter "in whom we live and move and have our being".[7] So asserts the philosophic apostle,[8] differing how widely from the theses of the modern mechanic school,[9] who consistently with their system must speak of the Supreme as of one from whom we *had* our being.[10]

^{a–b} ms: principle and [missing words supplied from *BL*]
^c ms: appicative

---

[1] The objection to Descartes' "I think, therefore I am" (*De Methodo* IV) appears in Leibniz *Nouveaux essais* bk IV ch vii 7. Cf *C d r V* (1st ed 1781) 355 (337).

[2] "For 'I think' is 'I am, thinking', but the 'thinking' is anticipated in the 'I am'".

[3] "He thinks therefore he is".

[4] "Whatever is (true) with respect to the genus is (true) with respect to the species. He is, thinking, therefore he is."

[5] "He is, therefore he thinks".

[6] "What is (true) with respect to the species is not necessarily (true) with respect to the genus".

[7] Acts 17.28 (var).

[8] St Paul.

[9] *BL* text adds: "(as Sir J. Newton, Locke, &c)". *BL* ch 12 (1907) I 184n. Cf C's letter to C. A. Tulk of Sept 1817 (*CL* IV 768).

[10] C's note is a variant on *BL* ch 12 (1907) I 184n.

[11] This paragraph is a variant of the final paragraph of "Thesis VI" ibid I 183.

or truth mediate, that is, of derivation ᵃdependent and conditional, certaintyᵇ which properly and originally belongs to A is attributed to B, and B is known to be true because in some sense or other it is one with A, being included in A it is concluded.ᶜ A chain without a staple from which the links collectively derive their stability, or a series without any first, has been compared not inaptly to a string of blind men each holding the skirt of the man before him, the file reaching far out of sight, and yet all the individuals moving without the least deviation in one straight line. That it was beyond the reach of sight would scarcely weaken our conviction that there was a sure guide at the head of the file. What if it were answered, "No—there is no head man. The blind men are without number and infinite: blindness supplies the place of sight"? Equally inconceivable is a cycle of equal numerically different truths without a common and central principle, and that the absurdity does not strike us with the same force as in the preceding instance of the line is owing to a surreptitious act of the imagination which automatically and without our consciousness not only fills up the intervening spaces and contemplates the *cycle* (of B, C, D, E, F, etc) as a continuous cycle, A giving to all collectively the unity of their common orbit, but likewise suggests and as it were supplies the one central power which gives to each its place in that circle and renders the movement of all cyclical.[1]

33   Lastly there can ᵈbe butᵉ one such principle, but one absolute truth, self-grounded, unconditional, and known by its own light, yet capable of communicating to other positions a certainty which it had not received. But this may be proved first *a priori*, for were there two or more such principles, and of course *ex hypothesi*[2] equal, they must refer to some other third and higher principle by which their equality is determined, or rather in which it is involved, consequently neither would be self-established, which yet is demanded in the hypothesis. And *a posteriori* it will be demonstrated by the principle itself as soon as it is presented to the mind. The principle itself, I say, which is here the absolute "I am", will be found to involve a universal antecedency and consequently to preclude both all precedency and all parity of any other in its very conception, and what is here affirmed metaphysically of the absolute "I am" is logically and scientially affirm-

---

ᵃ⁻ᵇ ms: dependent, and conditional certainty
ᶜ Ms unpunctuated   ᵈ⁻ᵉ ms: but be

[1] This paragraph is a variant of   [2] "According to the assumption". "Thesis II" ibid I 180–1.

able of consciousness generally. This will be admitted at once of contingent truths. They of course can have only a borrowed certainty.*a* If we affirm of a board that it is blue, the predicate "blue" is accidental and not implied in the subject "board". We know it to be true by having seen it. But even where the truths are necessary, they are not therefore, as we have already shown, independent. When I affirm of a circle that it is equi-radial, the predicate indeed is implied in the conception of the subject, but the existence of the subject itself presupposes the existence of a mind both as its cause and percipient.[1]

34   Before we proceed, in this our conversation at least, it may not be uninteresting or without its uses in preparing and familiarising the apprehension for after-truth to make a few remarks on the celebrated principles or rather principle of contradiction and identity which in all books of logic hitherto are stated as the ground and universal rule of all logical reasoning—in short, as that truth in which all other truths are contained as far as the form is concerned. But it is questionable whether even these principles properly belong to common or syllogistic logic, and during the disquisition which we have been carrying on lately I have been not unaware that I was anticipating what appertained to the last and concluding stage of our present subject, viz. the transition of the dialectic into the organic, and, with this, the subordination of logic to the noetic or formal science, to that knowledge in which truth and reality are one and the same, that which in the ideas that are present to the mind recognises the laws that govern in nature, if we may not say the laws which are nature. The principle of identity is "A = A" or, if we prefer the refinement of the *Wissenschaftslehre*[b] (Fichte has so called his peculiar system of idealism), "if A = A, then A = A", and the principle of contradiction that "A is [not] not-A".[2] Both amount, as we have seen, to the position "A is", and even this supposes an assumption of the latter word "is" as either one and the same with A, so that "A is" really means no more than a tautological repetition of "is, is", or in other words a mere and simple assertion of being universally, or that something must be, which again is equiva-

---

a Comma in ms
b Transcriber B has written "Wissens"; "schaftslehre" has been added in the space left for it, probably by J. H. Green

[1] This paragraph is a variant of "Thesis IV" ibid I 181–2.
[2] Fichte *Ueber den Begriffe der Wissenschaftslehre* 48–9. For C's early mockery of the passage, see *CL* II 673–4. He may have been reminded by Jäsche's mention of it in the preface to Kant *Logik* xvi–xvii.

lent to the following fact of our consciousness.[a] In order for me to attach any sense to the word "something", in order to the conception "something", I must have had the conception of "thing", and, in order to this, [a] conception which we will resolve into the "ing", that is, our English termination answering to the *ens* of school Latin.[1] Let us try this in another form, our present object being that of exercise and the agility and flexibility of mind acquirable thereby— it is not food, but as a game at tennis. "A is"—by this position I either assert necessary being and at the same time the necessity of being, by light[b] of reason [νους], and then it belongs to noetics (metaphysics *sensu[c] strictiori*),[2] or I speak of some fact in the light[d] of sense,[e] the inward or the outward, and then the position belongs to history (*sensu generalissimo*).[3] Now *toto genere* different[4] is the question "what is A?" To this question, "A = A", or "A is [not] not-A", would be no answer, for these are the same with the affirmation implied [in] "A is". "What is A?" resolves itself into two sentences, the former assertory, "A is", and the latter interrogative, "but what is it?" The answer must be some predicate of A as a subject and not of A as *ens absolute positum*[5] or that which is its own predicate and which is therefore no more a subject in relation to a predicate or object, for predicate is here but another word for object, its logical synonym. "I am that I am", where (as we have before more than once noticed) the simple term *sum* or *ego*[6] is equivalent to the whole position. Hence in the formula A = A, etc, representing principles of identity and contradiction, the subject (improperly so called) and its *predicate* are always convertible terms. Example: "Quid est spiritus?" Answer, "Ens se ponens". "Quid est ens se ponens?" Answer, "Spiritus".[7] But let A signify wood and B signify black and then A = B is far indeed from B = A. In the one case the predicate, whatever its grammatical form may be, is in sense and logical value a substantive, in the latter necessarily an adjective.

---

[a] Ms unpunctuated   [b] ms: right   [c] ms: penser
[d] ms: right   [e] Full stop in ms

[1] I.e. mediaeval Scholastic Latin. In classical Latin the suffix *-ens* corresponds to the *-ing* of the present participle in English; the use of *-ens* as present participle of the verb "to be" is lacking in classical Latin and was introduced in the Middle Ages and much used by the Schoolmen. Cf above, p 81 n 6, and below, pp 89–90, 130.

[2] "In the stricter sense of the word".
[3] "In the broadest sense".
[4] "Utterly different in kind".
[5] "Posited as an absolute entity".
[6] "I am" or "I".
[7] "What is a spirit?" "A self-positing being". "What is a self-positing being?" "A spirit".

Ebony is black, but we cannot say that black is ebony. And it is such positions alone that properly appertain to syllogistic logic. Thus if these famous principles have any property logical it can only be that the proper subjects of logic are λογοι, in distinction from ρηματα, φωναι, εἰδωλα;[1] but the λογοι are acts of the λογος or reflective mind, of which it is a constituent character, that in the act of knowing its own being it knows that it cannot at the same time and in the same sense deny what it affirms or affirm what it denies.

35 For the same reason, therefore, that in a former chapter we have omitted reflection in the list of the particular distinguishable functions of the understanding,[2] viz. attention, comparison, abstraction, because the reflection is the understanding itself, a synonym not a predicate, or at best a tautology, we here dismiss the principle of identity as having no other place in logic than as an assertion sufficiently superfluous, that the forms and functions of the understanding suppose an understanding as their ground.

36 The principle of contradiction is: *impossibile est idem simul esse* [*ac non*][a] *esse*[3]—well, this is a good definition of the impossible but is it therefore a principle? If it be a *princeps*,[4] that which is to go before, there ought to be something that should follow; but what is to follow in the present instance? How can we arrive from this negative to a positive? Through another negative? As whatever is not *ens* and *non ens*[5] at the same time is possible[?] But the rule that two negatives make a positive is grammatical, not logical. Besides, even this is not to be inferred immediately, for it requires an intermediate position, viz. that the contrary of the false is true. Both of them may be entitled axioms but neither of them can be named a principle. The rival position, the *principium identitatis*,[6] is in fact two positions. First, "whatever is, is". Secondly, "what is not, is not". Now the former is merely a repetition during the act of reflection of the term "is". I mean that it expresses no more than my consciousness that I am reflecting,[b] that is, consciously reflecting the truth of being. The term "is" being a verb substantive, we might without absurdity, though without any change or addition in our knowledge,

---

a Ms has dash in place of the words   *b* ms: *reflectius* [for *reflectens*?]

1 "Words, utterances, images". Cf N 29 ff 42–3 for material parallel to Paragraphs 34–8.

2 See, rather, Paragraphs 1–7 of the present chapter.

3 "It is impossible for the same thing at the same time to be and not be".

4 "A first [position]". "Principle" is derived from *princeps*, "first" in time or in order, a "leader".

5 "Being and not-being".

6 "Principle of identity".

convert the word "is" to a noun substantive in one case and a verb in the other and say, "is, is", and in fact we do what is tantamount to this when we say, "the necessary being is", or, "God is". Do not yield to the very natural temptation of impatience with these subtleties so thin that, strip them of their clothing, they totter on the edge of nothing. They, or rather the exercise of the mind in reducing them to their true value, will not have been useless if only it has put us on our guard against the frequent error in arguing, an error which has by no means become obsolete*[a]* with the schools in which it sprung and was reared, the error of presenting as particular truths the mere exponents of our universal or essential consciousness—such, for instance, as the one now under consideration, the being of being.*[b]* Instead of truth, principle, or axiom,*[c]* it is in reality a mere narration of a fact:*[c]* I reflect on being. The second position, "Whatever is not, is not", is either a μεταβασις εἰς ἀλλο γενος,*[1]* that is, the introduction of a heterogeneous term, or it is nonsense; for it either means that "A *non est* Y"*[2]*—Y being some predicate, as "ebony is not white" —and then indeed it may belong to syllogistic logic, but as a particular, consequently no principle; or else A stands as a universal, and then it amounts to, "omne ens quod non est ens, non ens est",*[3]* or "A which is no A, is no A", a precious principle which commences with a contradiction. In short, the substance of these boasted principles is a mere assertion of the act of reflection, implying the reason as one universal in all individual reasoners. The "is", we have before shown, is grounded, not in our reflection, or the analytic unity, but in the synthetic, which we do not give to ourselves but find given to us.*[4]* Though the contents as it were or matter of this datum may be given in the sense, but which, as*[d]* not being the product of any individual's faculty, we call common sense; yet the *form* and that which gives it immoveable reality for the mind, that is, certainty —*this*, I say, is a truth of reason. The striking analogies between reason and sense are among the most interesting subjects of philosophic meditation. The mathematic,*[e]* indeed, which has for its subject the forms of the pure sense and products of the active imagination, is not only the first pure science but supplies to all other sciences the most perfect model and exemplar.

[a] ms: absolute   *[b]* Comma in ms   *[c]* Full stop in ms   *[d]* ms: has
[e] ms: Mathematique [an attempt to follow C's pronunciation of *Mathematik*?]

[1] C's tr: a "Transition into a new kind". *AR* (1825) 215. From Aristotle *Posterior Analytics* 1.7 (75a). A favourite tag.

[2] "A is not Y".

[3] Literally, "every being which is not being is not being".

[4] See pp 76–7, above.

37   The highest compliment which we can pay to such truths as "whatever is, is", or, "if it is, it is", etc, etc, is to interpret them into these words, "if it be so judged by my reason, it is valid in all reason and for all rational beings who are gifted with reason". Though even here the negative part of the position (that the reason cannot at one and the same time, and of one and the same thing, deny what it affirms) seems to be little more than a way of generalising a form of words familiarised to us by the habit of comparing particulars with each other: e.g. I am accustomed to see jet, and while I am thinking of jet I happen to light on a piece of amber in very many points resembling jet, and with this thought present to my mind, "amber is not black", which in truth must be resolved into, "jet is black, and amber therefore is not jet". But here we are referred to principles of a very different order from those of technical arguing:[a] the metaphysical ideas of identity and alterity, the one and the many —principles, I say, of metaphysical ontology[b] as much presupposed in common logic as sounds are in grammar. And after all that can be said in favour of these abstractions, the habit of abstracting being perhaps their best purpose,[c] it is no slight objection that from their extremely vague nature the terms are unsteady and not marked by that plain and clear opposition which is essentially requisite in all logical antitheses: thus *nego*[1] is not the proper correspondent or antitheton to *affirmo*,[2] but really answers to *removeo*.[d] "I remove this while I place that". The rightful use therefore of these terms, as represented by + and −, is to be found in the doctrine of characters, best studied mathematically and during algebraic studies.

38   As, however, we have proceeded so far and while we are yet lingering on the origin and comport of the objectivity or affirmation of the same contained in the major of the syllogism, not as the συλλογισμος or ratiocination itself, but as its condition and presupposition . . .[e] the clear way of stating the true force of the negative is as follows. It is a fact of universal consciousness that man possesses the power not only of beholding A and B but noticing that they are two and different. Hence if he reflect on B in immediate succession to A, so that B comes while A is still present to his thoughts, in which memory and the condition of all comparison consists, he soon discovers an abbreviation for the two positions "A = A", "B = B" in the words "A is not B", this "not" having been

---

[a] Full stop in ms   [b] ms: autology   [c] Full stop in ms   [d] ms: removes
[e] Full stop in ms, but the sentence is incomplete. Ms then starts a new paragraph

[1] "I deny".   [2] " I affirm".

probably first derived from some painful feeling occasioned by his having looked for one thing which he was desirous to have and finding another which was nothing to his purpose—looking for parsley, for instance, and finding hemlock. The gesture, the motion of the head, the impatient shrinking from the object, and the correspondent motions in the organs of speech, produced, and still are found to produce in infants, that particular modification of sound which may be traced more or less distinctly in the simple negatives of all languages, the nearest being the Hebrew "ngain" or the "ng", the roughest and primitive digamma, the sound which, softened and made pronounceable by the vowel prefixed, we retain in the ἀγγελος.[a][1] It is not therefore so properly a *perception* as a *sensation* connected with some one perception, in consequence of some other having been and still being in the fancy, connected with the feeling of expectation. It is curious to notice in ourselves that preparation which we make for an increased degree of vividness which we expect from the senses when we are on the point of seeing something which is already present to the mind's eye; a feeling not unlike that which we experience the moment before the presentation of the moon through a glass.[2] But in proportion to the degree and pleasureableness of this expectation and preassurance is the disappointment, and when by the frequent repetition of such occasions the sensation is become evanescent and the tones of passion are no longer heard, that abbreviation, that compression and welding as it were of the two into one, remains in use from its convenience and the "not" becomes the mere sign or character of connection by comparison.

39   There are three assumptions then on which the solidity of logic as the science of conclusion is grounded. The first, the existence of mind absolutely, which we have agreed to distinguish by the term νους. We commenced, it will be remembered, with the division of philosophy into the speculative and the practical, and then announced our present object as belonging to the former. Next, we seek for some principle, from which we might proceed. But this, as a principle, and independent of the consideration whether it is to be a principle of speculative or a principle of practical philosophy, must be *absolute*. For how can that which depends on, or is bounded and qualified by, another and extrinsic power be a *principle*? In the strict sense of the word, I mean. Again: there cannot be two absolutes different from each other. The supposition involves an absurdity.

a ms: αμελλος

[1] See above, p 25 n 6.   [2] I.e. through a telescope.

It follows, therefore, that the principle must be the same for both divisions, that is, the principle of speculative philosophy is one and the same with the principle of practical philosophy.

40   Nevertheless, when, as is the case in all speculation, our attention is especially directed to the absolute as the principle of the ideal or intelligential, in distinction from the same absolute, considered as the source of being and action, we may allowably *confine* the term "nous" and its derivatives to the expression of this special direction, and appropriate the terms, "Supreme Will" or "Supreme Being" to the designation of the same Absolute, as the principle of ethics or practical philosophy. I need not say, however, that these distinctions of terms refer exclusively to differences in our own thoughts and their[a] validity is exclusively subjective and logical.

41(a)   Still the same essential character is intended, and the νοῦς is that in which the idea is at the same time the reality; the knowing is the thing known; the *scire* one and the same with the *esse*. This, then, is the first assumption. Secondly, it is assumed that the reason which is present to the mind of man or of which the human mind partakes (*vide* N.T.[b])[1] is one with the νοῦς; in other words, that the reason in[c] man as far as it is reason implies its own reality, and consequently that the truths of reason are essentially real—real in their own right, and not in consequence of any other thing being real.

41(b)   There are two things which we may contemplate as contraries. The one a whole, the parts of which are not necessarily homogeneous, and consequently a whole that derives its right to be so called altogether from the unity of the perception, and so that it supposes no unity in the object but only in the organ of sense through which that object is presented. A heap of corn or still better a heap of grains, chaff, dust, etc, etc, affords an instance. With regard to these we cannot conclude from the whole to the parts, or infer that because it is a part of that whole it is one with it; so that what is affirmed of the major or including shall be predicable of the minor or included.

42   In full contrariety to such merely subjective wholes stand those unities, the parts of which are not so properly called parts: for this term can be strictly used only of objects which in some way or other constitute units by aggregation, as they are repetitions of the units conceived as realising (in technical language putting themselves[d] under given relations). Purely for illustration's sake let us

---

a ms: its   *b* ms: N.P.   *c* ms: is   *d* ms: itself

[1] Another reference to Acts 17.28?

imagine space to possess real being and energy and that to its figurability were added the active power of figure—*vis se figendi relative ad formam et extrinsecam et interiorem*; that is, *ideam figurativam.*[1] The consequence would be that all the possible elementary forms with all their combinations would be contemplated as so many repetitions of space and at the same time representations of its figurability, all which would differ indeed from each other, but in no respect from the space which would be their common essence. Now what we have here imagined of space is actually affirmable of TRUTH the moment we have agreed to consider it as real, that is, as universal reason and not a mere logical whole having its unity in the analytic unity of the understanding, or reflection, as the heap of grains, etc, in the synthetic unity of the sense together with the organ of sense. Between these there is a third possible mode of existence partaking of both, which you will at once recognise under the name "organisation" or "organic body". In these there is a positive and intrinsic unity as well as the unity which is completed in the percipient and has its occasion only externally in the accidental juxtaposition of particulars, each of which, from the endless divisibility implied in body, is as truly a whole, as all collectively, and we need only alter our position or change our arrangement, as it were, and sphere of our attention, to convert the collective all into a part of some more comprehensive whole.

43   We have seen that a judgment or the act of judging consists in reducing a position to its primary constituent parts of subject and predicate, and that this presupposes the division into object and subject. Consequently the functions of logic commence when we consider the subject objectively, that is, as a something that is not the same with our own subject or our mind, but an object of our mind. Thus, for instance, when I think of my neighbour's soul I know that it is a subject in and for him; but relatively to me it becomes an object. While for that which, had it appertained to myself, I should have called an object, I am compelled to invent another name in order to distinguish it from the former. In order to this I call the former what it really is in itself, *the subject*, though in relation to me it is an object, and the object of that subject I name its predicate. Hence we may see the ground on which logicians have defined a judgment, viz. to compare a mark with a thing, that is, a predicate

---

[1] "The power of fixing itself relatively to extrinsical and inner form",   that is, "relatively to a figurative idea".

with a subject, is what we call judging;[1] the act of comparison being expressed by the intervening verb substantive. There is little perhaps to object to what is here meant, yet somewhat to the way of expressing this meaning. And I am anxious to impress this because more than any other point it is calculated to elucidate what has been before declared respecting the simplicity and universality of the syllogistic form as uniformly consisting of the three acts of the mind, clusion, inclusion, and conclusion. Strictly speaking, a judgment is the determination of a subject by a predicate, not always or necessarily to compare the one with the other. E.g. "a spirit is simple". "Spiritus est aliquid vere simplex".[2] No one will deny that this is a judgment, and yet it would be a strange abuse of language to say that we compared the word "spirit" with its own meaning. But, likewise, "a spirit is not compounded". "Spiritus non est aliquid composit[um]".[3] Now here we do compare or contrast the conception "spirit" with the essential predicate of a different conception in order to acquire at least a negative knowledge of spirit or for the purpose of enlivening our knowledge and bringing it into a distincter consciousness by adding an act of seclusion to that of clusion simply. This, however, is a question of language rather than of things inasmuch as it depends on the different extent in which we may use the term "compare". If it could be proved that other things besides spirit were likewise entitled to the attribute of simplicity in the same sense, we doubtless might[a] be said to compare "the one" with "us", a particular with a universal, or a minor with a major, in order to determine whether or no the former was contained in the latter. I am, however, inclined to think that instead of distinguishing judgment into affirmative and negative, both being considered as comparative, it would be more expedient to entitle the first positive, the other comparative, while determinative is the name common to both.

44   From this point we are now able to see the true use and application of logic; and this twofold. In the first the forms of thinking are realised in the objects of the thought, as that "all men are mortal and therefore Socrates, being a man, must be mortal". Here is an actual inclusion, and in all cases of this kind the process as far as it is a logical process is almost automatic or spontaneous and the

---

[a] ms: may

[1] E.g. Kant "Die falsche Spitzfindigkeit . . ." § 1 *VS* I 585.

[2] Literally, "a spirit is something truly simple".

[3] Kant's example "Die falsche Spitzfindigkeit . . ." § 1 *VS* I 585.

only question is respecting the truth of the original perceptions or apprehensions, whether ideas or facts, and not respecting the conceptions or comprehensions which follow[a] by the very mechanism of our intellect. It is a science of nature's rather than of our conscious self, or, as we commonly say, it is a natural logic.

45(a)   But there is another application which, though it may be called verbal, is of far greater need and more frequent utility. Nor will the epithet "verbal" degrade it in our minds who have learnt to distinguish words, λογοι, from articulate sounds, ρηματα, and to consider them as partaking of this communicative intelligence, του λογου, and of its ideas or communicable forms, των λογων, as the echo partakes of the original sound, and that sound of the power which modified while it impelled the motion of the air to its distinct conveyance; or rather as a portrait would partake of the person if we supposed the person contemplating the same and the image varying with the changes in the person produced by the contemplation.

> Like to Narcissus, on the grassy shore,
> Viewing his outward face in watery glass,
> Still as he looks, his looks add[b] ever more
> New fire, new light, new love, new comely grace
> To's inward form; and it displays apace
> Its hidden rays and so new lustre sends
> To its true shadow—[. . .]
>
> And this I wot is the soul's excellence,
> That from the hint of each self-issuing glance
> In shadows se[nsible][c] she doth from hence
> Her inward life and radiant hue advance
> To higher pitch, and by good governance
> [d]May weaned[e] be from love of fading light
> In outward forms having true cognizance
> That 'tis not these that are the beauty bright
> Which takes men so, but what they cause in human sprite.
>
> Henry More[1]

The first utility which I shall mention is that of which we have before given an instance, in which if we regarded the mark or predicate in the minor as the predicate of the subject [of the major] it would be a mere synonym of the predicate in the major instead of

---

[a] ms: follows   [b] ms: had   [c] Insertion, probably by J. H. Green
[d-e] Insertion by J. H. Green

[1] Henry More *The Argument of Psychozoia, or, The Life of the Soul* canto I sts 11, 12 (var): *Poems* (Cambridge 1647) 4. For C's marginalia to this poem, see *C 17th C* 623. Cf 617–18. Cf RS's adverse comments on it: *Omniana* II 157–8.

being included therein. In other words it would be a mere tautology,[1] thus: "God is simple". "God is noncomposite". Where the "non-composite" might be commuted for "simple", and "simple" for "noncomposite", and yet it may be of use both as an auxiliar and as a corrective, to remind a learner that God being simple cannot be sought after by the same organs as bodies or things that are compound. There results therefore a real addition, not indeed to the material truth, but to the mind's property in that truth. We acquire a sort of regulative knowledge from being thus made sensible that the simple is irreconcilable with the composite and inasmuch as the mere prefixing of the negative sign to the latter[a] renders it a synonym of the former.

45(b)   Now in the stricter use of the term "understanding" it has been defined [as] the regulative power or the faculty in which all RULES originate. On this being assumed, the judgment may [be] technically distinguished from the understanding, as the determinative faculty or the power of *determining* this or that under the condition of some rule; while the reason gives a necessity or universality to that determination under the condition of the rule, that is, the rule and the accuracy of the rule being taken for granted. Whenever therefore a predicate arises in my mind not self-presented but in consequence of some other predicate in which its truth is involved, or even when on consideration the former is found to mean the same with the latter, if only it requires consideration to be aware of the sameness, we are entitled in both cases in respect to the forms of reasoning to regard the one as included in the other, and such note, mark, or predicate is called by the logicians *nota intermedia*.[2] E.g. "necessary" is an immediate mark or predicate of God; but "unchangeable" is a mark of necessity, and therefore a mediate or intermediate mark of God.[3] We arrive at the truth of God's immutability by reflection that [that] which exists of necessity can neither have existed from any contingent cause out of itself, nor can it have been affected by any such cause, for then, [it] would no longer be an existence of necessity inasmuch as it must have been conceived to have been or become something that it was not, or something else than what it is. This intermediate

---

[a] ms: letter

[1] The example that follows closely resembles Kant's in "Die falsche Spitz-findigkeit..." § 1 *VS* I 585. See above, p 95].

[2] "An intermediate mark" or "attribute".

[3] The passage "such note ... mark of God" is translated from Kant ibid § 1 *VS* I 585–6 (Abbott 79–80).

mark, like the former or immediate, may be either positive by affirmation or comparative by negation. It may be either "God being a necessary Being, is therefore immutable", or "God being a necessary Being is therefore not subject to contingency";[1] and whether this conclusion by intermediate marks is more than tautological is determinable by no rule beforehand but by the state of knowledge and development of the faculties in the person respectively to the given subject for whom the reasoning is intended, provided only that it is possible to consider one or the other of the terms as the more comprehensive. Thus we should not hesitate a moment in rejecting the following as a logical conclusion. "This cloth is sky-blue and therefore it is cerulean"; though by reversing it, it might be a necessary grammatical instruction that when the cloth was described as cerulean it meant the same as its being sky-blue; but in neither case could the position be entitled a logical inference by[a] *nota intermedia*. Thus, then, we come to the real definition of a logical or rational conclusion. Every judgment by means of an intermediate mark is a conclusion. In other words, to conclude logically is to compare a mark or predicate with a subject by means of an intermediate mark, which in a syllogism is ordinarily named *terminus medius* or "middle constituent conception".

46   Logicians speak of immediate conclusions. The impropriety of the word "conclusion" we need not point out, it being evident that what is concluded must have been previously included, therefore affirmed by means of an intermediate—call them, however, immediate deductions or inferences, and still I much doubt whether they can be properly termed logical by any right of their own, whether they may not all be referred either to truths of reason or metaphysical facts, as in a former page we have already explained in our sceptical remarks on the principles of identity and contradiction,[2] or else to grammar as mere explanations of synonymous terms, or thirdly, and most often in conjunction with the first or second, to an enthymeme or abbreviated syllogism: in all which the process in the mind is the same as in the regular figure, only that some one term is passed over as obvious of itself, or, as the school phrase is understood, *subintell[ect]um*.[3]

a ms: be

[1] The sentence up to this point and the preceding sentence are a free translation of Kant ibid § 1 *VS* ɪ 586 (Abbott 80).

[2] See above, pp 87–91.

[3] "Understood (without being expressed)".

47 A single instance will set the preceding in full light: "all matter is mutable, therefore what is not mutable is not matter". This is a so-called immediate conclusion, of which the logicians enumerate several sorts—that of logical inversion and that of contraposition being the most important. It is difficult to determine how far such an inference deserves the name of inference, whether in reality it be logically considered anything more than repetition of the very same truth in other words: and whether so or not it is plain that the force of the deduction depends on a rule not mentioned, though understood, viz. that whatever contradicts the essential predicate of a thing contradicts the thing itself. We shall see this in what follows, though we need only alter the words without in the least affecting the meaning and make the "whatever" or logical sign of the universal what it really is, an indetermined particular, to find that this instance corresponds to our preceding assertion, viz. that it is but an abbreviated syllogism. "No matter is unchangeable"; then putting "A" for "whatever", "A is unchangeable", therefore "A is no matter". We have, I repeat, a regular syllogism.

48 A syllogism formed of three positions is a pure syllogism (*ratiocinium purum*) and necessarily affirmative, that is, in the form of affirmation or negation. Whatever is composed of more than three positions is a mixed or illegitimate syllogism (*ratiocinium hybridum*) and is not coercive by force of the terms or positions mentioned, others being always understood. This most frequently takes place by the interposition of some immediate inference or deduction, as above explained. We will suppose a friend to reason thus. "Nothing that is corruptible is simple. Therefore nothing simple is corruptible. The soul of man is simple. Therefore the soul of man is not corruptible." Now this contains four positions, but by reflecting on the true grounds of the conclusion we shall discover that this is nothing more than an ordinary syllogism grammatically disguised. "Nothing simple is corruptible" is precisely the same as "the simple is always incorruptible". "Whatever is simple is incorruptible. The soul of man is simple. Therefore the soul of man is incorruptible."[1] I have been perhaps unnecessarily prolix, but it has been to preclude the worse prolixity which the different forms of the so-called four figures of syllogism would have forced us to. It is a safe rule that a syllogism (*ratiocinium logicum*) consist of three acts. First clusion or seclusion, that is, universal or particular premise. Secondly, inclu-

[1] The paragraph up to this point *VS* I 592–3 (Abbott 82–3). is a free translation of Kant ibid § 3

sion, and thirdly, conclusion. And that whatever is affirmed on other grounds than by a conclusion rising out of an inclusion may be *truths of reason*, that is, those of which we render ourselves distinctly conscious by an act of evolution (which will be explained in the third part of this work, or the organon),[a1] or by equation as in the truth of sense—as in geometry—but are not properly logical. The same criterion may be expressed thus: "Whatever is predicated, the mark (say, B) of a mark (C) of a thing (A) belongs to the thing itself.

C   B

Whatever is rational is a spirit.

A   C

The human soul is rational.

A   B

Therefore the human soul is a spirit."[2]

49   This is Kant's rule, but some little obscurity may arise from the first position ("whatever is rational"), which stands as the subject of the major [and] is entitled a mark or predicate; but this we have before explained in the more intelligible rule that the subject of the major becomes the predicate in the minor and the conclusion. C has for its mark or predicate B. A has for its mark or predicate C. Therefore A has for its mark or predicate B.[3] I should prefer expressing the rule of the so-called first figure thus: when the subject in the major becomes the predicate of the minor, the subject of the minor acquires the predicate of the major, all apparent deviations being nothing more than grammatical equivalents or inversions, that is, saying the same thing in a negative form that had been before said in an affirmative, and vice versa. Now we assert that in this figure only and exclusively are the *ratiocinia pura* or legitimate conclusions possible: and that in the three other figures the syllogisms are mixed or illegitimate, *ratiocinia hybrida*. In the second figure mixed conclusions only are possible.

50   "The rule of the second is this: Whatever contradicts the mark of a thing contradicts the thing itself."[4] But this position is true only because whatever is contradicted by a mark contradicts that mark, that is, if A is precluded by B, B in like manner is pre-

---

a Parentheses inserted

[1] Another reference to the missing Part Three. See above, p 57.

[2] Kant ibid § 4 *VS* i 594 (Abbott 84).

[3] This sentence and the preceding one are translated from Kant ibid.

[4] Kant ibid § 4 *VS* i 595 (Abbott 84).

cluded by A. But again whatever contradicts the mark of a thing contradicts the thing itself, consequently that which is contradicted by the mark of a thing contradicts that thing itself. Here it is evident that the connection of the minor with the conclusion depends altogether on the convertibility of the major as a negative position, and that unless this conversion be mentally interposed the syllogism has no conclusive force. But this position expressing the inversion is, we have seen, an interpolation or a fourth term. In the technical language of logicians the syllogism has four judgments and is therefore a *ratiocinium hybridum*. For instance:

No spirit is partible,
All matter is partible,
Therefore no matter is a spirit.

Doubtless I have here inferred rightly, but the conclusive power consists in this—that out of my first position, "no spirit is partible", I mentally infer the inverse. "Therefore nothing partible is a spirit", and from this the remainder follows.[1] According to the universal rule, the syllogism falls under the first figure, consequently the second figure is no proper part of logic, but a disguise which belongs to grammar or rhetoric or rather to that science between both for which we have proposed the name "rhematic".

Nothing partible is a spirit,
All matter is partible,
Therefore nothing that is matter is a spirit.

The original major, by means of which it acquired its place as a second figure, being wholly superfluous to the syllogism, though possibly the occasion by which the reasoner came to the legitimate major, "no spirit is partible". Well! that is the same as "nothing that is partible is a spirit". We will substitute the latter:

Nothing that is partible is a spirit,
All matter is partible,
Therefore nothing that is matter is a spirit.

Ah, now we have a legitimate syllogism, but it is a syllogism of the first figure.

51 In the third figure likewise, the conclusive power depends always on a fourth or interpolated judgment. The rule of this third figure is: whatever belongs to or contradicts a thing, that likewise belongs to or contradicts some things that are contained under some

[1] From the beginning of the para- of Kant ibid (Abbott 84–5).
graph to this point a free translation

other mark of this thing. "All men are sinners." The "sinners" here belongs to "all men". "All men are rational." Here is another mark of "all men". "Therefore some rational beings are sinners." Now it is plain this conclusion is brought about *per conversionem logicam, per accidens*,[1] that is, a logical conversion partially of the minor position. I reason thus: "all men are rational"; but therefore "some rational beings are men". If the term "rational" expresses the whole sphere in which man is included, I do but say the same thing in other words when I assert that some part of that sphere is filled by men. But, this once granted, the whole follows regularly.

All men are sinners,

All men are rational,

And consequently some rational beings are men,

Therefore some rational beings are sinners.[2]

The force of the conclusion depends on the perception of the mind that the term "some rational" is perfectly equivalent to the term "men". It is therefore no syllogism [of the third figure] if you omit this and say, "All men are sinners". "Some rational beings are men, and therefore some rational beings are sinners." It is a legitimate syllogism; but a syllogism of the first figure.

52   The very same holds good of the fourth figure, under which, observe, no affirmative positions are possible. The rule for this fourth figure it is perhaps possible to give, but the mode of conclusion is so unnatural and depends upon so many interposed or understood inferences and equations that any universal rule abstracted from the possible instances would be a riddle or puzzle, the difficulty of which would stand in an inverse proportion to its worth. Instead therefore of a rule I will content myself with pointing out under what conditions the conclusive force is possible. Now this takes place when either by logical conversion or contraposition I alter the places of the constituent terms and therefore after each premise can think of its immediate consequence or rather equivalent, so that these steps of the conclusion acquire mentally the same connections which they would have had expressly in a syllogism under the first and in fact the only legitimate rule and figure. Of the first sort, and that by logical conversion, take the following instance.

No fool is learned,

[1] "By means of a logical conversion, *per accidens*". C, adding his own Latin to Kant's, means what is usually called *conversio per accidens*—i.e. a conversion in which the quantity is changed. Ibid § 4 *VS* I 596 (Abbott 85, 86).

[2] The paragraph to this point is a free translation of Kant ibid § 4 *VS* I 596–7 (Abbott 85–6).

Some learned men are pious,

Therefore some pious persons are not fools.

It would be quite sufficient to prove its want of all claim to the name of syllogism, that nothing is included, but the predicates are applied by mere accident. Piety, for instance, is no property of the learned as learned, and therefore the term "learned" is altogether idle and the bond of connection therefore, such as it is, is supplied by a word wantonly interpolated. But to adhere to our former test, we will take the thing as it is, inserting those mental interpositions by force of which there is any force in the conclusion.

No fool is learned—consequently

No learned person is a fool.

Some learned persons are pious—consequently

Some pious persons are learned, therefore

Some pious persons are not fools.

Substitute the parenthetic positions, omitting the major and minor of which they are the converse, and we have the regular syllogism with no fault in the *form* whatever. Ignorance as to the fact may be proved by the rash assertion that no learned man is a fool. Of the second sort take the following instance:

Every spirit is simple,

All that is simple is incorruptible,

Therefore something incorruptible is a spirit.[a]

The conclusion as it here stands cannot, it is plain, flow out of the premises; to see this we need only compare therewith the middle or common term. I cannot say "some incorruptibles are spirit"; because it is simple it does not follow necessarily it is a spirit. The syllogism ought to stand:

Every spirit is simple,

But whatever is simple is incorruptible,

Therefore whatever is a spirit is incorruptible.

But the whole includes its parts and therefore "some incorruptible is spirit". But then it is evident that, omitting the mental interposition or fourth term, it differs in nothing from the regular syllogism of the first figure.[1]

---

[a] The letters "a", "a", and "i" (identifying the form of the syllogism) are written beside the three lines of the syllogism in a different hand—Green's?

[1] This paragraph is a free trans-   (Abbott 86–8).
lation of Kant ibid § 4 *VS* i 597–600

[PART TWO]
THE CRITERION OR DIALECTIC

[CHAPTER 1]

1   The old and famous question with which it was once usual to puzzle the logicians and to force them either to a confession of their ignorance or to the necessity of answering in a circle is that which Pilate of old contemptuously [put] to Him who was indeed in the highest sense the reality of that concerning which he asked: "What is truth?"[1] The verbal definition, viz. the coincidence of the knowledge with its object, is here presupposed and admitted. But the querist wants to be informed and such is the purport of the question, "What is the universal and sure criterion of any and every knowledge?"

2   "Prudens quaestio dimidium scientiae", says Lord Bacon.[2] It is already a great and important proof of understanding and insight to know what can be rationally asked. For if the question itself be absurd[a] and an answer unnecessary, the consequence may be that the querist beguiling the respondent into an attempt precluded from the beginning, that of returning a wise answer to a senseless question, places the respondent and himself in a position which our ancestors describe by observing that the one milked the boar and the other was holding a sieve under to catch the stream.[3]

3   Harris has informed us that "the ancients divided questions into two kinds, the simple, which they call ἐρώτημα[b] or interrogative, and the complex, which they call πύσμα[b] or *percontatio*".[4] "The first consisted of such questions as permitted an answer, in the same words without addition when affirmative, and with the addition only of the negative particle when negative. 'Are these verses Homer's?'

---

a ms: observed [an example of mishearing in dictation?]   *b* Word in pencil

[1] John 18.38.

[2] *De augmentis scientiarum* bk v ch 3: *Works* (1740) I 148–9 (var). C's tr in *Friend* (*CC*) I 489: "the forethoughtful query . . . which is the prior half of the knowledge sought".

[3] The proverb has English predecessors (e.g. *Spectator* No 138 [8 Aug 1711]), but C is probably giving an English turn to Kant's version, which involves a he-goat; paragraphs 1 and 2 are adapted from Kant *C d r V* 82–3 (97).

[4] C is quoting Moses Mendelssohn (*Morgenstunden* notes p xx), who in turn is referring to a footnote in James Harris *Hermes* bk I ch viii: *Works* I 299–300n.

'These verses are Homer's.' 'Are these verses Virgil's?' 'These verses are not Virgil's.' 'Yes' and 'no' being the abbreviation or way of returning the same answer in the shortest possible manner; but if the question be complex, as, for example, 'Are these verses Homer's or Virgil's?' or, if it be indefinite, as, for instance, 'Whose verses are these?', it is evident that the former mode of replying would be inapplicable. A certain enquiry is more or less necessary; a choice must be made; the answer to the first instance may be either first, 'They are Homer's', or, secondly, 'They are not Homer's', or, thirdly, 'They are Virgil's', or, fourthly, 'They are not Virgil's', or, lastly, 'They are neither by one nor the other': and this may be pursued still further or rather without limit in the latter instance, 'Whose verses are these?', either affirmatively as, 'They are Virgil's, Ovid's, etc', or negatively, 'They are not Virgil's, Ovid's, etc, etc'. In all questions of this kind or *percontations*, the answer cannot be given in the same words without addition or with 'not' only added, though here too the language of mankind ordinarily furnishes appropriate abbreviations. Thus, if it were asked 'How many right angles do all the angles of a triangle contain?', we should reply by the single monosyllable—'two'; but unabridged,[a] the answer would be, 'All the angles of a triangle are equal to two right angles'."[1]

4　"Such is Harris's account, and it would be hard to say that it is not sufficiently accurate, and yet we may be allowed to complain that little or no additional light has been thrown on the subject. Perhaps we shall succeed better if we take up the subject at a somewhat earlier point and begin by asking not how many kinds of questions there are, but what is a question. Every questioner (if the convenience of this word may excuse this barbarism),[2] every questioner, it is plain, wants to know something by which a deficient or imperfect position or affirmation may be completed and rendered satisfactory. The answer supplies this defect and transforms the imperfect position of the questioner into a complete or perfect one. 'Who is the author of the *Iliad*?' The interrogative 'who' stands here in the place of the unknown subject. The answer names the subject 'Homer', and now the position is complete. 'Homer is the author of the *Iliad*.' 'What is the *Iliad*?' The interrogative 'what' stands here in the place of the unknown predicate. The answer names the predicate 'an epic poem of Homer's', and we have a

---

[a] ms: we abridged [an example of error in transcription?]

[1] A free translation of *Morgen-stunden* notes pp xvii–xx.　　　[2] For "jeder Fragende".

complete position. 'The *Iliad* is an epic poem of Homer's.' There is no necessity therefore to [?deal]*ᵃ* with any abbreviation,[1] as Harris has done, from the very definition of a question that the answerer needs only give that part of the position which the questioner wished and was unable to supply. The interrogatives have the same function here as the letters X, Y, Z, as marks of an unknown quantity in algebra. The answerer gives the value or determinal quantity which must be substituted for the undeterminate mark in order to render the position full and determined."[2]

5 "In like manner the case of the interrogative points out the defective part of the position—where the language possesses such cases. The nominative 'who?', 'what?', 'which?', signifies some main term of the position, subject, or predicate, as may be seen in the instances already given, while the accusative 'who[m]?', 'what?', informs us that an object is wanting, as in the following instances: 'Whom has Homer seen?' 'Whom has Homer taken for the hero of [the] *Iliad*?': answer, 'Achilles'. The ablative signifies the point whence, the dative the point whither, and the genitive the relation in which the subject or predicate stands with some other subject: e.g. 'Whose epic poem is the *Iliad*?' The original position contained in that*ᵇ* question was, 'The *Iliad* is an epic poem of X', that is, of someone but I know not whom. The subject and predicate are here given and determined; but the substantive was wanting with which the predicate is to stand in the required relation. The answer*ᶜ* supplies this substantive, viz. 'Homer'."[3] Respecting Harris's fifth possible answer to the question, "Are these verses by Ovid or Virgil",*ᵈ* "They are by neither of the two", is no[t] so properly [an answer] as a declaration that the question was absurd or incorrect inasmuch as it confined the doubt within narrower bounds than the truth permitted. [. . .]*⁴* That kind of question therefore, "which, according to Harris, the ancients called πυσμα*ᵉ* (*percontatio*), and which he describes as complex, belongs in truth to the ἐρωτημα*ᵉ* (*interrogatio*)*ᶠ* and is not complex but in and of itself perfectly simple. The number of possible answers exists" only in the indifference relatively to the logician who is supposing the case or in the indefiniteness of the

ᵃ Blank space left in ms   *ᵇ* ms: that is the   *ᶜ* ms: answers
ᵈ Full stop in ms   *ᵉ* Word in pencil   *ᶠ* ms: interrogative

[1] "Es ist also nicht nöthig, mit dem Harris eine Verkürzung anzunehmen": "it is unnecessary, therefore, to accept an abbreviation as Harris does". *Morgenstunden* notes p xxi.

[2] Ibid pp xx–xxi (var).
[3] Ibid pp xxi–xxii (var).
[4] "Respecting Harris's fifth . . . truth permitted" is a free paraphrase of ibid p xxiii.

example.[1] In reality the answer would be perfectly simple, either the name of the author or "I do not know", which of course is no answer at all. The questions which are properly entitled πυσματα,[a] and which again are no more characterised by their compound nature than the former, are such as these: "Are those verses Homer's?" "Have you seen the white bear?",[2] to which the answer is "Yes" or "No". On the conversion of the change of the personal pronouns or the position of the words, "Are these verses Homer's, yes or no?", or "These are or they are not Homer's". "Hast thou seen?" "Yes", "No", or, "I have", or "I have not", in English we might express the πυσμα[b] by "asking", the ἐρωτημα[c] by "enquiring", or simply by "questions" and "enquiries". The latter have acquired a certain dignity by their constant recurrence in the Socratic reasoning, it being the habit of this greatest of uninspired teachers "to determine at all times the subject and predicate of a position so exactly as to leave no other answer necessary on the part of the disciple but 'Yes' or 'No'. [. . .] These subtleties, which our Sterne has placed in so laughable a light in his example of the white bears, lead nevertheless to useful enquiries.[3] They remind us at least that all questions must be answerable, that they must consist of imperfect or defective positions which a possible answer may convert into perfect[ible][d] and conceivable positions.[e] As soon as it is proved that the position which the question intends to have completed is in its own nature incapable of completion,[f] the question itself must be rejected"[4] and instead of an answer the questioner, if he be in earnest and deserve a serious reply, must have this incurable defect in the question pointed out and explained to him.

6(a)   We will apply this remark to two or three questions which it is not uncommon to hear proposed and agitated in societies where the conversation turns on speculative subjects, and we will recommence with the question with which we introduce[d] the present chapter: "What is truth?" taken not in the sense of its verbal definition as the correspondence of an affirmation or particular knowledge to its object, or[g] as the test of such correspondence, but as a universal criterion, whether or no in any and every given case this coincidence exists. Now if truth consist in the coincidence of a knowledge with its

---

[a] Word in pencil   [b] ms, in pencil: ἐρωτημα   [c] ms, in pencil: πυσμα
[d] Ms leaves a blank space; C. A. Ward has inserted "sense"
[e] Ms unpunctuated   [f] ms: [?confution]   [g] ms: but

[1] A free rendering of ibid pp xxiv–xxv.
[2] The question is from ibid p xxiv.
[3] *Tristram Shandy* vol v ch 43.
[4] *Morgenstunden* notes pp xxv–xxvi.

object, this object must thereby be distinguished from other objects. For a knowledge is false if it does not coincide with the thing to which it is referred, though it may contain somewhat that might be truly affirmed of other things; but we are bound to demand of a universal criterion that it should apply to all knowledges indiscriminately, that is, without distinction of the objects severally appertaining to them; but in order to this we must abstract from all the contents or *material* of the knowledge, which material constitutes in fact what we mean by its relation or reference to the object, and it is evident therefore that as the truth consists in this reference, as this, the material, the substance, or "very stuff" of each knowledge, is what we understand by its truth, the question itself is absurd and rationally impossible. For it is to ask after a distinctive mark of the true contents and matter of each and every knowledge, when at the same time the abstraction from all contents is a necessary condition of the possibility of such a mark.*a*[1]

6(b)   To avoid the inconvenience from the awkwardness of the plural word "contents" and the ambiguity of the singular "content" we shall henceforward employ the term "matter" as the antithesis of "form" and as answering to the *Inhalt* (Inhold of the German). Question: "What is truth?" Answer: "If you ask for the meaning of the word, and this relatively to the human mind, I reply, 'the coincidence of the word with the thought and the thought with the thing'". Relatively to God the question has either no meaning or admits of but one reply, viz. "God Himself". God is the truth, the identity of thing and thought, of knowing and of being, and consequently the idea of God is presupposed in the coincidence of the one with the other, which implies the existence of each severally; but this was not the purpose of the question. You ask for some one test by which in all cases you can determine this coincidence between the word, the thought, and the thing, and in this sense the question implies a contradiction. For to be universal we must first abstract from all that is particular in each thought: but this consists in its reference to the particular thing at that time thought of, consequently we remove the very subject for which the criterion was required, and properly worded the question should stand thus, "What is the universal criterion of truth when all truth is out of the question?"

7   Truth, therefore, is its own criterion and, in the language of

---

a Ms unpunctuated

[1] The paragraph is a free translation of Kant *C d r V* 83 (97–8).

Augustine,[a] at once discovers itself and detects its opposite, even as
we discover darkness by light and the light by its own evidence[1]—
vide fol. third *ab hinc*.[2]

8(a)   So far on the supposition that the question respects truth
objectively: but there is another sense and a more fruitful one. We
may mean subjective truth, in which truth may be defined [as] the
coincidence between the thought and the thinker, the forms, I mean,
of the intellect. Now as far as concerns the knowledge of the mere
form abstractedly from the *matter*, it is plain that logic, inasmuch as it
presents the universal and necessary rules of the understanding, must
in these rules present likewise the criterion of truth, that is, of formal
truth, or truth relative to the constitution or constituent forms, laws,
and rules of the thinking faculty. For what contradicts these tests is
false, because the understanding contradicts its own universal rules
of thinking, and therein contradicts itself. And in truth there can be
no contradiction. These criteria, however, respecting only the form
of truth are in themselves infallible; but not of themselves sufficing;
for, though a knowledge may be in perfect congruity with the logical
form, and be free from all contradiction, it may nevertheless con-
tradict or be incongruous with the matter or real subject. The
logical criterion of truth or the harmony of an affirmation with the
laws of the reason and the rules of the understanding is the *conditio
sine qua non* but still only the negative condition of all truth, and
farther than this pure and proper logic cannot extend, and conse-
quently can supply no touchstone of error or falsehood, when such
error lies in the thing, fact, or reality, considered as the substance
and matter of the thought.[3]

8(b)   But there is a third sense in which the question might be
asked, as we have indeed implied in our last definition of truth, in
the communication of which always and in its evolutions and
presentations to our own minds most often a coincidence between
the thought and the word is likewise implied, and here the criteria
must vary with the occasion and the purpose. They may, however, be
reduced to two. First, common usage, and, in civilised and cultivated

---

[a] ms: Augustan

[1] Thinking, perhaps, of Augustine
on John 18.38: "When therefore
Christ bears witness to the Truth,
undoubtedly He bears witness to
Himself, seeing it is His word, *I am
the Truth*: and indeed He hath said
in another place, *I bear witness of*
Myself". Homily cxv 4 in *Homilies
on the Gospel According to St. John . . .*
(Oxford 1848–9) ii 1021.

[2] See above, pp 110–11—three folios
earlier in ms.

[3] The paragraph is a free translation
of Kant *C d r V* 83–4 (98).

societies, the usage and authority of the best writers; but where these[a] are imperfect, and not only different shades of meaning are found expressed by the same word, but even diverse meanings, then we have no other criterion than to determine the word to some one of these meanings and if there should be another word used synonymously and, as most often happens, equally equivocal and unsteadfast in its application, to appropriate this, and if there be not, we must either borrow a term from some other language or invent one in the mint and from the materials of our own, or lastly be content to convey our meaning in a periphrasis, and supply the want of the proper term by the definition. For rude and ponderous masses, our corn, hay, coals, and timber, the weighbridge will suffice, and for the commodities of the market generally the steelyard[1] and the ordinary scales differing more in their dimensions than their accuracy, but medicine must have its appropriate weights and the goldsmith and the jeweller their gold and their diamond scales, and the experimental philosopher seeks from the artist an accuracy yet more nice, even though at the cost of a more complex machinery and the final result not obtainable without the aid of calculation.[2] We may apply this to the investigations of truth speculative, moral, or historical. The common usage is but the weighbridge,[b] and even the authority [and] sanctions of celebrated writers [are] only the steelyards and the weights and measures of the market enjoined by public authority; the investigator must use the gold scales of precise definition; never, indeed, wantonly deviating even from the common usage, still less rashly rejecting the sense attached to the term by his more celebrated predecessors in the same pursuit; but yet preferring the interests of truth to all ("amicus Plato, amicus Socrates sed magis amica veritas"),[c][3] and well knowing that accuracy which in this case demands the fixation of the magnetic needle to one point, a thing possible, indeed, only when we are masters of our own poles and can, as it were, construct our own world, or, at least, to suffer no variation without giving at the same time the requisite warning.

9   The second instance: "What are the things in and of themselves

[1] An instrument for weighing luggage, etc.

[2] The metaphor is an elaboration of one used in *P Lects* Lect 12 (1949) 355, which in turn seems to be derived from Kant *Träume eines Geistersehers, erläutert durch Träume der Metaphysik*

(Königsberg 1766) pt I ch 4: *VS* II 304–5.

[3] "Plato is a friend, Socrates is a friend, but truth is a greater friend". Traditional adaptation of Aristotle *Nicomachean Ethics* bk I § 6 par 1.

independent of our sensations, representations, and conceptions?"[1] In this form an idealist would state the question. [a]"What [are] the things in themselves, independent of their qualities and properties, that is, what is the substance wherein the qualities and properties inhere? What is that to which they belong?" For so the materialist would state it. In either case, this somewhat, metaphysicians have named the thing-in-itself, *res in se, res ipsa,* or *res absoluta.*[2] Now before we think of the answer we will, according to the rule above given, transform the question into the imperfect position which it contains: the things independent of all sensations, representations, and conceptions (or independent of their qualities and properties) are = X. And for this unknown quantity X the respondent is to substitute some "A".[3] We will suppose this done. Now it is evident that this "A" can by no possible means represent anything by which it can be distinguished from the former X, for if it be a known quantity, there must exist some means of knowing it; but the means by which we can know an object are contained in our sensations, perceptions, representations, and conceptions wholly and exhaustively. Not only [b]are there[c] no other means, but no other is it in our power to imagine, even as possibility, and again, on the second statement, the means by which the thing here assumed as external and self-subsistent can make itself known to us are all contained in its qualities and properties, consequently the A is equal to X and therefore = to not-A. The question therefore supposes a contradiction, in other words, no answer at all, as the only answer of which it is capable.

10   A shorter, but less obvious, way of annulling the question would be found in the definition, and possibly in the etymology, of the word "thing"; for possibly the word itself is the same with the "ing", a termination frequent in the names of towns and districts in the countries in which the mother language of the inhabitants was a branch of the Gothic, whether Scandinavian or Teutonic, and a diminutive of which our own language retains in the word "ingle" for hearth, that is, a smaller inclosure within another space likewise inclosed. The "ing", therefore, is the universal exponent of whatever

---

[a] New paragraph in ms   [b-c] ms: there are

[1] *Morgenstunden* notes p xxvi. This is Mendelssohn's first instance of the class of unanswerable questions.

[2] "Thing in itself, thing itself, absolute thing".

[3] The passage "the imperfect ... substitute some 'A'" is from *Morgenstunden* notes pp xxvi–xxvii (var).

is inclosed, bounded; but what is inclosed, considered abstractedly, must be known by that which incloses it; and these are the qualities and properties or the correspondent acts or effects in the percipient.[1] It would be no less absurd therefore to enquire what a thing, that is, an inclosure, is, supposing the inclosure out of the question, as to ask what a circle is, exclusive of its circumference, or a square, exclusive of its sides and angles. I scarcely need warn the reader that the inclosure is here taken metaphorically, or that the external image, or particular in which all words originate, must lose its particularity when its sense is extended. Whatever may be thought of the etymology as an historical point, the sense is out of all doubt: a "thing" in all languages is that which is contained in the answer to the *quale* and the *quantum*.[2] And it is to the perception of the contradiction implied in the extension of the enquiry beyond the *quale* and the *quantum* that has occasioned the third interrogative term, *quid*,[3] under the name "quiddity",[4] to mean anything at once subtle and senseless.

11   In this instance, however, as likewise in the former, there is another sense in which the question might be asked, and to which the preceding reasoning would not apply. It is, however, full and conclusive in reference to the terms in which the question has been stated, of those things, namely, which are considered as objects of our sensations, perceptions, and conceptions, whether they are supposed to arise like the images in certain pieces of clockwork from the mechanism in the mind itself; or as holding the place of the reflection in a glass to the object, or of the object to the reflection; or lastly of the image in a picture to an invisible painter, under which illustrations we may accurately represent the systems of egoism or ultra-idealism; of Locke and Hobbes, and lastly of Berkeley.[5]

12(a)   The third instance: "'Has the universe any motion of place? or can the universe move out of its position, and change its place in empty space?' I ought to speak of this query with some hesitation, for it was proposed by the great Newton himself. And yet

---

[1] A discussion of the particle "ing" appears in a letter on elementary logic C wrote to his son DC in late Nov 1818: *CL* IV 885. Cf also his report of an encounter with Horne Tooke: *TT* 16 Aug 1833.

[2] The "what kind of" and the "how much".

[3] The "what".

[4] The term is used, e.g., by Berkeley *A Treatise* ... and *Three Dialogues Between Hylas and Philonous: B Works* II 75, 256. Cf *TT* 20 Apr 1811.

[5] I.e. the egoism exemplified by Locke and Hobbes, the theory that what "I" perceive conveys adequately the reality perceived; and the ultra-idealism of Berkeley, in which what is perceived by God is, by definition, reality.

it is evident that in order for the question to be answerable, the position 'The universe hath changed its place', must be distinct, and by some intelligent being or other capable of being distinguished from its contrary, 'The universe hath not changed its place'. Now this is impossible by the very terms of the proposition; for in the infinite vacuum there cannot possibly exist any mark by which the portions of space and consequently the differences of the places can be distinguished."[1] More plainly, we need only, as in the former instance, require a definition of the term "place", and when we find that it means no more than the change in the relations of space of one or more bodies to one or more other bodies, it is evident that by excluding the latter half of the definition, namely "other bodies", you destroy the meaning of the whole: for if the universe change its place, it must needs be in relation to some other bodies likewise under relations of space; but then it would be no longer the universe: and "Leibniz was justified in rejecting the question *a priori* as unanswerable".[2] If, however, it should be objected that the universe might change its space, though, supposing such a change, no human or even no angelic understanding could discover or detect the difference, it might perhaps be permitted, as with a smile, to recommend the propriety of suspending the question till it could be proposed to an intellect capable of returning the answer. But it would be wiser and more fruitful to demand of the respondent, which in this case may be one with the querist, by what right he assumes that a superhuman is not at the same time a supersensual intellect? But if supersensual, by what right he is entitled to suppose that a supersensual intellect contemplates the objects under the relations of space or with the predicates of inward and outward distance or proximity? I have said that this would be the more fruitful method, for it would lead us to an investigation of primary and indispensable necessity as the portal and even preliminary of all philosophy—of all speculative investigations, I mean, the object of what is conveyed in the heaven-descended precept, γνωθι σεαυτον.[3]

12(b)　We might increase the number of these instances almost indefinitely; these, however, would be sufficient for our present purpose, were I not tempted by the frequency of its occurrence to

[1] *Morgenstunden*　notes　p xxviii (var).

[2] Ibid p xxviii. See Leibniz and Samuel Clarke *A Collection of Papers . . . Relating to the Principles of Natural Philosophy and Religion* (1717) Leibniz's Fourth Paper §§ 6ff pp 94ff. See below, pp 159–60.

[3] "Know thyself". C is quoting Juvenal *Satires* 11.27—a favourite passage. See below, e.g., pp 143 and 205.

läutert den Grund des Wahren bey der ver=
schieden.n Einbildung sehr wohl. Es sey mir er=
laubt, ein Beyspiel dazu zu geben, mit welchem
ich mir die Sache anschaulich gemacht habe —
Die vierseitige Pyra=
mide A schwebe in der
Luft, so, daß sie von
allen Seiten gleich er=
leuchtet ist, und also
dem Auge nicht die
Vermuthung eines
körperlich.n Umfanges
darbeut, und nun
werde sie aus ver=
schiedenen Standpunkten betrachtet. Der eine
sieht sie gerade von unten in C und sagt: es ist
ein bloßes Viereck; der andere, der sie gerade
von einer Seite in B sieht, sagt: es ist ja ein
Dreyeck; (gleichseitig oder verkürzt, nachdem es
mehr senkrecht oder von der Spitze zu betrachtet
wird) ein Dritter sieht zwo Seiten D, es sind
zwey rechtwinklicht zusammengefügte Dreyecke —
Nein: nach E vielmehr zwey ungleiche Drey=
ecke — nach F ein Dreyeck mit angehängtem
Trapezio — nach G ein durchkreuztes Viereck
— nach H ein längliches Viereck, in drey Drey=
ecke abgetheilt — nach I drey ungleiche Dreyecke.
Alle diese und noch mehr Abänderungen lassen
sich

3. The example of a suspended pyramid in Moses Mendelssohn
Morgenstunden (Frankfurt & Leipzig 1790) notes p xvi. See p 117.

The British Library; reproduced by kind permission

add one other, different, however, from the preceding inasmuch as the questions are all answerable if only we take the preparatory caution of ascertaining all the senses in which the words may be used and to answer each separately: that if one answer only were demanded, the question would belong to the former class, and be fairly put aside by the old tale of the tailor who was required to make a suit of clothes for the moon which should fit her through her phases.[1] I think I have given the example elsewhere, but it deserves to be impressed on the memory, and for this reason I will repeat it more at large as I find it in the prelections[2] of the excellent Mendelssohn.

13(a) "Let a four-sided pyramid A be supposed to float in the air so as to receive the light equally on all sides and consequently not suggesting the notion of its solid figure and contents to the eye of the spectator. We will suppose eight or nine spectators in different positions, and the question afterwards arises what shape the phenomenon had. The one had stood just underneath at C and declares that it was a proper square; a second who stood just on the one side, *vide* B, assures them that it was a triangle that they had seen, whether equilateral or otherwise according as he had contemplated it more perpendicular[ly] or from the point downward. A third, D, saw two sides, and affirms the figure to have consisted of two right-angled triangles applied to each other. 'Nay', exclaims a fourth, E, 'two triangles there were, but two unequal triangles'. The fifth, F, has seen a triangle with a trapezium hung to it. A sixth, G, a quadrangle with a cross. A seventh, [H], a parallelogram divided into three triangles. The eighth, I, declared himself to have seen three unequal triangles. *ª*The student in perspective is aware that many more positions might be imagined."[3]

13(b) Now let us suppose the question to be, assuming no known difference in the competence and integrity of the eight contending evidences, which of these was the true figure. It is evident that in each the answer might be either "this" or "not this", and, to all collectively, "all and none". How, then, should we proceed? Contradic-

---

ª New paragraph in ms

[1] Traditional. Cf Burton *Anatomy of Melancholy* pt 1 sect 3 mem 1 subsect 4: "you may as well make the Moon a new coat, as a true character of a melancholy man . . .". C may have noticed its occurrence in Horne Tooke Ἔπεα πτερόεντα I 46.

[2] For *Vorlesungen.*

[3] *Morgenstunden* notes pp xvi–xvii. C also uses the example in a letter to Edward Coleridge on 27 Jul 1826 (*CL* VI 597) and in 1829 included the letter as an appendix in *On the Constitution of the Church and State* (*C&S—CC—* 178–9). See Illustration 3, facing this page.

tions cannot be true, and there is no possible way of avoiding a contradiction in this instance but on the supposition that there are two senses involved in the word "figure" in the question "Which is the true figure?", and our first endeavour must be to discover the possibility of this generally and then [to turn] to the application of the difference so discovered in the particular case. The general possibility has been already given in the different senses [?φαινομενα, νους], object and subject, objective and subjective; and in applying this difference to the particular case we shall have to examine in which of the senses of the terms we should be entitled to reply that B, C, D, etc, are objectively false but subjectively true. First we shall find that the term "subjective" is not used in any defective sense, in which, indeed, the word "true" itself would become equivocal: e.g., suppose the question instead of [to the] figure had related to the colour of an object, and that one of the dissentients had seen it as yellow or in that colour which is produced by the insensibility of the eye to blue. Here we might indeed say that the person had answered truly, but scarcely that the answer was true, or truth and veracity would be confounded, or the question at least would be shifted, viz. from "What colour is that object L?", to the query "Did the object L appear to the person M?"

14   There are then two modes of subjective perception, the one, which is in congruity with the object and finds its explanation in that object taken conjointly with its possible relations: and the other, in which the perception, that is, the phenomenon resulting from the perception, has no proper cause in the object, but must be explained, not merely by the opposition of subject and subjective to object and objective, but by the peculiarity of the individual subject. In the former instance the absence of all such peculiarities is taken for granted. The answers are therefore supposed to be subjectively true, and therefore the question leading to the final answer must be, "What figure is that which, being taken objectively, though different from any of the figures seen, will yet account for them all as the necessary consequences of the real figure under each particular relation?" And this, though in reality it might never have been, or be capable of being, an object of immediate vision for any human being, as, for instance, the true magnitudes of the sun, Jupiter, and the fixed stars, is yet not only an object of human experience, distinguishing it from mere images, and the fleeting stream of impressions connected with the sensation of their outwardness.

15   Having once mastered this general distinction, and having[a]

---

[a] ms: to have

filled up the outline sufficiently so as to put us in possession of the possible difference in the application of the terms, a new sense will arise in all or the greater number of the preceding instances, and this too of such importance as to leave no doubt of the correspondent use and necessity of tracing these differences, those, I mean, of the objective in the object, and of the subjective under the generic term of the subject, to their sources, and as far as is possible to causes and occasions. We have seen one proof of this in the question respecting the change of place of the material universe, and we may find another in our second instance; and for the more close investigation into this point we have an additional motive, inasmuch as the answer, or rather the negation of all possible answer, which, applied to things as phenomena, whether considered as outward images or impressions therefrom, as*a* true and conclusive, might give occasion to a dangerous error, if it were returned to the question, "What are things in themselves, as contradistinguished from appearances?" Nay! the most noticeable stratagem of the present age, the true *sophisma pigrum*, or sophistry of indolence,[1] and mode of justifying ourselves in the indisposition to any energy of reflection, much more to the yet higher effort of beholding the truths that have not even their origin in the senses, and in the contemplation of which the senses afford us either no assistance or an ambiguous and unsafe one, may be referred to one or other of the two maxims, the use of which we have ourselves exemplified in the instance preceding. The first is the way of settling the question by denying the difference, or in other words by reducing the difference to a mere difference of words. How often and in what self-complacent terms have I heard men, who had never troubled themselves with the first elements of self-knowledge, who had never looked at a Plato or an Aristotle, or any of their celebrated compeers in later times, except on a shelf, assure their auditors that all the points noted by the metaphysicians were mere disputes about words, utter logomachy, and these the men who would have stood silent to the simple question: "What do you mean by a word, or has it any other meaning than that of an articulated sound? Or lines in various connection or juxtaposition representing the same?" For should there be another and higher meaning, namely the meaning itself, should the word differ from the mind only as the breeze differs from

a ms: is

[1] Of which Leibniz gives a clear and amusing illustration in his *Theo-* *dicée* pt I § 55.

the air—should it, I say, mean the truth, contemplated as conveyed and communicated, and the truth itself be a living power, or, to bring all to the one point, should two diverse things be included in the common term "definition", which in one therefore must be the essence of the thing and in the other the mere accident, namely an articulated sound or[a] its visual representative, should the ῥήματα (flowing sounds) which are not λογοι (intelligible words) be distinguished from the latter, whether appearing with the accident of the former or otherwise, and, lastly, should all words have their ground and highest source in the "Word"[b] that was from the beginning,[1] it might appear that a dispute, if by dispute serious and earnest discussion only be meant, that a dispute concerning words is the most important subject on which the mind of man could exert its reasoning powers, a contemplation [c]worthy [of a Bruno],[d][2] and which might remind the objector and the educated worldling, wherever he be, of the truth that we do not live by bread alone, but by every word which cometh from the mouth of God.[3]

16   But I have been led unintentionally into too high a strain, and perhaps ill suited to a subject in the treatment of which the mind should not only remain dispassionate, but even free from emotion, however ennobling the latter might be on its own account and in its own connections. Neither is it from worldlings only, or as an excuse for indolence, or a trick by which ignorance is transformed into a merit, that we hear the same maxim from many excellent and intelligent persons who have taken up their notions of the Schoolmen and even of their master Aristotle on hearsay, or from books that have copied from copyists and repeated for the hundredth time the repeaters of Lord Bacon's assertions, and even men of philosophic minds, but who have taken up their first grounds too superficially, or at all events not at the true depth, have for the last century and more accustomed themselves to a mode of thinking and expression exactly coincident with the following sentence of Mendelssohn, himself an amiable and every way respectable representative of the class last mentioned. "You are aware", says he, "how inclined I am to consider the controversies of the philosophic schools as mere

---

[a] ms: of   [b] Ms lacks closing quotation marks
[c-d] ms: worthy   (I. Bruno) ["I. Bruno" inserted in a cramped and possibly different hand]

[1] John 1.1.
[2] I.e. of a philosopher concerned with reconciling opposites. For C's knowledge of Bruno, see Alice D. Snyder "Coleridge on Giordano Bruno" *MLN* XLII (1927) 427–36. See also Dorothea W. Singer *Giordano Bruno His Life and Thought* ... (New York 1950) 196–200.
[3] Matt 4.4 (var).

disputes about words, or at least to trace them up to some logomachy as their original first source."[a1] How predominant this maxim was in the mind of this philosopher may be seen in almost every page of his work; in all the polemic passages, I mean. I do not hesitate, however, in coincidence with the founder of the critical philosophy, of which Mendelssohn witnessed the dawn only, to express a very different and almost the opposite conviction.[2] I believe that the existence and number of false synonyms, that is, of different words in the same language used to convey the same meaning, as well as the opposite but always accompanying evil of one and the same word used at different times to convey very different senses, have been and are the growth of later times; and that the countervailing excellence we in no small measure owe to the labours of these supposed logomachists, the logicians, theologians, and divines from the thirteenth to the sixteenth century; but that the possibility of the remedy and the means of administering it were given by their labours and are to be found in the study of their works. I know of no controversy of any long continuance or which had excited any strong interest in the mind of the learned world that can be fairly reduced to a mere dispute on terms. On the contrary, whatever imperfections had previously existed in the language, whether in the Latin or vernacular tongue, these controversies were the surest and most efficient means and occasions of their removal, by forcing the controversialists to compare the term with the thought that had been conveyed or the object intended, and trying the consequences by this test, that is, truing them up to the thought or object from which they legitimately followed, to perceive the differences of the thoughts, and the correspondent necessity of a difference in the terms. But the difference of the thought once secured and in any language once fixed becomes a mark and a guide for all other languages.

17   The old mapmakers were allowed the privilege to fill up the interior of Africa with giants or pygmies, mountain or abyss, griffins, elephants, and wildernesses of land rendered doubly unin-

---

[a]   Closing quotation marks inserted

[1] Untraced. The sentiment, if not this wording, does appear in Mendelssohn: "Es wäre nicht die erste berühmte Streitfrage, um welche die Menschen sich veruneinigt, ja einander gehasst und verfolgt haben, und die am Ende auf eine blosse Wortfehde hinauslief" ("It would not have been the first famous subject of controversy over which people have fallen out, indeed have hated and persecuted one another, and which in the end resulted in an empty quarrel about words"). *Morgenstunden* 118–19.

[2] See, e.g., Kant *C d r V* 368–9 (309–10).

habitable by monstrous serpents. A liberty not altogether unlike this, the critics and metaphysicians of the last century and more have taken with the writers of the Middle Ages; or it would be incomprehensible how the charge could have originated against the Schoolmen and the earlier reformers, of neglect and laxity in the definition and discrimination of their terms. It is impossible to turn over fifty pages of any one of the Scholastic commentators on these sentences and not to perceive that the fault that might truly be laid to their charge lies in the opposite extreme—excessive anxiety in the detection and display of distinctions almost always just and subtle, but too often unfruitful.[*] It might seem as if the whole mass were crystallising into needles. I am not ignorant, nor unwilling to concede, that their premises too often stand in contrast with the process, as must needs be the case when the first ground is not taken at a right and sufficient depth: though even in this respect it would not be difficult to give the most convincing proof, by a series of instances containing the most important subjects of human disquisition, that[b] they are superior to the age that succeeded them, almost to our own days, in all questions properly philosophical, or when the subject does not consist in the objects or notices of the bodily sense. When, however, facts or matter of fact are concerned, the student would find it neither uninstructive nor unamusing to compare (I will not send him so far back as to the masters of the school, no, nor even to the systematised divines of the fifteenth or the former half of the sixteenth century), let him compare a volume of miscellaneous tracts published during the interval from the death of Elizabeth to the Restoration with a similar volume from the last century. I am much mistaken if there should not be found at least as marked a superiority in the logical connection of the sentences, in the correct use of the conjunctions and other exponents of the connecting acts in the mind, in short as marked a superiority in the propriety of the statement and the legitimacy of the consequences on the part of the elder writers as there is of good sense and accurate observation in those of our contemporaries.

18(a) From this digression, though in common justice I ought rather to term it a prolongation of the subject, we will return by

[*] For the point in question at least, but still most useful not only in possibility but by the actual effects in the gradual perfecting of language (and that which [is] the principal means of improvement in every language, in the desynonymising of words),[a] or by the disquisitions preparatory to the same.

 a Parentheses inserted   *b* ms. redundantly: that even, in this respect giving one striking example of the fallacy concealed in the maxim which occasioned these remarks, viz. that the controversies of most note [on] which the schools of philosophy and divinity have been divided are reducible to mere disputes in words. The same Mendelssohn from whose *Morning Hours* we have quoted this maxim[1] has applied it to the great and inveterate question or controversy on freedom and necessity, which whole dispute he would reduce to a mere equivocation in the word "must", or, as we might as well or better express it in our own language, to a neglect in distinguishing the difference between compulsion and obligation, a physical and a moral necessity.[2] But this is attempting to stop an inundation of the Danube or Ganges with a hay-band or a bundle of straw. It is most true that such an equivocation did exist, and perhaps in the minds of too many may exist still in the term "necessity" and, till the reign of Charles II, even in the word "compulsion". And Hobbes repeatedly speaks of the will as compelled by certain causes where an accurate speaker would now say impelled by such and such motives or tendencies.[3] But this ambiguity has long ceased to exist among men conversant with the history of this celebrated controversy and at all entitled to renew it, and its removal having been effected by and in consequence of the controversy furnishes a proof in point that the most noted questions in philosophy not only are not mere logomachies easily reconciled by showing that, though both parties use the same word, yet each understood it in a different sense, and thus that, like the two knights respecting the gold and silver target on the signpost, both were right;[4] but that the discussion of such questions is one of the most probable means of detecting and disarming all equivocal terms. And whether the controversy ends by the solution of the problem, or is still carrying on the pursuit, or is fairly tired out, yet it is almost sure during its continuance to remedy some one or

[1] C's only direct reference in the *Logic* to the *Morgenstunden.*

[2] *Jerusalem oder überreligiöse Macht und Judenthum* (Frankfurt & Leipzig 1791) 5–12. C's copy in the BM is bound with the *Morgenstunden.*

[3] C is drawing on *Jerusalem* 12 here. A favourite example: cf *BL* ch 4 (1907) I 64n and *P Lects* Lect 5 (1949) 174.

[4] Cf C's note on a flyleaf of Jacob Rhenferd *Opera philologica . . .* (Utrecht 1722) (BM copy): "The controversy . . . was like that of the gold and silver shield—the phrase meant either—and which of the two must be determined by the context." The fable of "The Party-colour'd Shield" appears in Sir Harry Beaumont [Joseph Spence] *Moralities: or, Essays, Letters, Fables; and Translations* (1753) 99–102; its moral is, "never enter into any Dispute . . . till you have fairly consider'd each Side of the Question". The story was a commonplace, however; see WW *Prelude* XI 79–82 and Scott *The Antiquary* (Edinburgh 1816) I 133.

more imperfections, and, as no important question having been once started can ever be more than suspended except by the discovery of a satisfactory answer, to shorten the labour and direct the attention of those who may recommence it, and to render our conceptions clear and more distinct even when it has failed in giving deeper insight or an enlargement of view.

18(b)　The several modes by which this is effected form one of the most important parts in the logic of discussion and can be here introduced only by anticipation. One mode is that of stating the question in a higher formula, that is, in such terms as to comprehend both of the two or more senses contained in the equivocal term complained of, and this was the mode adopted in the present instance —whether the occurrences in the world under which term the voluntary actions of men are comprised are or are not determined in the series of the antecedent causes. Now this is evidently no longer a mere strife of words, but a question of profoundest interest, which in all ages it has excited wherever the duty and tendency of self-knowledge is felt and allowed.

19　So much for the first maxim, which, we may be permitted to add, is calculated to produce different effects in different characters. To the idle and vain it furnishes a self-complacency with a pretext and a disguise for mental ignorance and a self-complacency in the ignorance resulting: but to individuals of active minds, more acute than subtle and not more agile than desultory, minds more delighted with the pursuit than intent on the truth pursued and fonder of beating up for the game than of being in at the death, it too often seduces into sophistry.

20　The works, but particularly the dictionary, of the celebrated Bayle furnish abundant instances how easily a man of an acute, quick, and discursive intellect in his eagerness to detect logomachy falls himself into the more dangerous fault of logodaedalism, that is, verbal sleight-of-hand and word-trickery.[1] He brings as it were two meanings together on a damp or sinking ground and when they run exclaims, "See, they are both one and the same."

21(a)　Before we conclude our reflections on this first maxim, there is one other caution to be noticed, of yet greater practical

---

[1] Pierre Bayle *Dictionaire historique et critique* (Rotterdam 1697). C mentions elsewhere Bayle's "acuteness and dexterity in the management of words and tricks of argument" (BM MS Egerton 2801 f 3), and calls him "the Founder and Father of Modern Scepticism and religious Indifference" (f 2ᵛ). Cf *AR* (1825) 119, BM MS Egerton 2801 ff 50 and 74ᵛ, and the early references in *CN* ɪ 277 and n, and 280.

importance and frequency of application: before we can safely decide whether a controversy is fairly reducible to a dispute about words, we ought to understand clearly and distinctly what is meant by "words", even when a word is proved equivocal and when the delusion is effected by placing the word in one sense in the premise while the conclusion [follows] from or on the supposition of the other. "Ridentem dicere verum/ Quid vetat?"[1] The mere wish of relieving the subject might be a sufficient apology if from the crowd that present themselves to the mind I select a trivial and ridiculous instance in preference, but in truth I have other and more serious purposes in view, and such preference forms part of my plan, for reasons which I shall hereafter explain. To the instance, however. A country squire, one of the reverend vegetables[*] so exquisitely portrayed in the 86th No. of the *Tatler*, having for the first time left his home, far inland, for Ramsgate, had been further tempted to join a sailing party in a trip to Calais. From the state of the weather the opposite coast was invisible till within a league of Calais. Our worthy voyager still keeping his face toward old England, when all at once the mists dissolved and the French cliffs bursting on the view, the master of the boat turned him suddenly round, exclaiming: "There Sir! that's France!" "You don't say so", quoth the Squire, "That's France! and pray, which is Spain?"[3] Now here it is pretty evident that the words "France" and "Spain" were both equivocal, each had two meanings, one the country so called, the other the portions of paper in the map of Europe or the world representing those countries, and that the good gentleman had started with the former, but was overtaken by the latter, that is, by the feeling that had been habitually associated with the image in the map and probably by some dim and imperfect relict of the image itself; but a moment's reflection will make it equally evident that the origin and proper cause of this blunder is to be sought for in the failure, irregular action, and faulty habit of the recollective, comparing, combining, and

[*] "I met him with all the respect due to so reverend a vegetable, for you are to know, that is my sense of a person who remains idle in the same place for half a century."[2]

[1] Horace *Satires* 1.1.24–5. Tr H. R. Fairclough (LCL 1966) 7: "what is to prevent one from telling truth as he laughs . . .".

[2] *Tatler* No 86 (27 Oct 1709).

[3] C heard the story told of Sir Gregory Page Turner (*CL* IV 942: 12 May 1819). He writes: "I would have given half a crown for such a Story when I was at Jesus. It is really an excellent one—I picked it up at Sir George Beaumont's last Monday." Sir Gregory (1748–1805) also appears in *The Watchman*, speaking in a debate on dog tax. *Watchman* (*CC*) 257.

concluding faculties, and above all in the too habitual passiveness of the mind to the automatic trains of the memory and the fancy, the sequency of which is mechanically determined by accidental proximity of time and place in the original impressions (*vide Friend*, volume third, page 138),[1] and that the words are merely the modes in which the errors in thought are conveyed and expressed, and so far from being in the first instance causes of the confusion the preexistence of such confusion is*a* the *conditio sine qua non of their own existence as equivocations.*

21(b)   Nor can we rest here, for it is in the exposure and detection of these ambiguities that we have the best means of making men sensible of the faulty and relaxed state of their intellectual powers and functions, not only in individual instances but to the enlightening of the public mind with and by the improvement of the general language. Were I asked what the most effective means would be, I should answer, as I have elsewhere already done, "a dictionary constructed on the one only philosophical principle, which, regarding words as living growths, offlets, and organs of the human soul, seeks to trace each historically through all the periods of its natural growth and accidental modifications".[2] A work worthy of a royal and imperial confederacy, and which would indeed hallow the science! A work which, executed for*b* any one language, would yet be a benefaction to the world, and to the nation itself a source of immediate honour and ultimate *weal* beyond the power of victories to bestow or the mines of Mexico to purchase. The realisation of this scheme lies in the far distance, but in the meantime it cannot but beseem every individual competent to its furtherance to contribute a small portion of the materials for the future temple, from a polished column to a hewn stone, or a plank for the scaffolding; and as they come in, to erect with them sheds for the workmen and tempo[ra]ry structures for present use.

22(a)   The second maxim will not long detain us, but the observation*c* which it suggests is most important. When, says the selfpresumed advocate of common sense, you have been told what a thing does or suffers, how it acts and how it is acted on, there is no sense in asking further what the thing is: it can have no answer because it is, properly speaking, no question. As by means of the former maxim the majority of the most celebrated philosophical

---

a ms: as   *b* ms: from   *c* ms: observations

[1] *Friend* (*CC*) I 456. C refers to the 1818 ed.   [2] See p 58, above. Cf *BL* ch 12 (1907) I 165n and, above, p 15 n 3.

disputes are settled by compromise, by means of the second maxim the remainder are to be got rid of by a nonsuit.[a] In the first instance, now, in the form in which we cautiously stated the question, this answer, or rather denial of the possibility of any answer, is strictly just. What the student has now to impress on his mind is that the question was purely logical, and not philosophical; for logic, we have long learnt, consists in the abstraction from all objects. It is wholly and purely subjective, and though in the preceding statement we had left it to the choice of the proposer whether he should say impressions and sensations, or properties and qualities,[b] nothing is more easy than to demonstrate that the latter are reducible to the former. As far as the understanding and the senses, or, comprising both in one, as far as experience alone is concerned, the least reflection will convince us that these qualities and properties supposed to inhere in, or proceed from, outward things are a mere inference from our sensations and impressions in connection with the forms of the mind, which it is supposed are called into action by them; but that this hypothesis is nothing philosophical, that is, that it has no respect to any reality independent of the mind or comprehending both the mind and outward nature, may be readily proved by substituting the mere term "cause" for these supposed qualities and properties, and the position would stand thus. The understanding is under the necessity of applying the notion of cause to all the images and thoughts on which it reflects, and when these cannot be referred to any volition of the mind itself, [to] the notion of an external cause. But this notion is itself abstracted from the forms of the understanding and consequently purely subjective. How else could it be accounted for, that this supposed object is in all instances one and the same with the supposed impression, and even in the images of memory a perfect duplicate? Can anything be more evident [than] that this hypothetical object is a mere projection of the image in the mind, not indeed ordinarily detected as long as the individual is in a similar state with that of other individuals around him, but recognised at once in fever, delirium, and even in dreams?

22(b) This remark contains the true answer to the Berkeleyan system.[c] It professes to be a subjective philosophy, the *perceptum* subsisting in the *percipi*,[1] and all the phenomena attributed to some outward reality under the name of nature or the material world

---

[a] Ms unpunctuated   [b] Full stop in ms   [c] Comma in ms

[1] The "thing perceived" subsisting in the "fact that it is perceived".

being mere modifications of the percipient's own being.*a* Now we reply that this may be logic; but it cannot be philosophy inasmuch as herein alone consists the difference between logic and philosophy, that the latter seeks for a truth which is not merely subjective. But again, though the Berkeleyan scheme, most inappropriately called Idealism, is logic in the extensive sense of the word, it is far, however, from being either a system or a science of logic, were it only that it takes its ground in the sensations, that is, in modes of consciousness that are utterly heterogeneous both from the understanding and from the pure forms of the sense. *Dantur non intelliguntur.*[1] Add to this that the deduction of visual forms from the mere cessation or diminished intensity of the stimulus of colour is one skimmed from the mere surface of the mechanical philosophy and which the admirable author would have rejected with contempt at a later period of his life, while at the same time it is an *argumentum in circulo,*[2] for as the sensations subsist only in the sentient, and as colour, according to Berkeley, is a sensation, it is evident that cause and effect are one and the same thing. To be sure, nothing can be more simple in appearance than the series of proof in support of this scheme. All sensations subsist in the sentient exclusively. All perceptions are modes of sensation, and all appearances are mere perceptions. (Their essence consists in being perceived.)*b* But by external nature which man knows, or is capable of knowing, we mean only the aggregate of appearance, therefore the so-called external nature subsists in the sentient and is merely and altogether subjective. Pity that the constructor of this scheme had not furnished us with his proof of the first position,[3] on which all that follow, together with the context, depend.

23   It is certainly no part of our immediate consciousness, and as little is it any part of the general belief of mankind, much less is it an universal belief, which it should be to be of any force at all in the present question. Now if instead of the assumption that the perceptions are forms of sensation we should take perception as the generic term and assume that sensation is a form or mode of perception, viz. a simple perception, or perception confined to one object, which

---

a Ms unpunctuated   *b* Ms unpunctuated

[1] "They are given, not understood". Cf below, p 162.

[2] "Circular argument".

[3] I.e. that "all sensations subsist in the sentient exclusively". See Berkeley

A Treatise Concerning the Principles of Human Knowledge: B Works II 42f. C's warmth comes from finding Berkeley trying to confute materialism with an inadequate argument.

in this case is the percipient's own being, while those involving the act of comparison and which may be called complex are perceptions commonly so called, the whole superstructure of Berkeleyanism would fall. Now we are perfectly entitled to do this, for the defect, if it be such, of removing the diversity which the common sense of mankind finds between sensation and perception, feeling and seeing, is common to both assumptions; the[a] results of the former are in direct contradiction to the universal and involuntary faith of man, while those of the latter would be found in perfect coincidence with it.

24 Add to this that the latter hypothesis has this advantage over the Berkeleyan in the very outset, that in agreement with common sense and all known languages it makes "feel" and "see" verbs active with a distinct objective case; while the philosophers who assert that all perceptions are to be resolved into sensations, and that sensations are but modifications of the sentient, ought not if they spoke consequentially to say, "I see a chair", but "I see or I see myself in the form of a chair", "to see", "hear", "touch", etc, being with them verbs reflex and intransitive.

25 Returning, however, to the second maxim, the validity of which we have admitted in all questions purely logical, but that it would be of false and most dangerous application if assumed as universally true, it would be only necessary for us to reflect on the way in which we form our idea of God as the highest intelligence. We contemplate in Him, pure, perfect, and proper reality, a something which is not merely real in opposition to pure negation of reality, but in opposition to the apparent, or phenomenal. Thus the motion of the sun, its rising and setting, are real appearances (*realitas phaenomenon*), but Copernicus, Kepler, and Newton[1] have taught all but the most ignorant that they are not the true reality. I beg leave to draw the student's attention more particularly to this remark, viz. that the opposition of real to not real, or mere nothing, is verbal and belongs to the grammar and the dictionary, not to logic; or to philosophy, if it were anything, it should be called the contrary of reality, not the opposite; but reality can have no contrary, and in accurate language we should say that "unreal" is the contrary word to the word "real". All opposites, like the extreme points of all lines,

a ms: while the

[1] For C's opinion of the relationship of Kepler to Newton, see *AR* (1825)   393–4 and *TT* 8 Oct 1830.

must have a mid-term common to both. Now in the present case reality itself is that mid-term; for what can we think of antecedent to reality out of which reality might proceed or be evolved? But this granted, we can at once perceive the nature of the two opposites, viz. substantial reality and apparent reality. A full illustration of which we have given in a preceding page in the example of the suspended pyramid.[1] Equally evident is it that all which we receive through the senses must belong to the latter kind, and indeed we comprise them all under the common name of *phaenomena*, that is, "appearances". It is probable that [the explanation of] the adoption of the Greek term when a term exactly corresponding was found in our own language and this too a word in common use, viz. "appearances", is that this word itself comprises, or rather is equally applied to, two species:[a] appearances that belong to mankind generally and constitute the common world of the senses and which under the name *phaenomena* we distinguish from appearances that result from accidents and peculiarities of the individual subject, and which therefore we do not honour with the name of real in either sense, but consider as closely bordering on pure nothingness, in the subtle language of the old Scholists as *non entia tantum non vere non entia*,[2] that is, nonentities that are only not quite not[b] absolute nonentities or[b] nothings next door to utter nothing.

26   A ghost and a shadow supply an apposite illustration. The shadow is a real phenomenon, though not a substantial reality. A ghost is a mere appearance, a fancy or disease of the individual beholder. But in the idea of the Supreme Reality we dismiss all that is phenomenal. He is invisible essentially and, in one word, absolutely supersensual; but, though we attribute to Him neither heat, nor cold, nor colour, nor shape, nor hardness, nor softness, is our idea merely negative? Does it consist in the abstract term "reality" without knowing what we mean by it, save only that we do not mean any one of all the realities of which we have any conception? Do we not far rather attribute to him intelligence, will, bliss, power, etc? We attribute these indeed to God in their absoluteness without limit in extension and unfathomable; but diminish these in the degree as much as you will, still they remain the same in essence, realities that are not phenomena, that are not appearances in any sense, even in the highest and that which comprehends all human beings, e.g. the aspect of the solar system as seen by an eye supposed to be placed in

a Full stop in ms   *b* ms: and

[1] See above, p 117.   [2] E.g. Duns Scotus.

the sun, which are not therefore merely subjective, for they must be presumed in order to conceive the existence of the subject; and as their substance or quality is not changed by differences in their degree, they may be attributed to other beings as well as to the Supreme; and in these therefore we possess properties of things, or rather the things in themselves, which are not only capable of being thought of, but which present the worthiest, nay, the only worthy, objects of the thoughts of a wise man, inasmuch as all others, if not directly or indirectly in reference to these as the ultimate aim, are vanity of vanities,[1] the dreams of an individual or the dreams of a multitude.

27   Still, however, our former speculation is not hollow, nor without its practical uses. Still it remains true that these realities, the first and the last of philosophy, are not objects of logic and therefore cannot be submitted to a discussion or reasoning purely logical. This for many reasons, one of which will suffice for the present and is, indeed, the only one suited to the present stage of our investigation. They cannot be submitted to logical reasoning because they are of necessity presumed and presupposed in the very first step, as the student will now recollect to have been proved by us in our analysis of the syllogism respecting the force of the copula "is" in every logical position, which communicates the reality to the subject and predicate. Before we could proceed to the sources of falsehood in subjects properly logical, it was necessary, for a moral expedience ought to be considered as a necessity, to establish those truths which, being transcendent to logic, are not deducible from it, and which because they could not be fairly deduced, and because every attempt so to do has been proved fallacious and sophistical, have been themselves regarded, nay! treated, as falsehoods. The first source therefore of falsehood in logic is the abuse and misapplication of logic itself. But if not of the understanding, of what other power are these truths the besetting objects? This is the question with which this second division of our work will end, the answer to it forming[a] the contents and subject of the third and last.[2]

---

a Remainder of sentence in Green's hand on the following page (II 174)

[1] Eccles 1.2.   [2] I.e. the projected organon again.
                                      See above, pp 57, 100.

^aCHAPTER [II]

On the Discussion of the PREMISES
in All Logical Reasoning

1(a)   What in ordinary language we call the "premises" of an argu-
ment is expressed technically by the major and minor of the syllo-
gism. Independent of the subject and the predicate, and, indeed, in a
certain sense antecedent to them, the student's attention was drawn
to the copula which, connecting both, asserts the reality of the whole;
and this copula we found expressed by the verb substantive, "is".
In what this reality consists was likewise declared, viz. that it con-
tained a truth which being antecedent to the act of reflection, and
of course therefore to all other acts and functions of the under-
standing, asserted a being transcendent to the individual subject in
all cases and therefore to all subjects thinking under the same laws.
Of this primary reality we discovered two sources—one above the
reflective and discursive powers,^b the other below them. The one was
the reason, and the other the impressions from the senses. Concern-
ing the reason, we have in the preceding chapter spoken sufficiently
for the purpose which we had in view, which was, to satisfy the claims
of morality, and secondly to prevent, though at the price of anticipa-
tion, any misunderstanding (which by the way is as often occasioned
by the absence of an important truth as by the presence of an error
or falsehood). We have therefore now to treat of the latter source,
viz. the senses.

1(b)   And yet a knot of uncommon difficulty meets us here at the
very outset, of such difficulty indeed that, if the reader will excuse
an apparent contradiction, resulting from the necessary inade-
quacy^c of every metaphor (*simile non est idem*, or as we say, no
likeness goes on all fours),[1] it must be first cut in order that it may
afterwards be untied.^d[2] We have used the term, "impressions on or

---

^a Transcriber A resumes at this point   ^b Colon in ms
^c ms: ~~dis~~⟨in⟩adequacy [correction resembles Green's hand]
^d ms: ~~united~~ ⟨untied⟩ [correction by Green]

[1] Cf above, p 11 n 4, and below,   [2] The Gordian knot. Cf p 235,
p 143.   below.

through the senses"; but what is impressed, as far as we have hither-to seen is[a] not the forms; for these the purely subjective nature of our science has compelled us to place in the mind itself, that is to say, either in the forms of the pure sense or in the forms and functions of the understanding, both which by a coarse metaphor indeed, but not more coarse or imperfect than the diversity between mental and material objects rendered inevitable, we attempted to explain by considering them as primary moulds or forms, conceived as the cause and origin of all shape, and consequently not subject to the necessity of having any shape of their own to be explained; for it would be absurd to speak of shape respecting a subject which we have assumed[b] as the antecedent of all shape, and not less contradictory than the question of ignorant atheists: "What was done during the time before time had a beginning?"[1]

2 If not the shapes of objects, what remains? Shall we answer, a sensation which, though of necessity inherent in the sentient subject itself, the subject cannot refer to any act or volition of its own and which being accompanied with the sense[c] of contingency and its succession being altogether irreducible to the spontaneous processes of the mind carried on under the law of association, seems to authorise, but at all events compels, us to consider in reference to something self-subsistent and present to us as other from ourselves and no less real. Such is the faith in the existence of an external[d] world, a faith confessedly pre-existent to, and, indeed, presupposed in, the arguments by which it is confirmed.[2]

3 We refer these sensations to objects without us; can we then divide or practically[e] distinguish the one from the other? I have a peculiar sensation, as, for instance, a thrill or any other feeling, and then infer that a table or house[f] is present and acting on me.[g] In all the objects with which the intellect is principally concerned, the very contrary is the known fact. In the impressions of sight as long as they remain healthful there is no appreciable sensation at all, and to distinguish the sensation in its latent mode of existence all languages have adopted a different word. And we say a sense[h] of sight and

---

a ms: ⟨are⟩ [added probably by Green]   *b* ms: assur⟨m⟩ed [correction probably by Green]
    c ms: ⟨sense⟩ [Green's hand over an obliterated word]
d ms: e⟨x⟩ternal [Green's correction?]   *e* ~~particularly~~⟨ractically⟩ [correction by Green]
              f ms: horse   *g* ms: us.
    h ms: ⟨sense⟩ [probably in Green's hand over an obliterated word]

---

1 Cf *CN* iii 3763 and n, where a version of this question is traced to St Augustine *City of God* 12.15 as being beyond "even the greatest fool ...".

2 Cf *BL* ch 12 (1907) i 177–8 and Schelling *System des transcendentalen Idealismus* 343–4.

[?cavil]*a* at a visual sensation as only not a contradiction. As little, on the other hand, can we in any particular instance detect or separate the share contributed by the mind itself, though, as in the kaleidoscope, we may have had it satisfactorily demonstrated how large a portion of all that we behold is given by the organ or machine itself.[1] What then remains but that in the first instance we should take the objects as universal nature and our own conjointly present then*b* to us? Enough that we have learnt that the unity in which all form and whatever can be called a whole must consist is not dependent on any power that we can call ourself. That whether in the mind or out of the mind or both at once, it is a nature and the only reality of objects considered in the primary antithesis of object and subject. It may not indeed be the primary reality, for in this the distinction of object and subject does not exist; but though in this sense a secondary and so far a derivative reality, we might even already anticipate that it would be found one and the same with the reality of the reason, and that the difference will be found in the different relations to the individual subject.

4　Our first rule, therefore, may be termed the rule of common sense, *nihil in intellectu quod non prius in sensu.*[2] In other words, that the objects must have been perceived aright before they can be rightly conceived, and, as a corollary, that they must have been rightly conceived before we can form legitimate abstraction or generalisation, and in like manner that we must have rightly abstracted and accurately generalised before we are in the condition of attaching appropriate abstract or general terms to the conceptions.

5(a)　Does nature, however, for by this term we have agreed to understand the cause and substance of all reality apprehensible by the senses and cognisable by the understanding—does nature, I say, present these objects to us without exciting any act on our part, does she present them under all circumstances perfect and, as it were, ready-made? Such may [be] the notion of the most unthinking; for even with these it is too opposite to their own experience to be a distinct belief: but our readers need direct their*c* attention, were it only to have the power of recognising it, or, as the phrase is, to bring it under their*b* cognisance when perceived; but the very senses

a Blank space left in ms　　　*b* for "them"?　　　*c* ms: our

[1] Cf *AR* (1825) 258n; *TT* 14 Apr 1833.

[2] Traditional summation of Aristotelian thought: "there is nothing in the understanding which was not previously in the sense". (C's tr; see below, p 226.) Cf pp 183-4, below, *BL* ch 9 (1907) 1 93, and *AR* (1825) 73.

by which we are to perceive will each again require the aid of a previous scientific insight—anatomical, physiological, and physical. Take, for example, the act of beholding: the instrumental agent of vision, viz. light, with its laws and properties, give[s] birth to the science of optics; yet these laws cannot be safely applied without an acquaintance with the laws and properties of the atmosphere together with the nature of vapours and their varying densities; and this again will be imperfect and insecure if the nature of transparence, translucence, and of transparent and translucent bodies generally be not understood, and the rule by which the phenomena are generalised grounded in some higher principle. Thus the several sciences of hydrostatics, aerology, crystallology, and chemistry, preceded and accompanied by a knowledge of the pure mathematics, may be all required in order to a legitimate judgment on a single phenomenon, i.e. before the image can be safely declared to possess objective reality—before it can be received with safety as a fact of experience. So erroneous would the assertion be that an object of the sense is the same with the impression made on the senses, or even that what we appear to see is the same with the image formed on the retina, if it were possible to conceive an act of seeing wholly separate from the modifications of the judgment and the analogies of previous experience. Nor have we yet enumerated all the requisites. A delusion might result, and in many cases necessarily would result, if the knowledge supplied by anatomy and physiology were wanting, and even with these the source of error is not yet wholly closed. All inattention to the laws and rules, pure and empirical, of the imagination, volition, and the feelings might occasion the beholder to mistake a product or disturbing force of his own being for the object which then only supports that name when it is contemplated free from all such preexistence of itself, as given to it when [?it has] attained the character of memory—thus in nature the germ presupposes the blossom even as the blossom presupposes the germ, numerically different indeed, and different in the relations of time and space, but essential and, in all its intelligible characters, the same. For an absolute first is a position with regard to which the understanding may submit in silence but which can by no artifice be thought of by the understanding or reduced under its forms. What follows? Even this—in order to discuss aright the premises of any reasoning in distinction from the reasoning itself, a knowledge of the matter is the first and indispensable requisite. This may appear a truism, but though equally certain it is not equally obvious that the same necessity applies to the very means and acts with and by which we acquire the materials of knowledge; not only must we have some scheme or general outline of the object by *a*which we could determine its nature,*b* informed that there is a previous discipline of the senses, that even in the general functions of touch and taste and smell and sight and hearing we pass from our birth into a school beginning at the lowest forms and at our death have not yet attained the highest. And as there is a seeing and hearing which belongs to all mankind, even so in the different kinds and species of knowledge there is a separate apprenticeship necessary for each. All indeed reducible to the common form of attention appropriately directed and rendered proportionally intense, but varying in degree of excellence with the greater or less knowledge already possessed by the observer of the object to which, the medium through which, of the faculty by which, and lastly of the state in which, the observer is while he is thus attending, for such is the mystery both of man and nature that every perception presupposes itself, and no knowledge could be acquired without subjective influences.

5(b)   We freely admit, or rather I have purposely introduced the preceding remarks for the purpose of announcing and impressing the truth, that in cases like those supposed in these remarks, where the reasoning is grounded on some distinct external object, the business of common logic is simple indeed, and that the application may be safely trusted to the common sense of mankind. For first the main end in investigations of this kind is most often the establishment of the object itself, which, once established, contains or rather is coincident with its inferences, and secondly, when this is not altogether the case, the sole logical exercise of the mind would be confined to the examination whether the second term was or was not included in the first, as the more comprehensive, or, which will more frequently occur, whether the application of the general rule is or is not legitimate. A power acting inversely as the square of the distance is the power of gravitation, but the law acts by a power, etc, therefore the law acts by a power of gravitation. We may now therefore readily understand the observation of Lord Bacon respecting the insignificance of common logic and its utter inadequacy in the investigations of nature, and, he might safely have added, in those of the pure reason, but let it not be forgotten that the great philosopher at the same time asserts its utility, nay, its indispensableness in all the moral

a–b ms: to which we could determine to not be

and forensic concerns of life.[1] But if we abstract all speculation and all discourse that fall under the class of moral, historical, and forensic, how small a portion shall we reserve for the majority of mankind. We need only reflect on the infrequency of any discussion in which the object is singly and directly presented to the sense or the senses.

6(a)   For the purposes of ordinary observation the few and safe rules generalised from uninterrupted experience, aided with a few of the principal results obtained by scientific investigation, and which are practically intelligible without any insight into the process by which they were[a] originally obtained, will be sufficient to give us a justifiable confidence in that which alone we men have a social interest to ascertain, viz. the coincidence of our individual perceptions with the average perceptions of our fellow creatures. Here indeed, plain and simple as these criteria are, spontaneously and almost instinctively as we apply them every hour of our lives, and simple as the rule pre-established in the logical canon [is]—that in order to a conclusion we must assure ourselves that A has been rightly secluded and that B is actually included in A—yet the habit of repeating this process consciously and on all subjects of importance, above all, and in all cases where the apparent conclusions of the understanding are at variance with our moral convictions or the persuasions of common sense, is[b] of vital importance and efficacy, for the results can be no other than that of a healthful dissatisfaction or premonitory discontent with whatever is vague or flitting. A mind so disciplined acquires not only a facility of recurring frequently to the sources and fountainheads of truth and there renewing the elasticity of reimpressing and sharpening the stamps of his intellectual being; but this process becomes a want, an habitual desideratum of his nature, the cause the more pleasurable because he progressively finds himself more and more amply remunerated both by the power which he acquires over others in anticipating the conclusions of minds formed in the same school with his own, and the delusions of others which he overlooks, as one[c] placed on an elevation in the centre of a labyrinth of paths not only sees his own future direction but can safely prophesy the entanglements and wanderings of the groundlings at every turn and in the whole detail of error.

a ms: even   *b* ms: [?all/ are]   *c* ms: our

1 See *Distributio operis* and *De*   *Works* (1740) I 13–14 and 137–8.
augmentis scientiarum bk V ch 1:

6(b)   Of the application of the rule implied in the canon as reduced in this work to the three forms of clusion, inclusion, and conclusion, we will give a single example as an instance of the mode [of] applying the rule and a proof of the services which it is capable of affording. In the writings of Plato we find the following apparent syllogism:

Ἔρως μεν ἀει φιλοκαλος

των δε καλλιστων Σοφια

Ἔρως οὖν ἀει φιλοσοφος:

i.e. "to desire beauty is the essential character of love. But wisdom is a thing of all other[s] most beautiful, therefore to desire wisdom is the essential character of love".[1] Now here it is plain that the minor[a] is included in part only of the major, viz. in the term "beauty"; and secondly, that the immediate consequence of the minor[a] would be therefore, "to desire wisdom is to desire beauty": but with this it would be a syllogism of four terms, which, where the result is not directly false, always proves that some one of the four terms [b]is out of place, and we must add[c] another syllogism in order to give the coercive power to the conclusion, for instance: "Whatever is harmonious in itself and in its relations is beauty. But wisdom is harmonious in itself and its relations. Therefore wisdom is beauty." "To desire beauty is the character of love. But to desire wisdom is to desire beauty. Therefore to desire wisdom is the character of love." Here the syllogistic reasoning formally considered is complete, and we have only to ask whether wisdom is actually included in beauty. Now a little reflection will convince us that wisdom is not a phenomenon, does not derive its being from relations, while beauty which is beautiful in itself is a nonentity or a mere lax and metaphorical use of words. For beauty subsists in relations and common sense. Sense instructs us that wisdom may be beautiful, i.e. may manifest herself in relations the constituent forms of which harmonise with each other and combine to a common unity in the total impression, yet we cannot say that beauty is wisdom or that the beautiful is necessarily wise. The conclusion therefore would be, not that love would desire wisdom for itself, but that it would affect the beautiful in wisdom; and this would be a mere movement in a circle. The minor was not included, and the apparent progression consists in nothing but a repetition of the major or original position in the different forms of words.

[1] *Symposium* 204B (var).

CHAPTER [III]

1(a) We have now reached the point at which it will [be] expedient to halt, though but for a moment, in order to review the road we have passed over, that we may thus be able to form a distinct conception of the journey that yet remains. For in order to see distinctly what a thing is we must ascertain what it is not. Hitherto, then, we have exhibited the essence, form, and rules of common or universal logic. Now the common logic is either pure or applied; in the first, which alone we have given in its completion, we abstract from all empirical conditions under which the exercise of the understanding takes place; we abstract from the influence of the senses, from the interference of the imagination, from the laws of memory, from the weight of customs, of inclination, of passion, and, inclusively, from the sources of human prejudices—in short, we abstract from all causes from which any given and particular cognitions^a arise, or out of which any counterfeits of knowledge proceed—because all these respect the understanding, circumstantially, under certain contingent occasions of its application, or of objects, to which and by which the application was determined. But in order to the knowledge of these, experience is required. But the pure common logic appeals wholly to principles *a priori*, i.e. to principles derived from the construction of the machine itself, not from its uses; from the construction of the understanding altogether abstracted from the materials on which it acts or the causes by which it is called into action. It is therefore, and so we have called it, a canon^b of the understanding. And inasmuch as the understanding is the organ of the reason, if not directly by affirmation yet indirectly by negation,* it is a canon^b of the reason like-

---

* When from two premises, both of which are affirmed with equal right by the understanding, the understanding itself by legitimate deductions can arrive at two contradictory conclusions, the only possible solution of the difficulty is found in assuming that the understanding has been applying its own forms and functions, or those which it has borrowed from the sense, to objects which do not fall under its cognisance; as when, for instance, the understanding applies the

^{a} Word inserted in pencil in blank space in unidentified hand, before ms came into Ward's possession. His guess that the insertion was C's was mistaken. It may have been Green's
^{b} ms: cause

wise, but only in respect of the formal, let the subject matter be what it may, drawn from outward experiences or from inward consciousness and reflection.

1(b)   By way of illustration we will take a sextant or other optical instrument. Now we may consider this in three different ways, viz. with regard to the objects and particular images which it presents, or, abstracting from these, with regard to the way in which it presents these images, however different in themselves, and which is common to them all, or lastly with regard to the construction and constituent parts of the sextant itself. But before we apply this instance it must be premised that in the mind the way in which the instrument acts of necessity, to a certain extent is determinable without the knowledge of the construction or constitution of the instrument, its exercise being inseparably accompanied with a sense of its necessity *inherent* in itself, and this necessity it is that forms the essence of a knowledge *a priori*. We do not say it has always done so and so, and therefore we have no doubt that it will continue so to do; neither ^athe analogy^b of the past nor the anticipation of the future enters at all into the contemplation. Proofs of which we have in every position of geometry and arithmetic as well as in pure logic. The mathematician rests perfectly secure that his axioms and propositions are necessary and universal truths, without troubling himself with any analysis of the faculties by which he constructs his figures and demonstrates their relations. With this previous explanation we may now apply the instance above given. A knowledge directed to the particular objects or images, as presented by the sextant—after the corrections and rectifications suggested by the variation from other optic instruments and necessary in order to arrive at a common result—such knowledge would represent the sciences of experience, though it might well

---

forms of time and space, of quantity, quality, and relation, to the idea of the Supreme Being, or of things themselves contradistinguished from the phenomena. In these cases, I say that the understanding is indirectly and by negation the organ of the reason, and the exercise of logic for this purpose by the understanding to prove the inadequacy of the understanding constitutes the Platonic dialectic which the divine philosopher calls the wings by which philosophy first raises herself from the ground.[1]

^{a–b} Insertion, possibly by Green

[1] Probably a reference to Plato *Phaedrus* 249c. "And therefore it is just that the mind of the philosopher only has wings, for he is always, so far as he is able, in communion through memory with those things the communion with which causes God to be divine." Tr H. N. Fowler (LCL 1926) 481–3.

happen that the knowledge of what experience itself is, wherein it consists, and under what conditions it is possible may form no part of this knowledge. Images which all men having their right faculties under the same given circumstances are capable of receiving passive[ly] or by reproduction and naming[a], i.e. referring to a class and in which each individual is conscious that the appearances with order of their sequence are not the creatures of his own volition, nor yet explicable by the law by which the spontaneous acts and products of his own faculties are determined, form the content and materials of experience, which, as is indeed involved in this view of its constitution, is as necessarily accompanied by a sense of a *contingency, as the truths *a priori*, from which the facts of experience are contra-distinguished, are characterised by a sense of necessity. The second sort of knowledge [is] that which respects the common way in which the sextant represents all images so that the image does not properly belong to the instrument unless it be so presented (e.g. in the case of an accidental speck or reflection on the object glass). This, we say, if applied to the forms of the pure sense, constitutes the sciences of measure and number, or geometry and arithmetic, and, applied to the understanding, gives the science of common or purely formal logic. There remains then one other knowledge, that viz. of the constitution and constituents of the instrument itself, without which we cannot certainly distinguish either what share the instrument itself has in the image presented by it, and, therefore, as little what it is that we are justified in referring to a correspondent object subsisting independent of the instrument through and by which we arrive at the knowledge of its existence. In the case of the sextant, we may indeed arrive at a probability which, sufficing for all practical purposes, may be called an empirical certainty, by comparing the result with those of other optical instruments, the human eye itself considered as one, in the same manner as we rectify the notices of one sense by those of some other or of all the other senses.

1(c)   But the instrument of the human mind is one and all, and

* I scarcely need inform the reader that this is to be interpreted relatively to the human understanding. By the Supreme Mind doubtless every object is contemplated with the same insight to its[b] necessity as the properties of [a] circle or the functions of an algebraic term are by the human mathematician. (*Vide Friend.* vol. III, p. 153.)[1]

---

a ms: ~~learning~~ ⟨naming⟩ [crossing out and insertion probably by Green]   *b* ms: their

1 *Friend* (*CC*) I 458–9. C refers to the 1818 ed.

when we have once learnt from experience, and with that degree of insight which experience is capable of affording, so far to generalise the operations of the mind as to distinguish the individual peculiarities or the accidental subjective, we are at the end of our resources. We know empirically that such and such (a way of perceiving, for instance, as when all objects appear yellow, or when no colour requiring blue for its composition is seen) do not belong to the perceiver as a man but as this or that individual in whom it constitutes such a defect or disease; or, when the difference existed in degree only and not in *kind*, possibly as an individual perfection; but whether the seeing of objects generally is an attribute of the object or a communication from the subject will remain uncertain as before.

1(d)   Now the desideratum is to distinguish the *subjective* from the *objective in toto*, not partially as hitherto in common logic by mere abstraction from the knowledge given by experience, by which we do indeed know [that] that to which we are exclusively directing our attention is purely *subjective*, but by no means that the matter or materials *from* which we have *withdrawn* our attention are properly and wholly objective—i.e. that they have a subsistence independent of the mind which contemplates them. They may for aught that the common logic can affirm or deny consist of a wonderful and seemingly indecomponible[a] union of the mind and an external agency, as the tune of the breeze and the Eolian harp.[1] It being of the utmost importance that the nature of this threefold distinction should be thoroughly understood, and even made familiar, let us attempt yet another illustration. We have heard of the automaton chess-player.[2] Let us imagine an automaton potter. While we are watching the procedure of the machine, we may either fix our attention on the different clays which by some machinery out of sight had been presented to the potter's hand, or rather to the vessels, inasmuch as according to our supposition the clay does not appear to us previously to its reception of the form, or we may fix our attention exclusively on the series of motions which the hands and arms of the automaton execute in all the different vessels which it is capable of forming. We abstract this action of the machine both from its effects

---

[a] Word inserted in another hand. Lucy Watson's conjecture (ms II 196) that it was Green's is probably correct

[1] Cf *The Eolian Harp: PW* (EHC) I 100–2.
[2] For a description, see Sir David Brewster *Letters on Natural Magic . . .* (1832) 269–83. An example was exhibited in London in 1819. Cf Descartes' discussion of automata in *Discourse on Method* (1637): D *Works* I 115–16.

or products and from the machinery which is its cause and agent.
Having thus abstracted its acts or motions we then generalise them,
i.e. we fix our attention on those of constant occurrence or bring all
the varieties under some common conception (as, for instance,
circles and ellipses may be brought under the common term of "a
revolving line"), or lastly we may examine the automaton itself, and
resolve the machine into integral constituents with their relation and
subordination, and again each constituent into its component parts,
co-ordinate or subordinate. We have before had occasion to remind
our reader that no simile quadrates:[1] but in questions that include
the powers and processes of the mind in the subject matter it is more
obviously true that every likeness must halt or be inapplicable in
some point or other. Thus in the preceding illustration the materials
on which the hands of the automaton work are supplied wholly from
without; but in the mind the machine itself and[a] all its acts and
processes are equally fitted to be the objects of its action as the vessel
with the substance from without that must be presupposed as the
basis and recipient of the form. But if only we bear this in mind, and
intellectually supply this defect, the illustrations will assist us both in
apprehending and remembering the several natures of the three
divisions of knowledge which we are here interested in rendering
perfectly intelligible. The vessels will represent all the knowledges
which we derive from experience. The constant movements of the
machine on the clay will represent the formal sciences generally: that
is, according to the faculty which we chose to represent by the hands
of the automaton. If we refer to the sense, these motions will repre-
sent the pure forms of the sense and the sciences of number and
measure. But if, as in the present instance, and in truth with greater
similitude and propriety from the narrow compass and simplicity,
both of the motions and of the science represented by them, the
understanding is the faculty in question, then these movements will
represent the science of common logic, the analysis of the automaton
itself. The investigation into the composition and constitution of the
mind itself yet remains the weightiest and worthiest of all contem-
plations if the poet have said rightly

e coelo descendit γνωθι σεαυτον[2]

and that the knowledge of our intellectual nature is the substance and

___

[a] ms: with

[1] See above, p 11 n 4.   [2] Juvenal *Satires* 11.27. See above,
                                    p 116 n 3.

life of all our knowledge and the ground of intelligibility of all other objects of knowledge.

1(e)   Were it only conceivable as an object of hope, instead of being, as indeed it is, a demonstrable truth, that the human mind is the compass in which the laws of all outward things are revealed as the dips and declinations,[1] this would of itself suffice to make the investigation to which we are now introducing the reader more than a subject of interest; it must make it an object of duty to all who, filling or destined to fill the higher and middle stations of society, possess opportunities of leisure which have been fearfully abused if they have not been made opportunities of reflection.[2] For these classes generally, though with especial reference to those who are forming themselves for public and professional life, the pulpit, the bar, the senate, the professor's chair, or for that which belongs to all and includes the qualities of all, the public press, this work was written, and to these I will now address myself as though they were personally present.

2   My friends! you enjoy an immunity from bodily labour and you are placed or seeking to place yourselves on an elevation to which the majority of your fellow-countrymen are to look up with respect and perhaps with reverence. The titles, the comforts, the revenues, which you possess or aim at, may designate your rank but cannot constitute your moral and personal fitness for it. Be it enough for others to know, that you are its *legal*, but by what mark shall you stand accredited to your own consciences as its worthy, possessors? Not by common sense or by common honesty; for these are equally demanded of all classes, and therefore mere negative qualifications in *your* rank of life, or characteristic only by the aggravated ignominy consequent on their absence. Not by genius or splendid talent; for these as being gifts of nature are objects of moral interest for those[a] alone to whom they have been allotted. Nor yet by eminence in learning; for this supposes such a devotion of time and thought as would in many cases be incompatible with the claims of active life. Erudition is doubtless an *ornament* that especially beseems a high station: but it is *professional* rank only that renders its attainment a duty. The rank in question must be so far *common* that we may be

---

[a] ms: these

---

[1] C quotes from *SM* (*CC*) 78–9. The quotation from Juvenal, in English, is given there a few lines later.

[2] Cf the audience addressed in C's second "Lay Sermon". See *LS* (*CC*) 119.

entitled to look for it in *you* from the mere circumstance of your situation, and so far distinctive, that it must be such as cannot be expected generally from the inferior classes. Now, either there is no such criterion in existence or the desideratum is to be found in an habitual consciousness of the ultimate principles to which your opinions are traceable.[1] Now, a steadfast reflection on the terms of the postulate might enable you to anticipate the conviction which the following section will, I trust, not fail to produce and perfect, that this is impracticable as long as we remain ignorant what, and of what kind, the senses are, and this again supposes a knowledge first of that which, though common in kind to all men, we yet, each of us, are entitled to call "mine", or "myself", as contradistinguished from that which is "not mine", "not of myself"—that, viz. which we have so often spoken of as a knowledge of the subjective in contradistinction from the objective. And secondly a knowledge of that which is not myself, or of me as contradistinguished from that which the mind possesses in itself or communicates from its own stores, i.e. a knowledge of the objective as contradistinguished from the subjective. And lastly a knowledge of that which is distinguished from both, as transcending both and [being] of both the root and identity.

3(a)   Now it is evident that the knowledge mentioned in the second place, which we may call the universal subjective, or that which is common to the race without distinction of individuals, must be acquired before we can form any judgment of the first, the properly objective. At least from the point on which we have hitherto stood and [are] still standing, viz. the point of reflection. This must be necessary inasmuch as our knowledge of [the] objective is merely negative. We affirm it to be objective—in other words, that the objects of such knowledge subsist independently of the mind—only because it is not accompanied by the mark of the subjective, viz. its validity *a priori*, and because it is not included and therefore not to be evolved out of that which we know to be the subject itself. But on the other hand, though less obvious, it is no less true that as the second or the knowledge of the constitution of the subject is a necessary precondition of any distinct knowledge respecting the object, yet this must presuppose the existence of that [first] and highest insight —an insight into the existence of a somewhat that is the common ground of the subject and object, were it only that it is in the

---

[1] Paragraph 2 up to this point is a free quotation from *LS* (*CC*) 121.

order of its formation anterior to reflection, in which power the antithesis of subject and object has its birth and origin.

3(b)   There is, as we have already learnt, a somewhat which, whether we refer it to an agency without ourselves or acknowledge it as an immediate presence to and as it were within the mind, we in both cases express by the affirmative "is". And hence we distinguish from the reflective faculty two species of reality—the reality in nature and the reality of reason. The one [is] characterised by its apparent contingency, as proceeding from a power separate from our own will and spontaneity, and the other by its absolute necessity, not the conditional necessity which inheres in the forms and functions of the understanding and the rules generalised from these, and which necessity with its consequence, the property of being affirmed *a priori*, we have aptly compared with the movement of a machine that results solely [and] inevitably from the construction of the machine, supposing it to act at all, though this is itself not universally necessary but must be limited to the mind from the faculties of which such and such cognitions result. Our present business is [?confined]*a* to the latter, and this again we must subdivide into two kinds, each forming a distinct science—these are, first, the universal forms of the pure sense and the knowledge [that] has been entitled "transcendental aesthetic", a term borrowed from a fragment attributed to Polemo, the successor of Speusippus, who succeeded Plato, the great founder of the Academic School. In order to distinguish the faculty of sense itself abstractly from the sensations and from the modifications of the senses or organs of sense, Polemo designated the former by the words Αἴσθησις ἐπιστημονικη,*b1* or sciential perception or apprehension. The term "transcendental" means the same as "sciential", but with an additional significance. All knowledge is excited or occasioned by experience, but all knowledge is not derived from experience, such, for instance, is the knowledge of the conditions that render*c* experience itself possible, and which must therefore be supposed to exist previous to experience, in the same manner as the eyes must pre-exist to the act of seeing, though without that act of seeing we never should have learnt that we possessed eyes. Now to distinguish the

---

a ms: compared   *b* ms: ἐπιστηματικη   *c* ms: renders

1 C appears to have confused Polemo with Speusippus here. Cf Tennemann III 8n, quoting Sextus Empiricus *Adversus mathematicos* VII § 145, which may be translated: "[Speusippus] said that the criterion of truths of reason (νοητων) is the sciential reason (ἐπιστημονικὸς λόγος) but of things sensible it is the sciential apperception (ἐπιστημονικὴ αἴσθησις)."

truths that are necessarily presupposed in all experience as its condition and co-cause, from the facts or knowledge not only occasioned *by*, but actually derived from, experience, whether it be the experience of the world without or the experience acquired by reflection on ourselves, and yet at the same time to distinguish the former knowledge from pretended cognitions and assertions that transcend our intellectual faculties or, what is equivalent, for which the human mind can be shown to possess no appropriate faculty and which assertions are therefore called "transcendent", the term "transcendental" has been chosen. And I have found it expedient to give this explanation, because the "transcendent" and "transcendental" are stated as perfectly synonymous.[1] In this, however, the lexicographer[2] was not justified by the usage of our own divines and metaphysicians in times past or by the present use in the continental schools. Transcendental knowledge is that by which we endeavour to climb above our experience into its sources by an analysis of our intellectual faculties, still, however, standing as it were on the shoulders of our experience in order to reach at truths which are above experience, while transcendent philosophy would consist in the attempt to master a knowledge that is beyond our faculties, an attempt to grasp at objects beyond the reach of hand or eye or all the artificial ends and, as it were, prolongations of eye and hand, of objects therefore the existence of which, if they did exist, the human mind has no means of ascertaining, and therefore has not even the power of imagining or conceiving; that which the pretended sages pass off for such objects being merely images from the senses variously disjoined and recomposed, or mere words expressing classes of these images and by addition of other words associated with obscure feelings, a process pardonable in poetry, though even there quickly degenerating into poetic commonplace, as, for instance, fountains of pleasure, rivers of joy, intelligential splendours, and the like, but as little to be tolerated in the schools of philosophy as on the plain high road of common sense.

4   The transcendental aesthetic is the first, and as there must be a perception, or, if we dared apply the word in this sense, a ception, before there can be a conception, the transcendental aesthetic must take place of[3] that investigation into the constitution and constituent forms of the understanding, which in analogy with the former is

---

[1] The distinction, as well as some of what follows in the paragraph, is based on Kant *C d r V* 330 (299).

[2] Samuel Johnson. Cf *BL* ch 12 (1907) I 164n.

[3] I.e. must precede.

termed transcendental logic or the λογος ^{a}ἐπιστημονικος[1] of
Polemo.^{b} However, though we deemed it expedient not to leave
unnoticed or unexplained the terms which the most profound of
modern logicians and the proper* inventor and founder of tran-

* I.e. unless the honours of discovery can be justly or honestly withheld from
the man who *first* saw and communicated the truths in their full extent, and
with systematic comprehension, under the pretence of a few scattered hints in
some ancient or modern books the report and bearings of which were not even
suspected by the writer himself. Such, however, is the destiny that with few or^c
rare exceptions has attended on the works and products of original genius. At
their first appearance, the new system is declared to be all jargon, a congeries of
useless, unintelligible phrases, either with no meaning or with a meaning that
outrages common sense. (The Copernican system Sir Thomas Browne describes
as a fit case for *a mad doctor*,[2] it being beneath the dignity of a philosopher to
confute the whimsies of a man *out of his senses*, for how should a man believe
in another's words who has given the lie to his own eyesight?) An interval takes
place, during which the higher and better minds have mastered the new system,
have recognised and proclaimed its value and importance, and their authority
with the increasing number and respectability of the new school has made a sen-
sible impression on the public opinion, and what follows? The doctrines are
true indeed, but without any claim to originality; and in proof of these assertions
the opinions of some former philosopher are wrested or wrenched into a coinci-
dence of meaning by critics who neither understand the one or the other, or who
from long prejudice and the indurate habit of thinking in some one particular
way are actually incapable of attaching any meaning to words representing truths
that suppose and require a different direction of the intellective faculty and who,
if able and inclined to learn at all, are too old and too indolent to learn where
the effort of unlearning is an indispensable preliminary: or lastly, some one or
two sentences which actually do *imply* the truth discovered by their contemporary,
but the force, pregnancy, and involved consequences of which no man had ever
seen, or perhaps could have seen, previous to the development of and expansion
on a systematic form, are extracted from some obscure book or perhaps torn
from their context in some well-know[n] books, and Harvey did not discover the

$a-b$ ms: ἐπιστηματικος of Palema c ms: of

[1] C uses the term in apposition to
"Discursive Intellect" in a note on
the endpapers of Tennemann VIII (pt 2).
See also p 146 n 1, above.

[2] C often attributes this view to
Browne (e.g. *CL* IV 864; BM Add MSS
36532 f 7^v; *C 17th C* 158, 395; *P Lects*
Lect 6—1949—200-1). He must have
had in mind *Pseudodoxia Epidemica*
bk 1 ch 5: "And therefore if any affirm
the earth doth move, and will not
believe with us, it standeth still;
because he hath probable reasons for
it, and no infallible sense, nor reason
against it, I will not quarrel with his
assertion. But if like Zeno he shall
walk about, and yet deny there is any

motion in nature; surely that man was
constituted for *Anticera*, and were a
fit companion for those who, having a
conceit they are dead, cannot be con-
victed into the society of the living"
(*Works*—1658-9, C's annotated ed,
now in the Berg Collection, NYPL—i
13) and have linked it in his recollec-
tion with comments of a similar
tendency, e.g. *Pseudodoxia Epidemica*
bk 1 ch 3, *Religio Medici* pt II § 13
(*Works* i 7, ii 28). A "mad doctor",
i.e. a doctor who treats the mad.
Browne usually speaks respectfully of
Copernicus himself, e.g. *Pseudodoxia
Epidemica* bk 6 ch 5 and bk 7 ch 18 § 6:
Works i 250 and 322.

scendental analysis[3] has adopted, we prefer the more intelligible and less uncommon title of the *critical* or judicial logic, i.e. a criterion of the general and particular judgments passed by the understanding as the faculty of reflection, derived from a knowledge of the constitution of the understanding itself and of the universal forms of the sense to which the legitimate exercise of its functions is[a] confined.

5   A criterion, indeed, and that, too, comprehended under the term "aesthetic" we have already given as an appendix to the common or syllogistic logic, i.e. the logic as a canon of reasoning;[4] but not a criterion, scientific and of course *a priori*, nor derived from the sciential or transcendental aesthesis, but abstracted and generalised from general experience and involving the exercise, active and passive, of the senses. Insufficient therefore for the safe application of common logic itself as being limited to those cases in which the affirmation as[b] the major and minor of the syllogism respect[s] the objects of the senses as concretes. These criteria therefore could not be omitted among the precognitions required as the tests of the material truth of conclusions formally legitimate, but holding a very subordinate place to the criteria which we are now about to investigate, whether we consider the extent and universal application of the latter, the weight and deep interest of the subject to which it is specially applied, or finally the circumstance that the former comes to us spontaneously at best with an accuracy sufficient for the ordinary purposes of life and as the necessary result of the comparisons and half-unconscious experiments which we are compelled by nature to make in order to exercise our senses for the purposes of self-preservation. Though in making this confession we are not to forget that the main point in the marks that distinguish the man of superior mind consists in his doing that consciously, in the light of distinct knowledge and the sense of pure agency, which the many do unconsciously or rather can scarcely be said to do at all, inasmuch as it is their common nature, rather, that does it in and for them.

---

circulation of the blood,[1] and Immanuel Kant stole the transcendental analysis and was not the founder of the critical philosophy. BUT "WISDOM IS JUSTIFIED BY HER CHILDREN".[2]

          a ms: are   *b* ms: is

[1] William Harvey (1578–1657) first made his thoughts on the circulation of the blood known in a series of lectures in 1616. In 1628 his *Exercitatio*

anatomica de motu cordis et sanguinis in animalibus was published in Frankfurt.

[2] Matt 11.19 (var).

[3] Kant.

[4] See above, pp 70ff.

CHAPTER [IV]

Judicial Logic,
Including the Pure Aesthetic

1 Among the consequences of the overbalance of the commercial spirit[1][—]not from any excess of trade and commerce in themselves, but from the decline or deficiency of the requisite checks and counter-forces, and among these more especially (for our present purpose at least) from the gradual neglect of all the austerer studies; the long eclipse of philosophy, the transfer of that name to physical and psychological empiricism, and the non-existence of a learned and philosophic class, constituting a *publicum in publico*;[2] and to all which we may add a cause which the age is accustomed to hail as a matter of triumph and self-congratulation, the aversion to theological controversy with the majority of well-educated Englishmen, and the revolution in the feelings and opinions of the public respecting the rank and value of polemic divinity[3]—among the consequences from the conjoint operation of the causes, we have had frequent occasion to lament the vague and equivocal import of the terms and phrases which we are obliged to use in philosophic disquisition, and which yet we cannot use without awakening the meanings en-grafted on them by the market,[a] or at least the confused state of apprehension, which the wearing out of the original impress and superscription by promiscuous handling is too well calculated to reproduce. Some advantage, however, will be derived from this inconvenience if it should work a conviction of the necessity of ex-amining into the original meanings of the words we have occasion to use, to compare these with what we ourselves actually meant, and thus to understand with a clearness and distinctness which cannot fail to produce a correspondent effect on our practice the full force of the words "*propriety* of language".

[a] Word inserted probably in Green's hand

[1] Which C had analysed in *LS* (*CC*) 169ff.

[2] "A public within the public".

Cf C's later calls for a "clerisy": *C&S* (*CC*) 53–4, 54n.

[3] To which C had referred in *LS* (*CC*) 199.

2(a)   If I mistake not, there are few words to which this remark is more applicable than "intuition" (and "intuitive").*a* The word is by no means of unfrequent occurrence in general conversation or in popular writings, but I have found it no easy matter to determine what the users exactly meant by it, except indeed that it seemed to be nearly, if not altogether, equivalent to instinctive, natural or innate; and yet, on the other hand, the proper sense of the term is one of prime necessity in all philosophical enquiries, and most of all in those that have the constitution of the mind for their express subject; and I know of no other convenient English word but "intuition" by which this sense is to be conveyed. Hooker, indeed, has expressed the meaning by an "immediate beholding",[1] but this, I need not say, is not so truly a proper term as the explanation of one and, like all periphrases, unknown in technical use. As an explanation we therefore adopt it, and "intuition", from the Latin *intuitus* or *intuitio*, from *intueor*, to look at or on a subject, to have it present to the sight, and then by a wider use, present to the senses generally, whether the outward or the inward senses, signifies a simple beholding, both the act of beholding and the simple product thence resulting, indistinguishably. Indistinguishably, I say, for we cannot separate the one from the other without reference to some hypothesis or theory. Our consciousness contains no such distinction, we are aware of no such twinship or duality, and it is a simple fact that we wish to convey, and for which therefore we must have a simple and perfect unequivocal term. It is on this ground that the words "intuition" and "intuitive knowledge" (and it is to be regretted that we have not a correspondent verb [such] as the Latin *intueor* and the German *anschauen*) are not superseded by the words "perception", "perceptive";*b* and "perceive"*c* not only nor principally appertains, it might seem, exclusively to the organs of sense *per quae* (through which) *sensa*

---

a Parentheses inserted   *b* Ms unpunctuated   *c* Comma in ms

[1] The quotation is attributed to Hooker elsewhere by C—e.g. "On the Principles of Genial Criticism" *BL* (1907) II 230 and *AR* (1825) 216. Was C thinking of the following passage: "The truth is, that the mind of man desireth evermore to know the truth, according to the most infallible certainty which the nature of things can yield. The greatest assurance generally with all men, is that which we have by a plain aspect and intuitive beholding"? *Of the Laws of Ecclesiastical Politie* bk II § 7: *Works* (1682) 119. If so, his rendering has acquired a Kantian turn; cf "Anschauung, unmittelbare Offenbarung" ("Intuition, immediate disclosure") in Kant *VS* III 80 and "Ein unmittelbares Bewusstseyn heisst Anschauung . . ." ("An immediate awareness is called intuition . . .") in Fichte *Das System der Sittenlehre* pt I ch 3 (Jena & Leipzig 1798) 50

capimus,[1] [a]but because the simple verb *capio*, *capimus*, anglicised by[b] the syllables "ceive", "ception", evidently refers to an act of the understanding or the reflective faculty. We have all had experiences[c] which we could no otherwise describe than by saying [that] such a thing was present to me and I must have seen it, for it has since recurred to me, that I was so lost in thought or my attention was so fixed on some other object that I did not perceive it. And indeed, though now it is not obsolete, degraded into a vulgarism, such is still the meaning of our native English of[d] *capio*. It is not uncommon either among our rustics or our more knowing Londoners to hear a fellow ask another, "Do you take me?" I.e. not, have you heard my words or seen my winks or gestures, but do you understand them— do you conceive me?

2(b)   Now we want an expression for the act of the sense and its accompanying product, independently of any other act or product of any other faculty; but in all beholdings or presentations by means of the bodily senses there is, we have seen, a sensation combined which escapes our consciousness, from use and the rapidity of the impression, but the existence of which is demonstrated by our perception of circular bodies and in general of densities[e] as distinct from surfaces, the counterfeiting of which, rendered possible by the law of association, constitutes the mechanical part of the art of painting (*vide* Berkeley's *Essay on Vision*,[2] or any popular work on optics).[f] Such presentations therefore we must entitle "mixed intuitions", or "empirical intuitions", to distinguish these joint products of the sense and its inherent forms, and laws of action, from[g] some other allied power acting from without and by its coincidence with, co-agency of, the sense, supplying the understanding with the ground and materials of experience. But as in the term "nature", or, in the equivalent terms, "from without" used in contradistinction to "from within", we include our own bodies and bodily sensations as far as they are not the creatures of our own will or the products of our own faculties either voluntary or spontaneous—these mixed intuitions are excluded from our present subject. To these indeed as well as to all other facts of experience the science of logic may be applied. Of course they must be known in each particular case before we can

---

a–b Inserted in another hand, probably Green's. A blank space large enough for two short words was available in ms
        c ms: experienced   *d* Inserted in another hand, probably Green's
e Inserted in another hand, probably Green's   *f* Parentheses inserted   *g* ms: &

1 "We take [i.e. receive] things sensed".   2 *An Essay Towards a New Theory of Vision* (1709).

judge whether a conclusion *formally* legitimate is likewise materially correct. Nevertheless, if we avoid the absurdity of giving an encyclopaedia under the title of logic applied, we must confine ourselves to the rules and maxims generalised from the common experience of mankind, and which refer to no knowledge that every man in possession of his human faculties is not supposed to possess. It would indeed be more accurate to say, the most important of these rules, of those the variations of applying which are of not frequent recurrence. Of those, the portion that refers to the objects of the outward senses we have already brought together under the title of aesthetic experiences, as an appendix to canonic or formal logic.[1] The remaining, and of greater claim to be inserted because less obvious, will be given as an appendix to the present section, under the head of psychological experiences.[2] We may now recur to our enquiry respecting intuitions.

2(c)   In whatever way and by whatever means any affirmation of the mind is referred to an object, that to which the last immediate reference is made is an intuition;[3] and in order fully to understand the nature of intuition *transcendentally* (i.e. where neither the thing nor the knowledge is the subject of investigation, but the faculty by which the thing is known, for this perhaps is the most intelligible explanation of the term "transcendental"), it will be expedient [to] throw ourselves back, as it were, into the ordinary apprehension and language of mankind, as if no question had been stated respecting the outwardness of things or of their being the perfect duplicates of the images by which they are presented to us. From this point of view it is plain that an intuition can take place respecting any natural object only as far as the object (or its component parts at least) is present to us.[4] But this again, viz. the object as the datum of the intuition, is only possible inasfar as it affects the mind in some determinate manner[a] (we use the word "mind" in this place as nearly equivalent to the soul,[b] as the sum of all our faculties, whether active, passive, or spontaneous).

2(d)   The capability of acquiring representations, which our elder logical and metaphysical writers entitled "receptivity", is what we call the sensibility or sensuous nature, or the property of

---

a Word inserted in another hand, probably Green's   *b* Ms lacks comma

[1] See above, pp 70ff?
[2] The missing appendix, presumably; referred to again on p 196, below.
[3] C is heavily dependent on Kant's "Transcendental Aesthetic" for much of what follows in this chapter and the next. Details are recorded in the notes.
[4] Paragraph 2(c) up to this point is based on *C d r V* 33 (65).

having the sense or sentient faculty called into action.*a* But this sensibility of course includes the sensations. When therefore we mean to abstract from the sensations, we want a distinct term to express this intent, and we then call this faculty THE SENSE. If we conceive this sense altogether and perfectly free from sensation (from the sensations, for instance, of pleasure, pain, heat, vividness, colour, and all the degrees and opposites of these) we obtain a notion of the *pure* sense. Either, however, by the pure sense or by the sensibility as including both the sense and sensation, the objects are given us, and consequently in this faculty alone are we to seek the origin of the correspondent intuitions.[1]

2(e)   The understanding, on the other hand, is the faculty that enables [us] to *think* of these objects.*b* As the sense is the *birth-place* of *intuitions*, the understanding is the organ of our *thoughts* and *conceptions*. We find, however, that we are incapable of presenting any object to the understanding by means of the sense except under the forms of space and time.

2(f)   We find, too, that these forms of space and time do not belong exclusively to our intuitions or perceptions of things as really present to us; we are equally incapable of *imagining* or *conceiving* any object otherwise than in time and space. Nay! so universally true is this that even objects to which our reason forbids us to attach either time or space we are still compelled to imagine and conceive as existing in both, and hence in the most awful object,[2] to which the attributes of time and space are both and equally inapplicable, reason and religion forbid us to imagine at all, but at the same time prohibit all attempts to *conceive* or *comprehend*.

2(g)   It must needs therefore be a question of deep interest (even were it not indispensable as the condition of all other insight, whether of positive insight into the nature of the things which are the proper objects of the sensuous intuitions, or, negatively, of those which transcend the sense) what time and space themselves are. Not what we *mean* by the terms: for this would be as absurd as to ask what we mean by the terms "yellow", "red", or "blue", if, as would be the case in the present instance, by asking for the meaning of a word we understand the being asked for some other words more plain or that more intelligibly would convey the same sense. No, our question looks in a different direction. Are time and space reali-

---

a ms: the human mind can be shewn   *b* Ms unpunctuated

[1] Paragraph 2(d) is closely related   [2] I.e. God.
to *C d r V* 34–5 (66).

ties subsisting for themselves independent of the mind? Are they subsistences? or, if not so, if they are only determinations or relations of other things, yet are they such as belong to things in their own nature abstractedly from their particular relation to *our* minds?[1] Dare we confidently affirm them as being the predicates and necessary attributes of the things in themselves as contradistinguished [from the] phenomena by which their existence is made manifest? (See pp [130–1] Introductory Chapter to the second section.) Or lastly, do they attach wholly to the form of the intuition, to the subjective nature of the mind, so that but for this constitution of our own faculties neither time nor space could have been predicated in any instance?

2(h) In order to arrive at some satisfactory answer to these questions we must begin with an exposition of the conceptions space and time. By an exposition we mean the removing the parts of anything from each other and again uniting them in order to form a more distinct notion of the parts and of the manner in which they are combined to one whole, to understand, in short, the composition of the thing and its components.[2] Thus we make our children take a map to pieces and then reconstruct it. Such is the literal sense of the Latin word *exponere* and such is the force of our own English "set out" or "set forth" and the German *auseinandersetzen*.

[Space]

3   First, then, space is not an empirical (experiential) conception. It is not a conception that has been drawn from outward experiences. For in order to my referring any given sensations produced in me to somewhat external to me, i.e. to somewhat in a different place of space from that in which I myself am, and in like manner, in order to represent the component parts of any total impression as[a] outward to and beside each other, therefore not merely as being different each from the other, but as being each in a different place or point of a given space—to be able to do this, I say, we must already have the representation of space itself to begin. The conception is evidently presupposed in the very question "Where is it?" It is presupposed in the universal sense of a thing out of us. If we ask ourselves what we

<hr />

a ms: is

[1] The sentence is translated from *C d r V* 37 (68).

[2] Paragraph 2(h) up to this point is translated from *C d r V* 38 (68).

mean by a thing, as opposed to a thought, we shall find that we mean
a somewhat extended—a somewhat that occupies a portion of space;
and in like manner in the division which experience has taught us to
make between objects, into those that merely occupy a space, as a
rainbow, and those which fill a space, as a solid body, both in the one
and the other the space itself is preconceived. The representation
space, therefore, cannot have been borrowed from those relations of
outward appearances made known to us by experience; but this out-
ward experience is itself possible only on the supposition of space.[1]

4(a)   2nd. Space is a necessary representation and, like all
representations combined with a sense of necessity, a representation
a priori as the pre-existing basis of all external intuitions. Try the
experiment: attempt to imagine that there is no space—try to fancy it
away[2]—you will find it impossible, though without difficulty you may
fancy away all objects and imagine a space in which there is nothing,
though it be altogether out of your power to conceive a form without
a space for it to appear in. Space therefore is the precondition of all
appearance. It is that without which apparent things could not appear.
Therefore it is no property of the things appearing, for, were it so,
they could no more be separated in the imagination (fancied away)
from space than the space from them. Besides, the appearances are
one and all accompanied by a sense of their contingency relatively
to us, but space we know to be a necessary conception forming no
part of our conception of the things existing therein but a representa-
tion necessarily and universally antecedent to all and every
appearance.[3]

4(b)   Now as by the world without us or outward nature we mean
only the sum and aggregate of appearances, and that as far as the
senses[a] and understanding are concerned we know of nothing which
is not either mind or nature, subjective or objective, what is proved
not to belong to the one must belong to the other. If space be neither
an outward thing nor any property of outward things, it must in
some sense or other be a quality or faculty or the necessary result of
some faculty or quality in the mind itself.*

---

* When taking our point of view from the above[b] understanding we divided
all things into subject and object, we did not disguise from ourselves that some-
thing far higher was presupposed, which was neither subject singly, nor object,

a ms: sensed   b Word very faint in ms

[1] Paragraph 3 is based on *C d r V*
38 (68).

[2] Here and throughout the para-
graph, C, paraphrasing Kant, un-

characteristically uses "imagination"
and "fancy" as synonyms.

[3] Paragraph 4(a) is from *C d r V*
38–9 (68).

5   3rd. Space is no common or general conception of the relations of things in general. Or rather, as all conceptions are discursive, and more or less general, it is, properly speaking, no conception at all, but a pure intuition—in other words, space is not a conception which we have generalised from any number of objects, like the conception of swiftness, whiteness, weight, and the like. For in the first place we can represent only*a* one single space: as, if ever we speak of many spaces, we mean only portions of one and the same space, or, more truly still, we speak only of things existing at certain distances from each other and attribute to the one undivided and indivisible space the diversion and plurality that belong to the things that appear in it. These universal parts cannot be presented for themselves antecedently to the conception of the whole as its components which can be imagined as brought together and constituting and composing spaces—we can merely think of them as parts by a play of the imagination, transferring the properties of A to its constant accompaniment B. If we talk of a space being separated from another by a wall, we know at the same time the wall itself occupies the space between and consequently thus there is a space to be occupied.[1]

6(a)   4thly. We represent space as an infinite given quantity.[*] Now were space a conception, an infinite conception would be one which consists of an infinite number of possible representations as the common character or mark of these. But no conception can be formed by the mind as containing in itself an infinite number of

---

nor a conjunction of both by adding the one to the other, but the identity of both, their common root. But to this we know that time and space are not attributable. As far, therefore, as either the one or the other is conceived, the former division stands good, and comprises all imaginable and conceivable things. And of these therefore it holds true that what cannot be referred to the object must be contained in the subject.

[* On the facing page the passage is clarified by an alternative wording:] 4thly. We represent space as an infinite given quantity. Infinity is its essential attribute, observe, not merely indefinite! The distance to which the fixed stars may extend is indefinite in our apprehensions: but we can without any contradiction conceive a limit, and thus at each successive distance from the earth we are nearer and nearer to this limit. I need not say that the very contrary is true of space. But an infinite conception is an impossibility; every conception is made up of the parts of which it is the common mark or predicate. But though a number may be indefinite it cannot be thought of as absolutely infinite, for then it would cease to be number. But, if space be no conception, as little is it, etc.—

a ms: only only

1 Paragraph 5 is from *C d r V* 39 (69).

possible representations. Yet this is the case with space in which an infinity of parts are thought of as simultaneous and co-existing.[1]

6(b) Space therefore is no conception; as little is it an eternal truth of the reason. For we are by no means permitted to assert or are capable of demonstrating that all things exist in space, nor even that anything always will so exist. That there may be a state in which time and space shall be no more, may or may not be a *groundless* assertion; but it is not nonsense, which every assertion must be that contradicts a universal truth of reason. But if neither a conception of the understanding nor a universal truth of the reason, it must be an intuition, and if not derived from particular things, forms, or images, it must be pure intuition *a priori*.[2]

Conclusions from the above

7 Space:

A. By space we mean no property of things in themselves, nor of any single thing, nor do we by space represent any relations they bear to each other arising out of the nature of the things themselves and which would remain after we had abstracted all the subjective conditions under which they are beheld. For neither absolute nor relative properties or determinations of things can be represented previously to the existence of the things themselves to which they belong, and cannot, therefore, like space, be contemplated *a priori*.[3]

8(a) B. Space cannot be contemplated as any single particular intuition. For it has been proved to pre-exist as the necessary condition or antecedent of all particular intuitions. The only remaining possibility is that space is nothing else but the common forms of all appearances of the outward senses—the subjective condition of that sense or sentiency, and that under which alone intuition is possible. Now since the receptivity of the subject, or the mind's capability of being affected by objects, must of necessity exist antecedent to all particular affections and therefore to all intuitions of these objects, we may easily understand how the form of all appearances, that which is the accompaniment of all alike, one and the same in all their

---

[1] Paragraph 6(a) is from *C d r V* 39–40 (69–70).

[2] Paragraph 6(b) is an expansion of the final sentence of the first paragraph of *C d r V* 40 (70).

[3] Paragraph 7 is from *C d r V* 42 (71).

particular differences, is to be assumed as previous to all actual perception of things, i.e. to all reference of particular intuitions to determinate objects.[1]

8(b) The difficulty that attends this conception arises from the impossibility of illustrating it by any particular image, but this difficulty will be [avoided][a] if only we reflect that we are not to seek after any image and then consider that every imaginable figure in which any image can be presented to us is a modification of its extension, but that [that] of which every particular form is a modification must be common to all forms and itself therefore the common or universal form. Or perhaps we may attain the same end still more simply by representing to ourselves any body of large extent and reflect[ing] on its extension before we have arrived at the boundary which constitutes its figure. Here in the first place we are conscious that the figure arises by a negation of the extension and not by anything added thereto, and, secondly, that the extension, considered independently of this, constituted a part of the image presented to us. But this extension is itself not a thing, in the sense of anything substantial; for this would be a contradiction in terms, the extension being equivalent to surface, and, if we may so say, essentially and exclusively superficial—but, if not substance, nothing[b] remains but that it is a form, not indeed as a shape, but that in which all shapes consist as far as they are shapes and not any particular shape. In common language we might say that space is the way in which we perceive all outward things.

9 It follows, therefore, that as little as we can attribute the form of a cast to the materials which had flowed into the mould, as little can we attribute space to the things that appear under the relations of space; and would we contemplate it as a reality in itself, as a thing outwardly subsisting, there would arise the absurdity of a thing having all the predicates of nothing, which in fact is the word used by the common people when they mean to speak of space as out of themselves. What is between me and yonder wall? "An empty space", might be the reply of the scholar. The common man would answer, "Nothing". Much less has been disputed respecting the ideality of space and of the celebrated controversy between Clarke and Leibniz[2] on this question, in which both parties were in the wrong. Leibniz was so far in the right that he denied the subsistence

---

a Blank space left in ms   *b* ms: nothing nothing

[1] Paragraph 8(a) is from *C d r V* 42 (71).   [2] Leibniz and Clarke *A Collection of Papers* (1717).

of space independent of the mind;[1] but he grievously erred in representing it as nothing more than a confused perception arising out of the indistinctness of all particular figures whether from the distance or the minuteness of the objects.[2] Clarke and the English philosophers rightly and unanswerably replied to this that space was preconceived in order to these very confused perceptions, that this very confusion supposed a space, in which it existed no less than the most determinate figures.[3] They contended with truth that space was not abstracted from any object nor generalised from any class of objects: but they erred in the too hasty conclusion that therefore it must itself exist objectively.[4] The truth is that it is the subjective condition of all objectivity, and whatever reality is attributed to outward experience must *a fortiori* belong to that without which no outward experience is possible. If therefore we use the term "real" in opposition to "fantastic", or if we use "objective" as the contrary of "accidental", in order to distinguish from the result of individual peculiarities, then space is in this sense an undoubted reality, and eminently objective; but if we use the word "real" in opposition to "mental", or "*obj*ective" in opposition to "*subj*ective" in its widest sense, then we must reverse the position.

Illustration

10   Those who cannot emancipate themselves from the notion that space, and the same we shall find hold good of time likewise, are inferences or adherences of things in themselves, may perhaps find some assistance in mastering a full conviction of the contrary by exercising their ingenuity on the following paradox. Suppose that two things, as, for instance, two conch[a] shells, in all circumstances, of quantity, and quality, and figure, fully alike, and only numerically different—it follows that the one might be substituted for the other without any possibility of discovering the change, and in fact so it is with two sovereigns from the same mint, as far as they appear only numerically different. If I had put down one sovereign on the table and my companion had left the room for an instant, he would not discover that I had changed it, nor should I myself afterwards be able to determine which of the two I had first put down, unless I had

---

[a] ms has French spelling: conque

[1] Ibid pp 57, 181–3.   [3] E.g. ibid.
[2] Ibid pp 195ff.   [4] E.g. ibid.

adopted some extrinsic means of securing the knowledge. It holds good indeed with all the plane figures in geometry. But various spherical figures afford proof, notwithstanding this perfect identity in all intrinsic characters, in every point that can be understood by the simple contemplation of the figure itself, [that there is] yet such a difference in outward relation that the one cannot be put for the other. Take, for example, two spherical triangles of both hemispheres that have an arc of the equator as their common basis. The triangles may be fully alike in respect both of the size and the angles, so that to describe each separately by itself, and this in the fullest detail, yet nothing will be found which will not be repeated in the very same words in a similar description of the other. The description in each case shall be adequate, nothing omitted which could be made intelligible as belonging to the object singly and without reference to any other object existing independently of the same. And yet we know that the one cannot be put in the place of the other, that which belongs to the one hemisphere cannot be transferred to the *a*opposite. There*b* is then some inherent difference of both triangles, which yet the understanding cannot represent as inherent—in plain words, which we cannot make intelligible, and which manifests itself to us solely*c* by the outward relation of each in space.[1] That it is a real, an *inherent*, difference will appear more readily perhaps if instead of the triangle we refer to a similar difference in the hop and scarlet bean, a difference which can be expressed by some outward comparison and which our gardeners do commonly express by describing the perfectly corresponding yet opposite w[inding] as with or against the sun,[2] yet the difference exists in the plants themselves (and there is of necessity an efficient ground and cause of this difference in the qualities and structure of the seed), but we cannot discover this otherwise than by submitting it to an act of comparison, each with the other,

---

a–b ms: opposite, here   *c* ms: solely to us

[1] Paragraph 10 up to this point is from *Prolegomena* § 13 (1783) 56–8.

[2] C refers to this difference between the hop and the scarlet runner bean (*Phaseolus multiflorus*, "one of the few plants that twine in a direction contrary to the apparent motion of the sun"—*EB* 11th ed article "Bean") for the same purpose in a letter to Thomas Clarkson of 13 Oct 1806 (*CL* II 1193). In each case he is drawing on an example in Kant *Metaphysische An-*

fangsgründe der Naturwissenschaft (Riga 1787) 7–8, from which p 161 line 22 to p 162 line 5 is freely translated. Kant attributes the phrases "with the sun" and "against the sun" to "Seeleute" (mariners) rather than to gardeners. Cf also Kant *Sammlung einiger bisher unbekannt gebliebener kleiner Schriften* (1800) 75 and *VS* IV 75. (C's copies of all three books are in the BM.)

and this too in order to place both in a relation of space. Thus we see that so it is and we know that there must be a ground, independent of ourselves and of our own faculties, of our being thus distinctly affected in each instant, but still we cannot *understand* the difference (*datur, non intelligitur*).[1] It is not therefore the understanding that is affected, for our conceptions remain unchanged and wholly alien from this knowledge. It is the faculty of sense alone that is affected, and the difference is made known to us as an immediate intuition, we *perc*eive it instantly, though we cannot *con*ceive it. Now, if space were an objective property and belonging to the things themselves, we should be able to describe this difference no less than those by which the two objects are both alike distinguished from others, as, for instance, the spherical triangles from plane, or the hop and bean from some other climber. A still more obvious example we have before us in the looking-glass. What can be conceived more perfectly like to my hand or my ear than its reflection in the glass, and yet the hand seen in the glass I cannot put in the place of the original. If it be my right hand, the hand in the glass is the left, the image of the right ear becomes the left. Here, it is true, there are no intrinsic differences that it is in the power of any understanding even to think, and yet the differences are intrinsic as far as our senses can teach us, for we well know that we cannot put [a] right-hand glove on our left hand, and know that we could not do it even if by some miracle we could substantiate that [?image]*a* perfectly identical of the reflection in the glass. What then is the solution of this riddle? No other is possible than that the difference in question, i.e. as seen by us, and not the cause of this difference, is neither to be found in A singly nor in B singly, but in C, as the result of the different relation in which A and B stand to it, as a third, affected at the same moment by both.

11(a)   What is this third corresponding to C? It is, evidently, the subjective sense, and the difference consists in an affection of the subjective sense calling forth that mode of action which results from its own constitution and characteristic property. This mode or form is modified. An unknown agency*b* from without is in part doubtless the modifying cause; but it is the faculty itself or its inherent mode of action that is the subject modified. That it is an affection of space is wholly owing to the sense. That it is that peculiar affection is

a Blank space left in ms   *b* ms: agency agency

1 "It is given, not understood". From this point on, paragraph 10 is based on *Prolegomena* § 13 (1783) 58–9.

inasmuch as in the instances above given, the Sense
is affected & its forms called into act while the
function of the understanding remain altogether
neutral & indifferent. I cannot conclude this chap-
ter without introducing one other at once the most
beautiful & the most simple elucidation of this
point. that which is presented to us in the well known
"Kaleidoscope," an instrument well calculated to
suggest thoughts, the interest of which will long
survive the innocent amusement to its powers of
supplying which the instrument owed its populari-
ty. We put into the instrument from 15 to 20
fragments, bits of coloured glass. a steel filing or
two, ends of thread— cuttings of wire, small pieces
of silk in short from 20 to 30. substances & at
every motion that we make there arises some new
& distinct form of beauty, in endless succession, the
number inexhaustible & all beautiful. though not
all equally delightful. We find the same diffe-
rences & the tastes of different persons differently

4. British Library MS Egerton 2826 f 240, in the handwriting of
Transcriber A. See p 163.

The British Library; reproduced by kind permission

derived contingently from the nature of the external object. In this simple contemplation, therefore, we obtain an insight, first into the difference of the subjective from the objective and in the purely subjective nature of space as an affection of the [a]subject; and secondly[b] into the differences in the subject itself, viz. the difference of the sense and its forms, from the understanding and its forms, inasmuch as in the instances above given, the sense is affected and its forms called into act while the function of the understanding remain[s] altogether neutral and indifferent.

11(b)   I cannot conclude this chapter without introducing one other at once the most beautiful and the most simple elucidation of this point: that which is presented to us in the well-known kaleidoscope, an instrument well calculated to suggest thoughts, the interest of which will long survive the innocent amusement to its powers of supplying which the instrument owed its popularity. We put into the instrument from fifteen to twenty fragments, bits of coloured glass, a steel filing or two, ends of thread, cuttings of wire, small pieces of silk—in short, from twenty to thirty substances—and at every motion that we make there arises some new and distinct form of beauty in endless succession, the number inexhaustible and all beautiful, though not all equally delightful. We find the same differences and the tastes of different persons differently affected, as if a series of beautiful *flowers* or *chefs d'*[*o*]*euv*[*res*] of jewellery were presented to the same person and to different persons. None could be denied to be beautiful, but we should hear the exclamations, "How beautiful!" "How very beautiful!" "This is pretty, but it does not strike me so much". "This is the most beautiful of all that I have seen", etc, etc. For my readers' recollections will present the delights of a kaleidoscope at its first introduction better than I[c] can dramatise them.[1] Let the twenty or thirty bits and fragments be removed from the kaleidoscope to a dice box and try as long as your patience will permit to throw them or any portion of them on the table so as to form a beautiful figure. You will in all probability waste an hour or a week

---

a–b ms: subject. And 2ndly   *c* ms: it

[1] C first mentions the instrument in 1818 (*CN* III 4411), hard on the heels of its appearance. See *Description and Method of Using the Patent Kaleidoscope, Invented by Dr. Brewster* (1818) —an attempt to market the device— and David Brewster *A Treatise on the Kaleidoscope* (Edinburgh 1819). In 1818, SH called it "entirely the plaything of the Adults" (*SH Letters* 144; see also 140 and 142), and Shelley mentions the rage for it in Italy (*The Letters of Percy Bysshe Shelley* ed Frederick L. Jones—Oxford 1964—II 69).

without succeeding in any single instance. The difference therefore in the former arrangements cannot arise out of the substances themselves, but is attributable exclusively to the instrument or medium through which they were seen and in which their arrangement was effected. What shall we call this difference, this property, I mean, common in kind to all the thousand successive figures presented to us? Evidently symmetry, and this subsists wholly in the instrument itself; in the constitution and constituent laws (or modes of action) of the kaleidoscope itself this symmetry originates and by these it is communicated not to the fragments themselves but to the figure in the beholder's mind resulting from this arrangement, and that they are all so arranged as to fall under one common form, viz. that of symmetry, is the work of the instrument itself. But further, the effect common to all, to what does it refer? Not to the sensibility considered as the capability of sensation. This indeed is affected, diversely affected, and it is its affections by which in great measure our preferences are determined and the greater comparative delight which we receive from one figure rather than from another—or from our selection of some substances rather than others; of bits of coloured glass, for instance, for common glass, or of the variety in colours rather than one or two kinds, and in some measure from the larger number of the substances included, though here the action of the instrument itself is concerned in the effect. If not to the sensibility, therefore to the sense. Instead of the kaleidoscope [as] the instrument of the sentient faculty let us take the faculty itself as its own instrument, or an instrument of the mind—instrument at once and a constituent part. In like manner, for symmetry or peculiar modifications of the relations of space, we will take space itself, and we may then apply the results without change. All intuitions of objects outwardly present have their origin both in the sensibility and in the sense. As far as the sensibility is affected we are justified in resolving this effect into an agency and[a] proper character of the *object*, modified, however, by the nature of the sensibility which it modifies. All else must be referred to the sense, with this exception, however—if indeed it is an exception and not included in the former class, viz. the affections of the sensibility—I mean the contingency of the determinate forms or the fact that the universal form, that of space in the present instance of the faculty, and that of symmetry in the presentations of the kaleidoscope, is[b] such at this moment, as far as it is not referable to an act of our own will, whether the external object be external in the ordinary use of the

[a] ms: & &   [b] ms: are

term or the spontaneous act of our own organisation as in our dreams. In all such cases, however, the determinable form subsists in and of the sense itself: whether the particular determination of the form originates in the will or the sensibility and again whether in the will, calling the sense into determinate act according to the laws of reason, or for the purposes of the understanding, or the will acting on the sensibility in wantonness or for amusement: and in like manner, the sensibility, whether affected by objects from without or by the organisation with which it is connected and on which it depends. The distinction [is] that the first only—the determination of the will according to the laws of the reason and arising from the constitution of the sense itself and the inherent properties of its constituent *a*forms—is*b* accompanied with a sense of necessity and capable of being known and determined *a priori*. The nature of these determinations we shall investigate after our enquiry into the remaining form of sense, viz. time, to which we now proceed.

Time

12　If space be then the *forma formarum*[1] or common form of the outward sense, it might be anticipated that time would be found to stand in the same relation to the inner sense. The process of proof must consist therefore in a repetition of the former and like the former will fall under two heads. First, the analytic exposition by which the constituent parts of the conception or intuition are *set forth*, so that a distinct attention having been given to each we may thereby obtain a more distinct and clear consciousness of the whole. Our purpose is not to attach a new meaning to the term but to reflect on that which we already possess *implicitly* so as to render it *explicit*. Not acquisition but explication of a knowledge already acquired is the aim of all analytic disquisition; not addition but distinctness. And secondly, the *transcendental* exposition or its relation to some faculty. For this, as we have before observed, is what is meant by transcendental.[2] We begin therefore with the analysis of the term.

13　Time is, first, not an empirical conception that has been or can be abstracted from any possible experience. For simultaneity or succession could not have been perceived if the representation of time did not pre-exist as its ground and condition *a priori*. How

1 "Form of forms".　　　　　　　　2 See above, pp 146–7.

should we distinguish simultaneity, or the being together in the same moment, from succession, if the idea of the same moment and not the same moment, of present or not present, and in the[a] not present as past or as yet to come, i.e. the idea of time itself, were not already in our possession? All knowledge from without must have originated in particulars and must be capable of reduction into the same. But no particular can be imagined or conceived which did not or does not presuppose the universal in this case. The utmost that can be attributed to the former is that they may have furnished the occasion of reflecting on the latter: and the first particular that does this gives us the consciousness of the whole, a consciousness not of something then given, but of a something already possessed.[1]*

14   Second. Time then is a necessary representation in which all our intuitions are grounded, or shall we say that it is the root of which all particular intuitions are the unfoldings under the influences of their exciting occasions. As in the instance of space, so in this: attempt to think away time itself while at the same time you present any number of phenomena co-existing and in succession. It is found impossible, though without difficulty [you may think] away any one

---

* "The intellectual seed must itself have its birthplace within, whatever excitement from without may be necessary for its generation. Will the soul thus awakened neglect or undervalue the outward and conditional causes of her growth? For rather, might we dare borrow a wild fancy from the Mantuan bard[2] or the poet of Arno,[3] will it be with her, as if a stem, or trunk, suddenly endued with sense and reflection,[b] should contemplate its green shoots, their leafits and budding blossoms, wondered at as then first noticed, but welcomed nevertheless as its own growth: while yet with undiminished gratitude, and a deepened sense of dependency, it would bless the dews and sunshine from without, deprived of the awakening and fostering excitement of which, its own productivity would have remained for ever hidden from itself, or felt only as the obscure trouble of a baffled instinct."[4]

a ms: the in the   *b* ms: rfection

[1] Paragraph 13 is from *C d r V* 46 (74).

[2] Virgil *Georgics* 2.80–2: "nec longum tempus, et ingens/ exiit ad caelum ramis felicibus arbos,/ miraturque novas frondes et non sua poma". Tr H. Rushton Fairclough (LCL 1940): "in a little while, lo! a mighty tree shoots up skyward with joyous boughs, and marvels at its strange leafage and fruits not its own".

[3] Dante. C is probably thinking of *Inferno* ii lines 127–30: "Quali i fioretti dal notturno gelo/ Chinati e chiusi, poi che il Sol li 'mbianca,/ Si drizzan tutti aperti in loro stelo,/ Tal mi fec' io di mia virtute stanca . . . .". Tr Henry Francis Cary (1814): "As florets, by the frosty air of night/ Bent down and clos'd, when day has blanch'd their leaves,—/ Rise all unfolded on their spiry stems,—/ So was my fainting vigor new restor'd". C quoted the passage in Lecture x of his 1818 series. *LR* i 160–1.

[4] The paragraph is from *Friend* (CC) i 513–14 (var).

or any number of the phenomena themselves. What is the reason? You cannot think away the thinking itself, for this is presupposed. Time, therefore, is given *a priori*, the *semper datum et suppositum*[1] by means of which all actual phenomena are possible.[2]

15   Third. In this necessity *a priori* or, if you please to vary the metaphor, in this necessity *ab intra*,[3] the possibility of demonstrative apodictic or self-evident principles of the relations of time, or what are called axioms of time generally, is grounded. Time has but one dimension. Different times are not co-present but follow each other. To suppose the contrary would be to assert that *different* times are the *same* time, an absurdity of which (otherwise than by a wanton abuse of words) it is not in our power to be guilty. And yet without any absurdity, or rather by a necessary insight, we assert that different spaces are not one after the other, but are together or co-present. These axioms cannot have been deduced from experience, for had that been the case they would possess neither strict universality nor demonstrative certainty. We should be able to say the common sense of mankind has hitherto coincided in this experience, and we see no reason for supposing that it will be otherwise for the time to come, but not, so it must be and cannot be otherwise for all beings that contemplate objects in the relations of time and space. We could only say, all the bodies that have hitherto come under the notice of my senses or my imagination have presented space to me as consisting of three[a] dimensions, while all the motions of bodies and all succession of bodies have presented time to me as having but one dimension, and I have no reason to suppose that the experience of any other man has been or ever will be different. But we mean something more and other than this when, with a sense of [the] necessity and universal truth of the position, we affirm that space has three[b] dimensions and time but one—that so it must be—for the contrary is an absurdity, i.e. an arrangement of articulated sounds or their representative characters, a collective[c] sense for which can neither be conceived nor imagined. Hence it is that these axioms of time and space serve as rules under which all experiences are possible. They are not borrowed from these experiences. For in all experiences they constitute the experience itself. What we experience may be the product of conceiving[d] causes; but that we experience at all is owing

---

a ms: their   *b* ms: 13   *c* ms: collection, ~~from~~   *d* For "concurring"?

1 "The thing always given and posited".

2 Paragraph 14 is from *C d r V* 46 (74–5).

3 "From within".

to time and space and presupposes them as its cause and necessary condition.[1]

16   Fourth. Time is no general conception representing any class of particulars. It is no conception that has been nor can be formed discursively by alluding to a number of particulars and then fixing the attention and reflection exclusively on some character common to all. Different times are only portions of one and the same time, the division of which does not exist in the time itself, but is attributed to it metaphorically from the objects existing in this relation to ourselves. They are not so properly parts of time as measures, each of which indeed is divisible *ad infinitum*. But a representation that can be given only by means of a single object is an *intuition* as contradistinguished from a conception. But this is true of time—it applies totally to each object to which it applies at all. Time therefore is an intuition, not a conception. Even the simple position that different times cannot be simultaneous cannot be deduced from any general conception. In order to give the words their full meaning we appeal at once to the intuition—simply and without exercising any one of the functions of the understanding, which are, and must be, exercised in the formation of a conception; we refer to no instance, we compare no number of instances, and consequently we neither abstract from that which is peculiar in each nor generalise anything that is common to all. The position is self-evident and admits of no further proof that it is so—if [for] no other reason than because so it is.[2]

17(a)   Fifth. The infinity of time signifies nothing more than that all determinate qualities of time are possible only by limitations of one single time supposed in all, which limitations, however, have no imaginable subsistence in time itself as the common measure and ground of all, but in the contemplation by occasion of the objects. Time is infinite in the sense that considered in itself, without reference to the object or its beholder, it contains in itself no bounds—*infinitum est, quia nullos habet fines in se*—and herein consists the difference in the infinity of time from the infinity of space. That of the latter is positive and essential. For where space is, it is essentially infinite. The infinity of time, on the other hand, is negative and consequent on the abstraction from all the boundaries or partial measurements that originate and exist in the objects only.[3]

[1] Paragraph 15 is from *C d r V* 47 (75).

[2] Paragraph 16 is from *C d r V* 47 (75).

[3] Paragraph 17(a) is from *C d r V* 47–8 (75).

17(b)   To give an insight, however, into the nature and ground of this difference would require an investigation beyond the bounds of a purely analytic enquiry and [one] which would not belong even to a transcendental exposition, which rests in the ascertainment of the faculty the existence of which we know only by means of reflection, i.e. by an exercise of one of the functions of the faculty. But to *understand* the faculty of the sense is impossible, for every act of the understanding presumes the sense as its datum. But to *understand* the faculty of the understanding is the same as to understand that which stands undermost—an attempt not more fortunate than that of the eastern speculators who having put the earth on a bull and the bull on a bear found it still necessary to put the tortoise under both.[1] Whether there exist any other source of insight, and [one] that can more properly be styled both a *source* and a source of *insight*, is an enquiry not included within the province of logic, in the stricter sense of the word, whether canonic or transcendental. If within the spheres of human knowledge at all, it appertains to the science of *pure* psychology, as a branch of metaphysics.

17(c)   Now it yet remains to be seen whether such a science as that of metaphysics (in the sense of a first philosophy) is *possible*,[2] or whether it be not *transcendent* of the human faculties instead of *transcendental*, i.e. referable to the constitution of these faculties; in which latter case it would be the same as transcendental logic and the name would be superfluous. But this possibility cannot be ascertained except by the means of transcendental logic, and the determination, whether affirmative or negative, presupposes the knowledge so obtained. There is indeed, as we have already noticed, a higher sense of the term "logos", in which it signifies the reason as including the understanding. On this assumption there would arise relations of the understanding to the reason and of the reason to the understanding, and the knowledge of these relations would constitute a higher, or rather the highest, branch of logic, viz. the logic of ideas and first principles.[3] But as distinct terms are often the condition, and always the assistant, of distinct conceptions, we have proposed to designate this branch by the name of "noetic" and have taken it as the subject of our last section, to the introduction to which the discussion of the question ("Is a first philosophy possible?") is deferred.

[1] Cf *CN* III 3973. A similar remark occurs in Locke *Essay on Human Understanding* bk II ch 23 § 2, and, following him, in Leibniz *Nouveaux essais* bk II ch 23 § 2.

[2] Kant's first question in the *Prolegomena* Einleitung (1783) 4–7.

[3] A fuller discussion appears in HEHL MS HM 8195, "The Divine Ideas".

Transcendental Exposition

18   What sciences derive their possibility as pure sciences from the notions *a priori* of time and space and law is an enquiry that strictly belongs to the transcendental exposition of these notions; but as I shall be under the necessity of treating the subject in the next chapter, to this I shall refer the student in order to prevent the waste of his attention by repetition[s] when they can be avoided with no greater inconvenience than a slight relaxation in the rigour of form. I proceed at once to the transcendental conclusions from the conceptions displayed in the analytic exposition.[1]

19   A. Time is not anything that subsists for itself or belongs to things as their own property or objective characteristic. In either of which cases the conception of time would remain after we had abstracted from all the subjective conditions of its intuition. For in the first case, that without any real object would nevertheless be itself real; and as for the second as a property or inherent order belonging to the things themselves, it could not possibly be conceived as antecedent to these things as their ground and indispensable precondition. But that so it is and must be contemplated we have already shown and shall further prove in the disquisition next following, from the nature of the sciences that peculiar evidence of which is grounded in this priority.[2]

20(a)   B. Time is the form of the inner sense, i.e. of the intuition that we have of ourselves and of our own inward state. It is this and nothing else. For time is no inherent property or quality of outward appearances. It belongs neither to shape nor position, while on the other hand it determines the relation of our representations[a] in the widest sense of the word, including both thoughts and feelings in our own inward being. So true is it that time has nothing to do with shape, position, and the like, because this inward intuition and universal form of all inward intuitions is itself shapeless.

20(b)   We seek to supply this defect by analogy, and as this is found in all known languages, we may say that mankind have been led as by a common instinct of their intellectual nature so to supply the defect and to represent the succession of time by a line proceeding infinitely in which the manifold constitutes a series of one dimension only, and out of the properties of this line all the properties of time

a ms: representatives

[1] Paragraph 18 is from *C d r V* 48–9 (76).   [2] Paragraph 19 is from *C d r V* 49 (76).

are concluded, with one exception, that [those of] the former, viz. the line, are simultaneous, while those of the latter, the moments or things signified, are necessarily successive. It follows too as a corollary that the representation of time must itself be an intuition inasmuch as all its relations are expressible in an outward intuition.[1]

21   At all events it is of the nature of an intuition, and to object to its being called an intuition would be little else than to quarrel with language itself and all the principles on which language is possible. (Instead of saying, what no one would deny, that we cannot actually have an intuition of time unaccompanied by some intuition of space.)[a] The mechanism or construction of the representations of time by space, and vice versa of space by time, belongs to another place; the fact only is mentioned here.

22   C. Time is the formal condition *a priori* of all phenomena universally. Space as the pure form of all outward intuition is, when considered as a condition *a priori*, confined to outward phenomena exclusively. On the other hand, as all representations, whether they have outward things for their objects or not, yet in themselves as determinations, or to use as [?affirmations],[b] of our sentient being, do of themselves necessarily belong to our inward state and as this inward state again falls under the formal condition of inward intuition, consequently of time, time must be the condition *a priori* of all phenomena, of all appearance, universally. It is the immediate condition of the inward proceedings of our consciousness and thence mediately of the outward phenomena likewise. An illustration of the nature of time (as given in §B) is suggested by the words "phenomenon", "appearance", as applied to the experiences of our inward state; as they fall wholly under the form of time, so, like time itself, they are in themselves shapeless, and, as in the instance of time, we are compelled to borrow the expressions from our outward intuitions, i.e. from the forms of space.[2]

23(a)   If we abstract from the way in which we intuitively contemplate our inward state and by means of this intuition are capable of representing to ourselves all outward forms, when we abstract from this and consequently speak of the objects as they are or may be supposed to be in themselves and independent of our mode of contemplating them, then time is nothing. And if we use the term "objectively" to express the object in the absence of, or perfect abstrac-

---

a Parentheses inserted   *b* Blank space left in ms [cf third paragraph of C's n to p 21]

[1] Paragraphs 20(a) and 20(b) are from *C d r V* 49–50 (77).   [2] Paragraph 22 is from *C d r V* 50–1 (77).

tion from, all that is communicated to the representation of this object by the mind or the subject as the instrument and medium of the representation—in the strictly *metaphysical* sense of the word— time is nothing objective, but wholly subjective.

23(b)   If, on the other hand, we take the word in the more usual and practical sense as applied to the phenomena themselves, and mean by it that such and such appearances are common to all men under the same circumstances and do not arise from any peculiarities in an individual subject or any particular sort and number of individuals, and that they may therefore be safely reasoned on and confidently anticipated—in this sense time has an objective reality, viz. the very same reality, whether it be of the appearances themselves [?or] of all [?of] which it is mediately or immediately the inseparable condition and constitutive form.[1]

23(c)   But we are not entitled to extend this assertion of its reality beyond these appearances, or beyond the human mind *a*collectively taken.*b* We are not entitled to assert that even all finite beings, whether higher or lower than*c* man, must necessarily perceive objects, or that the objects must necessarily appear to them under the relations of time; much less dare we thus limit the infinite mind. It is certain that we can neither conceive nor imagine any appearance not under the relations of time, and this is a sufficient proof that it is universally subjective as far as man is concerned, but it proves nothing more. It may, however, suggest a truth of the highest importance, that there are objects the existence of which we may hold with the clearest and most distinct insight of reason, though we are capable of forming neither a conception nor an imagination of the same. And this reflection we may make use of as a preservative from two opposite errors, both equally perilous. The one, that of attributing an absolute reality and self-subsistence to that which is subjective only and which therefore is real only as far as the mind is real, of the constitution of which it is the necessary result, and*d* this is what we mean when we say that time is subjective reality; or, real in relation to the human mind as the subject—and in this sense we may contradistinguish this subjective reality from the yellow colour of bodies to a jaundiced individual[2] or from the apparition of the late Mrs Veal

$^{a-b}$ ms: taken colectively
^{c} ms: the ^{d} ms: & &

[1] Paragraphs 23(a) to 23(b) are from *C d r V* 51–2 (77–8).

[2] The example of illusion used by Descartes in *Discourse on Method*: *D Works* I 105. Cf *CN* II 2439 (Feb 1805).

to her surviving laundress in St Bride's Lane, Fleet St, recorded by the Rev Dr Drelincourt, or the translator of his work,[1] which may or may not have been subjectively actual, i.e. have actually appeared to one individual subject, whether feverous or dreaming, but has no pretensions to reality, i.e. permanence and universality, subjective or objective, i.e. relative or absolute.[2]

23(d) From inadvertence to the truth that subjective reality does not cease to be reality arises the only plausible objection to the view of time obtained in this chapter. The changes of objects are real; we have the same experience and consequently the same evidence of these as of the objects themselves; but these changes we have ourselves admitted are not possible except in time, therefore time itself must be real. We answer the position by admitting it. Both the one and the other, the succession and the time, are real, and the experience and the objects of the experience, viz. the phenomena whether of the outward or of the inward sense, are real; but they are all alike subjectively so, and a moment's reflection on the meaning of experience itself will convince us that an experience not subjective would be a contradiction, or an experience which was no one's experience. But I refer the student to the beautiful tale in the *Spectator* of the line[a] of changes and successive events that happened to the Vizier in the interval between the immersion and emersion of his head in the cold bath.[3] These changes, it will not be denied, were subjectively actual, and the student has only to reflect what was wanting to make these subjectively real and which of these additions would in the least alter the subjective nature of the changes themselves. Will the subjective be done[b] away by multiplying the subjects, or will the rainbow be less a reflection by being reflected from a thousand waves at the same moment or from ten thousand myriads of dewdrops?[4]

---

a ms: life   *b* ms: done done

[1] Defoe's authorship of *The True Relation of the Apparition of One Mrs Veal* was known. See, e.g., George Chalmers *The Life of Daniel Defoe* (1790) 74.

[2] Paragraph 23(c) is from *C d r V*

52–3 (78). The examples of jaundice and of Mrs Veal are C's.

[3] Presumably a reference to the story of Alnaschar's daydream: *Spectator* No 535 (Thursday, 13 Nov 1712).

[4] Paragraph 23(d) is based on *C d r V* 53–4 (79).

CHAPTER [V]

Of Analytic and Synthetic Judgments[1]

1 We have hitherto directed our attention expressly to the distinctions of cognitions *a priori*, or cognition, and those *a posteriori*, or experience and facts of experience, i.e. between knowledge from [a transcendental point of view and knowledge from]*a* an empirical, the latter term taken in all its primary and indifferent sense, simply experiential. In our present subject, however, a new distinction will present itself. Whatever the origin of the judgments may be, whether their sense be transcendental or experiential, there is still a difference in the contents or matter of the judgment, so that the purport of the one is simply that of elucidation, while that of the other is addition or enlargement of knowledge. The former or the analytic process of the judgment we have explained at large in a*b* preceding page and illustrated by the case of the map.[2] The latter or synthetic process might perhaps be sufficiently defined by saying that it is the opposite of the former; but the import of both the one and the other term will be best and most easily shown by simply rendering the Greek word into its English equivalents—analysis being the resolution of a thing, image, or conception into its constituent parts, and distinguishing what it is made of, and synthesis, the adding of one knowledge to another, the putting of B to and with A. By the analytic process we know what we know *better*; by the synthetic we know more. If B had been a part of A, by distinctly contemplating A and*c* nothing else we could have become conscious of B. The affirmation of B would be an analytic judgment. "You saw the part of such a house?" "Yes." "Were the windows square or round?" "Let me reflect a moment. I did not particularly notice the windows, but now I bring the whole before me again I see they were square windows, but one in the middle was a bow window." This is properly an analytic judgment. But if I

---

a An example of the transcriber's eye skipping a line?   *b* ms: the   *c* ms: as

[1] The chapter is freely drawn from *C d r V* 10–14 (48–51). The examples of the house, the spark of fire, and the eyes of horses are C's.

[2] See above, pp 125–6.

asked concerning the furniture of the house, as, for instance, if I spoke of a picture in the room appertaining to the bow window, the answer might be, "How should I know, as I saw only the part of the house?"; or "Yes, for it was the first room I examined, after we had been shown the extent of the house." The judgment by which the picture is connected with the bow window is synthetic. It is most important to observe that the circumstance of the connection in this instance being accidental does not in the least affect the synthetic character of the judgment, neither increasing nor diminishing, least of all constituting, its synthetic nature. Instead of the bow window, etc, take the instance of the spark of fire from the flint of a gun in connection with the flight of the ball from the muzzle. The judgment, in this case that the fire-spark being known, the flight of the ball is known likewise, is no less a synthetic judgment than the former, unless it could be shown that a man who had simply seen the gun-lock, though he had neither seen the ball nor the powder, could yet, by mere increase of his attention to the image and conception which the lock itself gave, find*a* that the ball, powder, barrel, etc were all constituent parts of that image and conception, things that he had actually seen in seeing the gun-lock, though in consequence of his attention having been directed chiefly to the whole he had not made himself distinctly conscious of the component parts, but which parts nevertheless as soon as he attends to them he knows that he had seen and must have seen before. In short, [it is] not what may be deduced from any position, whether with or without a sense of necessity, whether the connection take place by the mere habit of seeing the one thing always or almost always co-present with some other, or the one immediately succeeding the other, though no interior connection is believed—as, for instance, in the connection of certain diseases of the eyes of horses with the wax and wane of the moon[1]—or whether in consequence of such concurrency we do attribute some interior connection, as, for instance, of the moon and tides;*b* [it is] not, I say, what may be *deduced* from B whether in consequence of a past experience which having associated C therewith induces me on the presentation of B to anticipate the occurrence of C; or as the result of a previous knowledge of A having both B and C among its constituent parts; or lastly, from my previous insight into some principle or law = X, by the application of which to B and C I

a ms: would find   *b* Full stop in ms

[1] For symptoms of the disease called "moon eyes", see Francis Clater *Every Man His Own Farrier* . . . (Newark 1783) 51–2.

determine that "B = C"; [that] makes my judgment respecting B an analytic judgment, or my knowledge a knowledge obtained by analysis, but what is *contained* in it. But even in this "it" there is a possible equivocation which it is important that we should remove. The conception may be[a] abstracted from the mind conceiving, and have a logical entity given to it, which but too easily may be mistaken for a real self-subsistence. Not that any rational man could deliberately and with distinct reflection form such a judgment; but that unconsciously such a confusion takes place is proved from the nature of the inferences drawn, which [have] no force, no legitimate consequence, except on the supposition of the conception being something more than an *ens logicum*, or product of the mind, as inseparable from the act producing it, as the act from the agent.

2   Now we affirm that[b] an analytic judgment extends only to that which is actually contained in the individual conception of the term, not in another's possible conception. For instance, in God's conceptions, if we dare attribute the term at all in reference to God, or in the conceptions of spiritual beings superior to man, though still, like himself, finite, the distinction of analytic and synthetic may not exist, or each conception might actually contain all other conceptions. But whether a knowledge of this description can without abuse of words be called conception is more than doubtful, and at all events they are not human conceptions and therefore are altogether alien from the present consideration. Once again therefore, and the student will find himself remunerated for the trouble and distaste which this perplexity and frequency of repetition may have occasioned him, that alone which I am able to learn from any given knowledge which I already possess by mere reflection on that knowledge and a distinct attention to the component terms or constituents—the import, I say, that these terms actually have for me—this alone is an analytic judgment. Of course whatever being resolvable into constituent parts and not a simple affirmation, and which therefore is neither analytic nor synthetic,[c] whatever is more than this, is synthetic. We will take an example. "All matter is extended."[1] I will suppose myself in the first place not to have distinguished between matter and body, but as is the case with the great majority of persons to have understood the terms as two words with one and the same meaning—I say, therefore, "all bodies are extended", and in so judging I form an

---

[a] ms: be be   [b] ms: than   [c] Full stop in ms

[1] Descartes' definition: *Principia* pt II princ ivff.

analytic judgment. For I have only to reflect on what I mean by matter or body to be made aware that extension was contained in my thought. In other words, that a something extended is the explanation of the word, whether wholly or in part; but in either*a* case inseparably so that matter or body could have no sense at all without extension. But when I say that some matter, or, speaking synonymously, some bodies are heavy, I here add a term, I assert a knowledge, which was not contained in my conception of matter or body, nor contained in the conception of extension that is contained in that of matter. This therefore is a synthetic judgment. I will now suppose myself to have reflected on the term "heavy" and to have multiplied my experiences respecting heavy things so as to have discovered that heaviness expressed merely a degree of a property far more general, and so general, indeed, that I found it expedient to determine that those matters only in which the property was discoverable should be called bodies. Thus "body" and "matter" would be terms of contradistinction in which "matter" would signify whatever phenomena were extended, either abstracting from (i.e. *logice*),[1] or in exclusion of (i.e. *physice*),[2] the property of weight, and body would signify the union or co-existence of extension and ponderability in the same phenomenon. Henceforward, for me, the judgment, "All bodies are ponderable", would be an analytic judgment, for to make myself aware of the predicate "ponderable" I have only to examine what I meant by the subject, i.e. "body", but then it is an analytic judgment that supposes a previous synthesis, and therefore for all our present purposes is equivalent to synthetic. (By which term therefore we shall characterise all judgments that could not have been formed without a synthetic act in the consciousness.)*b* The student will see my reason for adding the last words, by recollecting our observations, in an earlier stage of this enquiry, on*c* the necessity of a primary synthesis anterior to consciousness and as the datum on which the functions of the understanding are to be exercised.[3]

---

a ms: neither   *b* Parentheses inserted   *c* ms: in

[1] "Logically".
[2] "Physically".
[3] Above, p 78.

CHAPTER [VI]

Analytic Judgments—the Common Principle of

1   The principle common to all analytic judgments is that of which we have before spoken as the *principium identitatis et contradictionis*,[1] i.e. whatever is, is. Whatever can be said to be, cannot be said *not* to be, and vice versa; or it answer[s] our purpose to say that all analytic judgments are grounded on the principle of contradiction:[2] that which forbids us to assert contraries of the same object at the same time, or, in the language of the vulgar, to say black is white. Now as this principle is a principle of reason, [it is] not deducible from any special faculty of the mind, whether of sense or of understanding, but [is] necessarily presupposed in all the exercises of both and of either, and consequently in all the knowledge which we acquire by experience, i.e. the coincidence of contingent impressions with these faculties, and therefore in the highest sense *a priori*. All analytic judgments are cognitions *a priori*, whether the conceptions that constitute them, and as it were form*ª* the materials of the judgment, be empirical or transcendental.[3] That, I mean, which gives a necessity to the assertion is *a priori* and contained in the mind itself, and that which the mind derives exclusively from itself. X may in fact be black, or be white, or neither, and without experience I could not have known which of the two it was; but far beyond all contingency, and altogether independent of experience, I determine with the fullest insight into the necessity and universality of all truth that X being throughout black cannot be at the same time white. We will express the proposition and the reason for it in the technical terms of logic. As the predicate of an affirmative analytic judgment already thought in the thinking of the subject and thought of affirmatively, it cannot without a contradiction be made negative, i.e. denied or exchanged

---

ª ms: from

[1] "Principle of identity and contradiction".
[2] The paragraph up to this point is from *Prolegomena* § 2b (1783) 25–6.
[3] The sentence is from *Prolegomena* § 2b (1783) 26.

for its contrary, when it is represented by itself and distinctly. In like manner, the contrary in an analytic negative judgment is necessarily negatived of the subject in conformity with the same principle of contradiction—thus, "Every body is extended" is an affirmative analytic judgment. "No body is unextended." This is a *negative* analytic judgment.[1] Therefore all analytic positions are judgments *a priori*, however empirical the terms may be—for instance, "gold is a yellow metal"—in order to know gold I must indeed have had experience; but in order to the position, "gold is a yellow metal", I need no other additional experience. My knowledge of the predicate "a yellow metal" pre-existed and was contained in my knowledge of the subject "gold".

---

[1] The paragraph from this point on is from *Prolegomena* § 2b (1783) 26.

^aCHAPTER [VII]

Of Synthetic Judgments and Their Principle

1 *Synthetic* judgments require another principle beside the *principium contradictionis*.[1] They, no less than the *analytic* judgments, must be in conformity with this principle; but this principle is only the condition under which they are judgments at all, and *not* the ground on which they rest as synthetic judgments.[2] To the synthetic class belong all judgments of experience, that is, all positions in which the predicate could not have been attached to the subject but by means of an experience as distinct as that of the subject itself. As an instance of synthetic judgments take the following. "This person is a father." I might have a sufficient conception of the person, but without another experience, viz. that of another person as a child, I could not have brought the two terms into connection in the position, "the person is a father". This, however, is admitted on all sides. The very word "experience" implies it, and the common phrases "increased experience", "growth of experience", and the like, openly declare it. The existence of synthetic judgments *a posteriori* is beyond all doubt; but are these the only synthetic judgments, or do there^b likewise exist [synthetic] judgments *a priori*? And on what ground does their evidence and cogency rest, viz. as *synthetic* judgments? We have seen that all *analytic* judgments are judgments *a priori*, and that they rest on a principle *a priori*, and that this principle is the principle of contradiction. But synthetic judgments are contradistinguished from *analytic* by not resting on the principle of contradiction. And synthetic judgments *a priori*, if any exist, cannot rest on experience as their ground; for by not resting thereon, they *become* synthetic judgments *a priori* in contradistinction from judgments equally synthetic, but *synthetic* judgments *a posteriori*. Their principle therefore must be *a priori*, and in addition to the principle of contradiction; and what may this be then? [These] are questions of the highest importance, the solution of which we shall attempt to give in the following chapter.

^a Transcriber B resumes   ^b ms: these

[1] "Principle of contradiction".   [2] The paragraph up to this point is from *Prolegomena* § 2c (1783) 26–7.

CHAPTER [VIII]

On Synthesis *a priori*

1 Bishop Berkeley has[a] remarked, and, if I mistake not, an observation to the same import occurs in yet earlier writers, that in speaking of objects in nature as antecedents and consequents we might more safely and appropriately name the former signals rather than causes.[*]

2 Though this remark of the philosophic bishop contains the substance of David Hume's chapter on cause and effect, little or no attention was excited by it. It was reserved for the Scottish philosopher by the publication of his essays in the year [1748][c2] and for the celebrity given to these essays by the praises of [the] French, repeated and echoed (according to Gray)[3] by the *literati* of Britain, to bring the subject of causality into public discussion.

3 This second spark, therefore, cannot be said to have fallen on incombustible materials. It produced great heat and volumes of smoke; but in reference at least to the *literati* of France and Britain it kindled as little light as the former.[4] The reason is obvious: Hume's opponents came forward not as investigators but as adversaries who saw nothing in the subject that required investigation. Whether they understood Hume's intentions as to the moral and religious application of the result, it is most certain that they altogether misapprehended the nature and import of the problem itself. Accordingly, all which the most eloquent among them could effect was the demolition

[*] In lieu of this paragraph quote the passage from Bishop Berkeley—I believe that it occurs in his *Minute Philosopher*.[b1]

---

a ms: had   *b* Footnote in pencil   *c* Blank space left in ms

1 C's reference to *Alciphron, or the Minute Philosopher* for this remark is incorrect. He was probably thinking of the passage in *A Treatise Concerning the Principles of Human Knowledge*: "the connexion of ideas does not imply the relation of *cause* and *effect*, but only of a mark or *sign* with the thing signified". *B Works* II 69. In BM MS Egerton 2801 f 115, C compared *Alciphron* favourably with Paley's *Natural Theology*, but termed them "sophisms both".

2 *An Enquiry Concerning Human Understanding*.

3 See William Mason "Memoirs of His Life and Writings" in *The Poems of Mr. Gray* (York 1775) 384–5.

4 The image is based on one used in Kant's discussion of Hume. *Prolegomena* Einleitung (1783) 7.

of a man of straw or Guy Fawkes[a] of their own manufacture, after they had amused themselves in contrivances more or less successful, to make it look as hideous as possible.[1] Before we therefore proceed to the solution of the problem, it will be necessary to state the problem itself at large and to explain wherein the difficulty lies: and I cannot perhaps do this better than by following what the Koenigsberg philosopher supposes to have been the course of Hume's own reflections.[2]

4   It stands as an axiom in philosophy, which the metaphysicians assert and which naturalists have hitherto admitted to be of universal application, that "whatever is not the first cause has (or must have had) a cause"; or, as it is sometimes expressed, whatever takes place, *becomes* (γινεται) or *comes to pass*, has a cause. Now we may use the words "cause and effect" in two ways: first, in the abstract as *entia logica*; secondly, as things to which this name is given when they are described as standing one to the other in the *relation* of cause and effect. To make the subject as intelligible as possible we will take them both successively, beginning with the former. And in order to elucidate the full sense and scope of this axiom we will represent the relation of cause and effect, which we shall hereafter name the "*causal* relation", or more briefly still "causality", under the more general formula of A = B, that is: A, of which B is no constituent part, is nevertheless so connected with B, that if B be given A is of necessity presumed. In other words, the notion of a cause is that of an A which does not *include* B, but yet *infers* it; and the notion of effect abstractly is that of a B which not being included in A is possible only on the assumption of A.

5   This is the true force of the judgment contained in the axiom "whatever is has a cause, with exception of the first cause", or, to avoid the scruple which might be excited by a universal principle (that commences with an exception to its own universality), "all that takes place has a cause". And this judgment is evidently not analytic. The position indeed has neither meaning nor pertinence if B be not different from A. When, for instance, I affirm that all body is extended, no one who understands the meaning of his words would describe the connection subsisting between "body", the subject, and

[a] ms: Faux

[1] For a similar account of the opposition to Hume, see *P Lects* Lect 6 (1949) 202–3.

[2] Kant *C d r V* 788–97 (606–12).

"extension", its predicate, as a connection of *cause* and *effect*. In order to a causal connection, I must pass *out* of A and affirm some other not contained in the conception A, viz. B, and vice versa; in order to establish B as an effect I seek for a somewhat not contained in the conception B, but other and distinguishable therefrom (as a watchmaker from the timepiece) which is to be its *cause*. Now Mr Hume called on the metaphysicians of his age to make known by what right they asserted the existence and necessity of such a connection, in other words, he required of them to tell him how they came by their notion of effect and cause, by what right they affirm it in reference to natural objects as a *necessary* connection; and further, by what right they transferred it from physics, and the phenomena of the senses, to metaphysical deductions and objects assumed as *super*sensual, and affirm at last a *universal* principle.

6 In the second and improper acceptation of the words in which by "cause and effect" we mean only the "causant" and the "effected", that *res causans, res [causata]*,[a] as when we say of any two bodies *that* is the cause and *this* is the effect, the exposition may be given in few words. By A = B, in this sense, the metaphysician asserts the existence of a link = X, necessarily connecting B with A. This X is the *notion* of cause, which is here marked problematically as an *unknown quantity*, inasmuch as the notion of cause is incapable of any further real explanation. So true is this that even the words and terms of the *verbal*[b] definition (viz. the necessary connection between A and a B not included in A) derive their positive meaning and intelligibility from the notion of cause, and not the notion of cause from this definition.

7 Mr Hume denied neither the existence, nor the expedience, nay! not even the subjective necessity, of applying the notion of causality to the phenomenon of antecedence and sequence in nature. What he called on the metaphysician to do was to assign the origin of this notion, to give proof that it was not a mere prejudice, and to ground this *feeling* of a necessity on the rational conviction that accompanies insight. Nor ought we to forget that the metaphysicians on whom Mr Hume called were, for the far greater part at least, avowed disciples of Mr Locke—men who no less than himself had exploded the doctrine of innate ideas and had adopted without limitation the principle of "nihil in intellectu quod non prius in

[a] Blank space left in ms
[b] ms: *vechal*

sensu".[1][*] Hume, in short, took the very same position that had been previously taken by Berkeley in the introduction to his *Principles of Knowledge* and dialogue between Hylas and Philonous,[7] the crude yet *racy* first fruits of his philosophic speculations, and with a more vehement and prolonged pressure deepened while he refreshed the footmarks which his predecessor had left.[8] On the grounds contended for (and which at that time he doubtless considered as having been fully established) by Locke himself did our English metaphysicians attack Locke's abstract triangles or the abstract idea, triangle *in genere* (the main weight of the confutation resting on Mr Locke's own definition and usage of the term "idea"), and afterwards flashed forth the luminous remark cited at the commencement of this chapter. And on the very same *grounds* and with arguments derived from the same premises did the Scottish philosopher support

[*] If, indeed, in the sense in which the words are used by Mr Locke, any such doctrine ever existed, of which Hume himself expresses his doubts.[2] It is almost incomprehensible how a man of Locke's learning could have attributed the notion to Aristotle, of whom it is, however, insinuated at least. In Descartes, indeed, the words *"innata idea*[b] are found;[3] but accompanied by a definition word for word the same with Mr Locke's own "ideas of reflection".[4] It is curious that the Jesuit Voetius had interpreted Descartes' phrase in the same way,[5] and it is interesting to see with what contempt the philosopher repels a charge almost too ridiculous to need a serious answer. "Innatas non connatas dixi, locum non tempus oriundi",[6] etc. And in the same place apologises for the barbarous use of the term "idea" on the ground of his having employed it metaphorically. At the same time he observes that, strictly speaking, all ideas were necessarily innate, that is, had their immediate birthplace as images, conceptions, etc in the mind, and that the distinction was merely logical, not metaphysical or philosophical.

[a–b] ms: "innatu ideo"

[1] See above, p 134 n 2.

[2] David Hume *An Enquiry Concerning Human Understanding* § II 17n.

[3] E.g. *Meditationes* III: *D Works* I 170.

[4] *Essay Concerning Human Understanding* bk II chs 6 and 7.

[5] Gysbertus Voetius (1588–1676), the Dutch theologian, was in fact a Calvinist. Cf *P Lects* Lect 13 (1949) 377–8. One of Descartes' anonymous opponents was the Jesuit Pierre Bourdin (1595–1653), but the anonymous work to which Descartes was responding was by neither Voetius nor Bourdin, but Descartes' own disciple Regius—Henri de Roy (1598–1679).

[6] "I said innate not connate, I spoke of the birthplace not the time." C's tr in *P Lects* Lect 13 (1949) 377. The Latin seems to be C's summation of Descartes' answer to an objection made by Regius—see *Notae in Programma* art XII: *D Works* I 442. For C's early and similar discussion of Locke's presentation of "innate ideas", see *CL* II 679ff. For Locke's discussion, see *Essay* bk I.

[7] *A Treatise Concerning the Principles of Human Knowledge* (1710); *Three Dialogues Between Hylas and Philonous* (1713). C must refer specifically to *B Works* II 27–38 and 192–4.

[8] For Hume's acknowledgment of Berkeley's precedence, see *Treatise of Human Nature* (1739–40) bk I pt I § vii.

his sceptical queries concerning the idea of cause and effect; and however dissimilar, or even contrariant, the ultimate objects, the practical aims, of the two men may have been, I should be sorry not to believe that the interests of science and speculative truth were*a* common to both.[*]

8 It would be still more strange, though less uncharitable, to suppose that Mr Hume was ignorant of the actual import of cause, or that if he had needed the information he was so unread in books familiar to all men of ordinary learning as not to have known from Cicero that neither antecedence nor concomitance constituted the essence of the notion. "[Non] praeire sed efficienter praeire neque comitari sed efficienter comitari."[1] It would be too hard, I repeat, to presume Mr Hume ignorant that the phenomena*b* antecedence and concomitance might, and often did, exist without any notion of a causal connection, ignorant, in short, of one of the commonest rules of common logic by which every schoolboy of fifteen is guarded against the sophism, "*cum* hoc: ergo *propter* hoc": or "post hoc; ergo *propter* hoc".[2] No, Mr Hume was well aware that the notion of efficiency was involved in every assertion of a causal connection, nor did he deny that we were under a subjective necessity of applying this notion in all synthetic judgments respecting external objects. He knew too and admitted that judgments grounded on experience are always synthetic. It were absurd to ground our analytic judgment on experience, however certain it might be that to experience we owed our knowledge of the subject, concerning which the judgment was formed, for as that which we judge or predicate respecting the subject is actually contained and implied in the mere conception of it, on what ground should we go further? Would we seek the *radii* of a circle on the outward side of the circumference? That a man is a

[*] The ability to answer an objection and the talent of railing at the objector are very different gifts. Each may have its value—greater perhaps than I am aware of; and this may be the reason why they are so seldom dispensed to the same individual.

a ms: was   *b* ms: phaenomenon

[1] "[Not] to precede, but to precede effectively, not what is concomitant, but what is effectively concomitant." The same quotation is given in part in *SM* (*CC*) 32n and is attributed to Cicero. Cf *De fato* 15.34: "non sic causa intelligi debet ut quod cuique antecedat id ei causa sit, sed quod cuique efficienter antecedat . . .". Tr H.

Rackham in Cicero *De oratore* . . . (LCL 2 vols 1942) II 231: "'cause' is not to be understood in such a way as to make what precedes a thing the cause of that thing, but what precedes it effectively . . .". Cf *Topica* 16.61.
[2] "*With* this, therefore *because of* this: or after this, therefore *because of* this".

rational animal is a judgment requiring no other condition than that
of knowing what we mean by the word "man"; but that a man is a
father requires that with the subject "man" I should combine the
conception of another subject; it is synthetic and so that the latter
being given, viz. offspring, the former is necessarily supposed.
Therefore through the whole extent of human experience, Mr Hume
admitted the existence and validity of synthetic judgments, and
admitted too that by the same experience we were entitled, because
impelled, to apply the causal connection or notion of cause. Neither
did the difficulty which attended this conception escape, nor was it
indeed likely to escape, so acute a thinker, viz. that of explaining the
necessity involved in our conception of cause and effect. Now is it
possible that the phenomena themselves, viz. antecedence and
sequency, or concomitance, not merely exciting but being contra-
distinguished by a sense of their contingency, this contingency being
indeed the very mark and criterion of their objective reality, yet the
connection resulting from this, should contain a sense of necessity,
and this too in the very essence of the conception? No, he saw the
difficulty and proposed a solution. And this solution it is which I
confess, highly as I appreciate Hume's acuteness as a disputant and
his talents as a writer, makes me sceptical as to the depth and
comprehension of view which Kant, judging by the effect produced
or occasioned on his own prepared and susceptible intellect, has
attributed to David Hume on the score of this particular essay.[1]
Hume's solution consists in assigning the origin and ground of the
notion, and the necessity conceived therein, to custom, association,
thus confounding, in the first place, the conception of necessity as a
positive and essential constituent of the conception "cause" with a
confused negative inability to do otherwise; in the second place,
assigning as the cause of causality a something which itself pre-
supposes a something, which the writers deemed classical on this
subject, Hartley, Priestley, and Condillac, and before them Hobbes,[2]
had by reducing all the phenomena of association to the law of
contemporaneity reduced them under the common law of cause and
effect, but which phenomena, according to Mr Hume himself, who
has borrowed without acknowledgement a much more correct state-
ment of the laws of association from Aquinas's[a] commentaries on[b]
the *Parva naturalia* of Aristotle, do at least presuppose the principle

---

a ms: Equinus's [a mistake in dictation?]   *b* ms: or

[1] Kant *C d r V* 792–7 (609–12).   [2] Cf C's account in *BL* ch 5 (1907)
i 65ff.

they [are] thus brought*ᵃ* in to explain;[1] and, in the third place, [adopting a theory] irreconcilable with the facts and contradictory to the very experience which is asserted to engender this conception. This last point has been ably set forth by Brown, the son of the celebrated medical theorist.[2] He has shown what indeed needs but be mentioned to be remembered as the result of facts, that the function allotted to experience is that of checking and limiting the application of the notion, that children instinctively predicate a causal connection in almost every case of coincidence, that every influence which by withdrawing the mind from reflections on its actual experience produces the same effect on adults that the want of experience does on children, induces the same promiscuous attribution as superstition, hope, fear, etc from the purse or coffin from the fire,[3] the stranger on the filmy grate,[4] the letter and winding-sheet on the candle,[5] the numbers on the hackney coach which*ᵇ* my grandmother had twice dreamt of for the prizes in the lottery,[6] the gris-gris of the African[7] and the amulets and charms of the European empiric. In short, it seems like the air we breathe to be ready everywhere to flow in where not forbidden and absolutely excluded by experience, or rather, shall we say, like the faculty of breathing which it requires an express volition to suspend?

9   But a still stranger, though less obvious and less striking, confutation of Hume's solution is derived from the nature and construction of experience itself; and custom is but an abbreviation for a customary or repeated experience. It would carry us too far for our present purpose to enter fully into this subject, the necessity

ᵃ ms: [?wrought]   *ᵇ* ms: or which

[1] Cf *BL* ch 5 (1907) I 73. Cf "David Hume Charged by Mr Coleridge with Plagiarism from St Thomas Aquinas" *Blackwood's Magazine* III (1818) 653–7. Cf *CN* I 973An.

[2] Thomas Brown (1778–1820) *Observations on the Nature and Tendency of the Doctrine of Mr. Hume, Concerning the Relation of Cause and Effect* (Edinburgh 1804). Further comments on Brown are to be found in BM MS Egerton 2801 ff 118–20. His father was a clergyman, and not, as C suggests here, John Brown (1735–88), the founder of the Brunonian system of medicine.

[3] *OED*: "purse"—"A fragment of live coal starting out of the fire with a report: regarded as a prognostic of good fortune"; "coffin"—"An oblong piece of live coal starting out of the fire with a report: regarded as a prognostic of death".

[4] Cf *Frost at Midnight* lines 15–16: *PW* (EHC) I 240.

[5] *OED*: "winding sheet"—"A mass of solidified drippings of grease clinging to the side of a candle, and regarded in popular superstition as an omen of death or calamity".

[6] This story has not been identified, although C does refer elsewhere to the limits of her arithmetical skill (*CN* II 2064).

[7] Cf *CL* IV 863.

to, being in part [satisfied] by the preceding investigations respecting the intuitions[a] of space and time as necessary preconditions of experience. In like manner we have only seriously to suppose a time in which the notion of cause and effect, or, if you please, that necessary predisposition to the same which may be called into effect and into consciousness by occasion of impressions from without, but can be no more given by it than the specific form of an oak can be given to the acorn by the outward elements of air, light, and moisture. We have only, I say, to suppose the moment when this notion was yet to be formed, or, to use the language of Mr Locke, to be by means of the senses put or conveyed into the mind. And on what ground, in cases where the effect or impression is coinstantaneous with the phenomenon assumed as its cause, [b]should the mind[c] make this arrangement? Or better still, perhaps, remove altogether the conception of causality, and what do we mean by the mind itself? And what is the experience of the mind taken abstractedly from the mind but as empty a word as thoughts without thinking or motion without a moving body?

10   These remarks are not wholly digressive; for whether the manifest insufficiency and superficial character of the solution proposed by the propounder of the problem does or does not justify my scepticism as to his having seen the problem itself in its true bearings and import, there can be no doubt that the belief of having solved it empirically prevented him from adopting a necessary preliminary to a true solution, viz. that of trying whether the problem could not be presented under a higher and yet more comprehensive formula. Whether there were not other connections = X between A and B not included in A besides the causal connection. Whether causality or the relation of cause and effect be anything more than a specification or particular application of this higher formula which it shares only in common with other exercises of the judicial power. In short, the assertion of cause and effect is in every instance a synthetic judgment. This is universally admitted, or rather it is not in the power of any man who understands the meaning of the words "analytic" and "synthetic" not to admit it. But are there no other synthetic judgments? The application of the causal connection to the particular phenomena depends beyond doubt on the knowledge given by experience; but it cannot be legitimately concluded from this that the connection itself or that which forms the essence of the notion of cause is likewise derived from experience

[a] ms: intentions   [b–c] ms: the mind should

(given by it, I mean) in contradiction from merely occasioned by it, or called into definite act and distinct consciousness; for this would have been falling into the same confusion with which Mr Hume himself so justly charges Mr Locke's reasoning, or rather the impossible error which Mr Locke exerts himself to confute in his first book in the *Essay on the Human Understanding*. Nor in fact does Mr Hume rest his opinion on any such conclusion; he believed himself to have discovered a sufficient solution in the influence of custom and therefore sought for no other. He did not argue the connection = X is applied by the human mind to the data of experience, therefore it is itself a datum of experience and a judgment *a posteriori*, but the connection X is a synthesis or combination of the repetition of the same impressions and the *nisus* or feeling of the animal life. In other words, the causal connection is the bastard offspring (*progenies hybrida*) of definite impressions from without and indefinite sensation, that is, of outward and inward experience, and altogether therefore experiential or *a posteriori*.

11   On this view it is evident that the sensation being a mere subjective accident of the same necessity and of no greater value than the sensation of faintness in distant objects, or the *nisus* or effort of sight in the attempt to distinguish them, the experience itself is the sole ground in every instance of the legitimacy or objective truth of the conception. In all reasoning therefore the materials of which or subject-matter are*a* not drawn from experience, the notion of cause and effect is not only inapplicable but without meaning. Hume's premises once granted, the conclusion is inevitable. Nor will I disguise my conviction that it was the obvious consequences of this conclusion that gave it its chief value and interest in the eyes of the Scottish philosopher.[1] The opportunities, I mean, of applying it to the doctrines of religion and of using it as a means of undermining the foundations of our religious convictions or principles, at least *b*those that*c* theologians and metaphysicians had hitherto taken for such, and not of religion only, but the fundamental principles of morality likewise, if more be meant by that term than the dictates of worldly prudence and the necessities and sympathies of custom, and varying therefore as the custom[s] of one age and country differ from those of another. There are few readers who need be informed that this is Mr Hume's own statement*d* of his theory and these are

---

a ms: is   *b–c* ms: as   *d* ms: statement both

[1] Cf Kant's greater faith in Hume. *C d r V* 773 (597).

his own deductions, but to be consequent is the *first* requisite, the first and most important requisite, of the reasoner, were it only[a] that with our limited intellects it must often happen that it is a view of the consequences that impels us to doubt and re-examine the premises, and this praise with that of as great frankness in the avowal of his conclusions as was compatible with personal safety, and, I am willing to believe, with the still more honourable wish to have his purpose understood by those only who were competent to understand his arguments, this praise belongs to David Hume.[1] But the many and important advantages which truth and science have derived from strict consequence even in dangerous error would form a very instructive appendix to a history of philosophy, while the inlaying of infidel premises with pious professions and sentiments, or the conjuring of religious conclusions from Godless premises, is equally injurious to the interests of science and of faith. It tends beyond all causes to stop the progress of the former, and it is sure to sophisticate the latter for a time and finally to be made both the pretext and the instrument of attack and open hostility. However ingeniously the wholesome and nutritious fruits plucked from the tree of revelation and ancient philosophy may be threaded on the barren fig-tree or rather let me say on the poisonous manchineel,[2] they will be more or less injured by the damps and exudations of the supporting branches and sooner or later will fall off, yet leave in the mind of the passer-by a temptation to pluck the native products of the tree that have taken their place. If no connection can be affirmed unless where both *antecedent* and *consequent* are *alike* facts of experience, and no analogical conclusions are valid between subjects of diverse kind (*analogicae ratiocinanti non conceditur* μετάβασις εἰς ἄλλο γένος), a spiritual antecedent cannot be presumed from a material phenomenon. For necessary connection is not only exclusively applicable to known, or, by analogy, to possible, objects of the senses; but the supposed necessity which constitutes the whole cogency of the conclusion, the world, that is, the whole aggregate of sensible objects, must have a cause which cannot therefore itself be an object of the sense, is not a necessity of insight, but a necessity of feeling,

---

[a] ms: only that it often happens that

[1] C expresses himself more forthrightly in *SM* (*CC*) 22.
[2] C combines two favourite images here—fruit threaded on the barren fig-tree (cf *Friend—CC*—ii 314, i 315) and the poisonous manchineel (cf *Lects 1795—CC*—296 and *Friend—CC*—ii 261, i 568), in which C persisted in spite of Mr Boyer's interdict. See *BL* ch 1 (1907) i 5.

or rather of blind feeling of necessity, gradually engendered by a repetition of the impressions with which it gradually becomes associated. The same objection applies, and was in fact applied, to the truth of miracles; the testimony on which the truth of the miracle rests is historical, that is, experiential, but here one constituent only of the judgment is the legitimate or possible object of experience. The other half, the miraculous substitute of the antecedent, is not the possible object of human experience and therefore not a legitimate object of human history. Nay, even though the supersensual A were admitted to exist, there would nevertheless result no right of asserting a causal connection between it and the phenomenon B: for *this* would be an act of the judgment; but the necessity in the *causal* connection is, according to Mr Hume, no act of the judgment, far rather, it is no act at all, but a mere *affection* of the animal sensibility, a passive *feeling*.[1]

12   Were it not, as it is, of highest importance from the moral interest of the question, it would be indispensable in order to the establishment of [a] logical criterion by which the true nature of the premises may be distinguished that[a] rules (of undoubted legitimacy in forensic reasoning, when what is subjectively true is likewise practically valid)[b] should be prevented from being applied as principles to the determination of objective truth in real science and natural philosophy; [c]the importance of[d] this end, I say, among all the works of modern philosophy, Bacon's *Novum Organum*[e] has[f] the immortal merit of having first fully and worthily set forth. It is indispensable that this last point should be seen with the greatest possible clearness and distinctness. The student must be made to understand that not the relation of cause and effect applied to certain antecedents and consequents in nature in and for itself was the object of Hume's scepticism. What Hume doubted was the *necessity* of the connection between A and any given B not included in A, as a necessity of reason and insight, which connection the metaphysicians hitherto had indeed *exemplified*, and of course asserted to exist, in the relation of cause and effect, but which Hume denies *altogether*. He denies, I say, the right of asserting this principle of necessary

---

a ms: and   b Parentheses inserted
c–d ms: in order to
e ms: Arcanum [an error in dictation?]
f ms: have

[1] C is referring here to Hume *An Enquiry Concerning Human Understanding* (1748) Sects VI and X, "Of the Idea of Necessary Connexion" and "Of Miracles".

connection in any case, and that which in the particular case under discussion (namely where A = B represents cause and effect) had been advanced as such, and which he affirms to have been the ground and origin of the belief, this he declares to be a something of a quite different kind, referable to a different source and to be accounted for on an altogether different hypothesis. Mr Hume's argument may be exhibited to the eye in the following simple statement, in which the letter X (as before) stands for the idea of ~~necessary connection~~. There exists *no* X between *any* A and B, where the latter is not included in the former, and that which in the one instance of cause and effect you have mistaken for X is really only = 0, that is, a blind feeling, a delusion engendered by custom. But did Mr Hume deny the cogency, the apodictive necessity, of the mathematics, or did he, like the late ingenious but somewhat overhasty Dr Beddoes, gravely derive the evidence of the elements of geometry by Euclid from the very same source and place it on the same scale with the elements of chemistry by Lavoisier and [assert] that we have exactly the same certainty and the same kind of certainty in affirming that water is a compound body constituted by the combination of oxygen gas with hydrogen gas in the proportion of twenty-seven to seventy-three, as in the mathematical position that a circle is formed by the circumvolution of a straight line fixed at one end?[1] No, Mr Hume was not disingenuous enough to pretend the former and far too acute a thinker to have been capable of imagining the latter.[*] He neither denied the

[*] I trust that I feel in myself as little disposition to be influenced by, and as strong an inclination to repel, Mr Hume's attacks on the principles of religion and morality as the most vehement of his antagonists; and to such an *exposure* of the fallacy of his *conclusions* by a fair *exposition* of the assertions on which they are grounded, as the Archbishop of Dublin (Dr Magee) has given in his work on redemption I have paid my full tribute of applause.[2] But I cannot bring myself to believe that David Hume was either more deficient in common sense, or more likely to render himself ridiculous by outraging its dictates, than

[1] Thomas Beddoes *Observations*, esp 108–10 and 15. In *LS (CC)* 173, C probably had this book in mind rather than Dalton. Lavoisier's ratio was 15:85 (*Elements of Chemistry . . .* tr Robert Kerr—Edinburgh 1790—199); the correct one is 11:89 (J. R. Partington *A History of Chemistry*—1961–70—III 452). Cf C's marginal note in Hooker *Works* (1682) (BM copy) 71, where he gives the ratio as 23:77. C was attached to Beddoes and said of his death in 1809 that it took

"more hope out of my Life than any former Event except perhaps T. Wedgwood's". *CL* III 174.

[2] William Magee (1766–1831) *Discourses and Dissertations on the Scriptural Doctrines of Atonement and Sacrifice . . .* (1816) II pt i 265–97. For C's rather grudging applause, see *AR* (1825) 400–1. In BM MS Egerton 2801 f 260, Magee is called a "Prig of Preferment" and a "modern Episcopal Arminian". Cf the scornful reference to "Mageeites" in *CL* VI 902.

evidence of mathematics nor doubted the necessary conclusions of common logic.[*] Adopting the opinions first maintained by Sir

Messrs Reid, Oswald, Beattie,[1] or any other of his contemporary opponents on either side of the Tweed. Nay, I am almost tempted to whisper my suspicion that he understood the nature and value of historical testimony quite as well as Dr Priestley himself.[2]

[* The following passage in the text is surrounded by pencilled parentheses by Transcriber B, with the remark that "The whole within the pencilled crotchets appears to be intended for a note and not to be introduced into the text".]

But in order to grapple with the question, concerning which Mr Hume demanded satisfaction, in order to discover whether the principle of causality was a truth determinable *a priori*, possessing an intrinsic validity independent of experience and therefore a utility capable of being extended beyond the objects of experience, in order to *this* his opponents must have meditated deeply and dispassionately on the nature of the mind as far as the laws of *thinking* are exclusively concerned. An easier resource, and of a far more *popular* character, was at hand, the appeal to *common* sense and the common *feelings* of mankind! And this they accordingly adopted. In fact it is a great gift of heaven (says Kant) to possess a sound common sense.[3] But we must prove that we possess it by our actions and modes of acting, by the considerateness and rationality of what we think and say, and not by appealing to it as to an oracle when we have nothing else, that is, nothing to the purpose, to advance in support of our opinions. As long as these disputants have any facts or arguments to bring forward, as long as they have anything to say in the way of reason, we never hear a word of this θεος ἀπο μεχανης[4] that supplies the place of skill and contrivance in the original construction of the plot; we need only look attentively and narrowly into these invocations of common sense, these appeals to the inappellable censure,[a] to discover that it is in reality an appeal to the judgment of the multitude. Mere claptrap for suffrages at which the philosopher would blush, and, like Phocion, ask of some by-stander, "quid tum stultum dixi?",[5] but which makes the popular witling crow again.

To these remarks, in part translated from and in part suggested by the founder of the critical philosophy,[6] I will add the memorable words of his illustrious countryman, the great Kepler, addressed to the theologians of his age, who appealed to the common senses and the language of the Bible, constructed on the laws of appearance: "And what other language could have been universally

---

[a] ms: seizure

[1] Thomas Reid (1710–96), author of *An Inquiry into the Human Mind, on the Principles of Common Sense* (Edinburgh 1764); James Oswald (1715–69), author of *An Appeal to Common Sense in Behalf of Religion* (Edinburgh 1766); and James Beattie (1735–1803), author of *An Essay on the Nature and Immutability of Truth . . .* (Edinburgh 1770). C is drawing on Kant *Prolegomena* Einleitung (1783) 10.

[2] Joseph Priestley (1733–1804), author of *An Examination of Dr. Reid's*

Inquiry . . . (1774). Again from Kant *Prolegomena* Einleitung (1783) 10.

[3] Ibid 11.

[4] *Deus ex machina.*

[5] "What stupid thing have I said then?" According to Plutarch, Phocion, on finding the people agreeing with him, asked, "Can it possibly be that I am making a bad argument without knowing it?" *Lives* tr Bernadotte Perrin (LCL 1919) VIII 163.

[6] Kant *Prolegomena* Einleitung (1783) 10–12.

Kenelm Digby in his treatise of bodies and soul,[2] Hume considered both mathematical and logical reasoning as purely and merely analytical, and the whole mighty pile of science geometrical and numerical as a succession of analytic judgments, or, in the language of Digby and his followers, a series of identical propositions. This being the case, it is easily conceivable that it did not occur to him to enquire whether there were not other judgments standing in the same predicament with that of the causal connection. He received no memento or assistance from his antagonists, and it is no wonder therefore that the discussion dropped without having occasioned any increase of light either for them, himself, or the learned public. Such at least appeared to be the result, and such it would have been, had not the seed, which as it fell unprofitably from the hand of the sower and which wafted and tossed about on the winds of literary rumour, found at length a well-fitted and prepared soil in the mind of a Prussian philosopher who in earliest manhood had already distinguished himself not only as a profound mathematician by the treatise on the dead and living forces,[*] and as a natural philosopher

---

and permanently intelligible? What other language appropriate to the divine purposes of the sacred writings?"[1] Beware that in trying your axe against adamant you do not render it useless even for the woodcutter.

[*] *Gedanken von der wahren Schätzung der lebendigen Kräfte*,[3] etc 1747, with the significant and characteristic motto, "Nihil magis praestandum est, quam ne pecorum ritu sequamur antecedentium gregem; pergentes, non qua eundum

[1] No exact source has been found for C's reference, but if he was paraphrasing or quoting loosely the following is a likely original: "Gleich als wann der H. Geist in der Schrifft die Astronomiam oder Physicam lehrete, vnd nit viel ein höhers Intent hette, zu welchem er nicht allein deren Wort vnd Spraach, den Menschen zuvor kundt, sondern auch deren gemeinen popularischen Wissenschafft von natürlichen Sachen, zu welcher die Menschen mit Augen vnd eusserlichen Sinnen gelanget, sich gebrauchete?" ("Just as if the Holy Ghost were teaching astronomy or physics in Scripture, and did not have a much loftier purpose, for which he made use not only of the word and language already familiar to men but also of the common popular knowledge of natural things which men arrived at by means of their eyes and external senses.") The passage occurs in Johann Kepler *Tertius Interveniens. Das ist, Warnung an etliche Theologos, Medicos vnd Philosophos . . .* (1610). See *Opera omnia* ed C. Frisch (Frankfurt & Erlangen 1858) I 594. For other evidence of C's enthusiasm for Kepler (1571–1630), see *Friend* (*CC*) I 485–6. Cf *Omniana* § 174.

[2] *Two Treatises: In the One of Which, the Nature of Bodies; In the Other, the Nature of Man's Soule; Is Looked into . . .* (Paris 1644). C borrowed the book from the Carlisle Cathedral library in 1801–2. *CN* I 1004 and n.

[3] "Thoughts on the True Estimation of the Living Forces". C recommends the work in *AR* (1825) 392–3n. It is to be found in *VS* I 1–282.

and astronomer by his prophetic system of the heavens[2] (the germ and original idea of Laplace's *Céleste mécanique*,[3] and in which the existence and place of the Georgian *sidus*,[4] of the small extra-zodiacal planets, the duplicity of Saturn's ring, etc, were pre-determined from the theory, long before either had been discovered by observation);[a] but by the singular dissatisfaction with the existing state of metaphysics, the author declaring himself equally at variance with those who boldly asserted the negative as with those who took for granted the affirmative of the questions, "Is such a science as that of metaphysics possible?" and "Is it already in existence?"[5] Before his acquaintance with the writings of Hume and Berkeley, he appears to have convinced himself that the Epicureans and Sceptics had a great deal more logic on their side than the zeal of the religious party was willing to admit, and that the orthodox had a great deal more truth at the bottom of their opinions than the contemptuous spirit of the Sceptics and matter-of-fact men could bring itself to discover. What Hume had only begun, this philosopher began anew and completed; and what he did the student of judicial logic must now proceed to do.

13   The subject, as we have seen, falls into two questions. Are the mathematical judgments analytic only? For if this should have been a mistake on the part of Hume and his predecessors—if the mathematical reasonings both in the processes of arithmetic and the constructions of geometry be as the ancients, mathematicians, and

---

est, sed qua itur."[1] This juvenile work of our modern Aristotle may be safely ranked among our most perfect specimens of scientific arbitration, and of the satisfactory settlement of a dispute by taking from each party the *truth* that belonged to it, and then uniting the two portions by a third comprehending both.

a Parentheses inserted

[1] Seneca *De vita beata* 7.1.3 (var). Tr J. W. Basore *Moral Essays* (LCL 1935) II 101: "Nothing . . . needs to be more emphasized than the warning that we should not, like sheep, follow the lead of the throng in front of us, travelling, thus, the way that all go and not the way that we ought to go." The passage is quoted in conjunction with Kant's title in A. F. M. Willich *Elements of the Critical Philosophy* . . . (1798) 55. C's annotated copy is in the BM.

[2] *Allgemeine Naturgeschichte und Theorie des Himmels* (1755).

[3] Laplace *Traité de mécanique céleste*. C makes the same assertion in a letter to C. A. Tulk on 12 Jan 1818 (*CL* IV 808). For a full discussion of Kant's relationship to Laplace, see introduction to *Kant's Cosmonogy* . . . ed W. Hastie (Glasgow 1900).

[4] The planet Uranus, or *Georgium Sidus*, named in honour of George III by its discoverer, Sir William Herschel (1738–1822), in 1781. It was called "the Georgian" in English almanacs until the middle of the nineteenth century.

[5] See above, p 169 n 2.

in fact the whole scientific world till within the last hundred and sixty years had never doubted, should be *bona fide* synthetic judgments, then as their *a priori* character is above all rational doubt, and is fully conceded by Hume himself, there are synthetic judgments *a priori* and other synthetic judgments beside that respecting causality; and this leads to the second question. Are there yet other synthetic judgments not mathematical, but of the same class with that of the causal connection? For should we be able to point out such, then as the synthetic character is common to all, both to the mathematical and to those that fall under the same class with that of cause and effect, it would be incumbent on us to ask whether they are not all alike instances and proofs of synthesis *a priori*. And *this* Mr Hume himself could scarcely have denied, certainly not consistently with his own admissions. For as the difficulty in any instance consists in the essential character common to all, as expressed in the formula [A] = B by virtue of X, or the necessary connection of one subject with another not included in the former as its constituent predicate; and as this, it has been clearly proved by Mr Hume, is neither derived nor derivable from experience, *then* its existence being nevertheless ascertained, it has a ground independent of experience. But this is what we mean when we say that they are true *a priori*. We have therefore little more to do than to put the student in the way of proving for himself that all mathematical reasoning is truly synthetic or composed of synthetic judgments *a priori*. When he has fully satisfied himself on this point, he will seek to understand how this synthesis is possible, and for this insight we have already prepared in the chapter on transcendental aesthetic, or space and time as the forms *a priori* of the outward and inward sense.[1] Of other synthetic judgments we shall thus have the negative character, viz. that the synthesis is not conditioned by the pre-existing forms of the sense, and may therefore anticipate their positive definition, viz. that this latter class have their condition and ground in the *a priori* forms of the understanding, and with the enumeration and exposition of these forms, together with the rules deducible therefrom, we shall conclude the scientific part of judicial logic or logic as a criterion. The rules and cautions afforded by empirical psychology will form the appendix to this section,[2] distinguished from the rules that are properly scientific, and belong to the science of logic, e.g. the rules of definition, division, method, induction, etc, by the name of maxims. And with these [we shall conclude] the treatise itself, as far as it is a treatise on the

[1] See above, pp 150–73.   [2] The appendix is lacking.

causes or legitimate forms of conclusive reasoning and of the criterion of the truth or falsehood of the premises as far as they can be learnt *a priori*, that is, without a previous acquaintance with the particular subjects in question. But neither here can we take leave of the science of logic, in this its most scientific sense, without again calling on the student not to finish his review of what this logic *is* and can effect, without considering what logic is not, cannot effect, or without adverting to the opposite errors, the delusions of superstition on the one hand and the sophisms of a faithless sensuality on the other that have originated from the undue elevation of logic and the understanding as the logical faculty to an equal rank with philosophy and reason, or the undue degradation of the human soul by subjecting all truth to conceptions formed from the senses, or to the notions which the understanding marks for itself by reflection on its own processes.

CHAPTER [IX]

On Mathematical or Intuitive and ~~Logical~~
~~or~~ Discursive Synthesis *a priori*

1 We have said in the preceding chapter that Hume had *taken for granted* the analytic nature of mathematical reasoning. This is no arbitrary assertion, on the one hand, for there exists no proof nor hint in his writings of his having particularly proposed the question as a subject of any distinct enquiry; and on the other hand the omission is not to be wondered at, as it was an error which he had in common with all the logicians and analysts of the human mind in his own age and at least a century preceding. Add to which that the occasion of the error is obvious, and has been already mentioned. I refer to the confusion of the common condition with the particular ground, as explained page [154ff].[a] The proper ground of analytic judgments being the condition, though not the proper and sufficing ground, of synthetic judgments, as the latter could not be true except under the condition of their congruity with the so-called principle of contradiction and identity, these principles were considered as the positive grounds of their actual truth. The condition, I say, under which alone the truth of any judgment is possible, was mistaken for the ground of the actual truth of these particular judgments. Accordingly this is one among the many instances that might be brought to confirm the remark of the celebrated Paley, and which we may apply to logical, with no less reason than he to moral, enquiries, that in the majority of cases the solution is easy in proportion to the insight into the difficulty of the problem.[1] For supposing the problem (or question proposed) clearly and distinctly comprehended, "Is mathematical reasoning merely analytic or not rather synthetic?", is the B introduced by the "then" or "therefore"

[a] Blank space left in ms; the facing page bears a pencil note by the transcriber: "On the Analytic and Synthetic Judgments."

[1] William Paley (1743–1805) *The Principles of Moral and Political Philosophy* (2nd ed 1786) viii: "in discoursing to young minds upon topics of morality, it required much more pains to make them perceive the difficulty, than to understand the solution...".

of the demonstrator actually included in the preceding A, from which it is deduced? We need only refer to our explanation of the term*a* analytic judgments, p[p 174–7],*b* and then simply to ask ourselves whether by any exertion of our reflecting powers on the terms contained in the first proposition of Euclid, without adding any one form or relation not actually thought of by us in the act of representing the former to our minds, in the same manner as we are certain that in thinking of a circle we actually must have thought of the centre and circumference, or have used the word without meaning anything by it at all; we need only ask ourselves whether in this way we could ever have arrived at the properties of the cycloid or the proportion of the area of the curve to the area of the generating circle. In short, we have only to attempt raising our minds to a comprehension of the mighty pile and fabric of truth, which (faith in God and the moral law alone excepted) is the proudest honour and glory of the human intellect, that in which above all others it finds the clearest sense of its own permanency and at the same time the most infallible evidence of its progressiveness, its still organised and ever organising growth, to find the supposition monstrous, too monstrous to have ever been distinctly believed, though, however, the phantom or substitute of belief is rendered possible by the confusion of terms through the imperfection and unsteady flitting of the attention and memory.

Such is the rise of forms
Sequestered far from sense and every spot
Peculiar in the realms of space and time;
Such is the throne which man for truth amid
The paths of mutability hath built,
Secure, unshaken still; and whence he views
In matter's mouldering structures, the pure forms
Of triangle or circle, cube or cone,
Impassive all; whose attributes nor force
Nor fate can alter. There he first conceives
True being, and the intellectual world
The same this hour and ever. Thence he deems
Of his own lot; above the painted shapes
That fleeting move o'er this terrestrial scene
Looks up; beyond the adamantine gates
Of death expatiates; as his birthright claims
Inheritance of all the works of God;
Prepares for endless time his plan of life,
And counts the universe itself his home.[1]

a ms: terms   *b* Blank space left in ms

[1] Mark Akenside (1721–70) *The Pleasures of Imagination* bk II lines 131–49 (var): *Poems* (1772) 156–7.

2   But if the assertion were not that each successive turn of the geometrician is analytically contained in the preceding, but that each and all the terms are perfectly independent affirmations, that mathematical reasoning is no interlinked chain, but a rope of sand, or if, in the poetic tone inspired by the recent quotation from Akenside, we may venture to elevate the subject by recurring to our former metaphor, when the vast complex of mathematic truth was represented as a magnificent palace—if, I say, this whole pile be, in all its apparent orders, dependencies, insertions, but a phantom in the desert, when on the contingence of some I know not what whirl blast

> the desert sands rise up
> And shape themselves: from Earth to Heaven they stand,
> As though they were the pillars of a temple,
> Built by Omnipotence in its own honour!*a*
> But the blast pauses, and their shaping spirit
> Is fled: the mighty columns were but sand,
> And sophist snakes trail o'er the level ruins![1]

—if, in short, mathematical reasoning be no reasoning at all, if geometrical demonstration be *monstratio de nihilo*,[2] and the consequents [are] not only not contained and understood in the antecedent, but having no true or necessary connection therewith—to such an assertion, I say, no answer can be given. And were it not so, no answer ought to be given but that of requesting the assertor to make or renew his acquaintance with the elements of geometry or with any one proposition. For either the assertor, supposing him to understand what he asserts, speaks that which he himself knows to be false, or we must condole with his case as an anomaly no less strange than[b] that of the two men who had the misfortune, the one of losing his shadow, and the other his reflection in the looking-glass, and who were both perfectly persuaded, the one that what the rest of mankind called their shadows, and the other that what they took for their own image, were unconnected, independent, and self-grounded verities.[3]

a ms: hours!   *b* ms: then

---

[1] C's *The Night-Scene* lines 77–83 (var): *PW* (EHC) I 423. An earlier version appears in the fragment *The Triumph of Loyalty*: *PW* (EHC) II 1072.

[2] "A showing from nothing".

[3] C may be referring to Erasmus Spikher and Peter Schlemihl; see E. T. A. Hoffmann "Die Gesellschaft im Keller" and "Die Geschichte vom verlornen-Spiegelbilde" in "Die Abenteuer der Silvester-Nacht" in *Fantasiestücke in Callot's Manier . . .* (1814–15). If so, he has altered the case by making their condition subjective. There is a copy of the 2nd ed (Bamberg 1819) annotated by C in BM.

3 An easy experiment will convince us, that is, occasion us to be conscious, that even the simplest processes of common arithmetic suppose a synthetic judgment, and that the supposition of their being analytic only arises from the original facility of the operation, but still more the facility acquired by habit, and our incapability of remembering the time when it was not already habitual. Under this impression it might be supposed that the position or judgment "$7 + 5 = 12$" is a mere analytic judgment that follows out of the conception of a sum composed of 7 and 5 according to the principle of identity and *de non sibi contradicendo*.[1] But if we examine the matter more closely we find that the conception of a sum of 7 and 5 really in the first instance, and previously to the arithmetical operation, contained no more than the union of both numbers in some single[a] number without its being any actual part of this conception what this single number must be. The conception "12" is by no means thought of necessity at the time that I first put the question to myself, "What is the sum of 7 and 5?" Even what we have shown in a former chapter concerning the nature of a question will prove this; for there we saw that every question consisted in an expression of knowledge and an expression of ignorance and that the latter, that viz. of which we are ignorant, is expressed by the interrogation and in cases like the present by the interrogative pronoun.[2] Now here the knowledge already possessed, and which is contained in the conception, is simply, there is a sum of 7 and 5, or the union of 7 and 5 constitutes a sum. Our ignorance is expressed and acknowledged in the word[s] "What is it?" In order to convert this ignorance into knowledge—in order to perfect the position—we must call in the help of the imagination (*intuitio, vis intuitiva*).[3] The scholar will perhaps, if he begins with 7, take his five fingers, or as in some of our popular ciphering books five points,[4] and add them one by one to the original number, giving at each step to the number thus constituted its proper name. But if any[b] doubts remained they may be removed at once by taking very much larger sums as the component factors, as, for instance, $35,942,768,412 + 57,843,647$, and we shall be convinced at once that we might dwell for centuries on the two sums without

---

a ms: ~~higher~~ single   *b* ms: my

[1] "Of not contradicting oneself".
[2] Ch IV.
[3] "Intuition, intuitive power".
[4] Kant, from whom C is quoting here, attributes the term to Segner.

C d r V 15 (53) and *Prolegomena* § 2 (1783) 29. J. A. Segner *Elementa arithmeticae et geometriae . . .* (Göttingen 1739).

discovering what the product of both would be,[1] if we did not proceed to a third, and perfectly distinct, act of the intellect, the synthetic act, or that of putting the numbers together according to the laws derived from the inherent forms of the sense or intuitive faculty so that they must produce or, in the language of the mathematicians, generate a third intuition contained in neither of the former, and which could not have existed for the mind otherwise than by the synthesis or copula of the two, any more than water could have been known to the senses by the mere consideration of oxygen and of hydrogen gas separately, without the act of their combination by means [of], and in proportions agreeable to, the laws of chemical nature. Thus too with pure geometry there[a] is [not] even a single axiom or fundamental principle that is properly analytic—that a straight line between two points is the shortest: for the conception "straight" is in no respect a conception of quantity and of itself determines nothing respecting degrees of quantity, but expresses a particular quality only. The conception "shortest" is added to it or put in connection therewith, συντίθεται, by an act or, if I may so say, an experiment of the intuitive or imaginative power. We *find* that it is so, and we find too that we *can*not imagine it otherwise, and this not from any defect or deficiency of the power in us, but by the nature of the intuition itself, involving the impossibility of the contrary. Now this is what we mean by ἀπόδειξις, or "apodictic", and its Latin correspondent *demonstratio* or demonstrative reasoning.[2] Where I affirm that [a] tree grows on a given spot, and that it is an oak, and my companion being doubtful of the fact, I take him to the spot and show him the object, this is δεῖξις, *monstratio*, an evidence of the senses, but it involves no proof that the contrary was [im]possible, it is not *apo*dictic, not *de*monstrative. It does not even amount to a positive proof that the showing did not depend on some individuality, or peculiar state of my companion's senses, or of the medium through which they were thus affected. The evidence here is rather moral than logical, and rests on the senselessness of supposing the contrary on the ground of a mere possibility, without any reason for asserting its reality in the particular instance. It is true that certain assumptions or principles presupposed by the geometrician are actually analytic,

a ms: it

[1] From p 201 line 6 to this point C is translating *C d r V* 15–16 (52–3). Cf *Prolegomena* § 2 (1783) 28–9.

[2] From line 12 to this point C is translating, with variations, from *C d r V* 16–17 (53–4). Cf *Prolegomena* § 2 (1783) 29.

and rest on the principle of contradiction, but these serve only as identical positions, as when we say "A being A", or " +A not being −A", as links of method, ways of recalling and enlivening the attention and memory of the demonstrator, not as principles out of which there flows any increase of evidence. Such, for instance, are "A = A", "the whole is equal to itself", or "the whole is greater than its parts". And yet even these, though valid as mere conceptions and logically coercive, are admitted in mathematics on this account only, that they can likewise be presented to the sense, and have an intuitive evidence because we not only understand, but likewise see, that so it is.[1]

4 I have said, and I now repeat, that the distinction between analytic and synthetic, once admitted and fully understood, its [non-]application to the different classes of positions or judgments can be accounted for only by some confusion or rather entanglement of thought; and in minds acute and highly cultivated, [such] as that of the Scottish philosopher,[2] the occasion of this perplexity is to be found in an obscure sense (and, might I say, a dim half-consciousness, a felt anticipation) of a truth that has its source and derivation from powers higher than the understanding considered as the discursive faculty of truth, that can be duly contemplated only from a higher point of view than that on which the logician can make a firm footing, truths that have more than subjective reality. The condition of the error is the confusion of philosophy with logic, but the efficient cause of it is the dissatisfaction connected with confused recognition, for which we have no other than the popular term, the "feeling" of the difference between them. For while the naturalist seeks to remove as far as possible all mixture of subjective form and influences, and the logician with the same solicitude excludes all that is objective,[*] the philosopher seeks to raise himself into a sphere in

[*] That is, in the primary and antithetic sense of the term; the secondary and metaphorical sense of "objective", in which that which is universally and permanently subjective, that is, what all human subjects possess in common by necessity of their constitution, is so called, is not here under contemplation. This caution has been before given and need not perhaps have been repeated, yet the anxiety which has tempted the author to repeat it may answer one purpose, that of showing the inconvenience of terms in science capable of being understood in several and different senses (*vocabula multivoca*),[3] even when the greater inconvenience on the other side may render their retention expedient, or other causes have put it out of our power to do otherwise.

[1] From p 202 line 35 to this point C is translating from *C d r V* 16–17 (54). Cf *Prolegomena* § 2 (1783) 29.

[2] Hume.

[3] "Words of several meanings".

which both are one, and where of course the opposition ceases and the antithesis no longer has any meaning. In the same sphere, the antithesis of analytic and synthetic disappears likewise and loses all import; for it rises out of the forms of the understanding and of the sense, that are instruments for the knowledge of true relations, of *relative*, not *absolute*, truth, which latter appertains to a higher principle, which may enlighten the understanding that receives it as its base and centre, but which can neither be deduced by the understanding [n]or from the objects that properly fall under its cognisance. The Epicurean, whether sceptic or dogmatist, will admit nothing but the understanding, yet demands of the understanding what by its constituent forms it is incapable of realising, and makes this the pretext of denying it absolutely and altogether. *Non est ibi; ergo, nullibi est.*[1] He cannot find it where he expected it to have been found. It did not exist there, and therefore it does not exist at all. Thus, παντων ζητουντες λογον λογον αυτον αναιρουσι,[2] which equally to the purposes of truth, though not with equal fidelity, we may paraphrase either thus:

5   Seeking a reason *for* all things, they take away reason itself— and all the truths *of* reason, *for* which no reason can without absurdity be required, because they *are* reason. Logically speaking, they *constitute* the reason, but in the language of the philosopher, the reason affirms itself in them. Or, [a]seeking the understanding of all things, they render the understanding itself baseless and unsubstantial. [a]To which we may add, as a corollary, that logic by itself, except where logic itself (that is, the forms of the understanding and the rules grounded on the same) is the subject, is but a cabinet of many drawers and pigeonholes, all empty. But are we, therefore, to procure no cabinets, and content ourselves with lumber-rooms and slut-corners? And who are these that are most forward and frequent in depreciating the science and discipline of logic, whether its technical rules or the knowledge which the understanding acquires by reflection on its own processes? Those who will profess that the mere words "transcendental" and "aesthetic" are *quite enough for them*— the wax of Ulysses[3] not more potent? Why, the very men who, with

[a] New paragraph in ms

[1] "It is not there; therefore it is nowhere."

[2] Theophrastus *Metaphysics* 8.26 (var). Used as an epigraph in *Friend* (CC) I 464. C appears to have found it in Hooker *Of the Laws of Ecclesias-* *tical Politie* I 8: *Works* (1682) 80. Cf *CN* III 3574.

[3] The wax used to prevent his men from hearing the Sirens. Homer *Odyssey* 12.173–80.

keenest contempt and most confident self-complacency, reject and ridicule the supposition of any higher source of truth than that of the senses, or any higher form of knowledge than that which results from these very processes of the understanding, and from the mechanism and inherent constitution of the faculty, which it is the express object of transcendental research to discover and explain! Men who make a merit of not knowing the meaning of the terms which they ridicule, professors (but of no *Socratic* character) of the science of nescience, who measure their sense by their ignorance—the genuine successors of Mr Pope's "Coxcombs that vanquish'd Berkeley with a *grin*".¹ We, however, will endeavour neither to overrate nor to undervalue the science, but to take logic as it is, and use it accordingly. And consistently with this profession, we readily acknowledge that the distinction between analytic and synthetic judgments, on which, and its historic occasion, we have discoursed so largely, is of small importance except in the investigations of transcendental logic; that its utility and application is confined with few exceptions to enquiries, the subject of which is not the knowledge real or supposed, but the faculty by which, either as the source or instrument, such knowledge is rendered possible. But is this nothing or of small value? Does it form no part of that knowledge that ought most to interest us, if our great moral poet have truly said that*ᵃ* "The proper study of mankind is man"?² Is it not included in the heaven-descended precept γνωθι σεαυτον?³ As the critical inquisition into the constitution of the intellectual faculties is the proper sphere in which this finds its use and validity, it cannot surprise us that it is scarcely noticed by logicians and metaphysicians previously to the appearance of the *Critique on the Pure Reason*,[*] which in fact would have been open

[*] Locke's *Essay on the Human Understanding* is an enquiry respecting the (by him so called) ideas, that is, notions, conceptions,*ᵇ* as the immediate objects of the faculty, and not an enquiry into the constitution of the faculty itself. The categories of Aristotle, with the fragments attributed on very suspicious authority to Archytas*ᶜ* and the Pythagorean school,⁴ but above all the passages elsewhere

ᵃ New paragraph in ms   *ᵇ* Ms lacks comma   *ᶜ* ms: Archidas

1 John Brown (1715–66) *An Essay on Satire, Occasioned by the Death of Mr. Pope* line 224 (2nd ed 1749) 17. The poem was published in Warburton's ed of Pope's *Works* (9 vols 1751) III xv and in later collections, hence, presumably, C's misattribution. Cf *BL* ch 8 (1907) I 93n and *CN* III 4397.

2 Pope *Essay on Man* ep II line 2.

3 Juvenal *Satires* 11.27. See above, p 116 n 3.

4 Tennemann argues for the later origin of all the fragments attributed to Plato's contemporary, Archytas (I 77–84n and 114n). C's successor on the *Encyclopaedia Metropolitana*, Richard Whately, uncritically accepted the tradition in his *Elements of Logic*.

to fewer objections, had it been proposed by the author under the more appropriate name of "Transcendental Logic". For considered as *logic* it is irrefragable; as philosophy it will be exempt from opposition and cease to be questionable only when the soul of Aristotle shall have become one with the soul of Plato, when the men of *talent* shall have all passed into men of *genius*, or the men of genius have all sunk into men of talent. That is, *Graecis calendis*, or when two Fridays meet.

6 The ignorance, however, of this distinction is not only to be inferred by the absence of all reference to it in the writings of the metaphysicians, metaphysical divines of the dogmatic philosophy, but by the effects of this ignorance.[*] For had the distinction between synthetic and analytic judgments been present to their minds, they could not have thought of deducing the principle of the

referred to in the *Novum Organum* of Lord Bacon, may be justly considered as approaches to, and the latter as anticipations or an implication of, the transcendental logic; but as a distinct branch of speculation it did not exist before the publication of the *Critique on the Pure Reason*, though it must have been more or less clearly present to the author's mind when he wrote the delightful essay entitled *Dreams of a Ghost-seer Illustrated by Dreams of Metaphysics*, 1766, the most popular of Kant's works and in the best sense of the word "popular".[1]

[*] The dogmatic philosophy, as opposed to the sceptical and the critical, is opposed to both. The dogmatist asserts, the sceptic doubts and denies, the demonstrability of human *opinions* or dogmas which characterises the critical philosopher and contradistinguishes him both from the dogmatist and the sceptic: thus, Hobbes, Locke, Clarke, Hartley, Wolff, Baumgarten, are *dogmatic* philosophers. Huetius with many other eminent Roman Catholic theologians, David Hume, Abraham Tucker, Lessing, and the author of Aenesidemus[a] are *sceptical* philosophers.[2] Voltaire, Paine, and the rest of that drove are no

[a] ms: Onesidemus

Comprising the Substance of the Article in the Encyclopaedia Metropolitana . . . (1826) 5, and was anonymously taken to task for his ignorance of German scholarship by William Hamilton in his "Recent Publications on Logical Science" *Ed Rev* LVII (1833) 194–238.

[1] *Träume eines Geistersehers, erläutert durch Träume der Metaphysik.*

[2] Samuel Clarke (1675–1729), philosopher and theologian and defender of Newtonian physics against Leibniz; Christian Wolff (1679–1754), systematiser of Leibniz's philosophy; Alexander Gottlieb Baumgarten (1714–62), a follower of Wolff; Huetius—Pierre

Daniel Huet—(1630–1721), bp of Avranches, author of *Censura philosophiae Cartesianae* (Paris 1689) and the posthumous *Traité philosophique de la foiblesse de l'esprit humain* (Amsterdam 1723); Abraham Tucker (1705–74), whose pseudonymous *The Light of Nature Pursued* (1768–78) was abridged by William Hazlitt in 1805; G. E. Lessing (1729–81), author of *Anti-Goeze*—for which see *Friend* (*CC*) I 34n; the author of *Aenesidemus*—Gottlob Ernst Schulze—(1761–1833), whose anonymous *Aenesidemus oder über die Fundamente der von dem Herrn Prof. Reinhold in Jena gelieferten*

sufficient cause from the principle of contradiction and identity, on which alone the truths of the common logic rest, as both their ground and their condition. They must have seen that the principle of contradiction is the adequate ground of analytic judgments only, or identical propositions, as they are more commonly named by our English metaphysicians,*a* but that a cause implies a synthetic judgment or a position resulting from the conjunction of two subjects.*b* Yet on this mistake rest*c* all the pretended scientific demonstrations of the Divine Existence and all other fundamental truths of religion and of morality; an attempt and an assumption that has been injurious in more ways than one. For first it has given a wrong direction to the mind of the enquirer*d* by directing it to expect and demand a *kind* rather than a *degree* of evidence in moral and religious truths, which they could not possess without ceasing to be moral and religious, inasmuch as it would exclude all participation of the will, which constitutes the moral, without counteracting its own end, by sacrificing the life and freedom of faith to a worthless, because compulsory, acquiescence. Secondly, it is injurious to other truths differing from these supposed demonstrable ones, chiefly by their being less calculated to permit the same delusion, or because they stand in a more particular connection with the conscience and the experience of the moral state of mankind. These truths, though their grounds and justifications are essentially the same with those of the former, are henceforward contradistinguished from them as mysteries, the subjects of ridicule to those who will believe nothing but by virtue of some legitimate conclusion from premises cognisable by the understanding, and who profess that their belief is commensurate with their logic, and consequently therefore confined either to the

---

philosophers at all, but as disbelievers they are of course dogmatists,*a* their followers being in the ordinary and popular sense of the word dogmatical because arbitrary and bigoted misbelievers, bigots of a bad faith on the credit of worse evangelists. N.B. The sceptic is not necessarily even an unbeliever. Many sincere and learned Christians have admitted no higher assurance than *that* of probability or reasonable belief, and no genuine sceptic goes beyond simple unbelief. The apology for this note, if any be necessary, will be found in the introduction to the transcendental aesthetic.[1]

a Full stop in ms	*b* Ms unpunctuated	*c* ms: rests	*d* ms: enquirers

---

Elementar-Philosophie . . . ([Helmstädt] 1792) defended Hume's philosophy against Kant's criticism (the work is summarised briefly in Willich *Elements* 20ff).

[1] See above, p 150.

objects of their senses or to the mere forms of the understanding itself as notions formed by reflection, or a pretext of pretending (without any insight at all) to believe in the truth of words of which they confess they do not know the meaning—a pretext equally favourable to the ambitious fanatic and serviceable to the designing hypocrite.* And thirdly, these dreams of demonstration have this inevitable consequence, that the negative may be proved on premises equally undeniable by the understanding, and by deductions equally logical as the affirmative; and atheism, pantheism, fatalism, the nonexistence of a responsible will, and the absurdity of the orthodox faith in all its leading points, have had their demonstrations, which, if we could, as in speculative reasoning and on a question of demonstration we ought to, free ourselves from all influence of our moral feelings and associations, will be found as logically legitimate as those given in proof of the contrary. Or if there were any difference, I fear that in point of strict consequence, Clarke and Wolff would yield the palm to Benedict Spinoza,[2] and the dogmatic idealism, spiritualism, of Berkeley be found less acceptable to the majority than the dogmatic materialism of Hobbes. Such are the results of resolving a synthetic judgment into an analytic, and thus of confining the character of truth and rational convictions to identical propositions, which, however long the series may be, are in reality so many repetitions of A is A, and what *is* cannot be affirmed not to be. Thus it appears that one of the great uses of logic is, first, that of circumscribing its own application and, secondly, of determining the conditions and circumstances under which it can be productively applied even within this sphere; and in like manner, that one of the most substantial services which transcendental logic performs for philosophy is that it confines the plenipotentiary power, the conclusive evidence of common logic, to truths that can be made evident without any other aid than that given in the principle of identity: that is, to every subject there belongs a predicate that is identical with it, or the principle of contradiction, which expresses the converse, viz. to no subject can a predicate belong that is in contradiction with it. Now these principles taken together constitute the highest and most general principles of the forms of discourse. They are, I say, the two

---

* [Note in J. H. Green's hand:] *Vide* p 53–54 of the 2d Lay Sermon from "If acquiescence without insight" to "Knowledge" line 6, p 56.—[1]

[1] *LS* (*CC*) 175–6.
[2] Benedict Spinoza (1632–77)—"this Samson Agonistes of unen-lightened Reason". BM MS Egerton 2801 f 1.

universal principles of the understanding in the formal exercise of its functions; but they can prove nothing more than the legitimacy of the form. They enable us to ascertain whether the understanding has contradicted itself or no, whether it has affirmed something respecting the predicate which it had already denied in the subject (e.g., that a circle has three angles), but by no means can it prove that our assertion is consistent with facts of experience, or with substantial truths, whencesoever derived. We may be certain that whatever is incompatible with these two principles must be false, but we cannot infer that what is compatible with them is therefore true. Whatever is more than this must be either true by its own evidence, truths, I mean, in the sense of realities—truths as distinguished from mere general principles, if such there exist, which is a question of *metaphysics*, not of *logic*[—]or facts learnt from experience, or the necessary products of a combination which the mind is enabled to make by virtue of its own constituent forms, whether the forms of sense or the forms of the understanding; in other words, whether intuitions or conceptions, truths immediately or mediately acquired. The first of the three does not belong to logic at all, not even the determination whether it is entitled to presuppose them affirmatively (that is, otherwise than problematically) in the premise or major of its syllogism. The second and third are synthetic judgments, the former, synthetic judgments *a posteriori*, the latter, synthetic judgments *a priori*, and the materials of which *a*they consist*b*; and that in the latter case synthetic judgments mean and might be called conjoint propositions or propositions by union or conjunction, as opposed to identical propositions or judgments simply analytic, which neither have nor require any other ground than that of the two above mentioned.

7   It is indeed a singular fact that the distinction between these two judgments should have remained so generally unnoticed that the only exception is to be found in Locke's *Essay*, and even here in one passage only, viz. the third chapter of the fourth book.[1] In this chapter, however, our great essayist expressly distinguishes two sources of the mind's judgments, and two sorts of knowledge as resulting therefrom—the first being the agreement or disagreement of the idea with itself, that is, analytic judgments, and the other the combination of two ideas into one subject, that is, synthetic judg-

a–b ms: it consists

[1] *Essay on Human Understanding* bk IV ch 3 §§ 22ff.

ments.[*] And he adds that with regard to the latter the power of the mind, acting on its own resources, is very limited—but without particularising what the limits are, or what the knowledges contained within them. Had he proceeded to this enquiry, he must have been led to the transcendental logic, that is, a true analysis of the understanding and not a mere classification of the ideas; and would thus have rescued the truth, which he actually meant, from the attacks of Berkeley and others, to which it was exposed by the impropriety of the expression consequent on the want of distinctness and adequacy in the conception of it. We need not therefore find it wonderful that the distinction had escaped Mr Hume[1] even when the nature of the question started by him and the direction which his enquiries took seemed to have placed it within his arms, if I may borrow a metaphor from a game not altogether dissimilar from that of metaphysics, the game of blind[man's]-buff, or that with his collateral views and hostility to all superstition it should have rather led him on a false scent. With this great advantage, however, that what he caught was so worthless and so intenable that it induced a more patient and dispassionate huntsman to seek the scent again at the point from which his predecessor had flown off and, having again once more caught it on the breeze, he follows it undeterred by the steep and difficult uplands whither it leads him, and

> Along the mountain's breast
> Stretches secure, and leaves the scattered crowd
> To puzzle in the distant vale below.[2]

[* Transcriber B writes in pencil (on f 335ᵛ) "this note should be on the other side" (i.e. f 336ᵛ); his correction is adopted here:]

The question has suggested itself to my mind whether some confusion might not arise from the more common use of the terms "analytic" and "synthetic" as applied to modes of reasoning—the analytic, when we reason from particulars to the general or from the many to the one; the synthetic, when we reason from the one to the many, from the principle to the consequences, etc. To prevent this inconvenience, however, it is only necessary to remember the difference between the form[s] of reasoning.

The reader will be pleased to observe that "idea" and "ideas" are here taken in Mr Locke's sense of the term as including all the immediate objects of the mind.

[1] Paragraph 7 up to this point is based on Kant *Prolegomena* § 3 (1783) 31.

[2] Untraced. The passage bears an interesting resemblance to WW *An Evening Walk* lines 179–88, 196–205: *WPW* i 22, 23.

CHAPTER [X]

On Mathematical Evidence

1   We have seen that mathematical reasoning or all truths respecting measure, number, and motion, susceptible of strict demonstration from self-evident premises, consist of synthetic judgments *a priori*. We have now briefly to show by what means this is effected, and how it is possible. Observe, not *whether* it be possible; for we have proved that mathematical truths are synthetic *a priori*, and of the existence of mathematics we are quite certain, and it were idle to offer any further proof of the possibility of a thing than is contained in its reality. We have not, I say, here as in the instance of metaphysics to enquire *whether* such a science be possible, which implies that its existence hitherto may be questioned, but *how* are synthetic judgments *a priori* possible. And in the first place, how are those in particular [possible] which belong to the mathematical sciences? Here we have a most assured knowledge which, vast even to astonishment in its present extent, promises to enlarge itself without limit in the future[1]—a science of which it may with severest truth be said that it, "Hath made Earth's reasoning animal her lord",[2] hath enabled man to behold the ends of the earth, and to survey what is beneath the heavens! He measureth the sea, and appointeth laws to the flowing thereof, he unravelleth the maze of the moon. He foretelleth the courses of the stars, yea, he weigheth them out and doth compass them as with a line. And this too a science, in the pure and most perfect sense, that carries with it, throughout, demonstrative certainty, an absolute *necessity* of truth, resting therefore on no grounds of experience, which could at best only give us the knowledge that it is so, not the clear insight and irresistible sense that so it must be, which consequently must be a pure product of the intellect acting by

---

[1] The sentence up to this point is translated from *Prolegomena* § 6 (1783) 48–9.
[2] *Religious Musings* line 220 (var): *PW* (EHC) I 117. The rest of the passage has not been traced to any source and may be an example of C's pulpit manner. Cf his letter to Benjamin Flower of 11 Dec 1796 (*CL* I 267).

its own powers on its own wealth, and this science, moreover, wholly and in all its parts synthetic. It is the work of reason; for where, except in the reason, can necessity and universality be found? But by what means and instruments doth the human reason bring it to pass? Is it by means of the universal principles of which the reason itself is the immediate source, and which are therefore rightly named principles of reason, and distinguished from *material* truths from the same source (supposing such to exist) by being merely *formal*? But we know of no other *principles*, that is, universal *forms*, of reason but those of identity and self-contradiction, the congruity with which is indeed a necessary *condition* of *all* judgments but the immediate ground of the analytic only. They supply the sufficient ground of *logical* certainty alone and therefore not the ground of mathematic evidence, which is altogether synthetic. But if not wholly or chiefly by its *formal* principles, so neither does the reason effect it by its *material* truths, by I D E A S (*sensu Platonico*)[1] or supersensual realities, the very existence of which is not of universal admission but which if allowed to exist might constitute a *mathematical* certainty and give birth to a series of synthetic judgments *a priori*, the sum of which would constitute the science of *metaphysics*; but not to those that constitute the *mathematics*, which instead of being supersensual is the very purity and perfection of *sense*. A priori therefore (and all means and materials *a posteriori* are excluded from the problem) there remain only the constitutive *forms*, or constitutional acts and functions, of the SENSE and of the *understanding*, with the several products of these, as far as they are producible *a priori*: viz. the pure intuitions[a] of the one and the self-derived notions and conceptions of the other.[*] By which then, or if by means of both, in what characteristic relation and proportion of the one to the other, does the speculative reason bring about this its most magnificent work?

2   A few references to what we have already learnt will narrow still more the sphere within which the answer must be found. We have already seen that the right application of the mind to realities, and in order to the true knowledge of what really is, constitutes philosophy, which, according to the difference of the object, receives a different name, as natural, political, or moral, physical, or meta-

[*] This does not express, nor is it meant to imply, that their evidence is derived from the *knowledge* of this constitution. The principles and canons of common logic are evident independently of the insight given by transcendental analysis.

[a] ms: intentions

[1] "In the Platonic sense".

physical philosophy; that the knowledge of the constitution of the mental faculties forms the science of transcendental analysis; and lastly that the rules and methods of conclusive discourse resulting from the constitution of the discursive faculty of the mind (that is, the understanding), under the universal principles of reason in reference to the *form* of the reasoning, constitute the science of common logic. We have seen too that the transcendental analysis consists of two parts, viz. the transcendental aesthetic and the transcendental logic. Now we shall [?attain] to the point in view if we assume, and in the first instance hypothetically only, and as a possible case, that the transcendental aesthetic is subdivided into two parts, of such disproportionate magnitude and extent, the one too circumscribed and perfectible, the other indefinite and illimitably progressive, yet ever travelling in the same fullness of light and leaving the light steady and undiminished along the whole of the vast line over which it had passed—not like the glowworm or firefly bearing the light along with it, but like a living fire that engenders a permanent light at every point of its progression. It would follow of itself that this latter form a science of itself especially if it should be found that in this instance as in that of common logic the evidence is complete in itself and in no way dependent on an insight into the grounds of its possibility. This insight therefore, and the investigations necessary thereunto, would alone belong to the transcendental aesthetic, or analysis of the pure sense. On the other hand, we will suppose that the second branch in our primary division, viz. the transcendental logic or analysis of the pure understanding, is in its nature so circumscribed that not only its inherent forms or its several functional powers are capable of being enumerated and defined, which is the case likewise with the transcendental aesthetic; but that the pure products and the connections of these products as far as they are produced and connected *a priori* are likewise predeterminable, having their[a] *ne plus ultra* in an assignable boundary. In this case, where both the producing powers and the possible products are presentable in our [?panoptic][b] and may be harmoniously combined in the same panorama, there would be no adequate motive for disjoining them as in the former case into separate sciences. The same science, that is, transcendental logic, would comprise both. Not only would the same science comprise both; but even the pure aesthetic shrunken in its dimensions by the contrary circumstance, that is, by the separation of its more important part, and too small for practical

a ms: its   b ms: panoplis

insulation, may more conveniently sink into a subdivision and be contained under the name of its more comprehensive co-factor. The analysis both of the pure sense and that of the pure understanding would stand under the common head, and be distinguished only as the several chapters of transcendental logic. We have only further to assume that the science separated from the transcendental aesthetic by its own magnitude and the independency of its evidence is that of mathematics, and in order to discover whether our assumption is well grounded we have only to compare it with the fact, that is, whether the acts of the pure sense under the universal form[s] of space and time, and the immediate products in and by which these acts are made manifest and which are indeed one with the acts, form the subject-matter and determine the proper character of the mathematical sciences. For this comparison is in no other way possible but by reflecting on the way in which the mind proceeds and the means it adopts in mathematical reasoning; but the statement of the way and means in and by which they are accomplished contains the full answer [to the question] "How are mathematical judgments as one class of synthetic judgments *a priori* possible?" Nor can this be done without at the same time answering in part—that is, as far as the negative characteristics are concerned—and in part preparing for the answer of the other question which then alone will remain, viz. "How are logical judgments possible, that is, synthetic judgments *a priori* that are not mathematical?"

CHAPTER [XI]

Of the Ways and Means by Which the Mind Arrives at Mathematical Evidence[1]

1 We are certain, inasfar as we know that it is impossible that the knowledge should be false.[2] Certainty, however, is to be distinguished from evidence. Two positions may be equally certain and yet the one have the advantage in being more evident. Thus: the certainty is as great in the calculations of algebra as in the demonstrations of geometry; but the latter are confessedly accompanied with a greater evidence, and the truth in both is capable of being rendered more evident than the truths of metaphysics, on the one hand, while on the other, than[a] the truths of induction or the knowledge derived from experience.[b] [Not] by their certainty, for we cannot say that they are more certain. A truth may be more or less evident but in certainty there are no degrees.[3] What is it, then, that gives the certainty to mathematical truths? And secondly, what is it that gives to the mathematics generally their greater evidence (which, however, is not equal in all its branches)?[c] And thirdly, therefore, what is it that (the certainty being one and the same in all) makes the evidence in geometry greater than that of arithmetic, and the evidence of arithmetic greater than that of the higher calculus? First. In order to understand a thing we must know all its component parts, and to be certain that we understand it, we must be certain that all the parts that belong to the thing are present to our mind, and that no others are imagined to be there. This process, by which we determine that nothing is

---

a ms: from   b Ms unpunctuated   c Parentheses inserted

---

1 This chapter is based on Kant *Untersuchung über die Deutlichkeit der Grundsätze der natürlichen Theologie und der Moral: VS* II 1–54.
2 The sentence is from *Untersuchung* Betrachtung III § 1: *VS* II 35.
3 Cf *CN* III 3455: "Two kinds of proof equal in certainty yet leaving the mind in very different states—these

may be called the Algebraic & Geometrical proofs—in the one you see it is so, and so it must be—in the other, you see likewise, *how* it is so, & why it cannot be otherwise—". Cf the distinction made between certainty and positiveness in *Friend* (*CC*) II 7, *CN* II 3095, and *CL* III 48.

wanting, and nothing intruded, is called in technical logic the "exhaustion of the terms".[1] Within our own memory, theoretical chemists believed themselves to understand the nature of muriatic acid,[2] that is, they believed themselves to have enumerated all its components or constituents, to the exclusion of all that were not such, in the terms oxygen in combination with a peculiar base. A more exact analysis and multiplied experiments caused them to believe that water was present in all cases, and that no means existed of its entire detachment. It was then thought safer—in other words, it was thought that the nature of muriatic acid was more intelligible—by admitting water as a component part. And for more than thirty years, during which time, too, chemistry was most zealously and most successfully cultivated, the favourite science of the age, all the chemists of the civilised world coincided in this assurance as grounded on the evidence of the senses, or on inferences so immediate and necessary as to be no more than the exponents of the phenomena or the phenomena themselves generalised in the conception and this conception expressed in words. They asserted, in short, that the position "muriatic acid is[a] composed of oxygen with an unknown base and water" was the true and only *meaning* of the phenomena and that there was no other way of conceiving the facts experimentally ascertained. And yet at the close of this period it was (or what for our purpose is the same, it was and is believed to have been) incontrovertibly shown that pure muriatic acid contains neither water, nor oxygen, nor an unknown base.[3] Add, too, that after the *experimentum[b] crucis*,[4] the decisive proof of the accuracy of Scheele's opinion respecting the simplicity of the oxymuriate[5] had been published by Sir H. Davy,[6] the founder of philosophic, as

---

[1] *Exhaustio terminorum.*

[2] Now called hydrochloric acid or hydrogen chloride.

[3] See Humphry Davy "On the Fallacy of the Experiments in Which Water Is Said to Have Been Formed by the Decomposition of Chlorine" *Phil Trans* CVIII (1818) 169–71.

[4] The "crucial experiment", or "acid test".

[5] Karl Wilhelm Scheele (1742–86), Swedish chemist, whose analysis of manganese dioxide in 1774 led to the isolation of chlorine.

[6] A reference to Humphry Davy's Bakerian lecture of 15 Nov 1810—"On Some of the Combinations of Oxymuriatic Gas and Oxygene . . ." *Phil Trans* CI (1811) 1–35. Davy particularly discusses the impropriety of the term "oxymuriatic acid" ("its great discoverer", he says, "called it dephlogisticated marine acid") and proposes instead "chlorine" or "chloric gas" (p 32). C was an indefatigable reader of the *Phil Trans*, knew Davy well, and took a keen interest in his work. C appears to have felt personally involved with this discovery, however; on the endpapers of Steffens *Geognostisch-*

Wollaston[1] of scientific, chemistry, the truth was not acknowledged till after a long and obstinate controversy, in which the English chemists were by no means unanimous in receiving it, while the Scottish, German, and French chemists were almost unanimous in its rejection. And even at last the balance was determined, it is probable, by the discovery of an analogous body, viz. the iodine.[2] It is not without deep interest *a*that I can*b* reflect that the French or Lavoisier's system, the adhesion to which occasioned this reluctance, is founded on as gross a *quid pro quo*[3] and equivoque as is to be found in the *elenchi* or sophisms exposed in the old books of logic, viz. the confusion of a power or principle with the body in which it appeared to be most predominant or in which it manifested itself most obviously.[4] On the very same ground on which Lavoisier made oxygen the principle of acidification, and thereby of combustion, he might have made platinum the power of gravity and elevated musk into universal repulsion.

2   The first distinction, therefore, the first characteristic prerogative of the mathematician, is that having first demanded a power which no man can deny, he begins by making his own terms. In all philosophical and historical disquisition the definition most properly should form the conclusion, as the result of the reasoning. If the writer commences with it, it is either by anticipation for the purpose of determining the reader's thought to the especial object proposed by the enquirer, as if a man pointing with his finger to the distance should say, "Keep in this direction and at yonder point you will see a building", which the speaker proceeds to describe in its main characteristics. Strictly speaking, these should rather be called "declarations" than "definitions". In the mathematics, on the

a–b ms: can I

---

geologische Aufsätze, he has written: "Long before Sir H. Davy's attempts to establish the independent existence of the Oxymuriatic as Chlorine, I had anticipated it a priori . . .".

[1] William Hyde Wollaston (1766–1828). C refers to one of his articles in a note on the flyleaf of Tennemann III. His tribute to Wollaston is less personal; see *CL* v 410 (early Feb 1825): "I have not the honor of any such acquaintance with Dr Woolaston, having only occasionally met him at dinner parties . . .". Cf *Friend* (*CC*) I

471.

[2] See Humphry Davy's lecture of 20 Jan 1814, "Some Experiments and Observations on a New Substance . . ." *Phil Trans* CIV (1814) 74–93. Davy names the new substance "iodine" (p 91) and credits Courtois—Bernard Courtois (1777–1838)—with having discovered it about two years earlier.

[3] "A mistaken substitution".

[4] Cf *CN* II 3192 (Dec 1807), in which the French chemists' misapplication of the names "hydrogen" and "oxygen" is referred to.

contrary, I begin with the definition. By the postulates I assert my power of productive action; by the definitions I determine what the product shall be and by what name it shall be known. These elementary products and the simplest constructions and integrations of the same are my definitions. By an act of my will I think four straight lines that enclose a plane space so that the opposite sides shall not be parallel, and I call the figure that results from this construction a trapezium.[1] To this I confine myself; I say nothing of anything out of myself as corresponding to it. There may, for aught I know, be many bodies that might in part be described in the same words, but these bodies may have many other and, perhaps, more essential characters. But this creation of my own is this and this only. These components and this composition constitute the trapezium. And to suppose myself deceived, or to pretend any the least doubt, would convict me of the same absurdity as that of the simpleton in one of our old plays, whom the poet introduces fresh from the wonders and sight-baffling sights of a pretended magician and which have left him so doubtful respecting the evidence of his senses, and so proud of his newly acquired scepticism, that speaking of a blazing fire he exclaims, "This fire does not really burn; it only seems to burn; but it does not really seem, it only seems to seem."[2] Now there might be some pretence for the first scruple, but the second contradicts itself. The man that sees a ghost *actually* sees it, though it may not at all follow that really there was any ghost to be seen. Now in the mathematics the producing act and the product are one and indivisible. A cone may signify elsewhere what you will, but the geometrician speaks of a

---

[1] C's example is taken from *Untersuchungen* Betrachtung I § 1: *VS* II 5–6.

[2] The original of this remark appears in a letter of Moses Mendelssohn's in F. H. Jacobi *Ueber die Lehre des Spinoza ...* (Breslau 1789) 86: "Lessing lässt, in einem seiner Lustspiele, jemanden, der Zauberey zu sehen glaubt, von einem brennenden Lichte sagen: Dieses Licht brennt nicht wirklich, es scheint nur zu brennen; es scheint nicht wirklich, es scheint nur zu scheinen." ("Lessing, in one of his comedies, has someone who believes he is seeing sorcery say of a burning light: this light does not really burn, it only seems to burn; it does not really seem, it only seems to seem.") The comedy in question is the fragment *Die Matrone von Ephesus*, first published in Lessing *Theatralische Nachlass* (Berlin 1784); the remark occurs in the first scene, and the offerer of the suspect flame is a supposed ghost. C's substitution of a "pretended magician" and his "wonders and sight-baffling sights", whether deliberate or forgetful, has the advantage of applying the incident to an old joke about theories of perception. See e.g. *Guardian* No 24 (8 Apr 1713) and *Spectator* No 242 (7 Dec 1711)—both by Steele. The *Guardian* story is used for its philosophical implications by Dugald Stewart in "Dissertation First ..." *Supplement to the Fourth, Fifth, and Sixth Editions of the Encyclopaedia Britannica* (Edinburgh 1824 6 vols) I 97.

cone which he himself has created by voluntarily presenting to himself a right-angled triangle that turns round on one side. It is therefore a synthesis, a composition, a construction.[1] The construction takes place, the product has its birth and existence within the mind. It is therefore a synthesis *ab intra*.[2] But this power must be presupposed in order to the possibility of contemplating the outward objects in similar relations. (*Vide* [above, pp 198–210] Transcendental Aesthetic.)[a] It is therefore a synthesis *a priori*. It is necessary; for it is impossible and a contradiction to affirm that he has not exercised the act which he is exercising, or that the product can be other than it is. And lastly it is universal; for he knows infallibly and on the very same principle that he possesses this as a man, not as an individual, that he can with certainty anticipate the same result from every other man, that is, rational and intelligent being having the faculty of sense, on the single condition of inducing him to make the attempt. (*Vide* the *Menon* of Plato.)[b][3]

3   But secondly, and which distinguishes the mathematical evidence from the logical, as the former contradistinguishes it from the experimental, the mathematician *always* and essentially reasons intuitively. It is not only a synthesis *a priori*; but a synthesis *a priori* of intuitions, which (the act and the product being one) are themselves intuitions *a priori*. The conceptions of the logician and the philosopher may be accompanied with intuitions mixed or pure, may be illustrated by them; but those of the mathematician *must* be presented *intuitively*. *Immediate* presentation *et in concreto*, in contradistinction from the knowing a thing *mediately* by representative marks obtained by abstraction (which the logicians call *in abstracto* as the antithesis to *in concreto*),[4] is *essential* in mathematical evidence and *makes* the evidence mathematical. Now to contemplate our knowledge *in concreto* and this by an *act* of the mind is what we mean by construction. I contemplate my face *in concreto* in the looking-glass, but the concrete or image is no act of mine as far as I am conscious—and within the bounds of consciousness alone we are

---

a Parentheses inserted; blank space left in ms for page numbers
b Parentheses inserted

---

1 The example of the cone is from *Untersuchungen* Betrachtung I § 1: *VS* II 6.
2 "From within".
3 *Meno* 82B–85B. Cf *BL* ch 12 (1907) I 173: "Socrates in Plato shows, that an ignorant slave may be brought to understand and of himself to solve the most difficult geometrical problem." Cf *Friend* (*CC*) I 457.
4 E.g. Leibniz *Theodicée* Preliminary Discourse § 63 (quoting Bayle): "the reason of man, or reason *in concreto* and . . . reason in general, or reason *in abstracto*".

now moving. My mind is passive to the impression on my eye. We need only demonstrate the simplest proposition in Euclid to be made [to] know how different this is from the contemplation of the concrete by means of a constructive act.

4   But here the difficulty seems rather to increase than[a] diminish; how is it possible to contemplate anything, to have the intuition of an object, except by the immediate presence of the object; and what is this but experience, or at least the matter of fact of which experience is composed, but of which the intuitions in question are to be independent? And truly, if the intuition in question were of that kind that it represented the things or self-subsistents[b] as they are in themselves, it would be impossible otherwise than by experience. For what is contained in the object of itself I can know only as far as such object is present or given to me. It would be something worse than absurd to suppose in a finite mind the power of creating anything out of itself; but what I cannot create for myself I must have given to me if I am to have it at all. I confess that even under the condition of this datum it is altogether incomprehensible how my intuition of a present object should enable me to know it as it is in itself, or to know anything more than the relations in which I myself stood to the object thus given. For the attributes or properties of a thing cannot pass over like emigrants into my soul or sentient being.[*] If, however, the possibility of this be taken for granted, still this intuition could not take place *a priori*; for this would imply a right destructive of all reason and all philosophy—the right of asserting at will the commencement of a thing at any particular time without any assignable ground, cause, or occasion. In fact [this is] the doctrine of Malebranche and of some other Cartesians [who] have taken refuge in the hypothesis of inspiration or immediate acts of divine agency— which may be *piety*, which may even be *truth*; but which most certainly is not *logic*, or philosophy logically deduced.[2] In our knowledge

---

^a ms: then   ^b ms: self-subsistence   ^c ms: if

[*] How the *esse* assumed as it[c] necessarily is in the act of reflection and consequently in all reasoning merely logical which takes the necessary data of reflection for its premises. How the *esse* assumed as originally distinct from the *scire*. […]
Biog. Lit: Vol. I, page 130, to "every part" line 14[a], 132.[1]

[1]   *BL* ch 8 (1907) I 89–91. Did C wish to include the passage?
[2]   Nicolas Malebranche (1638–1715). C cites him in *BL* ch 12 (1907) I 187 to the effect that we see all things in God, but on that occasion he is merely paraphrasing Schelling (*System des transcendentalen Idealismus* 319). He refers to him in *CL* II 679 and *CN* III 3974. Cf Kant's similar dismissal of

a posteriori, or the image in the mind correspondent to the outward object consequent on the presence of that object, the fact may bear down the want of insight into the possibility of the fact. At all events it does not contradict the principle of the sufficient reason, or any other universal principle real or formal, which would be the case in the assertion of an intuition *a priori* of an object which is yet distinct from the object itself and its correspondent.

5   There remains therefore but one way in which it is possible that my intuition should, in its universal forms, be antecedent to the presentation of the object, and certain of my particular intuitions being independent of any outward object, viz. if the intuition and these particular constructions of the same contain nothing else but the forms of the sense, the sense itself in short, considered apart from the sensibility, the form in my own mind as the subject is anterior to all actual impressions from without as being that which predetermines within certain bounds the mode in which outward objects can be contemplated by me. In short, knowledge *a priori* is possible, but *possible* then only when the knowledge and the object known, the *scire* and the *scitum*, are one and the same.

6   We have now only to refer to the preceding chapters on space and time as the universal forms,[1] *that* of the outward, *this* of the inward sense, and then to any, the simplest, operation in mathematics, geometrical or arithemetical, in proof and illustration of the productive imagination by which the intuition of space and that of time are variously combined or constructed, to have afforded a complete solution of our three first questions, viz. "How are[a] *a priori* knowledge, or synthetic judgments not experiential, possible?" Secondly, "How mathematical knowledge in particular, as forming one class of synthetic judgments *a priori*, is possible?" And thirdly, "Wherein do these judgments differ essentially from others that are likewise both synthetic and *a priori*, that is, what is[b] the essential distinctive character of pure mathematics?"

7   Of the ordinary and indispensable proceedings of the mathematicians, let the following be taken as the illustrative instances. That a space, as far as it is the space, and not a boundary of any other space, has three dimensions, and that space in the absolute is a truth grounded on the position that not more than three lines can

---

a ms: is   *b* ms: are

Malebranche ("Principiorum . . . elu-   *intelligibilis forma et principiis* § 22
cidatio" § 3 II prop xiii usus par 6:   scholion: *VS* II 473–4).
VS IV 171 and *De mundi sensibilis atque*   [1] Ch IV above, pp 150–73].

cut each other at right angles in one point. But this proposition cannot be proved out of any conceptions. It cannot be logically concluded or deduced but rests altogether and immediately on the intuition: we *see* that so it is, and this [is] a pure intuition, an intuition *a priori*, arising out of the intuitive faculty itself, because it is a certainty accompanied with a sense of the impossibility of the contrary; because we do not confine ourselves [to affirming] that so it is in this instance and so it has been hitherto in all my experience, and in that of all other men as far as I know, and I see no reason for supposing that it will be otherwise in future, which is the utmost that knowledge founded on experience could warrant or excite; but so it must be, and if contemplated in sense it cannot be contemplated otherwise. But that such intuitions are pure and *a priori* is likewise proved, because the geometrician can, and often does, require that a line should be produced infinitely (*in indefinitum*) or that a series of changes, a series of spaces left behind in a given motion, should be continued *ad infinitum*—postulates which presuppose a presentation or intuition (or if I may use the language of the Cartesians without implying my assent to its appropriateness or expediency), *an innate idea* of space and time which subsists wholly in the intuitive faculty itself, as far as it exercises its power unaided and unbounded by anything out of itself.[1] In the same manner all the proof[a] of the perfect equality of two given figures rests wholly on the immediate intuition of their entire coincidence, or that they cover each other in all points, which as an image indeed might have been derived from experience, but not as a necessary truth.[2] It was the inadvertence to this distinction that misled the late Dr Beddoes to the strange assertion that the evidences[b] of the mathematician are of the same kind, derived from the same sources, derived from the same means, as those of the chemist.[3] To the strange position before mentioned, even suppose two bodies to be made [to] cover each other before our eyes, yet what could we say but that these bodies, as far [as] *I* see, coincide. In order to determine whether the equality grounded on this coincidence is a *necessary* and universal consequent, I must construct it in my own mind, and in *this* construction it is that I find the impossibility of the contrary. In fact the very words, "if these two surfaces cover

----

a ms: proofs   *b* ms: evidence

[1] Paragraph 7 up to this point is freely translated from Kant *Prolegomena* § 12 (1783) 55–6.
[2] The sentence is based on *Prolegomena* § 13 (1783) 57. Cf above, pp 160ff.
[3] See above, p 15 n 1.

each other they are equal", have no proper or immediate reference to the *bodies*. For I have no reason to suppose the existence or even the possibility of any two bodies or surfaces absolutely equal to each other, and if such did exist, yet I have certainly no means of ascertaining it, nor should I have, though my eyes were ten times more microscopic than Mr Pope supposes those of the fly to be.[1] The true meaning of the words refers to the constructive faculty itself, not to the image, no, not even to the image in the fancy, which is no other than the mental diagram, both it and that drawn on the slate or paper being alike pictures of the mathematical line generated by the mathematical points and of the mathematical surfaces generated by the lines, which, as the very definitions are sufficient to show, are acts and products of the active and productive imagination.

8   What the use of the picture is in aid of the evidence, and how little it is essential to the certainty of the intuition, we may find in going through any arithmetical operation—that $3 \times 3 = 9$ and $3 \times 9 = 27$ we determine in the first instance by the law of succession in ourselves, that is, by the intuition of time, and this [is] sufficient for certainty as long as we can attend to the progression with the recollection of what went before, or some mark representative of the same and a substitute for the recollection more secure than the recollection itself, the names, I mean, of each unit expressing and involving all that in the line of time had gone before; but yet in order to extend and facilitate the construction and for the purpose of increased evidence we express the intuitions of time by those of space. A 9 we call the square, and 27, the cube of 3; but which no more alters the nature of the former process or prevents it from being constructed intuitively, that is, a truth immediately grounded in the form and constructive power of the inner sense itself, than the notes of music cease to be auditual and successive by being entitled sharps and flats. The student, if acquainted with fluxions and the processes of integration and of differentials, will find the happiest and most perfect exemplification of the relations which the two forms of the outer and inner sense, that is, of space and time, are capable of bearing to each other. We reason algebraically and above all infinitesimally in order to give rapidity and sense of difference to our reasoning, and we translate it, where it is practicable, geometrically, that is, into the intuitions of space, in order to give it totality and greater evidence.

---

[1] *Essay on Man* ep I lines 193–4.   *Microscopic Experiments* in *AR* (1825)
Cf C's reference to the eyes of the   158 and n.
Aranea prodigiosa and to Baker's

9   We have seen, likewise ([above, pp 168–9], Transcendental Aesthetic), that the intuitions of time are higher and more comprehensive than those of space, the constructions of space, that is, figure, being inconceivable exclusively of the inner sense, while these may exist for themselves. In order to form a line we imagine the successive motion of a point; and to form a figure the lines must be finite in one direction at least; and if the figure is to be complete, a circle, square, ellipse, etc, and dependent for its degree of evidence on the forms of the outward sense, the component lines must be finite altogether. But figure is not necessary to the conception of motion, and it is by the sense of succession, that is, under the universal form of time, that we arrive at the motion *ad indefinitum*, whence we may comprehend the greater affinity which the intuitions of time and the constructions of the same have to the conceptions of the understanding than takes place in pure geometry. The higher we advance in the higher calculus, or in what is mathematically called the transcendental analysis, the more does the mathematical reasoning resemble the logical, differing from it, indeed, in this respect, that though the reasoning be *in abstracto*, yet this abstraction must be capable of being resolved into intuitions, or at least there must be a certainty that intuitions are the grounds and constituents of the certainty. Otherwise it would cease to be mathematical and be merely logical. The preceding remark supposes a greater acquaintance with the higher mathematics than I am entitled to suppose that my reader possesses or in fact than I myself possess, if the remark requires anything more than simply to know from other authority that so it is, and to understand that from the nature of the thing so it ought to be.[1]

---

[1] For C's regret at knowing so little mathematics, see his marginal note in Böhme *Works* published in *CN* II 2894n.

CHAPTER [XII]

On Synthetic Judgments *a priori*
Other Than Mathematical,
or on the *a priori* Connections of the Understanding,
or Logical Conceivability

1 We have seen, then, that MATHEMATICAL SCIENCE is grounded in the intuitive faculty itself, and consists of the acts and products of this faculty, that is, pure intuitions and constructions *a priori*; and that in this view, and this alone, we are enabled to comprehend how the positions or judgments of the mathematician should be *synthetic*, no less than the judgments *a posteriori* (that is, the combinations ascertained by *experience*), and yet necessarily certain and apodictic, which no judgments merely experiential are or can be. We have arrived at this insight by the transcendental deduction of our conceptions time and space as the universal forms of the sense, that is, of the sentient faculty considered abstractly from its objects; and we see that without this deduction, and without granting, moreover, the postulate which it suggests to us, that whatever is presented to our senses (to the *outward* senses in space, and to the *inner* sense in time) is contemplated and apprehended as it *appears* to us, not as it is in itself (*ut res* PHAENOMENALIS *et subjectiva, non ut res in se et seorsim a mente subsistens*).[1] We might indeed have found ourselves compelled to admit the *fact* of mathematical certainty, but how such a fact is *possible* we must have remained ignorant. We might have *known* it, but we could not have *understood* it. And lastly we have learnt the distinction between certainty and evidence; more than this is beyond the bounds of logic, either common or critical; the attempt if made at all belongs to *noetic*, or the doctrine of ideas.[*]

[*] The reader who wishes to enquire further and will either not wait for, or who deems himself entitled to reject *a priori*, such a doctrine, I can only refer to the concluding paragraphs of the chapters on transcendental aesthetic.[2]

[1] Literally, "as an apparent and subjective thing, not as a thing in itself and as subsisting apart from the mind".

[2] See above, pp 171–3.

2　The time is gone by when a few misinterpreted metaphors and symbolic expressions of the divine philosopher[1] induced the visionary Platonist to attempt the explanation of spiritual mysteries, and make discoveries in the spiritual world, by means of geometrical figures and mathematical numbers, and to find the originals and first parents of our human diagrams in celestial realities, angelic triangles, and arch-angelic circles. I need not in the present age instruct the reader that *mathematical* truths as the forms of the sense are exclusively applicable to the objects of the senses, and that these forms are realised, or possess a reality more than subjective, only as far as the observations of experience are found coincident therewith; and with what fortunate success our astronomic discoveries and both the discoveries and inventions in mechanics and statics bear witness. As little does the reader require to be informed that the mathematic is most applicable to those appurtenances or attributes of external nature that are most homogeneous with itself, viz. that which is most general and capable of being abstracted and generalised, [such] as extent, mass, weight, and motion. Before we proceed it will be expedient to guard against an error into which the frequent mention of pure and mixed intuitions, that is, immediate perceptions of the modifications of extension and succession, might mislead the student, as if in mathematical reasoning these were the only constituents. It will be useful, I say, to look somewhat more narrowly into the famous adage common to the Aristotelian school and that of Epicurus, "Nihil in intellectu quod non *prius* in sensu"—and not so much for the purpose of guarding against its undue extension by adding the Leibnizian postscript, "praeter ipsum intellectum",[2] which we have already done in general, and the particular explanation of which is the subject of the present chapter; but with especial reference to the word *prius*. "There is nothing in the understanding which was not previously in the sense", which, to an incautious mind at least, might seem to infer that, though in the exercise of reason there can be no conceptions formed independently of perceptions, yet we may reason by perceptions, that is, possess intuitive knowledge without the aid of conceptions. The error indeed would yield to the first attentive reflection, and with a thoughtful reader therefore could only be momentary. For it would give to the mathematician the power of knowing and of demonstrating his propositions, but deny him that of understanding them. The true distinctive character of mathematical

---

[1] Plato.

[2] "Except the understanding itself".

Leibniz *Nouveaux essais* bk II ch 1 § 8 (var). See above, p 134 n 2.

science lies in the necessary construction and essential constructibility of its conceptions in the forms of intuition. The presence of conceptions therefore is as truly presupposed as that of intuitions. In fact each supposes the other. And not only does this hold true in the instance of those conceptions which are properly intended in the Aristotelian adage and of which alone the assertion can be truly made, viz. the *quotquot* IN *intellectu*;[1] but likewise to those purely formal, which are included in Leibniz's cautionary addition, "praeter ipsum intellectum". Examine any synthetic judgment of whatever kind (or we might submit them all to an exact analysis), and we shall find, though in opposition to the common opinion, that they never consist of intuitions alone that are merely combined by an act of *comparison* or *equation* into one judgment; but that the synthetic judgment would be impossible if, over and above the conceptions abstracted from the intuition, whether it be the image of an outward object or the image itself considered as an object, there did not likewise supervene a *pure* conception of the understanding, not derived from any form of sense or representment of the senses, under which conception the former (those viz. abstracted from the objects of the senses, or expressed in the forms of the sense itself) are taken up or subordinated (which process is by the logicians technically called subsumption, or the act of subsuming). And when the conceptions and intuitions are thus subsumed under some pure conception, some one of the inherent and constituent forms of the understanding, then first are they capable of being combined into a judgment that has real validity and significancy.[2] And observe that this reality, or objectivity in the secondary sense of the word, is not confined to judgments *a posteriori* or to what we affirm or deny on grounds of experience. Let the image be the offspring of the intuitive faculty itself and the immediate product of its imaginative power called into action. Still, yet even here, the mind itself is assumed as the substance, the substratum of the form, and as far as this can be universally and permanently assumed in contradistinction from individual peculiar and contingent [considerations], the truths resulting are equivalent to those in which the substance or substratum of the forms is other than the subject engaged in contemplating them, or the mental subject, and because the two results are equal they have been expressed by the same name as judgments possessing objective validity. The reader will excuse me that I so readily avail myself of bringing back

---

[1] "As many things as are *in* the understanding".

[2] Cf Kant *Prolegomena* § 20 (1783) 83, and, for what follows, cf 82–3.

to his recollection explanations that have been so frequently given before, but the more nearly he approaches to the conclusion of our logical disquisitions, the more should his mind be prepared and predisposed to see and understand the utmost boundary as well as the legitimate extent of the antithesis, subject and object, subjective and objective; and that, both in the one term and in the other, different, nay, at first sight contradictory, senses, that at different times are expressed by one and the same word, are not to be attributed to any removable defect in the technical language of the science, or to an injudicious choice of equivocal terms; but from the necessary indifference of both in the point producing (or on each side produced into) the line of which they are the differentials or opposite poles: *opposita semper unigena. In omni oppositione datur suppositum in quo* (*seu, tenus quod*) *opposita unum sunt. Thesis = antithesis in aliqua prothesi*.[1] Terms that can be rightly opposed to each other in the evolution of a truth must be identical in the root, that is, radically one. These are different ways of expressing the same principle, a principle of paramount importance in philosophy no less than in logic, pregnant as an idea and infallible as a criterion.

3   We have said that synthetic judgments in no instance consist of intuitions merely nor of conceptions formed from them, but that in all cases, whether the judgments [be] *a priori* or *a posteriori*, there must be some pure conception of the understanding as the ground and condition of the former; even the positions of the pure mathematic in its simplest axioms form no exception. That the straight line is the shortest between two points presupposes that the line is subsumed under the conception of quantity, which most assuredly is no mere intuition but has its seat wholly in the understanding and in this instance exercises an appropriate function. There is first the intuition—the line, to wit—now this line cannot be reflectively contemplated but in relation to the judgments which the mind may form respecting it. And the conception in this instance determines this judgment in respect of the *quantity* of the line by which I judge that in any given image a number (plurality, multeity) of homogeneous points or spaces is contained in the unity of a given intuition.[2] The exceedingly abstract character of the words which on subjects so universal and abstract as the present must needs be, e.g., points,

---

[1] "Opposites are always of the same genus. In every opposition a suppositum is given in which (or insofar as which) opposites are one. Thesis = antithesis in some prothesis".

[2] Paragraph 3 up to this point is from Kant *Prolegomena* § 20 (1783) 84.

lines, surface, etc, give[s] the appearance of a difficulty which really does not exist in the conception itself.

4   Let the student try the experiment whether he can present a given line to his mind without some determination in his mind of its being longer or shorter, that is, containing more or less of an homogeneous extension, more or fewer of an indefinite multitude of homogeneous points, which it is in his power to conceive singly and successively, and so far as *many* that are not *one* but which here he contemplates as co-present, continuous, and as the *many* in *one*. But this unity depends, he will find, on determining the *quantum* of the *many* that have become *one*. Now this is not in the line; for it is out of our power to think it long or short, more or less, except in comparison with some other, but this again holds equally true of that other and of each and every possible intuition *ad infinitum*. But that which exists neither in A nor in B, and yet is such that without it neither A nor B can be contemplated at all, or consciously known as existing, must of necessity exist in C as a relation of A and B taken comparatively to some principle of comparison in C itself. Here, that is, in C, as the subject or mind contemplating A and B, there is no focus in which any imaginable rays converge and become intense. That which neither A nor B possess[es], neither A nor B can irradiate or give forth. The utmost that can be said [is] that it was called forth in C in consequence of A and B falling at one time under his contemplation, which is indeed proved further by the fact that one of the objects may have been noticed for the first and last time twenty years ago and in China, the other at the present moment and in Peru,[1] and the conception of their comparative quantity will take place equally well. But comparative supposes positive, and every finite a previous indefinite. We cannot conceive waves without a sea, lake, or river, nor a sea, lake, or river without the preconception of water, as the common term. The very terms "more" or "less", "larger" or "smaller", with all their definite determinants, of number, weight, and measure, inches, feet, miles, pints, gallons, etc, etc, presuppose that of which they are at once measures and parts, *measures* of quantity and themselves *quantities*, not parts, from the co-existence or proximity of which a whole results, as in a heap of corn or any other mere aggregate; but parts that owe their existence and their possibility to a pre-existing All, an ἐν καὶ πᾶν *ejusdem generis*,[2] to

---

[1] An echo of C's favourite example of redundancy—Johnson's *The Vanity* *of Human Wishes* lines 1–2. See *CL* IV 685 and n.

[2] "Homogeneous one and all".

which they have the same relation as the thoughts to the mind, as spaces to space itself, etc.

5   Might I again interrupt for a moment the disquisition, in order to address the student as if he were indeed present, I would say, "Do not let the newness and strangeness of these speculations discourage you or lead you to suppose that there is any difficulty in the thoughts themselves, anything abstruse in that which is really meant, otherwise than as all efforts are troublesome to which we are unaccustomed. They are hard only because they are strange. The unexpected, the unusual, oppresses and overbears us. And hence the origin of the word 'insolent', *insolens, quod maxime insolitum.*[1] Abstraction, indeed, in its highest degrees and when the process is not favoured by the senses (as in abstracting a colour, redness, for instance, from the many and diverse bodies that are so coloured,[a] but on the contrary we have to abstract from all the accidents of sense), is the most arduous function of the understanding, and the minds able and disposed to exercise it are comparatively rare. 'Peu de têtes sont faites pour une abstraction absolue, c'est à dire, pour une attention qui n'est dirigée qu'à l'être. Mais la vérité ne sauroit nous venir de dehors, elle est en nous.'[2] In other words, to abstract adequately is hard, but in scientific pursuits there is no getting at the truth without it. If we would emancipate ourselves from the tyranny of appearances, we must abstract. The abstraction, however sufficient for our present purposes, is trifling compared with what is required in the higher branches of the mathematics, and even with regard to the degree in which it must be exerted in making the experiment of the line in the last paragraph but one. If having read the paragraph two or three times attentively you either miss the meaning or find it dim and flitting and that it escapes a steadfast grasp, in this and in other similar cases I would advise you to desist from the effort and pass on. The few passages in which this is likely to occur, where there exists an actual wish to understand my words and a proportional vigour and

[a] Close of parenthesis in ms

[1] "Insolent, because most unusual". C is pointing out that "insolent" (Latin *insolens*) is derived from the negative prefix *in* and *soleo* ("I am accustomed"), so that its original meaning was "what is very unexpected or unusual".

[2] "Few minds are suited to absolute abstraction, that is, to directing their attention exclusively to being. But the truth cannot come to us from without, it is within us." The passage is attributed to Spinoza by Hemsterhuis in an imaginary dialogue; it appears, accompanied by a translation into German, in Jacobi *Ueber die Lehre des Spinoza* . . . 123–4. C has reversed the order of the sentences and moved the "mais" from one to the other accordingly.

continuity of attention, are in no instance, I flatter myself, indispensable. What follows or what has gone before may perhaps supersede the necessity of the particular argument or illustration, while the latter, perhaps, may have the same effect for some other reader with respect to a paragraph in which you had found no difficulty, but on the contrary a furtherance and the very light you were seeking. Desist, I say, from *trying* to understand; for first, it may not be necessary, and secondly, it is most probable that as so often happens with regard to names it will start up of its own accord when you are not thinking of it."

6 Retrace our recent exposition of quantity, and of quantities that are parts and measures of quantity. You observe at first sight that it cannot be *things* that are here spoken of and thus described, but *thoughts*, or modes and powers of thinking. If by a thing be meant a possible object of the senses, a whole, that is of necessity antecedent to its parts, cannot be a thing; it is impossible, for it is the very definition of a sensible whole that it is the sum, limit, and common result of its constituent parts. And therefore in direct contrast with a *whole* of the former kind, that which precontains its parts. This the student will have suspected from the instances given, [such] as the mind and its thoughts, space and the spaces, as compared with the illustrations and similes, the sea, for instance, and the waves, if what is said were to be understood of the things themselves and not of our thoughts respecting them. If I propose to myself in humble imitation of Archimedes the question of the number of drops in a tub of water,[1] it is most certain that the universal, or, if I might borrow a more expressive and more English [word] from our sister language the German, the allcommon (*allgemein*) term "water" precedes the given whole, namely the vessel of water, and the vessel, that is, the given total quantity, goes before the conception of the drops, and predetermines their number, though physically and matter of fact the vessel may have been put in the rain and the drops have been antecedent to the whole that results from them or which they have made. Do not misconceive me, I do not say that a whole necessarily antecedent to its parts must always be mere thought or *ens logicum*: for such a whole must life be, and every particular life.[*] But I say

[*] Which would perhaps be better and less equivocally named a "productive unity", and distinguished from a whole, as elsewhere I have proposed to use

[1] A reference to Archimedes' testing of Hiero's crown or a confusion of his work on hydraulics with his calcula- tion of the possible number of grains of sand in the universe? Cf *SM* (*CC*) 51n.

that it cannot be an object of the senses, and must, therefore, be a subject, or some act, mode, or attribute of a subject, whether it be a subject simply, as life, or a subject having its object in itself, that is, the mind, or some determinate act or product of the life or mind.

7 When, therefore, I say that every particular conception of quantity which I attach to particular intuitions pure or experiential presupposes the universal conception "quantity", and this as innate and *a priori*, I can by the latter form have but one meaning, viz. that my mind is so constituted as of necessity to contemplate objects in this particular relation to itself, that as a machine moving in a particular way, predetermined by the construction of the machine itself, describes of itself a particular figure and impresses this on any impressible body that comes under its action, so in the mind itself there is a self-determining predisposition to contemplate objects in certain ways, and, as far as they are its objects, to contemplate these its own acts and products in them.

8 "Well! This", the student may reply, "we can understand, and in this sense, as you have yourself informed us, Mr Locke himself admits the existence of innate conceptions under the name of

---

the term "form" as the technical antitheton to "shape".[1] As form = *forma formans*,[2] to shape = *forma formata*,[3] so the productive unity = *totum suas ipsius partes constituens*,[4] to the whole (mass aggregate) = *totum a partibus constitutum*.[5] The former is the same with the Leibnizian monad and the entelechy[a] of Aristotle,[6] which the famous poet, scholar, statesman, and patriarch, Hermolaus Barbarus[b] raised the devil to find the meaning of.[7] This was the first time that the devil served the purpose of philosophical dictionary, though some two centuries afterwards Voltaire and his friends proved how aptly and effectually a philosophical dictionary might serve the purpose of the devil.[8]

---

a ms: Enteuchè   *b* ms: Barbasus

[1] Cf "On Poesy and Art" *BL* (1907) II 262: "there is a difference between form as proceeding, and shape as superinduced;—the latter is either the death or the imprisonment of the thing;—the former is its self-witnessing and self-effected sphere of agency".
[2] "Form that forms". Cf the discussion on p 242, below.
[3] "Form that is formed".
[4] "A whole constituting its parts out of itself".
[5] "A whole constituted out of the parts".

[6] Cf Leibniz *Monadologie* § 18: "All simple substances or created Monads might be called Entelechies ...". Leibniz *The Monadology and Other Philosophical Writings* tr Robert Latta (1898) 229.
[7] Hermolaus Barbarus (1454–93). According to C. G. Jöcher (*Allgemeines Gelehrten Lexicon*—Leipzig 1750—1771), the devil answered "perfectihabia". The incident is referred to by Tennemann (III 183n).
[8] *Dictionnaire philosophique* (1764).

determine predispositions of the mind.[*] But with what propriety are they called 'conceptions', pure, general, *a priori* 'conceptions'? Even as in your former exposition of space and time, with what propriety is the power of contemplating objects immediately as objects of sense and the predetermination of that power—or more shortly, with what propriety is the law of the intuitive faculty itself entitled an intuition?" If in addition to what has been already urged by me in a former chapter, in which the subject was elucidated by the kaleidoscope, any answer is necessary, I know not how to reply but by the uncourteous way of retorting the question. With what greater propriety can they be called anything else but pure general conceptions? Nay! in strict propriety and with austere precision what else can they be called? Reflect for a moment, but first permit me to impose on you the trouble of turning back to and attentively reperusing the contents of [Part One Chapter ii].*a* What do we mean by a conception? Can we mean any more than the mind conceiving more or less determinately, more or less singly? I may form a conception of this ruby, or of a ruby, or of precious stones in general. In what other way am I to express these three several acts to which the mind by another simultaneous act of reflection gives unity and fixation? The result thus substantiated, or understood, or having an understanding given to it, becomes the product of the former act: but a

[* The following appears as part of the text, but seems to be intended as a footnote. At the end of it, a new paragraph opens with the words "Predispositions of the mind". These and the change of paragraph are omitted.]

Only they must not be called "innate ideas", though the difference assumed in the present treatise and hereafter to be more fully explained and, I trust, established, between ideas and conceptions, and intuitions, is not at all a point in question in Mr Locke's essay. "Idea" in Locke's use of the word, comprehending both the two latter, that is, whatever is the immediate object of the mind, though in point of fact and history, the word "idea" was, if not invented, yet as a *philosophical* term, first introduced, for the very purpose of expressing the pre-existing principles of particular thoughts, inasmuch as the ordinary language wanted a word that might contradistinguish these antecedent principles from their consequent εἴδωλον, intuition, image, or *particular* thoughts. But, on the other hand, had he not quarrelled with the phrase "innate ideas", there would have been nothing for him to have quarrelled with either in Aristotle or Descartes, nothing whereon to raise the glory of having overthrown and routed the logical and psychological principles of Descartes, as his great contemporary Newton had subverted the physical and astronomical system of the same philosopher. But for this accident, I do not say that we should not have heard much both of Mr Locke and of Sir Isaac Newton, but we should not have heard so often of Locke and Newton.[1]

b Blank space left in ms

[1] Cf C's letter to Josiah Wedgwood of 24 Feb 1801: *CL* ii 686.

single conception, a particular and a general? Or, if I composed the
series of more links, I might give to the highest and most compre-
hensive the name of "universal". Now it is evident that as these
characteristic names do not refer to the things in themselves, but
wholly to my thoughts and to the way in which I arrange them, the
names themselves are variable in their application so far that, when
I say, an "universal conception", I mean only that the conception
includes all of that space or number which I have circumscribed or
secluded. E.g.: this ruby, a ruby, a precious stone, a stone. The latter
would here be an universal conception, but if I had chosen to think
yet more comprehensively and had added the conception "an oxide",
the term "universal" must have been transferred to this, the concep-
tion "stone" would have become generic, that of "a precious stone"
specific, that of "a ruby" particular, etc. If, then, we are entitled to
call a conceiving and its mental product, which neither is nor possibly
can be any more than an act self-known, a "conception", what can a
mode of conceiving mean more than a series of such conceptions?
Or what the faculty of conceiving in this particular mode other than
a generalised term, an *ens logicum*, expressing at once the sum total
of these acts, their particular character, and the mind as the agent?
All language originates in reflection, and it is only by means of this
reflection, by which we represent the mind as a whole consisting of
all its thoughts as its parts, that we can form any conception of mind
at all. And if it were true that the human mind was limited to the
impressions on the sensibility, to the forms of the sense, to the con-
ceptions generalised from both these as the objects of the under-
standing, and lastly to the acts of the reflection itself generalised and
reflected on, if this were indeed true, our conception of the mind
would stop there. The mind could be thought of by us only as a
watch, a house, or any other mechanical whole, as the resulting mass
of its constituent parts, and in fact more than this could neither be
directly demonstrated nor coercively concluded from premises that a
man can be made to admit as truths passively known and the
knowledge of which it is not in his power to deny mentally or other-
wise than in words. Such, for instance, are the fundamental principles
of geometry, and, supposing the integrity of the senses, such are the
facts of immediate experience. If I can but once place the object
before his eyes, I can compel the man to know that I have a hand and
five fingers and that I hold it up in such and such a direction. His
free will is not at all brought into act. Hence, in asserting the existence
of a whole antecedent to and constitutive of its parts, I not merely

assert a something which by no effort of sense or understanding I could have acquired, and of which no logic will enable me legitimately to conclude for the information of another, but, in using the terms supplied by the understanding, I incur, or at least border closely on, a contradiction; for I speak of a whole the constituent parts of which are in no moment all present or all existing. But if, sensible of this, I substitute the phrase of "productive unity" as that which gives existence, I venture on a thought which, while it necessarily escapes the notice of the sense, contradicts the first axioms of the understanding, which as imperiously demands the stuff for the form, as the form for the stuff, and in whose creation a chaos necessarily precedes the world. From such contradictions there is but one way of escaping, viz. by assuming, by WILLING to assume, that the truth passeth all understanding, and that a contradiction exists in the heterogeneity of the faculty, not in the object; or rather in the misapplication of the faculty to an object for which it was neither adapted nor intended. It is a Gordian knot which it is incomparably more to our interest to cut than untie, even if the latter were as easy as it is in fact impossible. Above all let it be remembered that to draw strict conclusions from lax and accommodated terms is an outrage on the first principles of ratiocination. But if not *strict*, then no logical conclusions at all. For logic has no degrees. That which is not *strictly* logical is not logical; and how can a thing be at once logical and illogical? And what can be more illogical than to use the same terms in one sense in the premise and in another in the deduction?

9   In that higher department of logic which we are now investigating, we have two objects in view: first, to learn what the understanding in connection with the forms of sense and the affections of the sensibility *can* do; and secondly, and of no less practical importance, what it can*not* do. The former we may call the sphere of the understanding; and this alone is the rightful sphere of logic. As *logicians*, therefore, and even in opposition to our *philosophic* creed, we may[a] take it as the *total* sphere of the human mind; and we are induced to treat it as such not only because by thus insulating the subject we may contemplate it more distinctly; but likewise and chiefly because we cannot compel an opponent to admit the contrary by arguments purely speculative or on premises which it is not in his power to deny if it should be his choice. As long as we remain within the circle of a theoretic science—if I may venture on a pleonasm for

a ms: make

the sake of additional clearness—we must confine ourselves to that which can be theoretically and scientifically proved, and in the present instance therefore to the understanding, sense, and sensibility. But though we are incompetent to give a scientific proof of any other and higher source of knowledge, it is equally true that no logic requires us to assert the negative, or enables us to disprove that a position which is neither theoretically undeniable nor capable of being logically *concluded* may nevertheless be morally *convincing* or even philosophically evident.

10   There is one thing, however, that logic does peremptorily prescribe—or rather it is a requisition of common sense, the giving effect to which is one main end of the study of logic—namely, that whatever term we use, and whether we assert or deny a reality correspondent thereto, we should use it in some fixed and appropriate sense and consequently that we should predefine it when there is any chance of its being understood in any other sense. For this reason, therefore, and without even starting the question respecting their existence, I hold myself bound to inform the reader what and what alone I mean by "ideas". Those truths, namely (supposing such to exist), the knowledge and acknowledgment of which require the whole man, the free will, no less than the intellect, and which are therefore not merely speculative, nor yet merely practical, but both in one, I propose to call "ideas" simply because, of all the other meanings that have been attached to the word, I do not know one which has not already a word of its own more expressive, more appropriate, and far less liable to be mistaken. And it may perhaps be thought an additional recommendation to this proposal that its general adoption would do away with the half-meanings which seem to have rendered the word "idea" an especial favourite [with many] out of whose vocabulary it might be dropped without their sustaining the least damage or inconvenience.[1][*]

---

[*] *Vide* "Appendix" to *The Statesman's Manual*, page xxxvii:[2] "The term 'idea', is an instance in point; and I hazard this assertion, together with the preceding sentences, in the full consciousness that they must be unintelligible to those who have yet to learn that an 'idea' is equidistant [...] from sensation, image, fact, and notion: that it is the antithesis, not the synonym, of εἴδωλον. The magnificent son of Cosmo was wont to discourse with Ficino, Politian, and the princely Mirandula on the 'ideas' of will, God, and immortality. [...] But these lights shine no longer, or for a few. *Exeunt*: and enter in their stead,

[1] Cf *C d r V* 369–70 (310) and 376 (314).

[2] *SM* (*CC*) 100–3 (var and with an omission).

11   It will be expedient, however, to observe that the ideas are not distinguished from the notions of the senses, the intuitions of the sense, and the conceptions and notions of the understanding by their being referred to another and higher source; for this ideas have in common with all the TRUTHS of REASON. Now though ideas must needs be truths of reason, truths of reason are not all necessarily ideas. There are such that have their source in the speculative (or theoretical) reason alone, and these I have termed principles— principles of reason inseparably connected with the human understanding as a foundation is with its edifice, but yet like the foundation presupposed, and therefore not included in the latter; for what is assumed as the precondition of the understanding must in the order of thought be taken as antecedent to the same, even though there were not another and more obvious ground for referring these principles to the reason, that they are absolutely universal and unconditionally applicable, that is, equally valid, whether we apply them to matter or spirit, to beast, man, angel, or Deity. I will add the following remark, not so much for its intrinsic value, though even in this respect it may not be found useless, as that it leads us back at

---

Holofernes and Costard![1] masked as metaphysics and common sense. And these too have *their* ideas! The former has an *idea*, that Hume, Hartley, and Condillac have exploded all *ideas*, but those of sensation; he has an idea that he was particularly pleased with the fine *idea* of the last-named philosopher, that there is no absurdity in asking, 'What colour virtue is of?'[2] Inasmuch as the proper philosophic answer would be black, blue, or bottle-green, according as the coat, waistcoat, and small-clothes might chance to be of the person, the series of whose motions had excited the sensations, which formed our *idea* of virtue. The latter has no idea of a better-flavoured haunch of venison than he dined off at the Albion.[3] He admits that the French have an excellent *idea* of cooking in general, but holds that their best cooks have no more *idea* of dressing a turtle than the gourmands themselves, at Paris, have any *real idea* of the true *taste* and *colour* of the fat!"

[1] For whom see *Love's Labour's Lost.*

[2] C refers to a passage in Condillac's *La logique* . . . pt I ch 6—see *Oeuvres complètes* XXII (1798) 55–6. C is not quite fair to Condillac, who was countering the objection that moral ideas seem to be independent of the senses. Some philosophers, he says, would ask "de quelle couleur est la vertu, de quelle couleur est la vice" ("what is the character of virtue, what is the character of vice"). His answer is: "la vertu consiste dans l'habitude des bonnes actions, comme le vice consiste dans l'habitude des mauvaises. Or ces habitudes et ces actions sont visibles" ("virtue consists in the habit of doing good deeds, as vice consists in the habit of doing bad ones. But these habits and deeds are visible"). Cf *C d r V* 376–7 (314) and *P Lects* Lect 12 (1949) 363.

[3] Probably the Albion Tavern, Aldersgate-Street, which became famous for its cuisine under John Kay. See Kent's *Original London Directory: 1827* (1827) 202.

once to our proper subject. If these, as a portion of that light which is to the understanding what the material light is to the eye, and so far therefore extrinsic, be termed principles of reason, there would seem to be no impropriety if the forms belonging to the understanding, on which the exercise of its functions is grounded, were called analogously the principles of the understanding, and in like manner if the universal forms of the intuitive faculty were entitled the principles of sense, and, should this be thought a more natural or more readily intelligible expression than that of "pure conceptions" and "pure intuitions", there can be no objection to the change capable of outweighing its convenience—provided only that the point be considered as a question of taste and expediency and by no means a correction required by the nature of the things meant—provided that it does not lead us unaware into the error of supposing a conception to be a something in nature different from conceiving, or conceiving a something different from the mind that so conceives. And now then we return to the scientific and didactic, our subject being henceforward, directly and exclusively, of the human understanding and its constitution, that is, the elements of transcendental logic, in the strict and most proper sense of the term, and as a positive science.

CHAPTER [XIII]

Of Transcendental Logic Positively

1   The understanding is the substantiative power, that by which we give and attribute substance and reality to phenomena and raise them from mere affections and appearances into objects communicable and capable of being anticipated and reasoned of. The way in which the understanding effects this is by judging according to certain principles and forms inherent in its own constitution.

2   The understanding therefore may be defined as the faculty of judging;[1] for it understands only as far as it judges that to such and such appearances there belongs a ground, an hypostasis, or supporting reality.

3   The proper and immediate substance, or hypostasis, is the understanding itself—the three words being indeed the literal rendering each of the other, or the Greek, Latin, and English sounds of the same mental word. We may, therefore, distinguish *power* from *faculty* in the present instance so far as to say that the understanding is the substantiative power. The substantiative power is its essence; or rather the latter is the meaning of the former. But this power again may be considered in relation to its proper characteristic end and object; and in this point of view we may say that the understanding or substantiative power of the mind is likewise, or exercises itself as, the faculty of judging, and namely of judging concerning the substantiality of phenomena in that further sense in which substantiality is the same with objectivity, or correspondency to a real object. Therefore we said that the understanding hath a twofold character. It gives and it attributes substance. The first is its essential act, without which it could not act at all; there would be nothing for it to act on. We mean the same power when we speak of the unity of consciousness. It follows, therefore, that all objects of the understanding must be likewise and previously *entia logica*, or logical entities, having their substance in the understanding itself; but it does not follow that all

---

[1] Cf *C d r V* 94 (106).

logical entities are *entia realia*, that is, having a correspondence to realities out of the mind.

4   It has been shown in a preceding chapter[1] that this substantiation consists in the power and necessity of reflecting under the forms of quantity, quality, relation, and (in especial relation to the reflective acts themselves and rather as a syllepsis of the three former) mode or, to speak scholastically, modality. What the understanding cannot conceive responsively to the *quantum*, the *quale*, in what case or relation and in what mode the understanding itself is placed, it cannot conceive at all. Consequently the understanding cannot judge of its own different judgings in any other way or by any other rule. We are now speaking of the mind, not in respect to the *quid est*, or what it is, but to the *quo fungitur*, or what offices does it discharge, in other words, not with regard to its constitutive but its functional powers. And if in this sense it be rightly defined the faculty of judging, our first question must be, "In what way are these judgings characterised?" Are they capable of being distinguished, classed, and specified? And in order to this, it has been shown under the necessity of substantiating the acts of judging into logical entities and to contemplate the act as a product, the judging as a judgment.

5(a)   Dry as this subject is, and as the writer himself feels it to be, it is yet of such extensive application that the student will be well repaid for the trouble of impressing it on his memory, for it lies at the bottom of universal grammar as well as of logic. In order to reflect on any series or collection of similar acts, we convert the verb or participle into a noun;[a] thus, to determine the character of a given continuous act of moving, we represent it under the abstract term "velocity". And even so, any given act of judging must be represented as a particular judgment. And when we affirm anything universally, without exception or confining what we affirm to any part or particular number, the so judging is on the same principles called an universal judgment.

5(b)   What we would examine steadily we must first fix—even though, as in the instance of the firefly fixed in the microscope and examined by daylight, we too often destroy the essential quality that had excited the desire of examining it at all.[2] But this makes the

---

a Ms unpunctuated

[1] There is no such previous discussion; C seems to be referring to the material that appears later, on pp 254ff, especially the table on p 256. Cf *C d r V* 95 (106-7).

[2] Cf WW's "we murder to dissect", in *The Tables Turned* line 28: *WPW* IV 57.

difference between logic and philosophy, and the knowledge of the difference is, as we have before had occasion to remark, not the least among the uses of transcendental logic. The student therefore will soon overcome the strangeness of finding the character of objects relatively to the human understanding predicated of the judgments themselves and severally assigned to them as their characteristic names. He will see that this is no figure of speech, no arbitrary pedantry of Scholastic logic, but that from the constitution of the human mind it cannot be otherwise. When a verb has been changed into a noun, it must observe the proprieties and cases of a noun. To continue the metaphor, we must decline the *entia logica* in the present case, the judgments concerning objects, by the same accidents or predicaments as the *entia realia*, or the objects themselves concerning which we judge. And there will be this further advantage, that the process will serve as a test or proof of our former position; for if it have been truly asserted by us that quantity, quality, relation, and modality are the sum of the constituent forms or most general and innate conceptions of the understanding, we shall be able to class all the possible judgments according to one or the other of these. No sort of judgment or way of judging will be adducible which will not have been found characterised under one or other of these four predicaments as being one or other of the three species comprised under each.

6   N.B. The singular circumstance of this threefold division or trichotomy obtaining throughout the analysis of the mind, and which the founder of the critical philosophy contents himself with noticing as being singular and worthy of notice, and which he supposes himself to have noticed first,[1] may be found in a much earlier writer, our own celebrated Richard Baxter.[*] Any attempt to explain

[*] It is no more than common justice to this acute and if too often prejudiced yet always sincere, pious, and single-hearted divine, to say that he saw far more deeply into the grounds, nature, and necessity of this division as a *norma philosophiae*[2] and the evils and inconveniences of the ordinary dichotomy when carried from its proper province, that of common logic, into philosophy and divinity than Kant did more than [a] century after. The sacred fire, however, remained hid under the bushel of our good countryman's ample folios.[3]

[1] Kant does not claim to have noticed it first. For his mentions of trichotomy see *C d r V* 110 (116) and *Critik der Urtheilskraft* Einleitung § ix n.

[2] "A norm of philosophy".

[3] C has been taken to task for this statement (see e.g. *Kant in England* 86), but he was probably more anxious to introduce an obscure but deserving Englishman to his fellow countrymen than to diminish Kant's glory. A marginal note on *Reliquiae Baxterianae* bk I pt 3 (1696) ii 69 (C's copy at

it would be out of its place in the present disquisition. It is a primary datum of the understanding, the *way in which* we reflect, proved to us by the pure *products* of reflection, as the existence of the *forma formans* must in every case be manifested by and in the *forma formata*, but [is] not to be explained by them.[1] Its purpose is to *account for* the results of reflection, and it would be preposterous to expect that these should account for it. Briefly, in common logic the fact has no interest: in transcendental logic it is a necessary element, but its explanation belongs to neither, as transcending the faculty of which the one gives the results and the other the analysis.

7   Here the student may expediently halt for a moment and, before he proceeds to the analysis of the understanding in the detail of its constituent members, collect and bring to his distinct consciousness a few positions from preceding chapters that may assist in warding off any confusion or misconception of the terms adopted in that which is to follow.

[Memento 1]

8   First, words, that in their proper and primary sense express relations of space, are likewise used sometimes *for* and sometimes inclusive of the relations of time. The language of *sight* is transferred to the affections and objects of the other senses, and of the inward experience. (See Aesthetic[a] Chapter   *ad finem.*)[2] In disciplining his mind one of the first rules should be to lose no opportunity of tracing words to their origin, one good consequence of which will be that he will be able to use the *language* of sight without being enslaved by its affections. He will at least secure himself from the delusive notion that what is not *imageable* is likewise not *conceivable*. To emancipate the mind from the despotism of the eye is the first step towards its emancipation from the influences and intrusions of the senses,

---

[a] ms: A S T H O P E [seemingly a mistranscription of "Æsthetic"]

Harvard) explains the nature of C's enthusiasm: ". . . Baxter *grounded* it [trichotomy] on an absolute Idea *pre-*supposed in all intelligential acts: whereas Kant takes it only as a *Fact* of Reflection—as a singular & curious Fact, in which he seems to anticipate or suspect some yet deeper Truth latent & hereafter to be discovered". He adds,

"On recollection I am disposed to consider *this* ⟨alone⟩ as Baxter's *peculiar* claim." (Published in *C 17th C* 119.)

[1] Cf above p 232 nn 2, 3.

[2] The reference has been left incomplete, but it could well be to the material that begins on p 71 line 4.

sensations, and passions generally. Thus most effectually is the power of abstraction to be called forth, strengthened, and familiarised, and it is this power [of] abstraction that chiefly distinguishes the human understanding from that of the higher animals, and in the different degrees in which this power is developed the superiority of man over man mainly consists. Hence we are to account for the preference which the divine Plato gives to expressions taken from the objects of the ear, as terms of music and harmony, and in part at least for the numerical symbols in which Pythagoras clothed his philosophy.[1]

9 On this principle I do not object to the extension of the term "image" (or "idea" in Hume's usage) from the *re*-presentations of the sight to the analogous relicts of the other senses—and if other reasons had not induced me to reject the *Humian* terminology of "impressions" and "ideas", the same concession would have been made to the phrase "auditual and tactual *ideas*"—a phrase, the use of which by one of our greatest living philosophers, then in the early morning of his manhood, and his fame only beginning to dawn did, as I well remember, give occasion of surprise and scandal to a veteran metaphysician in my presence.[2]

10(a) I will conclude this first Memento by the following extract from the Latin dissertation delivered by Immanuel Kant, 20th August, 1770, on taking his degree as professor ordinarius of logic and metaphysic, the (afterwards justly celebrated) physician and physiologist Marcus Hertz,[3] the friend and townsman of Moses Mendelssohn, being the respondent; and I cannot too earnestly recommend the student by careful and repeated perusal to impress the contents both on his memory and his understanding.[4]

---

[1] Cf BM MS Egerton 2801 f 121 for C's sympathetic view of Pythagoras' "numerical symbols". Cf *CN* III 4436: "The more I reflect, the more important do both the Pythagorean or arithmetical, and the Platonic or harmonical Schemes of Nature present themselves to my mind."

[2] Story untraced. Could the philosopher have been Davy and the metaphysician Beddoes? C himself used the phrase "visible & tangible Ideas" in a letter to Josiah Wedgwood in Feb 1801: *CL* II 699.

[3] Marcus Herz (1747–1803), Kant's friend and correspondent. Author of *Betrachtungen aus der spekulativen Weltweisheit* (Königsberg 1771) and other works.

[4] *De mundi sensibilis* § 1: *VS* II 439–40. "Hence it is clear, from what cause many reject the notion of the continuous and the infinite. They take, namely, the words irrepresentable and impossible in one and the same meaning; and, according to the forms of sensuous evidence, the notion of the continuous and the infinite is doubtless impossible. I am not now pleading the cause of these laws, which not a few schools have thought proper to explode, especially the former (the law of continuity). But it is of the highest importance to admonish the

10(b) "Hinc patet, qui fiat, ut *cum* irrepraesentabile et *impossibile* vulgo ejusdem significatus habeantur, conceptus tam *Continui*, quam *Infiniti*, a plurimis rejiciantur, quippe quorum, *secundum leges cognitionis intuitivae*, repraesentatio est impossibilis. Quanquam autem harum e non paucis scholis explosarum notionum, praesertim prioris, caussam hic non gero, maximi tamen momenti erit monuisse: gravissimo illos errore labi, qui tam perversa argumentandi ratione utuntur. Quicquid enim *repugnat* legibus intellectus et rationis[, utique est impossibile; quod autem, cum rationis]¹ purae sit objectum, legibus cognitionis intuitivae tantummodo non subest, non item. Nam hic dissensus inter facultatem *sensitivam* et *intellectualem* [. . .] nihil indigitat, nisi, *quas mens ab intellectu acceptas fert ideas abstractas, illas in concreto exsequi et in Intuitus commutare saepenumero non posse.* Haec autem reluctantia *subjectiva* mentitur, ut plurimum, repugnantiam aliquam objectivam, et incautos facile fallit, limitibus, quibus mens humana circumscribitur, pro iis habitis, quibus ipsa rerum essentia continetur."

Memento II

11 "Image" involves the existence of a correspondent. Hence, though I should not object to the word in the same extension in which Mr Hume and his followers use "ideas", as opposed to (or at least distinguished from) "impressions", I would not ordinarily employ it to express the *pure* constructions of the intuitive faculty, that is, the immediate products of its productive acts. I would say,

reader, that those, who adopt so perverted a mode of reasoning, are under a grievous error. Whatever opposes the formal principles of the understanding and the reason is confessedly impossible; but not therefore that, which is therefore not amenable to the forms of *sensuous* evidence, because it is exclusively an object of pure intellect. For this non-coincidence of the sensuous and the intellectual (the nature of which I shall presently lay open) proves nothing more, but that the mind cannot always adequately represent in the concrete, and transform into distinct images, abstract notions derived from the pure intellect. But this contradiction, which is in itself merely subjective (i.e. an incapacity in the nature of man), too often passes for an incongruity or impossibility in the object (i.e. the notions themselves), and seduces the incautious to mistake the limitations of the human faculties for the limits of things, as they really exist." C's tr in *BL* ch 12 (1907) I 190n, where he quotes the same passage. In Apr 1818 he recommended the essay to a Mr Pryce (*CL* IV 851). Part of the same passage is quoted in BM MS Egerton 2801 f 159.

¹ The missing passage is probably an example of the transcriber's eye slipping from "rationis" to "rationis". The underlining follows *BL* closely.

the image *of* a thing, but not (except for illustration, *et* PER REGULAM *falsi*[1] as it were) the image *as* the thing. If there be felt an uncouthness, which the student finds it difficult to overcome, in the use of the plural term, "intuitions", for the mathematical concretes (e.g. the figures of pure geometry) I should prefer "theoremes" (θεώρημα, *contemplamen*), and in this sense the word actually occurs in one of the noblest passages of Plotinus,[2] or "forms", or even "sensuous ideas", to "images".

Memento III

12   We commenced by adopting the old division of knowledge into the theoretic, or intellective, and the practical, or that which respects the acts of the will, the judgments of conscience, the rules of conduct, and the laws of the practical reason; and it was settled that, as far as the present enquiry was concerned, our attention was to be given exclusively to the former, that is, the theoretic.

13   It was next determined that we should confine our inquisition to the data[a] presented to us by *reflection*, and as[b] they appear to us in the act of reflecting; or to the immediate inferences from these made necessary by the laws of reflection. What these[c] laws are is a subject for future enquiry, but be they what they may, it is easy to imagine some superior being capable of contemplating at once an individual mind and its objects, of judging how far and in what manner the objects are modified for the human mind by[d] its own mechanism, and lastly of looking at the objects independent of such modification. Now he who disclaims all pretensions to any prerogative of this kind, or who, though believing that a *substitute* or [e]a something *analogous*[f] to it subsists even for the human intelligence, nevertheless *abstracts* (that is, voluntarily withdraws his attention) from it and agrees to reason as though no such power existed, is said to stand on *the point of reflection*. And here we agreed to take our position, that is, to take things as they appeared from the point of reflection, and to assume nothing that by sense and reflection alone we could not have discovered to exist. And as every disjunctive[g] position is more readily recollected and acquires the semblance at least of additional clearness when a distinct name is assigned to that from which it is dis-

---

| *a* ms: date | *b* ms: as | *c* ms: those | *d* ms: in |

e–f ms: something analogous   *g* ms: distinctive

1 "And by way of controlling error".   2 *Ennead* 3.8.4. Cf above, p 74 and n 1.

joined, we contradistinguish the point on which we do *not* stand from the point on which we do stand by designating the former as the "ideal point" and the latter as[a] the "point of reflection".

Memento IV

14   Our next step was that of abstracting from all objects existing out of the mind—and these *collectively* we entitled the "objective"; and this is the primary sense of the word as *technically* used. What remained, and to which alone our attention was to be given, we consented to call the "subject", or the "subjective" collectively.

Memento V

15(a)   Yet not all that might be comprised under this head did we propose to comprehend in our specific enquiry. In the subject itself we abstracted from the *affections* of the sensibility, and the passive impressions on the senses, and agreed to regard the sensibility (in this *restricted* sense and the self-active power of sentiency *not* included) as the common boundary, or neutral ground, of the objective and subjective. What remained after this last abstraction we found to be the powers of perceiving and conceiving, the faculty of contemplating *in concreto*, and that of *thinking* generally or *in abstracto*. I contemplate the essential properties of the triangle; I think of the Divine Attribute. The first we named THE SENSE or "intuitive" power, the second THE UNDERSTANDING or "reflective" faculty. The knowledges possessed by the understanding, whether derived from the sense (that is, grounded on "intuitions") or acquired by reflection on its own acts and processes, these and these only are the admissible data of our intended disquisition and form the subject matter of logic.

15(b)   But we were made aware that among the data of reflection there were a few the peculiar character of which suggested, even if it did [not] necessitate, the assumption of a higher origin than either of the two faculties, taken with the abstractions above noticed; and that in point of fact the understanding in all its acts does *pre*sume them, as the indispensable conditions of its own existence as well as of its exercise of each particular function. These, therefore, as having

---

[a] Word inserted in accordance with a ms of Mementos III, IV, and part of V in C's hand, in the Beinecke Rare Book and Manuscript Library, Yale University, for which see frontispiece. The corrections recorded in notes *b–g* on p 245 are also made on the authority of this ms

the distinctive character of absolute universality and unconditional necessity (that is, not merely necessary in relation to the human sense and understanding), we named "principles" and (yet without *deserting the point of reflection*) "principles *of reason*". For they are *data* of the understanding, made known to us in and by reflection, though there may be ground for considering [them] as the offspring of a higher source, which for distinction's sake we named "the reason". Of these principles we found no more than two, entitled the "principles of identity and incompatibility"; and in thus admitting them as principles of reason, we were made distinctly [to] understand that as *logicians* and from the point on which, as such, we had placed ourselves, we meant no more by "reason itself" than the source of absolute principles, as inferred from the fact of their existence.

16   P.S. The knowledge thus obtained by the understanding we entitled "discursive", in distinction from the "intuitive" knowledge given by the sense; the understanding itself being named by elder logicians the "discursive" faculty, and, as far as its processes are grounded on the principles above mentioned, by our great dramatic poet "discourse of reason".[1]

Memento VI

17   Having thus separated the sense from the sensibility, and the subjective,[a] now comprising the sense and the understanding, from the objective, and further the sense, as the source of *intuitive* knowledge, from the understanding, as the source of *discursive* knowledge, we took the latter as the especial subject of the science we had chosen for our present study. The temple of Truth has two main portals, the first and more magnificent being the science of intuition, or MATHEMATICS, the other and narrower but not less necessary, the science of discourse and the discursive faculty, or LOGIC.

Memento VII

18(a)   The very title of our science leads us naturally to the two parts into which it is subdivided: viz. first, the necessary *forms* and connections of all legitimate discourse and the *rules* generalised from

[a] ms: subject we

[1] Shakespeare *Hamlet* I ii 150. Cf *SM (CC)* 69.

the same, resulting indeed from the constitution of the discursive faculty itself, but evident of themselves and therefore capable of being given independently of the knowledge of the latter; and secondly, the analysis of the understanding in order to a knowledge of its constitution. Which, however, could not have been effected or made intelligible without a previous analysis of the sense: both conjunctively taken forming the science of *transcendental* analysis, so called from the character of its aim and object, which is to rise from the *knowledge* or *matter* of consciousness to the *faculty* by which it is known or presented.

18(b)　The former of these two main divisions we passed through under the name of the "common" or "syllogistic logic", or the "logical canon"; and of the latter, first introduced as the pure "logical criterion", and then more definitely named the "science of transcendental analysis" comprised under two heads, "transcendental aesthetic", or the analysis of the pure sense, or *faculty* of intuition, and "transcendental logic", or the analysis of the understanding, or discursive faculty. We have completed the first head (namely the aesthetic) and prepared for the accomplishment of the remainder by a large declaration of the historical origin and true nature of the question, an exact exposition of the terms to be employed in its solution, and by such other notices and reminiscences as seemed calculated to facilitate our progress either directly and, as it were, *propulsively*, or indirectly, by the removal of possible obstacles, misconceptions—for instance, the errors of prejudice and the mistakes of inadvertence.

18(c)　There remains then but one additional Memento, if it may be so named; it being in part only retrospective and in part preliminary—but equally with the seven preceding belonging to the purpose of this review of our past labours, as being preparative for the work immediately before us.

Memento VIII

19　Hitherto the understanding (see Memento v) has been only negatively defined by its distinction from the sense. It is a faculty of knowledge that is not sensuous. (N.B. As we took the sense abstractedly from the sensibility, so in order to distinguish the adjective corresponding to the two terms we adopted the unusual but highly sanctioned word "sensuous" for the former and appropriated to the latter the more common word, namely, "sensual", though without any mixture of the moral meaning ordinarily connected with it.[1] We should use the word, if we used it at all, as expressive of the *kind* and not of any *excess* or *blamable degree*, though even in *kind* we have generally included it in the wider term of "empirical", having at the commencement—*vide* Memento v—abstracted from the sensibility, and put the sensual relatively to our science on the same ground with the outward objective.)

20   The understanding is an unsensuous faculty of knowing, or whereby knowledge is acquirable. Now independently of the sense we can have no intuition or intuitive knowledge. Consequently the understanding is not a faculty of intuition; its knowledge is not intuitive, not sensuously presentable or constructed *in concreto*. In plain English, we do not perceive by means of the understanding. But besides perceptions (that is, intuitions pure or mixed) there exists no other way of knowing, or sort of knowledge, but by means of conceptions. Therefore the knowledge of every understanding that is the same with the human is a knowledge by means of conceptions, not *intuitive* but *discursive*[2] (*vide* Memento VI). "In varios docto discurritur ordine gyros". (Claudian.)[3] Our perceptions as far as they are sensual are grounded on the affections of the sensibility; as far as they are the pure and immediate products of the intuitive faculty, in which sense we, for distinction's sake, have most commonly called them "intuitions",[a] they are grounded on the productivity or productive acts of the sense. It will be expedient therefore to carry on the same purpose of distinct terminology by grounding the conceptions on the functions of the understanding. This latter term is a word in common usage, and we must all, therefore, have some conception of what is meant by it, more or less precise, more or less in our power to communicate. This, however, will not suffice for the exact analyst. He must ascertain the full, distinct, and proper meaning of the word, and then determine whether it apply in the instance before him and this, too, adequately, so far at least as to justify its selection as the best and most applicable word.

21(a)   We have already had occasion to distinguish the unity of

a Full stop in ms

[1] Cf the distinction made in *BL* ch 10 (1907) I 109.

[2] Paragraph 20 up to this point is from *C d r V* 92–3 (105).

[3] Claudian *Panegyricus de sexto consulatu Honorii Augusti* line 633.

Tr Maurice Platnauer (LCL 1922) II 121: "wheeling and counter-wheeling with ordered skill". More literally: "there is a running about in various circles in disciplined ranks"—C linking "discursive" with *discurritur*.

totality, the oneness which we connect with the conception of a whole—of a watch, for instance—and which we may denominate the consequent or resulting unity, from the productive or producible unity—that of the proper germ, or *heart,* or plantule of a seed, apart from its lobes, eye, and coat, as the ground and productive principle of the future whole, and which we may call the "antecedent" unity. (Not forgetting, however, that the antecedence here spoken of is a priority in order of thought, and [not] necessarily a priority in time, and that as a memento of this we have recommended the occasional substitution of the phrase, *ab intra* or *ab intimo*[1] for that of *a priori*.)

21(b) This twofold unity is comprised in the definition of the term "constitution". *Constitutio fit ubicunque unum e pluribus* (= *unitas* CONSEQUENS) *et plura in uno sunt* (= *unitas antecedens*).[2] And the relation of the latter to the former [is described] in the somewhat unpoetic line of a philosophic poem accidentally lying open before me,

—the constitutive one
Present to all that doth make all one whole.[3]

We have only to add that, as the result or consequent is necessarily a harmony of differences, the antecedent must be a unity of differential powers; for though an effect is not always an adequate or exhaustive measure of the cause, yet whatever exists in the result as an effect or product must have been contained in the antecedent as an attribute or productive power. And this is what the Scholastic logicians meant by "existing eminently", *Quicquid existit in consequenti realiter, vel manifeste, existit in suo antecedente eminenter.*[4] Nor does a plurality of interdistinguishable attributes in the antecedent interfere with the conception of its unity. Far rather it is requisite to its being conceived; for without distinction conception cannot exist, and in this consists the important difference of positive unity or oneness from indistinguishable unicity[*] or negative sameness.

[*] New things justify new terms. *Novis in rebus licet nova nobis verba confingere.* We never speak of the *unity* of attraction, or of the unity of repulsion, but of the unity of attraction and repulsion in each one corpuscle as the twin attributes of its οὐσία or constitutive essence. The essential diversity of the ideas "unity" and "sameness" was among the elementary principles of the old logicians; and

[1] "From the innermost part".

[2] "A constitution arises whenever one [is formed] from many (= *consequent* unity) and whenever many are in one (= antecedent unity)."

[3] *Religious Musings* lines 130–1 (var): *PW* (EHC) I 114. Comparison

with the original is instructive: "But 'tis God/ Diffused through all, that doth make all one whole . . .".

[4] "Whatever exists in the consequent, really or apparently, exists eminently in its antecedent."

22(a)   Having thus removed, we trust, all ambiguity from the two extreme terms, we shall pursue the attempt with the word in question as an intermediate between both and then illustrate the whole by an example, premising only, what must indeed be evident on the first serious reflection, that every such attribute, considered as a differential force, must of necessity be contemplated as an unity. Else it would not be the attribute of an antecedent one but a factor or component part of a consequent whole. Hence as it is a distinct unity manifesting a *difference*, so must it be a reduction of differences to a distinct and several unity, or, to use the technical and more precise term already explained, it is that by which any number of *differents* are at once *differenced* and subsumed under a several unity. Now this is a FUNCTION.[3] And the function of a power is the unity of any given class or series of its actions by which a difference is manifested and communicated. And observe that this unity, though we could not have conceived it but by the aid of abstraction, is, however, not to be conceived as being itself a mere generalisation or expression of coexistence; for this would be in effect to fall into the delusion exposed ([?σοφισμα]) and convert actions into things separate from the agent or supposed to constitute the agent as the result of their composition.

22(b)   On the other hand, however, a different error lies in our way against which it is no less important that we should be on our guard—an error sufficiently glaring, indeed, when it has been once detected and presented in its nakedness, but which under various disguises and by means of indistinct and fluctuating conceptions has imposed on doctors of no small celebrity and lies at the bottom of more than one theory, physiological and medical as well as psychological and metaphysical. I allude to the confusion between distinct inherence and dividuous or separate subsistency and to the consequent treatment of the attributes and faculties of a mind as if they

---

the sophisms grounded on the confusion of these terms have been ably exposed by Leibniz in his critique on Wissowatius.[1] This note and the sentence in the text to which it refers are transcribed from the author's (second) Lay Sermon, page 55.[2]

[1] "Defensio Trinitatis per nova reperta logica . . ." in *Opera omnia* ed L. Dutens (6 vols Geneva 1768) I 10–16. Cf *AR* (1825) 202n. C recommends the work in *CL* IV 851 and cites Lessing's article "Des Andreas Wissowatius Einwurfe wider die Dreieinig-

keit" (*Sämmtliche Schriften* VII 65–102). Wiszowaty (1608–78) was a Polish Socinian.

[2] *LS* (*CC*) 176, 176–7n.

[3] Cf Kant's definition: *C d r V* 93 (105).

were so many several minds in miniature. In like manner with respect to the understanding itself and its co-ordinate faculty of sense, metaphysical writers have too often expressed themselves as if they were speaking of so many different *persons*, the *homunculi*[a] as it were, of which the integral man was composed, and thus seem to renew the whimsy of the old homoeomerists, according to whom the heart was an architectural structure of little hearts.[1] But still more obviously does this confusion remind us of the craniological theory, at all events of a very frequent misconception of the same, in which the various convolutes of the brain not only act the part of so many several brains, but of so many several and altogether different souls actuating and as it were playing upon them—the total brain representing the orchestra in which some thirty and odd musicians are seated each in his own stall and at his own several instrument.[2]

23   There are many things not necessary and yet not superfluous, and in this list we may place the repetition of the same caution in proportion to the frequency with which the error guarded against is likely to occur. On this account we are not unwilling to be again reminded that, as men or as philosophers, we do not speak even of the understanding itself; no, nor even of the mind including both sense and understanding, as of the man or personal being; but as an attribute of each individual person common to him and to all other men, as far as they are *men*, that is, possess the characteristics of *human* nature. Only as our particular science had for its exclusive object the mind abstractedly (*vide* above, pp 110–11[b] and we are therefore understood to speak as *logicians* merely, for *us*, I say, and as long as we are understood to be using a *technical* language, the *mind* is the vicegerent and representative of the man or of the soul. And we personify the mind without incurring or occasioning delusion. Thus in the administration of justice, the ultimate power and *real substantive* is supposed to be the king, and the court is the representative of the royal person; yet we speak of the court itself as of a person and assign to it all the forms, acts, and attributes of personality. And observe, this is no mere generalisation (or, as the grammarians say, a

[a] ms: Themunculi

[b] ms: (*vide*   123) [The reference is to ms II 125, previously numbered 123 in pencil]

[1] Stanley e.g. discusses Anaxagoras and his "homoiomora" p 63. See also Tennemann I 308–11.

[2] Public interest in craniological theories was revived by George Combe (1788–1858) in his *Elements of Phrenology* (1824). The 2nd ed was attacked by Francis Jeffrey in *Ed Rev* Sept 1825 and the controversy was joined by Sir William Hamilton in addresses to the Royal Society of Edinburgh in 1826 and 1827.

noun of multitude); the court is a real personal power, and that power a real unity. And we have only to contemplate a court exercising at different times several different sorts and forms of judicial law, and we shall have the example or illustration that our subject requires. We have seen that it is a true personal power and likewise a true unity; but not a true personal or individual unity. What then is this unity? We reply that it is the unity of the action by which the representative of a more comprehensive or manifold power exercises a given portion of that power, or that power in a given direction and determination, and in this unity of action corresponds to the personal unity from which its personal power is derived and of which it is consequently the representative. Now this is a "function", and the algebraic use of the term is substantially the same with that here given. First a variable undeterminate quantity is assumed = X. With these, other quantities having determinate and invariable values are joined, and the expressions that result from such conjunction are called "functions" of X. Now a function comprehending several functions whether in *co*-ordination or *sub*ordination may be distinguished from the ultimate power and personal unity whose function it is by the name of "functionary", and this may be allowably done whether the manifold function be placed in a single individual, as in the instance of the Lord Chancellor, or in many persons, as the House of Lords or the Board of Admiralty, or lastly, by the law of reflection which we have elsewhere called "substantiation", in a personal power or faculty. Thus if it were my intention to carry the analysis no farther I should say that the sense and the understanding were functions of the soul; but, if I meant to enter into the analysis of the understanding into its component powers, then, to avoid confusion and in obedience to the old adage, "qui bene distinguit, bene docet",[1] I might find it expedient to designate the component powers alone as functions and to impersonate the understanding itself as the functionary. It is a matter of indifference as long as we are aware that it is a matter of words, decided wholly and exclusively by considerations of convenience. But above all as long as we see and understand that the *function* is *the unity of the action*, whether we are thinking of the functions of the Lord Chancellor or of the Court of Chancery, in both alike we abstract from personal individuality. But though the function be the unity of the action only, yet it is an antecedent and not a resulting unity (*unitas collec-*

---

[1] Source untraced. C uses it in *CN* III 4058 and 4418. "He who distinguishes well teaches well". Said to be a Scholastic maxim.

tiva), an active and communicating, not [a] passive or received. Therefore it was said that though we arrived at the thought by aid of abstraction it was still something more than a mere abstract, and, if we may call in the aid of analogy and of the sense, in the attempt to master and fix this conception, only substituting the spontaneous for the mechanical, we might refer to the movements which without much impropriety we might consider as the functions of Brewster's kaleidoscope, or Mr Asa Spencer's geometrical lathe,*ᵃ* by which an endless variety of beautiful patterns is successively produced, transferred, and retransferred.[1] For here too [there is] a unity of the act, and this real, antecedent, and operative.

24(a) We may now, with increased confidence in the intelligibility of our words, repeat that images are grounded on affections of the sensibility; pure intuitions on the productive self-representing energies of the sense; and the conceptions on the functions of the understanding. Again, the acts of the will and of the reason, when we speak of the reason not as a presence only but as an agency (though perhaps it would be better to say the acts of the man), are characterised as voluntary, the functions of the understanding as spontaneous. Our conceptions therefore originate in the spontaneity of the thinking or conceiving faculty, and now what use does or can the understanding make of these its conceptions? A moment's reflection convinces us that it neither does nor can make any other use of them but that of judging thereby. And as no representation refers otherwise than mediately to the object and immediately to the intuition or affection, it follows *a fortiori* that a conception never refers immediately to an object but to some other representation of the same which may be either image or perhaps some previous conception. This, then, being understood, we can be at no loss in defining a judgment of the understanding. A judgment is the *mediate* knowledge of a thing and consequently the representation of a representation of that thing.

24(b) In every judgment there is a conception that is common to, that is, equally predicable of, a number of things, and*ᵇ* this number

---

ᵃ ms: laugh [an error in dictation? Did C pronounce "lathe" with a short *a*?]
ᵇ ms: and in

[1] For Brewster's kaleidoscope, see above, p 163 and n 1. The geometric lathe was an automatic engraving machine, one of a number of devices designed to put a stop to the counterfeiting of banknotes. The lathe and its development are described by its inventor in "Vindication of Claims to Certain Inventions and Improvements in the Graphic Art" *The American Journal of Science and Arts* XLIV (1843) Appendix to No 1 (between 216–17 in some copies) 1–12. Spencer states that the machine was known in London in 1820 (11).

comprehends likewise a certain given representation which latter is then referred immediately to the object in point. A single example will suffice to give the meaning of these words. I judge that all bodies are partible, and in this judgment, "All bodies are partible", the conception of partibility, or that which can be divided into parts, is applicable to several other conceptions, but out of these it is here especially referred to the conception of "body", and this conception again to certain appearances and affections which have occurred to us. These which are the ultimate immediate objects of our consciousness are represented or mediately presented by the conception of partibility. All judgments are therefore functions of unity in our representations or official acts by which a unity is effected among our representations, inasmuch as that instead of an immediate representation, and of course therefore a representation *in concreto*, a higher one comprising (or, in logical language, comprehending under it) these and others is employed in order to the knowledge of the object, whereby several possible knowledges (cognitions) are contracted into one. But all acts of the understanding subsequent to the operation essential to and one with the faculty itself and implied in the term "understanding", subsequent to that, namely, for which we have appropriated the term "substantiation" (*seu actio hypostatica*),[1] are reducible to judgments. And the understanding therefore or substantiative power may be adequately defined as the faculty of judging; for it is a faculty of thinking or of discursive thought and thus*a* a knowledge by means of conceptions; and conceptions as predicates of possible judgments refer to some representation or other of some object not yet determined. Thus the conception of "body" refers to something that by means of this conception can be known and judged of—to metal, for instance. But it is a conception only inasmuch as several other representations are comprehended under it by means of which representations it can be referred to existing objects. Did it not contain such representations under it, it would not be a conception, but a form, image, or feeling. The conception "body" therefore is the predicate of a possible judgment, for instance, "every metal is a body". Previously therefore to the consideration of the functions of the understanding relatively to its objects and purposes, it will be advisable to consider the judgments in their own character and relatively to the faculty or as far as the understanding itself is

a ms: this

1 "Or under-standing action". See above, p 239.

alone concerned.[1] It may well happen that the attainment of the one may discover, if not make a road to, the attainment of the other; and that from the forms more strictly subjective we may find the means of deducing the laws on the subject by which objectivity is judicially given and attributed. In other words, the laws under which alone objects are representable as *objects*.

25   Here then we end our retrospect and recommence our progress. We will first enumerate these judgments in a tabular form and annex the few explanations that may appear necessary or expedient.[2]

The judgments are characterised according to

1
Quantity
Universal
Particular
Single

2
Quality
Affirmative
Negative
Limitless

3
Relation
Categorical
Hypothetical
Disjunctive

4
Modality
Problematic
Assertional
Apodictic

Remarks

26   One use of this table is that it gives us an opportunity of pointing out certain differences between common logic, or the canons of the understanding, and the transcendental logic, or the analysis of the faculty itself.

27   First. In common logic, which enquires into the use of the different judgments in connection with each other, the judgments according to quantity are divided into two, the universal, or what we affirm of all in common, being the same with the single. It is indifferent whether I speak of a subject as having no particulars included, an

---

[1] Paragraph 24(b) and the final sentence of paragraph 24(a) are from *C d r V* 93–4 (105–6).

[2] The following table is from *C d r V* 95 (107). Cf *Prolegomena* § 21 (1783) 86. '

atom, for instance, or of all without occasion to particularise any of its parts either by exception or by attributing to one more than to another—as "the ocean" or "the world". It is indifferent as to the use, and of course as to the rules concerning the use of such judgments, whether I think of a thing, or *all*, as *one*. But if I am to speak of the judgment itself in each case in its own nature, in respect, namely, to its own quantity, it would be strange indeed to assert that I form the same judgment where I affirm of a number that it is one and of another that it is infinite. The rule in common logic depends on the principle that the one, or the single point, can have no circumference because it has no extension, while the infinite quantity can have no circumference inasmuch as it has no boundary. Hence the dictum *de judiciis singularibus* and *communibus eadem est ratio*.[1]

28 Secondly. In like manner, respecting the quality, the third species (though limitless) has no place in common logic, which knows only of affirmative and negative, the limitless being comprehended in the former. The reason may be easily understood. In common logic we abstract wholly from the matter or purport of the predicate which may perhaps be negative and consider only whether it be attributed to the subject or opposed to it, or denied with regard to it. But the analyst or transcendental logician contemplates the judgment likewise with respect to the value or purport of this logical affirmation by means of a really negative predicate, and thus, if possible, to determine what advantage is obtained thereby with regard to our knowledge of the subject in general. An example will make this plain. "The soul is not mortal." Here a negative predicate is attributed affirmatively, and by means of this negative I have at least prevented an error; but still I have said no more than this—of the whole extent of possible beings, the mortal forms one division, and the not-mortal another, with the addition that the soul is one of that infinite number of things that remain after I have subtracted all that is mortal. The boundless sphere of the possible is so far therefore decreased that I have excluded from it one portion, the mortal.[a] The remainder, however, still remains boundless, and many other portions might be supposed excluded without the least positive access to my knowledge of the soul or what it positively is, and without my judgment being in itself actually affirmative as well as *formally*.[2]

[a] ms: not-mortal

[1] "For singular and general judgments the reasoning is the same". Paragraph 27 is based on *C d r V* 96 (107).

[2] Paragraph 28 is based on *C d r V* 97–8 (108).

29   Compare with this the position, "the radius of a given circle is curveless". Here the predicate, though as in the former instance negative, is actually affirmative. I acquire a definite and positive knowledge of the line, viz. that it is straight. But in common logic, which respects only the forms of discourse, the two judgments fall under the same character, both are formally affirmative or affirmed of the subject, and with other than formal affirmation the common or formal logic has no concern; but in reference to the judgments themselves and the knowledge derived or derivable therefrom, that is, in transcendental logic, I need not say that it is far otherwise.

30   Thirdly. All relations of the thought in our judgments are: A. The relation of the predicate to the subject. B. The relation of the antecedent to the consequent. And C. That of the division (or distribution) of the contents, and the numbers of the division or distribution to each other. In the first (A) there are two *conceptions*; in the second (B) two *judgments*; in the third (C) *several* judgments are contemplated relatively to each other. "The moral government of the world is marked by perfect justice." This is called a categorical relation, or a relation categorically stated. "If a perfect justice obtain in the government of the world the impenitently and persever-ingly*a* wicked do not escape punishment." This is an hypothetical judgment or position, and as the former contained two *conceptions* in relation to each other, so the latter contains two *judgments* in similar relation, viz. "There exists a perfect justice", and secondly, "the perseveringly wicked are punished". Whether both or either of the positions are true, severally considered, remains undetermined. It is the *consequence* only which is thought of at the moment that we form this judgment.[1]

31   N.B. It is called hypothetical or suppositive (*not* in the popular use, as when we say, of a report, it is only a *supposition*; but) in reference to the primary sense of the word, namely, to put one thing under another, as its ground or basement. Hence this, being the relation of *the antecedent* to the *consequent, or of the ground* to that which it is made to support, is named hypothetical—from ὑπο, "under", and θεσις, "position".

32   Of the third species called the disjunctive judgment, the following is an instance: "The world exists either by blind chance, or by necessity in itself, or by a cause out of itself".[2]

a In ms the letters "ly" have been erased

[1] Paragraph 30 is based on *C d r V* 98–9 (108–9).   [2] Paragraph 32 is excerpted from *C d r V* 99 (109).

33 In this judgment the number of the positions placed in relation to each other is indifferent. There may be two or three or several; but we may still more clearly distinguish it from the second and preceding judgment by the difference in the relation itself, which is not that of consequence to ground but in the first place that of exclusive opposition inasmuch as the one position excludes the other. But in the second place, and when all the positions are taken conjointly as a single judgment in the relation of community—a phrase which I have tried in vain to exchange for a more expressive one—it means, however, that the several positions taken collectively fill the whole sphere of our knowledge on the given point, inasmuch as the sphere of each part is a complement of the sphere of the other. But how, it may be asked, can the same positions be at the same time exclusive each of the other and yet supplemental each of the other? We reply that the first, that is, the character of reciprocal exclusion, holds good in reference to the positive knowledge and the thing itself: thus chance excludes the position of an inward necessity, and an inward necessity that of an external cause. But the same positions are supplemental of each other in reference to the mind and to the possible knowledge or the sphere of possibility. All the knowledge I can acquire is contained within a determinate sphere consisting of three or more spheres. In which of the three it lies is not determined, but that in some one it does exist, and consequently my judgment would be defective if I had omitted either, though at the same time I understand that the knowledge can lie in one only, to the exclusion of the other.[1]

34(a)   This third species is not properly a part of syllogistic logic, though it may at first sight appear to constitute a syllogism in exception or even opposition to the canon which in the first section of this work is laid down as universal—that of clusion, inclusion, and conclusion. Major. "The world exists either by chance or inward necessity." [Conclusion.] "Therefore it exists by an outward cause." In this syllogism the minor is evidently an act of exclusion, and the consequence, instead of being concluded with the major, asserts an absolute identification with a part only of the major. But in fact the reasoning here is not properly logical, that is, discursive and consequently syllogical or syllogistic;[a] as far as it is logical it is a repetition of single positions affirmative or negative; but as far as the conse-

---

[a] Ms unpunctuated

[1] Paragraph 33 is based on *C d r V* 99 (109).

quence and connection of the positions are[a] concerned, it is purely intuitive and mathematical.

34(b)   Take two from three, and one remains. Nevertheless, the disjunctive judgment itself is formed discursively, hath its origin in the understanding, and belongs, therefore, to the analysis of the understanding, that is, transcendental logic, though it does not form the ground of any reasoning purely and exclusively logical. And herein we discover an important distinction between the common and transcendental logic: that the former abstracts from all materials of knowledge and considers the form only. The contents or real import it receives or is supposed to have received from other sources previously.[1] In other words, the common logic employs itself on conceptions already formed and concerns itself with them only as conceptions without reference either to the products of the sense or the affections of the sensibility out of which they were formed. On the other hand, the transcendental logic contemplates the formations of the conceptions and is enabled so to do by including the transcendental aesthetic, and hence, though equally with the common logic it abstracts from mixed intuitions and the affections of the sensibility; yet the pure intuitions and the intuitive constructions lie before it and within its sphere, and from these it is enabled to derive a proper and actual import and substance for its conceptions; and consequently is concerned with judgments that are not merely formal.

35(a)   Fourthly and lastly we are to speak of the modal judgments or judgments expressive of the mode of thinking. A species already by Aristotle accurately mentioned and distinguished[2] and only too prolixly treated of by all his commentators. The mode, say they, refers neither to the subject nor to the predicate, nor to the copula between both, but to the understanding itself; or the mode may be defined as that which expresses the value of the copula in reference to the way of thinking, or the way in which we think it. The judgments in the sentence above given, "The world exists, etc", are problematic, problematically stated. "The girdle of trees below the snowy region of Etna consists chiefly of oak":[3] this is an assertory judgment. "All the angles of every triangle are equal to two right

[a] ms: is

[1] Cf the definition in *C d r V* 102 (111).

[2] *Prior Analytics* 1.2; Aristotle treats of them further at 1.3, 8–22 (25a–b, 29b–40b) and *On Interpretation* XII–XIII (21a–23a). See Kneale 81–96.

[3] C remarked of Mt Etna in 1804: "The fertility at its feet was dimly visible". *CN* II 2202.

angles": this is an apodictic or necessary judgment. The difference between this and the preceding is evident, but yet does not at all concern the use made of them in common logic; the apodictic being treated in the same manner as the assertory and consequently holding no place in its catalogue.[1]

35(b)   When these remarks have been thoroughly considered, the student will do well to revise[2] the table of the judgments and experimentally to convince himself that in it all the functions of his understanding are contained—in other words, that he can form no judgment which, taken in and for itself abstractedly from the matter judged of, or the matter of the judgment characterised either by its quantity, its quality, or relation, or mode, which[a] is not in respect to the first either universal, or particular, or single; in respect to the second, either affirmative, or negative, or interminable; in respect to the third, either categorical, or hypothetic, or disjunctive; and in respect to the last, either problematic, assertory, or apodictic. We may then proceed to the forms of the understanding in relation to the object as far as these forms pre-exist in the mind itself as the conditions under which alone phenomena can *become* objects of the understanding. We suppose the student to know that the accusative case is the same with, and in many grammars called, the "objective", and in one of the oldest, the "predicamental", and that the Greek words answering to predicamental or object predicamental and objective are κατηγορια and κατηγορικος, that is, "category" and "categorical". And lastly, that this word as expressing the fundamental conceptions of the understanding was introduced by Aristotle, and has been continued by all logicians from the time of that great father and founder of logic to the present day, and the differences, important as they are, between the views of the Peripatetic logic[3] and ours do[b] not necessitate and therefore do[b] not appear to me to warrant a change in the name. Our next chapter therefore will contain a table of the categories or pure conceptions with remarks.

a ms: and which   *b* ms: does

[1] Paragraph 35(a) is based on *C d r V* 99–101 (109–10).

[2] In the sense of "review".

[3] I.e. Aristotle's.

CHAPTER [XIV]

1   We will in the first instance present the table of categories, which we assert, and the student will for a while consent to assume, as correct and complete, borrowing a metaphor from the genealogists, only imagining a tree, the trunk*a* of which, as the reader perhaps may have noticed in the gigantic hollies of the New Forest or the cele-brated yews of Borrowdale,[1] the trunk of which is formed by the convolution of several distinct stems rising from a common root; we may consider these categories as the stems or stem conceptions of the tree of knowledge, out of one or other of which all other concep-tions of the understanding arise as far as their essential form alone is spoken of. For it need not be said that whatever is derived [from] without and answers to that which in the physical plant [is caused] by the outward elements and the accident of place and position does not belong to our enquiry; but that we still contrive to abstract from every consideration that cannot be traced to the mind as its source and constitutive principle.

2(a)   Table of categories, being a register of the primitive or stock conceptions of the understanding.[2]

1	2
Conceptions of Quantity	*Conceptions of Quality*
Unity or the one	Reality
Plurality or the many	Negation
Omneity or the all	Limitation

3
Conceptions of Relation
Inherence and subsistence
(Substance and accident)
Causality and dependence
(Cause and effect)
Community (reciprocity of action between the agent
and patient), or the equality of action and reaction

a ms: trunks

[1] Cf WW   *Yew-Trees* lines 16–17: "each particular trunk a growth/ Of intertwisted   fibres   serpentine...".

WPW II 210. C first saw the yews of Borrowdale in Nov 1799. *CN* I 541.
[2] The table is from *C d r V* 106 (113). Cf *Prolegomena* § 21 (1783) 86.

4
Conceptions of Modality
Possibility—impossibility
Entity—nonentity
Necessity—contingency

2(b) This we affirm is the inventory of all the original pure conceptions or synthetic forms that the understanding contains in itself and *a priori*, and by virtue of which alone it is capable of being contemplated as a pure understanding (*intellectus purus*), that is, a faculty having a proper subsistence and not merely a receptivity or passive result of other powers. For by these alone we understand a something by the manifold that is presented to it by the sense, the sensibility, and the senses as the union of the two. But to understand a thing is to think of it as an object. The light streams variously from a thousand surfaces on the infant's eye, which the mother or nurse has brought out into the open air, and doubtless produces the correspondent impressions and sensations; but these exist for the infant only as a chaos or confused manifold which hereafter he will understand, as a tree, a garden, or the like;[1] he will think of the phenomena as objects, and this he cannot do but by a synthesis or union of these with the forms of the understanding itself. But as there can be no conceptions but by thinking of the phenomena under these forms; or, rather, the reduction of the manifold of sense and sensation to these forms constitutes thinking and is what we mean by the word; the forms themselves are properly entitled conceptions.[*] The student will do well to familiarise this truth experimentally for himself by fixing his attention successively on any number of appearances within sight and asking himself, "What is it?" And then examining the grounds on which the answer rested as far as the answer determined the point of its actual existence. Or he

[*] None but the thoughtless (Dr Darwin observed) can consistently talk against theory: for to think at all is to theorise.[2] It would be little more than a faithful version[3] of this remark into the language of logic if to those who railed at conceptions *a priori* we replied that to think of a thing at all is to superinduce some *a priori* conception on the phenomenon that occasioned and excited the act of thinking. And that then, and not till then, the impression became a thing as far as the beholder was concerned.

[1] Cf *The Nightingale*: *PW* (EHC) I 267.

[2] Erasmus Darwin (1731–1802) *Zoonomia; or, the Laws of Organic Life* (3rd ed 1801) I ix: "There are some modern practitioners, who declaim against medical theory in general, not considering that to think is to theorize . . .".

[3] I.e. translation.

may perhaps arrive more easily at the same end by merely examining whether the answer could have been returned, whatever it might be, whether a tree or a clump of trees, a man, a flock, etc, etc, supposing him to have abstracted from all the conceptions specified in the preceding table: whether he could have returned the answer, that is, have determined the phenomenon to be some object, without thinking of it as one or many or all, as real or the mere effect pro-duced by the absence of reality (e.g. in the words, "it is merely an interspace between the clouds") or as partly one and partly the other, which exists in all cases of limitation (e.g. in the so-called "looming" of objects when ships or houses appear in the air above the horizon),[a] or the remaining conceptions found under the category of relation; and, in like manner, whether he could have arrived at any such determination without considering the answer in reference to the mind or conceptive power itself under the so-called category of modality. Is it possible—is it actual? If actual, might it have been otherwise? Or is it necessary? In either way the student will convince himself of the actual existence and necessity of these conceptions if he will reflect and give sufficient attention to his reflections, especially on occasion of appearances strange, or from whatever cause of a doubtful nature, in which the operations of his mind may be suffi-ciently slow for the mental eye to watch them, where the wheel from the impediment or[b] deficiency of the impelling power moves slow enough for the spokes to be distinctly noticed as they follow each other. Let him then try if he can think of any primary conception, that is, of any one which in the first place is a conception and not, like time and space, or *ubi* and *quando*,[1] modes of intuition. And in the second place, primary, that is, not derivable from any higher and simpler one, which is not to be found in the preceding catalogue: and should his attempt be unsuccessful—should no conception answering both these marks occur to him—he will by this negative proof of its completeness be disposed and prepared for proofs positive, any one of which if well grounded will in addition to the former suffice to mature the justifiable anticipation into a rational conviction, viz. that the conceptions contained in the above table *are* and are *all* the stem-conceptions of the understanding in its determination of objects and at once the necessary preconditions and the essential forms of such determination.[2]

---

^a Parentheses inserted　　　　　^b ms: of

[1] "Where and when".
[2] Paragraph 2(b) greatly expands

C d r V 106–7 (113–14); the examples are C's.

3   Now it is evident that this proof must be derived from the mind itself, for we have abstracted from all else. But, if so, it is equally clear that it must be derived by a deduction of these primitive conceptions from some other manifestation of the thinking faculty, by some other agency, act, or product, by which the constitution of the understanding is manifested. But again we know of no other but the judgments or the logical functions exercised in judging. In order therefore to a positive proof of the correctness and completeness of the second or categoric table, its contents must be deduced from those of the first or the table of judgments, and such deduction will give the proof required; for what is deduced must have been implied, but as this deserves to form a chapter by itself we shall fill up the present with a few observations in part explanatory of what has been already said and in part preparatory for that which is to follow.

Remark the first

4   As the character of the mind's judgments is, such or correspondent thereto must be the character under which the phenomena are judged of, that is, objectively determined, or, again, under which alone they become objects for the mind. Let the student refer to the table of the logical functions and compare the several judgments with the table of categories and its contents severally, and he will not only observe the correspondence of the latter to the former, but a little reflection will show him that it cannot be otherwise—that it is almost an identical proposition. For if the impressions (or by whatever name we may designate the materials supplied to the understanding by the sense and the sensibility) become objects in and by the mind's judgments and modes of judging, the mark or stamp (*nota sigellaris*)[1] of objectivity must needs be a counterpart of the seal by which it is communicated and from which it is transferred. Therefore when we have once established the conviction that the radical or most general conceptions of quantity, quality, and relation [and modality] are derived from the mind itself[*] and not communi-

[*] Here it may be well to remind the student that whatever hypothesis he might adopt as a man, whether he stands on the higher ground of philosophy, seen from which mind and nature, subject and object, are one (that is, anterior to that evolution of the prothesis in which mind and nature first appear as the thesis and antithesis), or whether he resolves the former into the latter on the theory of materialism—in both cases, even in the last, even though he should

[1]   "A mark made by a seal".

cated by the phenomena to the subject, but by the subject as to the raw material on which the specific mark of objectivity is to be stamped—when this conviction, I say, has been established, it is evident that the mind having acquired the first table—the table of judgments—by virtue of its self-consciousness by continued reflection on its own acts is[a] in possession of a principle that both guides and predetermines it in the construction of the second or the table of categories.

Remark the second

5 The inherent constitutional forms, or species, of the understanding are evolved out of one[b] common ground or principle, namely, the analysis of the understanding itself, as of the judging faculty (or what is the same, the faculty of thinking).[4] Hence both the

---

be as staunch and contemptuous a materialist as ever sprung from the union of atoms and vibratiuncles,[1] still as a logician he must consent *scientia[e] causa et per hypothesem instrumentalem*[2] to receive the several conceptions specified in the table of predicaments and their pure derivatives as innate, in the alone rightful and alone intended sense of inherent in the constitution of the understanding, or as constituting what we mean by the understanding, whatever it may be in other respects, whether a self-subsistent soul, or a function of the same, or a mere modification of matter, or a common result of two co-agents as the tune from a musical instrument. For the difference of these elementary conceptions from the products of empirical generalisation which always presuppose them, e.g. from the generalised conceptions of whiteness, vegetation, organisation, or from the nouns of multitude, as a flock, a herd, a people, etc, is a fact of consciousness—a primary datum of reflection. As long as we reflect, the categoric species must necessarily appear as the inseparable accompaniments of reflection, as the means by which, or the modes in which, we reflect, and not as the contingent objects of our reflection, not as the materials on which we reflect, and consequently therefore must appear not only different but diverse from these, as long as both the one and the other are contemplated from the point of reflection. But this is as essential a postulate in the science of logic as it is in the sciences of geometry and arithmetic, to contemplate the subject-matter from the point of the pure sense or intuitive faculty. As we cannot become mathematicians but by reasoning according to the laws and necessities of the primary imagination, so neither can we be logicians or discourse logically, but according to the inherent forms and necessary data of the understanding or reflective faculty. What should we think of a man who in proof of the worthlessness and falsehood of arithmetic should assure us that there were no such units in reality, *neque in rebus naturae neque in natura rerum*,[3] as 5, 7, 9?

[a] ms: and   [b] ms: a one

[1] The "atoms" of Democritus and "vibratiuncles" of Hartley.

[2] "For the sake of science and as an instrumental hypothesis".

[3] "Neither in the things of nature nor in the nature of things".

[4] From this point to the end of paragraph 5 from *C d r V* 106–7 (114).

contents of our table and their distribution are systematic and not brought together by luck or chance during the hunt of induction while the mind is beating about for *most general* terms—or (what it may please to consider) *pure* conceptions—without any ground of certainty that the induction is complete and the whole number of such conceptions included in the list, and unable to assign any reason why precisely these and no other should be declared innate or pure conceptions. Herein consists the difference of the preceding table with that under the same name in Aristotle. The mere thought and purpose of seeking and collecting the primary and fundamental conceptions was indeed worthy the great founder or at least the first systematiser of logical science. But as he had no principle to guide his pursuit or predetermine his choice, he took whatever had the appearance of being such as they occurred to him and in the order in which they happened to occur; in this way he ra[n]ked together in the first instance ten such, and called them "categories", which his Latin commentators rendered by "predicaments". Afterwards he believed himself to have discovered five others, which he annexed to the former under the name of [μετα τας κατηγοριας] or "post-predica-ments".[1] Still, however, his table remained imperfect; nor is this all. Not only it did not contain the whole number that should have been comprised in it, but it contained heterogeneous articles that did not belong to it. Thus we find sundry modes of the pure sense in this classification of the forms of the pure understanding, viz. *quando, ubi, situs, prius, simul*.[2] And there is one empirical conception in the list, viz. *motus*,[3] and lastly several secondary or derivative concep-tions are classed as primary, viz. *actio, passio*.[4]

Remark the third

6   Since in these categories we present the genealogical tree of the pure understanding as far as the trunk is concerned, or the stem-conceptions of which the trunk has been found to consist, there can be no doubt that the derivative conceptions if pure are entitled to a place in a complete system of transcendental logic as the branches and boughs of a tree.[5] And this we have in part effected in our

---

[1] Chs 10 to 15 of Aristotle's *Categories*.

[2] "Time, place, position, priority, simultaneity".

[3] "Motion".

[4] "Action, passivity".

[5] The image is Kant's: *C d r V* 108 (114).

glossary, though only in part.[1] For as in the present work we aim chiefly at the exhibition of the main principles of the science, and even by preference to leave for the student what being master of the principles he will himself be equally able to perform, we shall deem it sufficient to give as specimens a few of the most obvious utility and importance, after we have finished an exposition of the categories or predicaments themselves. And as we have adopted the Peripatetic name for the primary conceptions, viz. "predicaments", we follow the example of the modern Aristotle, the founder of transcendental logic, and first scientific analyst of the logical faculty, in designating the derivatives or offsets by the term *predicabilia*,[2] that is, the characters predicable, or which may be affirmed respecting objects in consequence of the predicaments. That the student, however, may not be left altogether without the opportunity of fixing the meaning of the term generally, we will refer him to the predicament of causality, or the causal relation, and by reflection he will soon discover that the notion of power, of active and passive, *agere et pati*, are all reducible to the primary conception of cause and effect, and logically therefore to be considered as derivatives therefrom. If I were to express this technically I should say that the terms *vis, actus, passio*,[3] are *predicabilia* under the predicament of causality, and in like manner that the conceptions "presence" and "resistance" are *predicabilia* under the predicament of community, or the third species under the head of relation.

Remark the fourth

7 The table of categories consists of four kinds, by an attentive consideration of which it will be found that they fall again into two classes, the first of which are appropriate to objects of the sense or senses, that is, to intuitions and images, but that the second have a reference to the existence of these objects or their way of existing, either relatively to each other or relatively to the understanding. The first order may be aptly entitled that of the "mathematical" cate-

[1] This reference to the glossary may have been prompted by a comment of Kant's that appears just after the passage in *C d r V* on which C has been drawing. Kant mentions that "a complete glossary, with all the requisite explanations, is not only a possible, but an easy task". *C d r V* 109 (tr Kemp Smith 115). C changes the remark to an unfulfilled promise, but he may have intended something on the lines of Willich's glossary in *Elements of the Critical Philosophy* . . . (1798) 139–83. Cf also *SM (CC)* 43 and 113–14.

[2] *C d r V* 108 (114).

[3] "Force, action, passivity". C is rendering Kant's German terminology in Latin. The sentence is translated from *C d r V* 108 (115).

gories. The second that of the "dynamic". And in this form we will repeat the specification. The categories are divided into two classes, the mathematical and the dynamic, each containing two kinds, and each kind three species.[1]

8 Table of the elementary conceptions entitled categories or predicaments.

1

The *mathematical,* or those having reference to the sensible forms pure and empirical, are those of quantity and quality.[2]

1	2
Quantity	*Quality*
One	Reality
Many	Negation
All, or the whole	Limitation
In abstract terms, or the	
categories of unity, multeity	
(otherwise called "plurality"),	
and totality.	

2

The *dynamical,* having reference to the existence of objects, are likewise of two kinds, the categories of relation and those of modality.[*]

1	2
Relation	*Modality*
Inherence and subsistence	Possibility—impossibility
(*substantia*[a] and *accidens*[b]	Entity—nonentity
of the elder logicians)	Necessity—contingency
Causality and dependence	
(cause and effect)	
Community, reciprocity of	
action between the agent and	
patient, or the equality of	
action and reaction.	

[*] For the purpose of reference, especially in conversation, it will be easier to quote them by the names rather than by the number of their kinds, e.g. the first, second, and third species of the categories of quantity or of modality, rather than by the first, second, or third of the first or of the fourth genus, or than by the first of the mathematical and second of the dynamical.

[a] ms: Substantive   [b] ms: Accedans

[1] Paragraph 7 is from *C d r V* 110 (116).

[2] Paragraph 8 and its table are from *C d r V* 110 and 106 (116 and 113).

Remark the fifth

9   The first class, or the mathematical categories, have, we see, no correlatives, these being found in the dynamical alone. Thus: accident is the correlate of substance, effect of cause, and necessary of contingent. For this point of difference between the two classes there must be some ground in the nature of the human understanding which by further research we may reasonably expect to discover. For the present it will suffice that we have directed the attention to the point as to a problem which we are to bear in mind [so] that whenever the requisite data turn up we may avail ourselves of the same for its solution.[1]

Remark the sixth

10   Under this head we refer to a former chapter in which we have spoken at some length on the noticeable trichotomy both in the table of judgments and in that of the categories.[2] The circumstance, I mean, of there being the same number of species, three to wit, under each of the four heads, whereas in the common or canonical logic, that is, in all classification *a priori* by means of conceptions, the form of dichotomy obtains. But in addition to this remark we have now to observe another not less noticeable circumstance, viz. that the third category arises in all cases out of the conjunction of the first and the second of the same genus. E.g. unite the conception of the *many* and that of the *one*, and there results the conception or predicament of *all*. So by the conjunction of reality and negation we obtain the notion of limitation, as in the instance of light, darkness, gloom, or twilight.[*] Thus too, community or reciprocal action is but the notion of substance conjoined with that of causality, which is possible only by two or more substances all equally in the relation of causality. And lastly, the notion of necessity or the third species of modality is nothing more than an existence, the affirmation of which is contained in its possibility, or, as the common phrase truly as well as happily expresses it, the very notion of which supposes its reality. But here we must be on our guard not to infer from this fact that the third category in each of the four kinds is a merely composited

[*] Memorandum. "Notion" to be used instead of "conceptions" when predicaments are spoken of.

[1] Paragraph 9 is based on *C d r V*   [2] See above, pp 241–2.
110 (116).

thought, or what the followers of Mr Locke would call a "complex" in opposition to a "simple" idea, that it is a mere general term or term of remembrance, or mark common to two things by means of which we remember both, and consequently that it can have no place among the elementary notions or preconceptions of the understanding.[1]

---

[1] Paragraph 10 is based on *C d r V* 110–11 (116–17).

EDITOR'S APPENDIXES

GREEN'S TABLE OF CONTENTS

GREEN'S TABLE OF CONTENTS

Coleridge's Logic—

A PRELIMINARY OUTLINE OF THE *LOGIC*

A PRELIMINARY OUTLINE
OF THE *LOGIC*

Ff 34–6 of BM MS Egerton 2801 provide a sort of plan for part of the *Logic*, and seem to represent an early phase in C's preparation of the book. They are written in C's hand on leaves measuring 22.4 × 18.4 cm (ff 34 and 35) and 22.0 × 18.4 cm (f 36); f 35 is watermarked BATH 1822.

I. Pre-advertisement—as the terms of the Compact between the Author and the Readers of the Work. 1. The particular *Object* of this Treatise: or *why* the Author wrote it. 2. For *whom* it was written—or the supposed Object, Character and Qualifications of the Readers, to whom as a *Class* of Pupils and Fellow-students the Author, ~~during~~ in the act of composition, conceived himself as speaking. 3. The Nature and extent of the ~~Advantages~~ final results promised on the Author's part: and 4. the conditions on the part of the Reader, under which he stands pledged for the fulfilment of the promise.

II. Sketch of the *History* of the Art of Reasoning, treated as a separate Discipline. Its direct and positive advantages extravagantly overprized in the middle ages; but as much undervalued and its indirect results forgotten, of late times. The Causes and Consequences of the two Extremes. Presumptions in favor of Logic, and the restoration of the same to its former rank as a regular and important part of a liberal Education; but its true Value best appreciated and characterized by a brief Statement of what ⟨(when rightly understood)⟩ it proposes and promises to the Student. The Author's motives for undertaking the Work—1. the non-existence of any work (in our language at least)[1] answering, or even pretending to answer, the same purposes; & 2. The conviction, grounded on observation & his own personal Experience, of the futility of the Objection, that men may be logical Reasoners ~~and~~ without studying Logic, and acute and powerful Debaters without entering into "the Elements of Discourse, or the Criteria of true and false Reasoning deduced from an Analysis of the ~~Discursive~~ Reasoning Faculty".[2]

[1] See above, pp 6ff.
[2] The title C used for the *Logic* in 1823 and 1824. See above, Editor's Introduction, pp xxxix, xlvii–xlix.

III. On Education. The Origin, proper import, and limits of the Term. ⟨Artificial Education prepared and suggested by the Education of *Nature*.⟩ The plan of Education adopted by our Forefathers vindicated against ~~our~~ modern Objections and Improvements, ⟨its several Periods or Epochs enumerated and described;⟩ and not only its superior but its *exclusive* claims to the name demonstrated. The decisive superiority of our great Schools, in which the essential ~~parts of the old plan are still more or less faithfully retained. The~~ defects of the Education there received: and that they are attributable to a departure from the *spirit*, and the too general Omission of one important Division & Constituent Part, of the old Scheme. Improvements and Furtherances in the Art and method of educing and training the mind in accordance with the [?~~true Idea and point~~ . . .] *philosophy* or true Idea of Education; of which the higher Branches of pure Mathematics on the one hand, and the three Divisions of Logic on the other, form the completion & conclusion.

IV. The etymological history of the Word (Logos) from which the Science, ⟨that treats⟩ of Words in relation to connected Thoughts, derives its *technical* name—and the several successive meanings of the word from the visual image, in its simplest and primary Signification, to its last and highest sense in the Christian Theology. The sense of the term as expressing the ground or faculty by which men are enabled to connect words conclusively, that, namely, which our great Dramatist with a happy fullness yet precision names DISCOURSE OF REASON[1] (the *Discursus*; *Vis discursoria*; *Cognitio discursiva*; of the Schools) and to which sense the Author confines himself in the two first Divisions of his Work, determined and explained. The term, *Reasoning*, ~~the~~ by which we *english* the Greek Logismos, apt if not previously explained to suggest a false notion. The Logos, when the *human* mind is the subject, answers to the Understanding, this word being used to express the Faculty of *reflectionng* and *judging* exclusively.—The high importance of Words, and the incalculable moral and practical Advantages attached to the habit of using them definitely and appropriately/ the ~~evil~~ ill consequences of the contrary not confined to Individuals, but extending even to national Character & Conduct. The term in question (i.e. the Understanding) an instance of this: and the contra-distinction of this Faculty from the Sense on the one hand and from the Reason (mens *absoluta*, lumen *siccum*)[2]

---

[1] Shakespeare *Hamlet* I ii 150.

[2] "Mens *absoluta*"—mind in the absolute sense; "lumen *siccum*"— "dry light", for which see Bacon *Novum organum* bk 1 aphorisms 49–50: *Works* I 279; cf *AR* (1825) 207–8 and *Friend* (*CC*) I 482 and n.

on the other, ~~ranks the~~ stands foremost among the eminent services rendered to Philosophy by Lord Bacon. It is indeed the main Object of his Novum Organon, and the ~~Basis~~ central Idea of his System. To the ~~indistinction of~~ unsteadiness in the application of words; especially the use of ⟨"the⟩ Reason" and ⟨"the⟩ Understanding" indifferently ~~and as synonymous~~ for one and the same Faculty, and this for the faculty, the imperfections and narrow limits of which he himself displays with ~~much~~ a depth of insight and a clearness of demonstration hitherto unrivalled; and the consequent adoption of mystical phrases, as Lumen siccum, Visio lucifica,[1] and the like, in order to distinguish the Reason from the Understanding;—to these, aided by ~~some the inconsistencies with the truths asserted in the Novum Organ, that occurs here and there in the~~ ⟨his⟩ other ~~treatises~~ some actual and more apparent ~~contradictions to the Principles Works~~ inconsistencies scattered thro' his numerous Treatises and Outlines, far more than to the Aphoristic form of his great Work, ~~or is it on~~ ought we to attribute the undeniable fact, that ~~Bacon~~ this pre-eminent Philosopher is more talked of than read and more read than understood, or read to any worthier purpose than that of finding quotations and mottos for ornament or authority.

I have enlarged on this point far beyond the bounds of a mere Chapter of Contents; because the hope and persuasion, that the Work, to which and to the preparation I have devoted so many years of Meditation and Research, will, where ever the *desire* exists, supply the *means*, of deriving the full profit from the study of Lord Bacon's writings, that mine of enkindling Truths and pregnant expressions! this hope, I repeat, came in aid of the main Object, that I had proposed to myself, and formed my strongest *supplementary* Motive. What the main Object is, and that which I have kept steadily in view from the title-page to the concluding period, I will explain as briefly as I can, consistently with my purpose—for ~~in~~ from this the Reader of the present Outline, if only he assumes for the moment that the execution [?is ⟨of the⟩ work] corresponds to the Plan, will form a clear conception of the character of the entire Work.

Let me only premise, that in what follows I am speaking of educated men, and that tho' the Remarks more particularly apply to Individuals in public or professional life, they concern all men, whose words are of any importance to themselves or to other men: "In all Discourse and Intercourse of Mankind (says Jeremy Taylor)

---

[1] "Light-making Vision".

by *Words* we must agree concerning each others' meaning":[1] and how is this possible, unless we first determine, each of us what he himself means by them? And how, again, is this to [be] expected where the Individual has never been taught or accustomed to put the question at all? Or, worse still, ~~and a sure way of passing off~~ (tho' one of the most common and approved Recipes for Self-delusion in modern times!) to ~~seek for the~~ *meaning* find out the *explanation* ~~in an English Dictionary, or to learn it (as we say)~~ *by heart* i.e. one or more other words—a scheme of conveying the *meaning* of each term, that might perhaps have answered at the Tower of Babel during the interval between the confusion of Tongues & the Dispersion of the Speakers;[2] but which in any cultivated Language can answer no other end but that of passing-off dim, vgague or confused

---

[1] C quotes the same passage in "The Divine Ideas" (HEHL MS 8195 f 750) and attributes it mistakenly to Taylor's *The Real Presence*. Source untraced.

[2] Gen 11.1–9.

REFLECTIONS ON THE BEGINNING
OF ARISTOTLE'S *CATEGORIES*

REFLECTIONS ON THE BEGINNING
OF ARISTOTLE'S *CATEGORIES*

Ff 36–9 of VCL MS BT 16 are in Coleridge's hand; the paper is not watermarked and the leaves measure 16.5 × 19.8 cm. The first paragraph is devoted to Aristotle *Categories* I 1a and the second to *Categories* II 1a–1b.

Aristotle begins ~~with a~~ by noticing certain differences in the uses of words/ namely, I. Homonymes, ⟨or words of equivocation,⟩ ~~thus~~ when a living & ⟨a⟩ painted animal are both called by one name/ "It is a Dog". The same word demands a different *Definition* in the one case, from what it does in the other. 2. Synonymes, ⟨or univocal words,⟩ when a man & a Lion are both called, animal. By Synonymes Aristotle means Generic Terms.—3. Paronymes, or Denominatives, such as Grammarian from Grammar, Astronomer from Astronomy.*

~~The next~~ He next divides all the objects of the human mind into the two Classes of ~~Predicate, and Subject~~ ⟨Universals & Particulars,⟩ ~~under the names of τα~~ the Λεγομενα, i.e. what ~~is~~ are *said*, and ~~τα~~ the

---

* This short first Chapter, containing in the original not more than a dozen Lines, conveys the *purpose* that accompanied the mind of the Philosopher, during the whole of the work, namely, the ready detection of Sophistry. All just reasoning is confined to deductions from Terms truly generical, or what Aristotle calls Synonimes/ for these the Sophists introduced Homonymes, & produced ~~thus~~ by ~~theiris~~ theirs means the most ludicrous sophisms—ex. gr.—

Omnes canes*a* latret.[1]
Canis cœlestis est canis.
Ergo Canis cœlestis latrat—

And in the like manner ~~by~~ another sort of Puns sophisms were made by the ~~intro~~ substitution of Paronymes for Synonimes—a species of nonsense, to which the Greek Language is more obnoxious, than ours.—I remember that at college we used to call a remarkably dull & prolix Talker the Spectator, because he was *genuine Prose*; which was the cant phrase for a dull converser. Yet it is difficult to conceive, how ⟨such⟩ Conundrums & could ever have formed the subject of serious, philosophical Detection/. This is however the fact, as Aristotle's Book De sophisticis Elenchis sufficiently proves.

a ms: Canes omnes [with a mark indicating that the words should be transposed]

[1] For "latrant".

Οντα, i.e. what ~~really~~ *is* are. ~~the one referring to an act of the mind, namely, a generalization, the other to an external reality.~~ The first ~~class~~ may exist either ~~singly or in connection~~—as Man, ~~or man reasons. As ⟨A⟩ Man—⟨a man conquers⟩~~ We may venture to translate τα ⟨the⟩ λεγομενα general ~~Terms~~, and τα οντα by Entities. unless indeed the first period of this second Chapter belongs, as I suspect, to the first.—It is in the character of the first, ~~& simply divides "what we say"~~ into things said with, ~~or~~ & without connection. The ~~Entities~~ Onta he subdivides, I. into ~~habitual, and accident~~ such as can ~~neither~~ not be called ⟨either⟩ a part or property, but comprize the whole; thus the man, is neither in Plato nor ⟨any way⟩ a part of Plato. 2. into such as are in the Subject, but cannot be affirmed of the Subject—and in the Subject, not as a ⟨discernible⟩ part, but as a quality or property—for instance, ~~such grammatical notions are~~ Geometry is, in the mind, but ⟨it⟩ cannot be ~~affir~~ said, ~~of/~~ the mind ⟨is Geometry,⟩—then too you cannot affirm that White is the essence of any thing, but you say, ~~that thing is white~~ the Board is whiteness, therefore Board is white. 3. Such as are ~~said~~ both said of a subject, & are at the same [time] in a subject—thus Science is in the soul, & ~~is affirmed of Geometry~~ Geometry is Science[a] 4. Such as are neither in ~~any~~ a subject, nor said of ~~any~~ a subject, ⟨but the subject itself.⟩ for instance, ~~a certain~~ any one man, ~~a certain~~ any one Horse.—This is ~~the substance~~ almost a Translation of the second Chapter—~~General . . . terms~~ The Legomena are distinguished from ~~Entities~~ the Onta; and ~~Entities~~ the Onta are divided into such as refer the mind to the whole Class, to the which the Subject spoken of is subordinated—for instance, the man, Plato—these ~~were~~ are called by after logicians, Substantia universales.—2. into ~~accidental Properties~~ particular accidents, as my knowlege of Geometry. 3. into universal accidents, as knowlege—it belongs to the very nature of mind, yet still you cannot say that the Mind is knowlege—4 into particular Substances —Thomas, John, Peter.—(We must not therefore translate Legomena by General Terms, and τα οντα by ~~real Existence~~ things ~~really~~ actually existing—for the three first divisions of the Onta, are clearly nothing more than ~~complex~~ General Terms—the *Man/* ~~Science~~ Geometry/ Knowledge. ~~And~~ this[b] explanation ~~of the Mind~~ seems in the original ~~almost~~ to border at least on an equivocation/ τα δε, καθ' υποκειμενου τε λεγεται, και εν υποκειμενω εστιν, οιον η επιστημη εν υποκειμενω μεν εστι, τη ψυχη, καθ' υποκειμενου δε

---

[a] C has inserted a mark (†) here, probably to link it with the passage that is similarly marked below; ~~see~~ note *b*

[b] C has inserted a mark (†) here; see note *a*, above

λεγεται, της γραμματικῆς.[1] The word επιστημη appears to be used in a different sense relatively to the mind, from that in which it is used relatively to the art of Grammar—S̶c̶i̶e̶n̶c̶e̶ or else it is only another word for the art of Grammar. If we translate it, Science—it seems a strange a̶b̶u̶ Play upon words to say, that Science is a property of the mind, & Grammar is a Science/—and if we translate it, the Science, which i̶s̶ indeed would be clearly false, it says only that Grammar is grammar/ & so would belong to the further division.— To answer this objection we must c̶o̶n̶ think of Grammar or Geometry, not as a *book* or *thing*, but as it exists in the mind of the Grammarian or Geometrician—in this sense, we may justly say, that Knowlege is a property of the mind, & that Grammar is knowlege.—/ The distinction of the Dicta from the Entia, I confess, I cannot at all understand—or why the phrase "Man runs", should belong exclusively to the former and S̶c̶i̶e̶n̶c̶e̶ Knowlege is a property of the mind, s̶h̶o̶u̶l̶d̶ to the latter. But it by [no] means appears, that Aristotle meant a̶d̶i̶s̶t̶i̶n̶n̶ absolute distinction. You may have two separate Classes; & t̶h̶e̶ many of the subordinate individuals, according to the view taken of them, may be found in both. Animals —& Spirits—Man would be found under both— —/

---

[1] "We find there are some things, moreover, not only affirmed of a subject but present also in a subject. Thus, knowledge, for instance, while present in this or that mind as a subject, is also asserted of grammar". Aristotle *The Organon* tr Harold P. Cooke (LCL 1938) ɪ 15. On Aristotle's ambiguities here, see Kneale 25-7.

A NOTE
ON THE DIVISION OF THOUGHT
INTO METAPHYSICS AND PHYSICS

A NOTE
ON THE DIVISION OF THOUGHT
INTO METAPHYSICS AND PHYSICS

In the *Logic* (above, p 44), C draws upon the following fragment in order to distinguish between "The sciences pure and mixed . . . in the order of their senses". The fragment, in C's hand, is BM MS Egerton 2801 ff 85–8ᵛ (the leaves measure from 18.4 × 11.0 cm to 18.4 × 11.2 cm approximately; f 86 bears the watermark "Ruse & Turners 1821").

Μετα Φυσικα[a]

A Noetics = the evidence of Reason*
B. Logic = the evid. of the Understanding
C. Mathematics = the evid. of Sense

Φυσικα

D. Empiric = Evidence of the *Senses*†
Scholium. The Senses = Sense + Sensation + Impression

---

* Noetics: or Truths of Reason applied
     1. to Being = Ontology
     2. to the Will = Theology   *real*
        i.e. to both, as absolute.   Science[b]
     3. to the finite and
        individual Will = Ethics

† The Empiric, ⟨D.⟩[c] brought under the Rules of the Understanding, ⟨B⟩[c] and the Forms of Sense (= Intuitus puri) ⟨C.⟩[c] becomes Experience.

α. Experience in ~~relations~~ application to Figure, Number, ~~succession~~ Position, and Motion successive or co-existen⟨t⟩ee = Physiography: i.e. Description of Nature, as the Aggregate of objects, or Natura *naturata*.

β. Experience; in application to Acts—i.e. manifestations of a Will—simultaneous or su⟨cc⟩essive, of Men; or of Nature considered as an Agent (Natura *naturans*) = History.

Experience, in application to the Laws and Principles of α and β acquires according to the matters so treated the names of

Phaenomenology
Physiology, including Somatology and Psychology
Anthropology
&c &c

a Greek words in pencil   *b* Both words in pencil   *c* Pencilled insertion

293

Now with none of all these, have we at present any immediate concern, B. only excepted. We are now exclusively seeking that evidence, which arises from the perfect coincidence of a Conception or Proposition (i.e. Words intended to express Conceptions,)[a] with the Laws of the Understanding, or the Rules that result from the Constitution of the Understanding itself, considered abstractedly from the its Objects—even as the Mechanist would examine an Engine, previously to its use—or an Astronomer a Quadrant or Telescope.—

It is the same whether we say the Constitution of the U. being considered as the Band or Copula of these. Thus a Steam-engine of course comprizes all the component parts; but these parts considered, in themselves, as individual things, do not involve or constitute the idea of the Steam-engine—the Steam-engine = the Parts + the Copula of the Parts—*Hæccëity* and *Alterity* (Hæc et Altera sive res sive forma)[1]

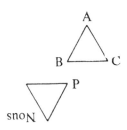

to Being, absolutely considered =
to the Will as absolute and one with the Supreme Reason—=
to the finite Will =
The Truths of Reason are Reason—Therefore we cannot in Noetics as we may in *Logicis* require a Reason for a truth: for it is Reason.——

---

[a] Parentheses inserted in pencil

[1] "The One and the Other, whether a thing or a form".

AN INTRODUCTORY DISCUSSION OF THE SYLLOGISM

AN INTRODUCTORY DISCUSSION
OF THE SYLLOGISM

Ff 1–17 of VCL MS BT 16[1] are transcribed, probably from fairly fluent dictation, in an unidentified hand, and seem to belong to one of C's classes for young men. The paper has no watermark date. A short passage on f 14, dealing with a Latin sophism, is in C's hand. The fragment is of particular interest in connection with the *Logic* because it shows C trying to treat the syllogism in terms of common sense rather than adopting Kant's dry and austere account.

Must not therefore the whole idea of the superior genus be involved in the inferior, and this again in the individual thing? No doubt. But does the converse of this hold good, does the idea of the individual exist entire in the species? the idea of the species entire in the genus? In short is the particular idea completely implied in the generic? No, for in the generic there are wanting many particularities of the individual and it is indeed formed by having these out. You see, then, that you cannot conclude from the particular to the universal, but that you must always conclude from the universal to the particular. You cannot say, since every square has right angles, therefore every four-sided figure has right angles, but we may with truth conclude, since every four-sided figure has four angles, therefore the square has four angles. And yet perhaps this deduction from the universal to the particular will not always hold good. A four-sided figure may have unequal sides? No doubt—the rhomboid has them. What, then, if we were to say a four-sided figure may have unequal sides, therefore a square has unequal sides? Here the deduction from the general to the particular would be false. And why here and not in the former instance? In the former conclusion it was affirmed determinately, it has—since every four-sided figure has—four angles; in the latter it was left indeterminate, since a four-sided figure may have unequal sides. The conclusion therefore from the universal to the particular is false whenever we are speaking of mere possible determinations of the generic idea. In reality here the first proposition no longer contains a generic idea in reference to the

[1] For mention of this ms in Editor's Introduction above, see p xli n 1.

square; [a] four-sided figure having unequal sides is not the generic idea of the square. But perhaps we make this rule too hastily? I think not, for the cause lies implied in the very definition of ideas, the particular idea contains more than the general; but under the attributes which the particular has in addition to those that belong to the general, there may be such, as in this instance of the square, incompatible with the nature of a general idea. There is yet another instance in which the deduction cannot be made from the general [?to] the particular. Can a generic idea, as far as it is generic, have existence? No. Why not? Because it wants the entire determinateness or particularity which all existing things have; therefore, out of the mind, every generic idea is a nonentity, hence said by the old logicians to have their beings in thought, *entia rationis*. What if we were to say, whatever is true of the generic idea may be likewise affirmed of the particular, but every generic idea is a nonentity, therefore every individual subordinated to it is a nonentity? This would be manifestly false. Compare, then, the two cases. In the first case you will find that the contingency implied in the term "may have" applies to a generic idea, only as a generic idea—a four-sided figure taken generally may have unequal sides, but any particular four-sided figure either has them or has not them. So in the second instance you will perceive in like manner that nonentity is, to use the logical phrase, predicable of a generic idea only as a generic idea. You may deduce the following rule: all that holds good of a generic idea only so far as it is a generic idea, or more generic than any other given idea, that does not therefore hold good of the subordinated specific or individual ideas. You will no doubt have heard the name of this sort of argument. Yes, a syllogism. The word simply signifies a connected reasoning. The subject has been enveloped in many learned words, yet nothing in nature can be more simple. You have acquired the habit, we will suppose, of directing the attention of your understanding to the points of resemblance between a number of individual images or sounds or, to comprise all in one, between a number of individual objects, and you have called these acts of your mind by certain names. You remember ⟨no doubt⟩ what you are said to have attained by this process. Yes, we attain by it universal ideas which are likewise called generic ideas, abstract ideas, representative ideas, or general ideas. Quite right. And you remember too that the nature of these universal ideas had been a subject of controversy among metaphysicians, but that such controversy left the logical use of them entirely unaffected. Now a syllogism consists in this: I have agreed to call one class of resemblances or of phenomena having some one point of resemblance by some one name—I see some individual object and I conclude from an examination of its characteristic properties that it is an object to which this name is applicable, and this constitutes a syllogism. Now, for instance, we have all agreed to call that somewhat, which makes the surrounding objects visible, to call [it] light. Now I find by experience that the moon makes every thing visible about me, I therefore conclude the moon is a light; in other words, I mention the class under which a particular object is arranged with reference to some one of its properties. So again, bodies that reflect light without transmitting it we have agreed to call opaque bodies. I perceive that the moon reflects light and that it is not transparent—here again I call it by another name and arrange it under another class. I will multiply examples, for I think it important to impress the truth as strongly as possible that all logical reasoning is simply classification, or adding to the common name which designates the individuality and consequently the differences of things, the generic name which expresses their resemblances. There is an individual man, John Woolman[1] by name; he followed nature in all his actions. All men who do this we arrange under one class and call them the virtuous. John Woolman therefore is virtuous. I have learnt by experience that warmth rarifies the air; I know that the sunbeams are warm; I arrange them, therefore, under this class, and say that sunbeams rarify the air. In some part or other of every syllogism we declare or imply the character of the class, we assume that the individual belongs to this class and we conclude, therefore, that the individual must have this character. But is not this merely repeating the same thing in other words?[*] Some have thought so and in consequence have asserted that all reasoning is made up of identical propositions. How far they speak truly you yourself have seen. Still, however, it appears to me a wanton abuse

[*] [The following passage in C's hand appears on the facing page:] Is this a Syllogism/ John Williams committed murder/ That man ~~com~~ is John Williams/ Therefore That man &c—[2]

1 John Woolman (1720–72), the American Quaker opponent of slavery. In a letter to Thomas Wilkinson on 31 Dec 1808 (*CL* III 156) C uses Woolman as an example of a man who not only believes in "the Voice within" but lives by it.

2 The name of C's murderer is carelessly written and could be Willis or Wilkes, but it seems likely that he was thinking of John Williams, whose exploits have been recorded for us by De Q in "On Murder Considered as One of the Fine Arts". See *De Q Works* XIII 9–124. For De Q's account of C's opinion of the Williams murders, see XIII 75–6.

of language, for though ⟨in every syllogism⟩ I do in reality repeat the same thing in other words, yet at the same time I do something more; I recall to my memory a multitude of other facts and with them the important circumstance that they have all some one or more property in common. The phrase "identical proposition" should be applied exclusively to those propositions which occasion in the mind no recapitulation and, as it were, refreshment of its knowledge and of the operations by which it both acquires and retains it. If you could take away from the human mind the power and the habit of classing its experiences according to its perceptions of likeness, you would sink it to the level of the brute; in all probability far below brutes. Whatever, therefore, keeps alive this habit and intends to invest it with a mechanic facility cannot be said to be barren of good effects. Now identical propositions are likewise called barren propositions, and should therefore be confined to such as are indeed barren. If A is A, A is A. But A is A, therefore A is A. A learned physician tells us the body cannot have the smallpox twice because it is in the first instance rendered inirritable to that particular poison. Now this is repeating the same thing in other words, but this of itself would not constitute it an identical proposition—but it does nothing more, it introduces no third idea, it makes no reference to a class, therefore we may with justice say that the medical philosopher in this instance imposed upon himself and his readers an identical proposition in the place of a reason—that particular poison is another phrase for the smallpox; that the body is rendered inirritable to it in the first instance is again but another set of words signifying that the body cannot have it twice. If the philosopher had said there exists a class of poisons which having once acted on a living body introduces a specific inirritability, and it is probable that the smallpox belongs to this class, he would have given the grounds of the phenomenon and the solution would be satisfactory in proportion to the number of individual instances contained in the class. Nor would it be any objection that he had not enabled us to conceive the manner in which this inirritability was produced.[a] A reason is given—whenever we can classify the fact—but two or three instances will form not a class but an anomaly. In this instance the fact stands single, and the translation of the sentence is given as the cause of the phenomena. But when the same physician says that brandy quickens the pulse and assigns as the reason that it belongs to the excitantia, he here does give a logical though not a philosophical reason—that 500 other

[a] Ms unpunctuated

things have the same property does not indeed enable me to perceive how such a property is possible, but nevertheless my understanding is improved and I gain valuable practical knowledge by being informed that 500 other things very different from brandy in colour, taste, form, etc are connected with it by this one important point of resemblance. Thus too, syllogistic reasoning, by which I desire to imply the substance and not the technical forms, has been called a mere act of memory, and no error will result from this—if only we are made to feel the full importance of such an act, made to understand that in this act our rational nature has its subsistence, that we both reason and act by it and would not act reasonably without it. It would perhaps lessen the reluctance of the imagination, which receives its chief delight from the contemplation of the concrete, if we were to detail the foundation that there is in nature for classification. All the plants of a certain class have hitherto been found poisonous. I am shipwrecked; I find a plant with fruit on it; I have never seen the plant before; I examine the number ⟨and position⟩ of its germens, and its pistils, and by these and other characters I find that it belongs to this class and I reason in this way: if in ninety-nine instances which from the whole of our experience hitherto the species of a certain [plant] have proved to [be] poisonous without exception, there is such a probability as ought to be acted upon that the hundredth will prove poisonous, consequently that I ought to ascertain it by experiments made on some inferior animals, not on myself or any of my fellow men. The plant is the hundredth species of this class, which is therefore sufficiently probable that this too will prove to be poisonous, and I must not ascertain the fact by an experiment on myself. This is an instance of complex ⟨hypothetical⟩ syllogism grounded on a classification of nature's own making. Whether or no all reasoning is syllogistic will be a subject of investigation with us hereafter—at present we will recur to technical language and detail the nature and contents of a syllogism as logicians in scholastic phrase—that by means of which we discover why a predicate is affirmed or denied of a subject is the reason or ground of the judgment. The whale (this is the subject) is improperly called a fish (this is the predicate), for it has hairs on its body and suckles its young (this is the logical ground). A judgment, when at the time we make it we think of the ground of it, or a proposition, i.e. a judgment expressed in words, to which we annex the reason, is called a syllogism. The ground or reason why a predicate belongs to a subject, why anything is affirmed or denied of any other thing, is in all possible judgments the following: because the subject is in reference to the predicate in the same class with some third idea to which the predicate belongs. The mammoth must have been a carnivorous animal, for it has the sharp and jagged teeth which carnivorous animals possess and which distinguish them from the herbivorous animals whose teeth are broad and furrowed. Consequently all syllogisms are formed on this rule: if the subject of the judgment is in the same class with a third idea with respect to a given predicate, then the predicate belongs to the subject, and vice versa. Animals with sharp jagged teeth are never herbivorous; the mammoth having jagged teeth is consequently not herbivorous; consequently the mammoth is not of the elephant class. You will perceive that I purposely avoid the common forms of syllogistic reasoning that you may more clearly understand the [? substance] and its frequent recurrence in the ordinary reasoning in common life.

I will now make you acquainted with the technical forms as far as they are connected with the laws of reasoning or explanatory of them, as far, in short, as they imply anything more than the passion of giving hard names to simple things. Logicians, then, have divided syllogisms into three head classes, the first of which is called the ordinary categorical syllogism; the second, the cryptical or abbreviated syllogism; the third, the compound syllogism. The word "categorical" signifies nearly the same as generical. The categories in Aristotle, meaning those highest abstractions of which he counted ten, but which later writers have reduced to four, under which all ideas may be brought, and before which they may be, as it were, cited before the assembly of the people or supreme judicature (the ordinary meaning of the word κατηγορεω is to denounce before the assembly of the people and thence used for accusation in general). Hence, when I say I demand a categorical answer, I mean such an answer at once deliberate and determinate and final, as you would be obliged to give to a supreme judicature before whom you had been cited. The ordinary categorical syllogism contains the proposition, ⟨or judgment,⟩ and two premises, and altogether three terms; the third term with which the subject of the judgment is classed in the one premise, and to which the predicate is attributed in another, is called the middle term. Thus, in the good old example "every animal is a living thing, every man is an animal, therefore every man is a living thing", the animal is here the middle term. The subject of the judgment which makes its appearance in one of the premises as subordinated to or at least in the same class with the middle term is

called the minor term, and thus in the above syllogism man is the
minor term, and the predicate which in another premise is attributed
to the middle term is called the "terminus major" (both the major
and minor have the common name of "termini extremi"). Of the
two premises, that which attributes the predicate of the judgment to
the middle term is called "enunciatio major", and that which classes
the subject or minor term with the middle term is "enunciatio
minor", or the "assumption". The proposition which declares the
subject itself is called the conclusion. "Every animal is a living thing"
is the enunciatio major; "every man is an animal" is the minor
enunciation or assumption; and, therefore, "every man is a living
thing" is the conclusion. The major enunciatio does not always
appear the first in the syllogism; consequently it is not essential that
the major term should make its appearance in the first or the minor
term in the second premise. This, however, affects the grammatical
form, not the logical substance, of the syllogism. The grammatical
forms of the ordinary syllogisms are 19; and 20, if we include the
form attributed to Galen,[1] but logically there can be but two sorts.
For the minor term is classed either as a species with its genus, and
in this case the conclusion is drawn from the universal to the sub-
ordinate particular: "because every animal is a living thing, there-
fore man, who stands to animal in the relation of a species to a
genus, must be a living thing"; or the minor term is classed as a
genus with its species, and then the conclusion is drawn from the
subordinate to the universal: "every animal is a living thing, every
animal is a substance, therefore certain substances are living things".
The common books of logic following Aristotle give three figures or
head classes of syllogisms. It [the third] differs in nothing essential
from the first; the conclusion is made from the genus to the species,
it concluding indeed always by a negation, but this it has in common
with modes of the first and third Aristotelian figure. We therefore
adhere to our division into two main classes, which,[a] in compliment
to the received terminology, we will henceforth call figures. The first
syllogistic figure draws its conclusion from the genus to the species,
⟨more accurately [. . .] from the more general to the less general⟩:
"all men are fallible, Titius is a man, therefore Titius is fallible".

---

[a] ms: wch. we

[1] C refers to the moods of the three
figures of the syllogism (for a descrip-
tion of which, see H. W. B. Joseph
An Introduction to Logic—Oxford
1966—262ff). The tradition that the
physician Galen (c 129–199) added a
fourth figure of the syllogism, thus
necessitating an extra mood, is now
thought to be untrue. (See Kneale
pp 183–5.)

The second class draws its conclusions from the less general to the more general, from the individual to the species, or from the species to the genus: "every animal is a living thing, every animal is a substance, therefore a certain substance is a living thing". I confess that this second figure appears to me a mere barren and identical proposition. The meaning of the word genus is that under a certain word we class a number of others of more specific meaning than itself, and this second figure appears merely to assert that the component parts of a class are more specific than the class itself; in other words, that genus is genus and species is species. We should not do wrong therefore if we affirm that there really is but one kind of syllogism and that if we exclude propositions perfectly barren from the idea of reasoning, all syllogistic reasoning concludes from the more to the less general. We have, however, retained the division, and if there can result any advantage from this introversive act of the mind we shall not fail to discover it in the course of our logical investigations. The utmost that can be said in favour of it seems to be this, that by reminding us that the genus not only does not exclude but implies certain particularisations in the species which belong to it,[a] it may prevent rash and precipitate judgments, and it has been noticed by accurate observers that men are more often wrong in what they deny than in what they affirm. However this may be, whether we consider syllogistic reasoning as one figure or as two, it is subjected to the following general rules. A proper syllogism contains only three terms. If it contains fewer, some one other is always implied; as when I say, "Titius must be fallible", I imply that Titius is a man. Titius might be the name of a god or of some infallible being. I imply, therefore, the third term, that of the genus or species. If the syllogism contained more than three terms, it is either a compound syllogism, that is, two in one, or it is a sophism built on equivocation. "The virtuous Titius will not frequent the company of Sempronius the drunkard, virtuous men avoid bad company, Titius is a virtuous man, therefore Titius avoids bad company; Titius avoids bad company, but Sempronius is bad company, therefore Titius avoids Sempronius." An instance of the sophism from equivocation. [b]Omnes canes latrant. Sirius est canis. Ergo Sirius latrat.[1]—This in the Latin

[a] Full stop in ms [b] The passage in C's hand begins at this point

[1] The Latin is preceded in ms by a cancelled attempt to make the point with a translation of the example: "All Dogs bark, but Sirius is a Dog, therefore Sirius barks—Here is contained under Dog two Ideas i.e. the Animal Dog & the name Dog."

is a sophism—& sophisms will oftentimes endure translation as little
as Puns. In English we call it not the Dog, but the Dog-star, & even
tho' we had called [it] the Dog, still the use of the article *the* would
have baffled the Equivocation. In the Latin the word "canis" has
two meanings—the animal, Dog, & the constellation called, the Dog
—consequently, here are two Terms in reality, tho' only one ver-
bally.—[a]The first rule, then, is that a proper syllogism must contain
only three terms. In order, therefore, that you may see the whole
process of the reasoning, if there be fewer terms expressed than three,
you must supply the term implied. If there be more ⟨you have detected
an equivocation or⟩ you must new mould the compound syllogism
into two or more simple syllogisms. The second rule is, no conclusion
can be drawn from two particular propositions. "Titius is a red-
haired man" is a particular proposition. "Some men are red-
haired" is another particular proposition, but we cannot conclude
that Titius is red-haired because some men are red-haired, because
here the words "some men" refer you to particular individuals. But
you may conclude that since the man Titius is red-haired, therefore
some men are red-haired, because, in this latter instance, the words
"some men" are only verbally a particular, but are in substance a
universal proposition, a proposition referring to the genus. We may
therefore express the rule thus—in every syllogism, one of the
premises must refer to a genus, for ⟨one of⟩ the premise[s] must either
say that the predicate of the conclusion universally belongs to the
middle term, as in the first figure, or that the minor term is a genus
to which the middle term is subordinated, as in the second figure. In
both cases, one of the premises must be generic. The third rule is,
from two negative propositions nothing can be concluded, for in all
negativing conclusions the contradiction between the subject and
the predicate of the conclusion is no otherwise conceivable than
because the subject is subordinated to some middle term to which the
predicate is contradictory, consequently one of the premises must be
affirmative. There are little grammatical tricks which dress up
affirmative propositions in the language of negative ones, but it is a
trick which common sense will at all times detect without much
difficulty. The fourth rule is, if one of the premises be particular, the
conclusion must be so likewise, for if the subject of the conclusion is
subordinated to the middle term to which the predicate belongs only
as a particular or species, as in the first figure, or when the predicate
belongs to the middle term only as far as it is considered specific, as

[a] The amanuensis resumes

in the second figure, the word "substance" is rendered specific, or, if I may so say, degeneralised, by the prefix "some". In either case, it is alike impossible that the predicate can belong universally to the subject: "every animal is alive, a certain substance is an animal, therefore a certain living thing is a substance". The fifth and last rule is this: if one of the premises is in the negative, the conclusion must be so likewise, for if the subject is subordinated to some middle term to which the predicate does not belong, or if it have the middle term subordinated to it as one to which the predicate does not belong, in either case the predicate must wholly or in part be denied of the subject likewise. You and I are by this time equally tired of thus wrapping up plain truths in technical terms. The truths are indeed in the concrete or particular instances so palpable that it is scarcely possible to make any mistake respecting them; the technical terms, on the other hand, so remote from our common habits of conversation and writing that it is scarcely possible not to confound them. It cannot be denied, however, that it is not possible to generalise completely without the use either of technical terms or of particular instances which are in their nature perfectly representative or generical, such as lines, figures, or the letters of the alphabet, which are as difficult to be remembered as technical or abstract terms. You are well aware of the importance of generalisation and the advantages of being able to express such generalisations in appropriate and perfectly unobjectionable language. You will therefore consider the last seven or eight pages as containing mere exercises to try your patience, if you please, in the steadiness of your attention. Permit me to repeat that I have thus introduced and thus clothed them not so much for the truths which you will learn from them as for the habit which you may exercise by them. When you are by yourself you will read or perhaps write them over again, adding in the margin such particular instances as may illustrate and, as it were, construe, each abstract term, writing in the first place two complete syllogisms, one of the first class, the other of the second, taking care that the terms in each shall be different words from those in the other, and these words and particular instances being added marginally to the abstract term in the rule will keep your attention steady, as an orange and a lemon placed on the table while we were discoursing[a] on the difference between orange and lemon colour, and, at the same time, familiarise you to the valuable habit of seeing the universal in the particular, the abstract in the concrete. Some men are the slaves of

[a] ms: discoursing while we discoursing

their senses, others the dupes of words; to prevent both the one and the other of these diseases we should to every general rule annex in our minds one or more particular instances, and often, though not universally, make or remember some general rule at the time that you are noticing individuals and particulars.

I have expressed a doubt concerning the second figure, which is, you remember, the third figure in Aristotle. We will consider this as *sub lite*;[1] all the rest, however, involved in technical language, and whether wisely or unwisely involved in it, do nevertheless detail and illustrate the actual processes of human reasoning. The other rules and terms, respecting judgments, propositions, the figures of syllogisms and the modes of those figures, appear to me, I confess, a mere farrago of hard names, a lust of classification where classification can answer no one wise purpose, where, in short, class itself can never be mistaken, while the logical exponents or technical phrases expressive of the classification will never be remembered. I will not, however, anticipate the discussion which we have promised ourselves respecting the value of logic as it at present exists, and that we may be the better prepared for it I will at our next meeting give you a short history of the Aristotelian logic, preferring the historical mode of explaining to you terms which can have no interest unless historically considered.

---

[1] "In dispute".

A DRAFT OF A SECTION
OF THE *LOGIC*
IN COLERIDGE'S HAND

A DRAFT OF A SECTION OF THE
LOGIC IN COLERIDGE'S HAND

Two pages of manuscript in Coleridge's hand have been found that show him in the midst of composing the *Logic*. They are in the Beinecke Rare Book and Manuscript Library of Yale University, labelled "Mementos III to V". The first of them appears as the frontispiece of this volume. (For the text see pp 245-6.)

Memento III.

We commenced ~~our present inquiry~~ by adopting the old division of Knowlege into the Theoretic, or intellective, and the Practical, or that which respects the Acts of the Will, the Judgements of Conscience, the Rules of Conduct, and the Laws of the practical Reason:—and it was settled, that as far as the present inquiry was concerned, our attention was to be given exclusively to the former—i.e. the Theoretic.

It was next determined, that we should confine our inquisition, to the data presented to us by *Reflection*, and *as* they appear to us in the act of reflecting; ~~and~~ or to the immediate inferences from these, made necessary by the laws of ~~the~~ Reflection. ~~What⟨ever⟩ these Laws are ⟨may be⟩, we are to learn hereafter, but~~ What these Laws are, is a subject for future inquiry; but be they what they ma~~d~~⟨y⟩e, it is easy to imagine some Superior Being, capable of contemplating ~~both the~~ at once an individual Mind and ~~the~~ its objects, ~~and of seeing~~ judging, how far and in what manner the ~~latter was~~ objects are modified ~~by the mechanism of the former;~~ for the human mind by its own mechanism; and lastly of looking at the Objects independent of such modification. Now he, who disclaims all pretensions to an⟨y⟩ ~~power, such as we have hear⟨re⟩ imagined in the high~~ prerogative of this kind, or who, tho' believing that a *substitute*, or a something *analogous* to it, subsists even for the human ~~intelligence, respond consents to reason without reference to it, ⟨yet wholly abstracts from it, and reasons as tho' it did not⟩ and in the same way as he would~~ intelligence, nevertheless *abstracts* (i.e. voluntarily withdraws his attention) from it and agrees to reason as tho' no

311

such power existed; is said to reas ⟨discourse⟩ or reason of things stand on *the point of Reflection*. And here we agreed to take our position—i.e. to view assume take things as they appeared from the point of reflection, and to assume nothing that by ⟨sense &⟩ reflection alone ⟨⟨including, however, the notices of Sense⟩⟩, we could not have discovered to exist. The problematic superior. . . of ⟨station we may designate as⟩ contra-distinguish from the *ideal point* of Reflection by the designating it as the ideal. And as all *disjunctives acquire an additional* every disjunctive position are is more readily recollected, and acquires the semblance at least of additional clearness, when a distinct name is assigned to that from which it is disjoined, we contra-distinguish the point, on which we do *not* stand, from the point, on which we do stand, by designating the former as *the ideal point*, and the latter as *the point of Reflection*.

Memento IV. Our next step was that of abstracting from all objects existing out of the Mind—and these *collectively* we entitled *the Objective*; and this is the primary sense of the word in the ⟨as⟩ *technically* use used. What remained, and to which alone our attention was to be given, we consented to call the Subjective, or the Subjective collectively.

Memento V. Yet not all, that might be comprized under this head, did we propose as the matter propose to comprehend in our specific inquiry. In the Subject itself we abstracted from the

EDITOR'S ANALYTICAL OUTLINE
OF THE *LOGIC*

EDITOR'S ANALYTICAL OUTLINE
OF THE *LOGIC*

None of the topics discussed in the *Logic* is particularly obscure, and some parts of it are simple enough and clearly enough stated for a child to follow them; nevertheless, the *Logic* is a difficult work to read through. The uneven demands made upon a reader by *Biographia Literaria* are repeated here in an exaggerated form. We may suppose that Coleridge would have improved its consistency if he had revised it. Coleridge's own advice, in Part Two Chapter xii, is sound:

If having read [a] paragraph two or three times attentively you either miss the meaning or find it dim and flitting and that it escapes a steadfast grasp, in this and in other similar cases I would advise you to desist from the effort and pass on.

In many cases Coleridge repeats a position with different examples, and where the first leaves us baffled the second sometimes clears the matter up. The *Logic* offers several kinds of difficulties. One is unavoidable—it is hard to think abstractly, and the subject is essentially abstract. Another is that by translating passages unaltered from the *Critique of Pure Reason* Coleridge has introduced philosophical explication of an advanced and concentrated sort into a treatise that is avowedly elementary. A third is that Coleridge's own exposition does not maintain a steady level of difficulty. Finally, unless one is already fairly familiar with Kantian philosophy (and consequently not in need of the *Logic*), the progress of the work is not made sufficiently clear. It is hard to be sure, especially at the outset, what is digression and what is main theme.

For these reasons an analytical outline of the *Logic* is provided as an appendix in which the progress of Coleridge's main arguments is summarised and separated from what in the editor's opinion is not essential to it. Some examples are introduced for the sake of clarity.

The *Logic* consists of three sections and was evidently intended to contain a fourth. The "Introductory Chapters" are not essential to the case made in Parts One and Two, although they are referred to in both. Parts One and Two belong together in a more conventional manner. In the "Introductory Chapters" Coleridge discusses education and language and the history of the emergence of philosophy. In Part One he begins with an analysis and definition of the syllogism (in the Preface and Chapter i). He moves on to a discussion of perception (in Chapter ii) and returns to the syllogism by giving an account of the four figures. In Part Two, "The Criterion or Dialectic", Chapter i restricts the domain of logic by considering what sorts of questions can justifiably be asked;

Chapter II comments briefly on perception; Chapter III, also brief, refers to the distinction between subjective and objective. With Chapter IV the presentation of the "transcendental aesthetic" begins. Space and time are discussed at some length, and Hume's analysis of causality is refuted. Chapter V distinguishes between analytic and synthetic judgments; Chapter VI describes analytic judgments, and Chapter VII synthetic judgments. Chapters VIII and IX expound synthesis *a priori* and mathematical synthesis *a priori*; Chapters X and XI deal with the nature of mathematical evidence. In Chapter XII, the series of Chapters V–XII is brought to a conclusion with the argument that nonmathematical synthetic judgments *a priori* are possible. Chapters XIII and XIV contain retrospective summaries of important points and introduce the table of judgments (Chapter XIII) and the table of categories (Chapter XIV) by way of anticipation of the unwritten Part Three.

ANALYTICAL OUTLINE

INTRODUCTORY CHAPTERS

Chapter I. Sketch of the History of Logic

1–2(a)   The importance, in the development of civilisation, of defining, distinguishing, and setting boundaries between the various sciences. Modern naturalists and Aristotle are praiseworthy examples; modern French and English works professing to discuss logic (Condillac and Watts) are instructive failures. The defining habit of mind is a mark of intellectual superiority; its rules belong to logic.

2(b)–6   The question of the level of the assumed audience; it is impracticable to suppose that the student knows nothing. Children learn in a desultory and omnivorous way before they are given formal instruction. The length of infancy allows for habits of orderliness to be acquired; the first effort made to help the child is to enable him to make himself understood.

7–12   The origin of the word "educate" in the word "educe"; the way in which rain helps a flower to grow compared with the way in which a teacher should help the child to learn. The first step the naming of things; it is followed by a comparison of the things named, or the noting of their likenesses. The stuff of our knowledge of external nature complete by the time the child has become a boy.

13(a)–13(b)   At this point formal or "artificial" education begins. Its aim, to continue the process already begun and gradually to enable the mind to reflect upon this process. To achieve this end the various faculties of the mind need to be disciplined, just as the body is disciplined by physical exercise. The intellectual powers should be awakened so that they become objects of reflection in themselves. The subject matter chosen for this exercise should be the one derived from the function of the human intelligence. Language is such a subject.

13(c)–15   The comparison of things in infancy involves unconscious abstraction. Artificial education induces the child to reflect upon the way in which he abstracts. Abstraction takes place according to rules, and it is a mental process that is independent of the objects abstracted.

16–18   Recapitulation: it has been found necessary, "in order to call forth, to strengthen, and discipline the powers of the intellect", "to consider them apart from all particular occasions and subjects". Our learning of words prior to our formal education and their being the first subject matter of abstraction makes them an appropriate vehicle for education. Civilisation begins with an alphabet and an accidence, and so should the education of children.

19–22(a)   The origin of language. The parts of speech are derived from a single source, the "verb substantive" ("to be"), and "express either being or action or the predominance of the one over the other". An explanatory diagram is provided; examples of English infinitives that may be regarded either as verbs or as substantives. Reminder that this discussion does not claim to be historical: grammar is being used here as an abstract science.

22(b)–24(a)   The discussion of education resumed. The human intellect differs in kind from that of the animal. The traditional English method of schooling with its emphasis on arithmetic, the alphabet, and the rudiments of grammar as subjects worth study in themselves is justified. It is not the usefulness or applicability of the accidence but its usefulness as a mental discipline that is valuable.

24(b)   The topic of the verb substantive. Instances of the predominance of being and act respectively.

25–29   Conclusion: a summary of the subsequent progress of the pupil through the arts of what C calls "rhematic" (or the art of "arranging words and sentences perspicuously"), rhetoric, and finally logic. A table of these. Although the study of mathematics is undoubtedly valuable to the philosopher, grammar, rhematic, rhetoric, and logic are not only sufficient but indispensable for the practical demands of life "whether for the bar, the pulpit, or the senate".

Chapter II. The history of certain Greek words, showing how their meanings became more precise and how new words were pressed into use to express distinctions between things previously thought to be identical.

1–7   The word "logic" derived from λεγω (I speak). Brief discussion of the Greek language and of the original sense of the letter λ. The original sense of λεγω had to do with picking up, choosing or weighing; λογοι (words) were the results of the choice or weighing.

8–15   Fables, which are oblique expressions of important matters, "words of weight", were also called λογοι. Λογοι came to be thought of as chronicles. Λογοι in this sense were distinguished from artfully arranged speeches or events, επεα (epic poems), whose authors were ποιηται (poets). The nature of poetry distinguished from chronicle. With the introduction of intelligent research, chronicles elevated into ιστορια (history). The poet and the historian having each acquired a distinctive name, the derivatives of λογος were now used to indicate people who were highly informed, intelligent (but not learned). The terms λογιοι and σοφοι (the wise) were still used synonymously.

16–19 Σοφοι were people inspired by a special gift, with which vice was incompatible. Learning was regarded as being irrelevant to wisdom and of little value. Under the influence of Pythagoras and others, learning came to be thought of as useful. The distinction between learning and wisdom was deeply ingrained; it was reintroduced in the term νους (pure reason), which was distinguished from λογος.

20 Λογος came to be thought of as the understanding or "intelligential faculty". It could be considered from three points of view: as distinguished from νους or pure reason; as distinguished from θεωρια or the faculty of sense; or, without reference to either the pure reason or the sense. Logic concerned with understanding considered from this third point of view.

21–23(b) A diagram of the relationship of νους (pure reason), λογος (understanding), and θεωρια (sense) to one another. From these three arise noetic, logic, and mathematics, all of which belong to metaphysics.

23(c)–25 This definition of terms does not imply that they represent truth or reality. Examples of the problems that a discussion of reality would involve: the materialist hypothesis about the mechanism of the brain; the idealist problem of the relationship between what is perceived and what is; alternative theories about reality that can be held.

26–28 The Greeks began by assuming that nature (or the objective) preceded the mind (or the subjective). Experience soon taught them that the senses are fallible and that the objects of the senses are inconstant. They turned to the alternative hypothesis, that the mind or subjective came first. This important step led to the development of a formal knowledge that referred to the mind alone, independent of the world around it. The logician must follow in the same path.

29–31 A synopsis of the main points covered so far. First, we have been asked to consider the mind (or the subjective) independently of nature (or the objective), without committing ourselves to either the materialist or the idealist philosophy. Second, we have been asked to distinguish between formal knowledge and real knowledge. Third, we have been asked to regard the mind as having three aspects: the νους or pure reason, the λογος or understanding, and the θεωρια or sense. A table of the sciences, metaphysical and physical, follows.

32–35 We are concerned with the laws of understanding only, with the way in which it works and not with its subject matter. Some examples of the ways in which we understand. An apology for using unfamiliar technical terms.

Part One

Preface

1–4 Logic that is independent of reality (the objective) consists wholly in the form of the syllogism. It is, therefore, neither a means of discovering truth (organon) nor of distinguishing truth from falsehood (criterion). It is rather a form (canon) to which all valid constructions of the understanding must adhere. Proposes to begin with the canon and then to proceed to the criterion, and finally—a promise that is left unfulfilled—to the organon.

Chapter I. Pure Logic or the Canon

1–2(c) An example of the way in which we come to conclusions. The three steps involved—"clusion" (or "seclusion"), by which we fix our attention upon a particular object out of the manifold around us; "inclusion", by which we note a part of this object, and "conclusion", by which we conclude that what is true of the object must also be true of the part of it. The technical terms for these elements of the syllogism (major premise, minor premise) and the rule that the subject of the major must be the predicate of the minor.

3–6(a) Explanation repeated. A first-figure syllogism used to demonstrate the common-sense implications of the rule that the subject of the major must be the predicate of the minor. The steps of the syllogism rehearsed with the aid of a diagram. All other figures of the syllogism are derived from the first.

6(b)–7 The truth of a legitimate (valid) syllogism depends upon the truth of its premises. An example of a valid syllogism that is manifestly false. Mendelssohn's analogy of the tree whose fibres run from the trunk through to the twigs, and in which what is true of the trunk must therefore be true of the branch, and what is true of the branch must be true of its twigs, but in which what is true of the twig need not be true of the branch.

Chapter II. On the Logical Acts

1–2 Human beings, unlike animals, exert an energy when they perceive things. An object to which we attend may either be really separable from other objects or not really separable, and it may occupy all our attention (clusion) or share it with other objects (seclusion). Seclusion implies comparison.

3–7 When the object is not really separable (e.g. a red tablecloth), we "abstract" from it and by the power of "substantiation" convert the "red" of the tablecloth into the abstraction "redness". The abstraction does not depend upon our having an image of it in our minds. It differs from a "generalisation" and from an "idea". A generalisation involves noticing essential likenesses without ceasing to be aware of accompanying differences (e.g. noticing that a group of animals of different colours and sizes can be generalised under the term "sheep"); abstraction, by contrast, requires that the differences be left out of account. An idea differs from both an abstraction and a generalisation in that it must exist prior to any image (e.g. the idea "philosopher" is prior to our image of Socrates). Some philosophers have failed to make the distinction.

8–9 What is true of a whole must be true of a part of the whole. This modest truth should not be underestimated; being an immediate truth of the mind, it has a higher certainty than evidence of the senses. (E.g. the difficulty of resolving Berkeley's problem about the relationship between what we perceive and what is.)

10(a)–12(a)   What distinguishes the understanding from reason. The understanding has to do only with means, the reason with ends (example of confusing them—the misapplication of the classical unities to Shakespeare's plays). Reason produces ideas, the sense provides us with perceptions, the understanding provides us with conceptions. What are these conceptions? How do we arrive at them?

12(b)–13   A conception is the product of an act that unifies a multiplicity of objects or thoughts. This unifying act takes place at two levels—the level of primary perception and the level of derived perception (e.g. what we perceive unconsciously and what we become conscious of by reflecting). Logic is concerned with only the second of these. The "common conceptions" of derived perception (misnamed "complex ideas") are unified, as the primary perceptions from which they are derived are unified; the unity of primary perceptions has been called the "synthetic function of the understanding", and the act of conscious reflection on them, the "analytic function of the understanding".

14–18   The nature of primary perception is active (the synthetic function); we do not receive sense impressions passively. (Examples, the geometrician's concept of a circle or a line; analogies from everyday experience—the thought of a line connecting two adjacent stars, the lines that seem to be formed by the rapid flight of a cloud of insects, and the effects observed when a piece of glowing charcoal is whirled rapidly about in the darkness). The activity of mind apparent in geometry (which is independent of the senses) must be assumed in the perception of objects too. The relationship between the resulting perception and the objects an important subject, but we are concerned for the time being with the more limited question of the unity presupposed by the action of consciousness.

19–22(a)   The unity of primary perception is contributed by this activity of the mind; we know nothing of what it unites except that (from the point of view of the mind) it must be opposite to unity—the many, manifold, multeity. The act of reflection, which brings to consciousness what has been perceived, shares this unification of the many into one, resolving it into the terms "subject" and "object", and this resolution holds true of all positions.

22(b)–24   The fact that every constituent of conscious thought has been subject to the unifying activity of the mind prior to its becoming conscious is the principle on which all analysis of thought should be based, a principle of reality for the mind independent of whatever is not mind (e.g. nature). A paradox is involved in the independent reality of mind. If reality involves a subject and an object, and the mind is the subject (or object), where do we find the object (or subject)? The paradox is resolved by the supposition of something that is at once subject and object—the self-consciousness of the mind. In grammar, the verb substantive ("to be") reflects the special nature of the position "I am" by requiring that its predicate and subject should have the same case. To say that the position "I am" is the ground of all truth, however, invites the errors into which the dogmatists and the Stoics fell.

25   The dogmatist affirms that the "primary underived truth" begins in self-consciousness. But our self-consciousness is derived or secondary

and presupposes an antecedent act of synthetic unity. The consciousness of a finite being cannot be taken as an absolute (even if the "I am" attributed to God by Moses and the importance of the verb in language might encourage us to suppose that self-consciousness had a significance beyond the finite). We are confined to analysis of the way in which we know things—the principle of the reality of the things themselves is beyond our ken.

26–33 Recapitulation. In seeking a principle on which our certainty can be based, we have rejected the absolute priority of object to subject and of subject to object; the two are dependent on one another as antitheses. The self-consciousness ("I am") combines both. (The principle of our knowing must not be taken for the principle of our being, or reality; the principle of our being belongs to another sphere and we postulate it in the self-consciousness of God.) But the distinction between mediate and immediate truth remains crucial. A series of mutually dependent truths means nothing if it is not based upon an immediate truth. There can be only one such fundamental truth—self-consciousness. What we postulate of God may be asserted (within the limited sphere of logic, or the rules of the understanding) of the mind.

34–38 The traditional logical principle of identity and contradiction (that a thing cannot at the same moment both be and not be) either strays beyond the bounds of logic or is a superfluous tautology. It amounts to no more than the assertion that the act of reflection is the same in all of us. Nor are the terms (what is, what is not), strictly speaking, antithetical. Some of the psychological features of negatives.

39–41(a) Logic depends on three assumptions. First, that the mind (in the sense of pure reason, νοῦς, or God) depends upon a single absolute principle in which knowing and being are identical. Second, that the human reason partakes of this pure reason, and that, although we cannot know to what extent our knowing and being may be identical, the truths of our minds too are independent of the reality of any other thing. (The third assumption is not given.)

41(b)–43 Two ways of defining terms. An object may be unified in itself (e.g. an organic body, or space), or it may owe its unity to the unifying act of the subject that perceives it (e.g. a heap of dust), or it may be both unified in itself and unified by being perceived. A subject (perceiver) may be regarded as an object (thing perceived) by another perceiver; similarly an object may be regarded as a subject from the opposite point of view. These terms depend upon the relationship of one to another and not upon the identity of either. The relationship is reflected in the logical terms "subject" and "predicate". Joining a subject to a predicate by the verb "to be" we call an act of "judging"; it implies an act of comparison.

44–47 Logic has two applications. The first is the almost automatic one in which the form of the syllogism (clusion, inclusion, conclusion) literally reflects the objects thought about (e.g. "All men are mortal, Socrates is a man, therefore Socrates is mortal"). The second, which is sometimes underestimated as being merely verbal, appears in statements such as "God is simple, something simple is noncomposite, God is noncomposite". Even if this syllogism is regarded as tautologous ("simple" being equivalent to "noncomposite") and as adding nothing material to our knowledge, it may be useful by adding to the way in which we know what we know. Whenever a predicate arises in the mind (e.g. the "mortality" of Socrates or the "noncompositeness" of God) as a consequence of another predicate (e.g. the "man-ness" of Socrates or the "noncompositeness" of something simple), even if upon consideration the predicates are judged to be synonymous, the first predicate may be called the "intermediate mark" or "middle term". What logicians call "immediate conclusions" do not differ essentially from the conclusions of a regular syllogism except that the middle term is passed over as being obvious.

48–49   A syllogism of three positions is called a pure syllogism; one of more than three is called a mixed or illegitimate syllogism. Kant's rule for a syllogism of the first figure is that whatever is predicated of the predicate of a thing is predicated of the thing itself. A clearer way of putting this might be to say that when the subject of the major premise becomes the predicate of the minor, the subject of the minor acquires the predicate of the major. Only in syllogisms of the first figure are legitimate conclusions possible; in other figures the conclusions are mixed.

50–52   The second, third, and fourth figures of the syllogism are all merely the first figure in disguise. In the case of the second figure ("No spirit is partible, all matter is partible, therefore no matter is a spirit") the first position has been mentally converted into "nothing partible is a spirit". In the case of the third figure ("All men are sinners, all men are rational, therefore some rational beings are sinners"), the position "all men are rational" requires the inference "some rational beings are men", which, when substituted for it, produces a syllogism of the first figure. The fourth figure is more complicated ("No fool is learned, some learned men are pious, therefore some pious persons are not fools"); the first position must be converted to "no learned person is a fool", and the second position to "some pious persons are learned", and then we have a syllogism of the first figure once again.

Part Two. The Criterion or Dialectic
Chapter I.

1–3   When attempting to answer questions it is essential to know what can rationally be asked. The ancients divided them into two kinds, the simple (which can be answered affirmatively in the same words, or negatively by the addition of "not") and the complex (which cannot).

4–5   It may be more helpful, however, to consider not how many kinds there are, but what a question is. A questioner wants to know something that will allow him to complete an imperfect position ("Who is the author of the *Iliad*?" "Homer is the author of the *Iliad*"). The interrogative word is like the "x" of algebra, and its case further limits its nature ("who", "whom", etc). Even so-called complex questions are really simple, therefore, requiring merely the name of the unknown "x" or the reply "I do not know". All questions must be answerable in these terms—if a question is incapable of completion, the defect must be pointed out to the questioner.

6(a)–8(a)   This conclusion applied to some common metaphysical questions. The question "What is truth?", taken in an objective sense, is absurd, because it requires the answerer to provide at one and the same time a universal criterion (abstracted from particular objects) of the relationship of knowledge to particular objects. Except in the case where God is said to be Truth (the identity of Being and Knowing), the question is self-contradictory. If the questioner asks after truth in a subjective sense, however, we come within the domain of logic. What is valid in logic is subjectively true no matter what its relationship to real objects may be.

8(b)–12(a) There is a third sense of this question in which the relationship between word and thing is sought. The question, "What are things in themselves?", is defective because we have no means of knowing things except subjectively. It is as if we were to ask what a circle is exclusive of its circumference. Newton's question as to whether or not the universe can move in space is also a contradiction in terms because the movement could only be detected in relation to some other object in space and by definition any object in space is part of the universe.

12(b)–14 One more example of the difference between objective and subjective truth is Mendelssohn's instance of the four-sided pyramid suspended in air and looked at by different observers from different positions. To the question "What is its shape?", a variety of answers will be returned, depending on the position of the observer. We must, of course, distinguish between the subjectiveness of the position and the sort of subjectiveness that might arise from peculiarities in the individual observers (e.g. defective eyesight). The question in this example should really be "What objective figure will account for the variety of figures subjectively perceived?"

15–17 The distinction between the subjective and objective ways of looking at things and the dangers of confusing them are sometimes dismissed as merely verbal (although disputes about the Word of God are the most important disputes of all). In fact, as Kant has maintained, disputes about words are an essential part of philosophy. Only ignorance can explain the charge that the mediaeval philosophers used words loosely— indeed, their fault was too great a subtlety in definition. Whatever their deficiencies, they were superior to their modern successors in all philosophical (nonscientific) fields, and even the tracts of the first half of the seventeenth century show a better grasp of logical connection than the writings of our contemporaries do.

18(a)–18(b) The maxim that philosophical controversies can be reduced to disputes about words is common but false. Mendelssohn's application of it to the controversy over necessity and free will, in which it is asserted that the controversy arises out of a confusion between obligation and compulsion. The confusion did exist; it is now avoided, but the controversy that gave rise to it has not been resolved. The detection of equivocal terms is indispensable to the solution of philosophical controversies but it is not a substitute for it. One way in which discussion can be advanced is to restate the question in different terms.

19–21(b) The danger of dismissing philosophical problems as mere disputes about words is that to the idle it provides grounds for self-complacency, while the active (e.g. Bayle) are seduced by it into sophistry.

One other warning must be added. When words are used equivocally they may reflect a confusion of thinking (a comical example is provided). The exposure of such ambiguities should make us all more aware of the slack way in which we think. A dictionary that traced the development of words historically, taking into account both their natural development and the accidents that befell them, would be of immense benefit to society. The realisation of such a dictionary lies far in the future, but those who are competent would do well to contribute materials towards it.

22(a)   The maxim that once you have learned how a thing acts or is acted upon it is unnecessary to ask what it is is also false. The question, "What are things in themselves?", as we have seen, is (from the limited point of view of logic, which abstracts from objects) unanswerable by subjective means. It would be equally inappropriate to attempt to apply the wholly subjective requirement that things should have a cause to things beyond the domain of the subjective.

22(b)–24   Berkeley's argument that "nature" or the "material world" is only a modification of the perceiver's being fails entirely to apply beyond the domain of the subjective. He never establishes his first position —that "all sensations subsist in the sentient exclusively". If, instead, we were to regard sensation as merely one of the modes of perception, the superstructure of Berkeleyanism would fall. (Language too is against it, in that the verbs of sense—"feel", "see"—are transitive.)

25–26   The second maxim is valid in logic. The danger of assuming a wider validity for it will be apparent if we consider how we form our idea of God, in which we distinguish between His reality and the reality of appearances (which can themselves be distinguished into different kinds— e.g. the suspended pyramid, a shadow, a ghost). Some of the attributes of the reality of God.

27   This reality, however, is not within the domain of logic—it is assumed in the "is" of each position in a syllogism. This reality cannot be deduced from logic, not because it is false, but because it transcends logic.

Chapter II. On the Discussion of the Premises in All Logical Reasoning

1(a)–3   We have seen that we have two sources of knowledge of objective reality, the reason and sense impressions. In sense impressions what is impressed is not the forms (for these we have discovered are properties of the mind itself), but in sensations that seem to be independent of our own acts we refer them to objects outside us. It is difficult to separate what is contributed to the sense impression from outside from what is contributed by the mind itself.

4–5(b)   What we know of nature enters our consciousness by way of the senses (and must be accurately observed before we can arrive at appropriate conceptions), but our previous knowledge contributes to the accuracy of our observation. In the case of a single distinct external object the use of logic is restricted to examining the validity of the syllogism in which it appears—a limited usefulness. But the subject of human discussion is rarely a single, distinct, external object.

6(a)–6(b)   For ordinary purposes the process of arriving correctly at a conclusion by way of seclusion and inclusion is almost instinctive, and yet to reflect upon it consciously, especially when the conclusion is at odds with our moral convictions or with common sense, is of great benefit to the mind (e.g. a concealed fallacy in Plato).

Chapter III.

1(a)–1(c)   Common logic can be either pure or applied. In pure logic we abstract entirely from empirical conditions and restrict our attention to the construction of the understanding. Take the sextant as an analogy. It may be considered in three ways: first, with regard to the objects at which it is aimed (e.g. stars); second, with regard to the way in which it presents them (i.e. by reflection in a mirror); and, third, with regard to the construction and parts of the instrument itself. The first way of considering the sextant is analogous to the empirical sciences; the second, if applied to the pure sense, constitutes geometry, arithmetic, and, if to the understanding, logic; the third can be applied to the sextant but not to the mind.

1(d)   What is wanted is a means of telling the subjective share in perception from the objective share. Another analogy would be provided by an automaton potter. We can consider the vessels it produces (it is assumed that we are allowed to see the products only and not the raw materials); we can consider the series of motions that it can perform; or we can consider the construction of the machine (the mind differs from the potter in that its materials may be furnished to it from within as well as from outside). In this analogy, the vessels represent knowledge derived from experience, the constant series of movements represents the formal sciences (geometry, arithmetic, syllogistic logic), the construction of the machine represents the highest of all contemplations.

1(e)–3(a)   This knowledge of the constitution of the mind is the key to all knowledge, and it is the duty of the professional classes to pursue it. They should become conscious of the ultimate principles to which their opinions are traceable, and they can only do so if they learn: first, what the senses are (including the subjective as distinguished from the objective); second, a knowledge of the objective; and, third, a knowledge of what transcends both (i.e. God). Our knowledge of the subjective must necessarily precede our knowledge of the objective (the objective being merely the nonsubjective) but it presupposes the prior existence of a somewhat prior to both.

3(b)–5   This somewhat is expressed in the word "is". Reality, as we have seen, may be the contingent reality of nature or the absolute and necessary reality of reason. We are restricting our enquiry for the time being to the science of the universal forms of the pure sense (what has been called "transcendental aesthetic") in which, not experience, but the conditions that render experience possible are concerned. (A distinction is made between this "transcendental" knowledge and a "transcendent" knowledge, the latter being beyond human capacities.) The transcendental aesthetic, or critical or judicial logic, must take the place of investigation into the constitution of the understanding.

Chapter IV. Judicial Logic, Including the Pure Aesthetic

1–2(b)   One of the most regrettable results of the absence of a philosophical class in England is the vagueness of terms. The words "intuition" and "intuitive" provide a case in point. Strictly speaking, although intuition implies "beholding", it differs from "perception". In beholding by means of the bodily senses, other acts of the mind (of which we are unaware because they are so rapid and because we are used to them) are combined. These intuitions through the bodily senses are therefore called "mixed intuitions". Since what we call "nature" includes our bodies, and bodily sensations so far as they are not the products of our own faculties, these mixed intuitions are outside our present topic. Our attention is confined to knowledge that all human beings share.

2(c)   The pure intuitions of space and time must be distinguished from these mixed intuitions. An intuition is a representation in the mind that is immediate (e.g. the image of a tree), immediate in the sense that it is not arrived at by intermediary steps. An intuition may be related to the object (tree) or independent of it (e.g. the tree may be imaginary). An intuition with which sensation has nothing to do is a pure intuition.

2(d)–2(h)   When we perceive an object, the faculty that permits us to receive the intuition is the sentient faculty, or sense. If we intuit something free from sensation, the faculty involved is the faculty of "pure sense". The understanding allows us to think of these objects. The sense can only present an object to the understanding under the forms of space and time, and we cannot imagine any object (even God!) independent of space and time. Space and time should therefore be of great interest to us. Are they realities independent of the mind, to be conceived of in relation to things in themselves, or are they merely features of the constitution of the subjective mind? It will be necessary to give an exposition of them.

Space

3–6(b)   Space is not a conception derived from experience. It is presupposed in referring any sensation to a cause external to us—outward experience is dependent on the notion of space and not vice versa. Space is a precondition of all experience—we cannot think a form without a space for it to appear in. Space must be a quality or faculty of the mind. It is not a conception (generalised from objects), it is a pure intuition. Nor are we justified in supposing space to be an eternal truth of reason. If space is neither a conception of the understanding nor a universal truth of reason, it must be an intuition. And if it is not derived from particular forms or images it must be a pure intuition.

7–9   We may therefore conclude: first, that space is not a property of things in themselves; second, that space cannot be contemplated as a single particular intuition, for it is the antecedent of all particular intuitions. Although a certain difficulty arises in our not being able to illustrate space by a particular image, we must nevertheless resist the temptation to attribute space to the things that appear under the relations of space. The errors into which Leibniz and Clarke fell in their discussions of space.

10(a)–11(a)   Examples of things that appear to be identical (e.g.

spherical triangles of identical dimensions) and that yet cannot be put in place of one another (e.g. in the opposite hemisphere); in such cases the relation of space reveals that they are different. The faculty of sense alone is affected by the comparison involved, not the understanding. This illustration should help us to see the difference between the objective and subjective as well as the difference between the sense and the understanding.

11(b)   The example of the kaleidoscope. In it, the beauties that we see depend upon the symmetry with which the instrument displays its materials and not at all on the nature of the materials themselves. What symmetry is to the kaleidoscope, space is to the faculty of sense.

Time

12–17(b)   Time stands in the same relation to the "inner sense" as space does to the "outer sense". It is not an empirical conception, but a ground and condition of our observation of simultaneity, succession, etc. Further, time is necessary to our intuitions—as was true of space, we cannot think it away. Time is one-dimensional (i.e. different times cannot be copresent), whereas space has three dimensions. Time is not a conception generalised from particulars, it is an intuition. Unlike space, the intuition time has no limits; however, the investigation of this difference would take us beyond the scope of the present enquiry.

17(c)   It remains to be seen whether metaphysics is possible. The possibility can only be assessed by means of transcendental logic, and the question is therefore deferred to the third part of this work (which is lacking).

Transcendental Exposition

18–23(d)   Time is a form of the inner sense (i.e. of the intuition we have of ourselves and our own state), it is not a property of outward appearances. It is the formal condition *a priori* of all outward phenomena. Time is wholly subjective in the metaphysical sense of the word, but it is a universal subjective (i.e. common to all normal human beings). We cannot assert that it is a condition of the inner sense for all finite beings, and certainly not for an infinite being. The objection that time must therefore be real is met by admitting that time is real but pointing out that its reality is subjective.

Chapter V. Of Analytic and Synthetic Judgments

1–2   Whether judgments are *a priori* or *a posteriori*, they may be distinguished from one another as "analytic" (those which elucidate what we already know) and "synthetic" (those which add to what we already know). Examples.

Chapter VI. Analytic Judgments—the Common Principle of

1   The principle of identity and contradiction is common to all analytic judgments. This principle is a principle of reason; it is not derived from sense or from understanding. All analytical judgments, therefore, are *a priori*, no matter how empirical their terms may be.

Chapter VII. Of Synthetic Judgments and Their Principle

1   Synthetic judgments require another principle besides the principle of identity and contradiction. All judgments of experience (those in which the predicate could not be attached to the subject but by means of experience) belong to the synthetic class. Synthetic judgments, therefore, can be *a posteriori*.

Chapter VII. On Synthesis *a priori*

1–6   The implications of Hume's discussion of cause and effect have been obscured by the misplaced zeal of his religious opponents. As Kant has pointed out, it is an axiom of metaphysics and of science that whatever is not the first cause must have had a cause. Cause and effect can be thought of abstractly as logical entities or concretely as things that stand in a relation of cause and effect to one another. The logical entities can be expressed thus: A (of which B is not a constituent part) is so connected to B that if B is given, A is necessarily presumed (e.g. A = father, B = son). This is a synthetic judgment. Hume asked why the relation of cause and effect should be accepted as necessary with relation to natural objects.

7–9   When Hume asked for proof of the notion of causality, he did not question its expediency, nor did he confuse cause and effect with antecedence and concomitance. He did not question the existence and validity of synthetic judgments, or the difficulty of explaining away what seems to be the necessity of causality. His solution was to attribute the notion of cause and its necessity to custom. His conception was confused in three ways: in his taking necessity to mean merely a vague inability to do without; in assigning a cause to causality that itself presupposed something else; in being at odds with the very experience to which he appealed (e.g. that experience teaches children *not* to suppose that coincidence necessarily involves cause). The notion of cause and effect could not come into the mind from outside.

10   Hume's belief that he had found an empirical solution prevented him from seeking a higher one. If his premise that the notion of cause and effect is derived from experience be granted, his conclusion (that cause and effect is not a necessary connection) must be admitted.

11–12   The theological consequences of this conclusion. Hume denies that there is a necessary connection between A and B when B is not contained in A (i.e. analytic). He did not deny the necessity of mathematics or of common logic, but he regarded both as merely analytical. It was not until Kant suggested that other judgments were of a kind with cause and effect that progress could be made.

13   Two questions are involved. First, are mathematical judgments analytical only, or are they not rather synthetic *a priori*? And, second, if they are synthetic *a priori*, are there any other such judgments besides the mathematical? To confute Hume we need only prove that these questions can be answered affirmatively. The previous discussion of the *a priori* forms of space and time has been preparatory to this end.

Chapter IX. On Mathematical or Intuitive and Logical or
Discursive Synthesis *a priori*

1–3   Hume and his contemporaries assumed that mathematical reasoning
was analytical. The question as to whether it might be synthetic only
needed to be asked. The Euclidean geometry clearly cannot all be implicit
in its first position. By way of experiment, however, consider the position
"$7+5=12$", or, more dramatically, consider the sum of 35,942,768,412 and
57,843,647—it is plain that only by a synthetic act can the answer be
arrived at, the act of combining these numbers according to rules derived
from the inherent form of the intuitive faculty. The same is true of the
fundamental principles of geometry (the few that are analytic, e.g. the
whole is equal to its parts, are merely reminders).

4–5   The failure to apply the distinction between analytic and synthetic
can best be explained by the philosopher's wish to occupy himself with
metaphysics, a realm beyond the understanding, in which the antithesis is
resolved. The Epicurean, by demanding more of the understanding than it
is capable of, finds it wanting and dismisses it as useless. Logic too can be
underrated. It is like a cabinet of empty drawers, but it provides us with a
useful way of arranging and categorising our thoughts. The distinction
between analytic and synthetic knowledge is limited in its application to
the study of the faculty by which such knowledge is made possible. Its
proper sphere is in the critical examination of the constitution of the
mental faculties; it was first adequately exploited in Kant's *Critique of
Pure Reason.*

6   The absence of the distinction in earlier writers gave rise to all the
mistaken scientific demonstrations of the existence of God and of the other
truths of morality and religion—with bad effects, first, because they
sacrificed the challenge of faith to the necessity of assent; second, because
they brought religious truths not susceptible of "demonstration" into
disrepute; and, third, because they could be used just as effectively to
prove the nonexistence of God, etc (indeed Spinoza and Hobbes are more
likely to persuade the majority than Clarke, Wolff, and Berkeley are). The
great advantage of syllogistic logic is that it defines the limits of the
understanding; the transcendental logic further limits the conclusive
evidence of common logic to the truths based on the princples of identity
and contradiction. Truths beyond these are not within the domain of the
understanding.

7   Had Locke carried his enquiry into the limits of the mind's power
to make synthetic judgments a little farther, he would have been led into
the transcendental logic. It is not surprising that Hume missed the import-
ant distinction; fortunately the barrenness of Hume's conclusions inspired
Kant to rethink the whole matter.

Chapter X. On Mathematical Evidence

1–2   We have seen that mathematical judgments are synthetic *a priori*.
How are they possible? Mathematics is the great example of a science of
human reason independent of empirical evidence. It is based neither on the

principles of identity and contradiction nor on supersensual ideas. *A priori*, only the constitutive forms of the sense and understanding and their derivatives are left. If we hypothesise that the transcendental aesthetic has two parts—one circumscribed and perfectible, the other indefinite and illimitably progressive—the latter would form a science by itself. We need only assume that it is mathematics. By way of testing the assumption we shall examine whether or not the subject matter of mathematics is the acts of the pure sense under the universal forms of space and time.

Chapter XI. Of the Ways and Means by Which the Mind Arrives at Mathematical Evidence

1–5   There are no degrees of certainty, but certainty may be more or less evident. What gives mathematics its certainty? First, our knowledge of the component parts is complete (cf chemistry, in which any change in our knowledge of the elements may alter our conclusions) because we define the constituent terms. In mathematics the possibility of being deceived by one's terms is removed. The constructions of the mathematician's mind (triangles, cones) are syntheses *a priori*. Further, this synthesis *a priori* is always pure intuition. The problem as to how we can have a pure intuition in the mind prior to a mixed intuition is solved by the supposition that the pure intuition is composed of the forms of the sense.

6–9   Reference back to the chapter on space and time and the consideration of a simple mathematical operation will show us how synthetic *a priori* knowledge is possible, how mathematics—which is synthetic *a priori*—is possible, and how mathematics differs from other synthetic *a priori* knowledge. Take, for instance, the pure intuition that space has three dimensions; this truth is grounded on the position that not more than three straight lines can intersect each other at right angles at one point. Or, again, the perfect equality of two given figures can in no way be learned from experience of them, but it can be intuited. And although geometry furnishes us with helpful illustrations, arithmetic shares its certainty. In the position "$3 \times 3 = 9$ and $9 \times 3 = 27$", the intuition of time is involved. Algebra and calculus are equally certain.

Chapter XII. On Synthetic Judgments *a priori* Other Than Mathematical, or on the *a priori* Connections of the Understanding, or Logical Conceivability

1–2   It is possible for the judgments of mathematics to be synthetic *a priori* because mathematics is grounded in the faculty of intuition. The truths of mathematics are only applicable to the objects of the senses (being derived from the forms of the sense). Before we proceed farther, however, we should bear in mind that conceptions are necessary to mathematical reasoning as well as intuitions. Synthetic judgments all require not only intuitions but a pure conception (not derived from experience). Only then can a judgment of real validity and significance result.

3–4   Even in the simple positions of mathematics a pure conception is required. E.g. the axiom that a straight line is the shortest between two points involves the intuition of the line but also presupposes that the line is comprehended in the conception of quantity. One cannot think of any given line without determining it as being longer or shorter. But this determination depends on a comparison with a line not present to the mind, and its length in turn depends on a comparison with another, *ad infinitum*.

5   One should not be discouraged by the unfamiliar difficulty of abstract thought; if a paragraph does not yield its meaning after two or three readings it is better to press on. The difficulty will often be dispelled later.

6–7   In the discussion of quantity, thoughts and not things were referred to. For instance, a whole that is antecedent to its parts cannot be an object of the senses, but only a thought. When we say that the universal conception, quantity, is innate and *a priori*, we mean that the mind is so constituted that it must contemplate objects in this relation.

8   The objection that quantity need not be a pure conception is based on a misunderstanding of what a conception is. A conception has to do not with things but with the way in which things are arranged by the mind. If conceptions were merely generalisations of sense impressions we should be obliged to think of the mind as a merely mechanical thing. To refuse to acknowledge the possibility of a whole that is antecedent to its parts because we cannot be shown one is to be wilfully blind to a solution that is of the highest importance for us.

9   We are trying to learn, first, what the understanding in connection with the forms of sense and the affections of the sensibility can do, and, second, what it cannot do. The former is the sphere of logic.

10–11   Ideas may be defined as truths acknowledged by both our free will and our intellect. The terms "principles of the understanding" and "principles of the sense" are introduced.

Chapter XIII. Of Transcendental Logic Positively

1–4   One of the functions of the understanding is to decide which of the phenomena we perceive are objects. It is therefore a substantiative power, and it exercises itself in the faculty of judging. The understanding both gives substance and attributes it. Substantiation, as we have seen, consists in the necessity of reflecting under such forms as quantity. Can our judgments be classified?

5(a)–7   All judgments can be classed under one of the following forms: quantity, quality, relation, and modality. Each of these "predicaments" is comprised of three species. A trichotomy may be observed throughout the analysis of the mind.

8–10(b)   Memento I. One of the first things the student must learn is to trace words to their origin—one good effect being to emancipate his mind from the senses and develop the power of abstraction. On this principle, the word "image" may be used for representations of senses other than the sense of sight. As Kant points out, it is not always possible to express abstract notions with images.

11   Memento II. The term "image" may be used by way of contrast to "impressions", but ought not to be used to describe pure intuitions.

12–13   Memento III. We began by dividing knowledge into two parts, the theoretic and the practical, and confined our attention to the theoretic. We confined it further to what we learn from reflection. By disclaiming any insight (such as God might be thought to have) and seeking merely a human analogy to it as a substitute, we agreed to assume nothing that we could not learn from sense and reflection—we stood on the "point of reflection".

14   Memento IV. We abstracted from all objects outside the mind (the objective) and confined our attention to what was left (the subjective).

15(a)–16   Memento V. From our consideration of the subjective we excluded the affections of sensibility and the passive impression on the senses. The powers of perceiving and conceiving were left, the sense and the understanding. The subject matter of logic was to be the knowledges possessed by the understanding, whether derived from sense (from intuitions) or from reflecting on its own acts. We also found two principles (called principles of reason, for their peculiar character suggested a higher origin—the reason), the principles of identity and contradiction. The knowledge thus obtained was called discursive.

17   Memento VI. Truth may be approached in two ways—by the science of intuition (mathematics) and by the science of discourse (logic).

18(a)–18(c)   Memento VII. Logic is divided into two parts: first, the syllogistic, which is concerned with the forms of discourse and the rules generalised from them; second, the transcendental logic, or analysis of the understanding.

19–20   Memento VIII. Understanding has been distinguished from sense. It is a faculty of conceptions, not of intuitions. Our perceptions, insofar as they are sensual, are grounded on the affections of the sensibility; insofar as they are pure intuitions they are grounded on the productive acts of the sense.

21(a)–22(b)   We have already distinguished between the unity of totality and antecedent unity. The term "constitution" expresses this twofold unity. Although totality, which is the consequent of an antecedent unity, need not contain all that was in the antecedent, it can contain nothing that was not. The antecedent unity may consist of various attributes (indeed, the term unity implies a combination of different elements). The constitution of the mind is intermediate between the unity of totality and an antecedent unity. The differents unified in the constitution are manifested by its "function". We must guard against either forgetting the differents that are unified or supposing that they are divisible or separate (i.e. that understanding and sense are really independent of one another).

23   It is worth reminding ourselves that we are only speaking of the understanding as an attribute. We can personify the mind without involving ourselves in a delusion. Consider the analogy of king and court in which we personify the court and attribute unity to it and its actions. The unity of action of the court is its function. The sense and understanding may be thought of as functions of the soul. The function (unity of action) is an antecedent unity. A mechanical analogy may be found in the kaleidoscope and engraving machine.

24(a)   Our conceptions originate spontaneously in the understanding. The understanding uses its conceptions by judging by them. As all representations refer immediately to intuitions or affections (of the sensibility) and only mediately to objects, no conception refers immediately to an object, but either to an image or a previous conception.

24(b)   In every judgment (e.g. "all bodies are partible") there is a conception equally predicable of a number of things (i.e. partibility), and this number comprehends a certain given representation (i.e. all bodies), which is the one referred to. The conception "body" is combined with the conception "partibility" (both mediate and not immediate representations) by the function of unity in a judgment. All acts of the understanding are reducible to judgments, and understanding may be defined as the faculty of judging. Before considering the functions of the understanding, it will be advisable to consider judgments.

25–35(a)   The table of judgments, containing four headings, each with its three species: quantity (universal, particular, single); quality (affirmative, negative, limitless); relation (categorical, hypothetical, disjunctive); modality (problematic, assertional, apodictic). The following difference between syllogistic logic and transcendental logic emerges: that in each case the distinction between the first and third term (e.g. universal and single) in transcendental logic is not made in syllogistic logic.

35(b)   The reader is advised to review the table and to convince himself by experiment that it is complete.

Chapter XIV.

1–2(b)   The categories may be considered as the stems or stem conceptions of the tree of knowledge. They are conceptions of quantity (unity, plurality, omneity), of quality (reality, negation, limitation), of relation (inherence and subsistence, causality and dependence, community), and of modality (possibility—impossibility; entity—nonentity; necessity—contingency). These are all kinds of pure conceptions *a priori* contained in the understanding. An infant may perceive a mere chaos in the manifold around him; when he begins to think of its components as objects he can only do so by a synthesis of what he sees with the forms of the understanding itself. The forms are conceptions. Again, the reader is invited to test the completeness of the table for himself.

3   Proof of the completeness can only be derived from the mind itself, and the categoric table must be deduced from the table of judgments. First, however, some observations, in part preparatory for what is to come (the missing Part Three), and in part explanatory of what has gone before.

4   Remark I. Phenomena must be judged of in a way correspondent to the character of the mind's judgments (cf the two tables). If once the conceptions, quantity, quality, and relation, are shown to be derived from the mind itself, the categories will follow.

5   Remark II. The forms of the understanding are derived from analysis of the understanding itself. They are systematic, not experimental, and that is why they differ from those of Aristotle.

6   Remark III. We are concerned here with the stem conceptions of the tree of pure understanding. The derivatives (*predicabilia*) may be affirmed as a consequence of these, however (e.g. the notion of power is reducible to the conception of causality).

7–8   Remark IV. The four kinds in the table of categories fall into two classes, the mathematical (intuitions and images) and the dynamic (exist-ence of these, or their way of existence). The table follows: 1) mathematical—quantity (one, many, all or whole), quality (reality, negation, limitation); 2) dynamic—relation (inherence and subsistence, causality and dependence, community), modality (possibility—impossibility; entity—nonentity; necessity—contingency).

9   Remark v. The mathematical categories have no correlatives, where-as the dynamic have—a difference that must have a ground in the nature of the human understanding.

10   Remark vi. Note again the trichotomy of species in each table—by contrast with the dichotomy of syllogistic logic. Further, the third species always arises out of a conjunction of the first and second, but we must not suppose that the third is merely a composited thought.

INDEX

INDEX

act(s) (*cont.*)
232, 298, 326; of moving 240; of own organisation 165; passive separated from 75; of perception 38, 71, 77, 78; of personality 252; of position 73; of precluding 63; primary a., of apperception 78, of seclusion 55; primary mental 76; producing 218; as product 240; productive a., of intuitive faculty 244, of sense 249, 332; pure a. inconceivable 21; of pure sense 214, 330; of reason 254; of reflection 46, 57, 78, 79, 90, 132, 220*, 233, 240, 245, 311, 320, 321; reflection on own 246; of seclusion 60, 95; of seeing 135, 146; self-conscious 74; of sense 152; simultaneous 45*, 141, 165; spontaneous 141, 165; of subject 75, 133; of substantiation 61; of subsuming 227; successive 45*; synthetic 77, 177, 202, 329; of understanding 60, 61, 68-9, 70*, 77, 78, 132, 152, 169, 246, 255, 333, essential 239; unity of 254; verb expresses 82; of will 164, 218, 245, 254, 311; *see also* action(s); process
actio 267 and n
hypostatica 255 and n
action(s) 317
community or reciprocal 270; conception of 267n; of consciousness 320; determined 124; expression of 16, 21; geometrical 74; indifference of being and lxvi, 17; laws of 152; of machine 142-3; moral responsibility for lxiv; productive 218; and reaction, equality of 269; reciprocity of 262, 269; separated from agent 251; source of being and 93; understanding 255n; unity of 251, 253, 332; voluntary 124
active and passive 268
activity, conscious 66
actus 268 and n
adage, Aristotelian 226, 227
adamant
axe against 194*; gates of 199
Addison, Joseph (1672-1719)
Spectator 107n, 173 and n, 218n, 287*
ad indefinitum, motion 222, 224
adjective 21*
conversion of a. into substantive 61; in grammatical form 88; *see also* adnouns

Admiralty, Board of 253
adnouns 16, 20
adverbs 16, 20
Aeolian harp *see* harp
aerology 135
Aeschylus (525-456 B.C.) 67
aesthesis, sciential or transcendental 149
"aesthetic" 149, 204
aesthetic, the
pure 213, 326; transcendental 146, 147, 213, 214, 248, 260, 316, 325, reference to discussion of 196, 207*, 219, 224, 225*
affection(s) 255
of sensibility 164, 191, 235, 246, 249, 254, 260, 331, 332; of space 162; of subject 163; of subjective sense 162
affirm, to 21*
affirmation(s) 89, 98
"is" in 77, 146; and laws of reason 112; mental 79; metaphysical, logical and sciential 86-7; universal 240
affirmo 91 and n
Africa, interior of 121
African(s)
empiric of 187; palavers of 27
age(s)
curriculum for different lx; Hume's 198; present 226
agency
derived from act 83; divine, immediate acts of 220; external 142; reason as 254; sense of pure 149; sphere of 232n; unknown 162
agent(s) 262
act inseparable from 176; in act of combination 80; actions separated from 251; external 77; instrumental, of vision 135; nature as 293*; originates act 83
agere et pati 268
aggregate 229
of appearance(s) 128, 156; of ideas, conceptions, images 37; of inferred powers 45n; mass 232*; of objects 45*, 190, 293*; of phenomena 14, 45n; units by 93
"ain" *see* "ayin"
air 83, 188, 299
difference of breeze from 119-20; globules of 22*; motion of 96
Akenside, Mark (1721-70)
The Pleasures of Imagination q 199 and n, 200; *Poems* 199n
Albion 237* and n

COLERIDGE, SAMUEL TAYLOR (1772–1834)

faculties (*cont.*)
153; sum of 153; of thinking 246, 255, 265, 266; of understanding 178, 205, 242, 255, 256; understanding appropriate to human 60; unsensuous f. of knowing 248-9; voluntary 152; *see also* intuition(s); judging; sense(s)
faintness, in distant objects 189
Fairclough, Henry Rushton (1862-1938) *see* Horace; Virgil
faith
absurdity of orthodox 208; distinguished from intellectual procedure 66; in existence of external world 133; expecting proofs for 207-8; in God 199; interests of 190; involuntary 129; life and freedom of 207; negative 41n; pre-existent to confirming arguments 133; universal and involuntary 129
fallacy
about disputes about words 123; in Plato 325; *see also* error(s); sophism(s)
fallibility 303-4
false, the
contrary of f. true 89; definition of 122; objectively 118
falsehood(s)
of arithmetic 266*; in logic xlix, 131
falsity 71
fanatic 208
fancy/fancies 53, 92
act of 61-2; automatic trains of 126; of beholder 130; half 39; image in 223; subjective 38; survivors of ancient facts 40; task suited to 39; trying to 156 and n; wild 166*
"fantastic" 160
fashion 19
fat 237*
fatalism 208
father 180, 186
Father, Our lxvi
Fawkes, Guy (1570-1606) 182
fear 187
"feel" 129
feeling(s) 170, 255
of animal life 189; blind 192; common 193*; of difference 203; of disgust 24; of expectation 92; of hatred 24; intense 24; laws and rules of 135; necessity of 190; of necessity 183, 191; negative arising from painful 91-2; passive 191; and seeing 129

feet 229
fence, ring 54 and n, 55
fever 127
healthful 8
fibres 58
Fichte, Johann Gottlieb (1762-1814) 14n
error of Germans since lxvi; on intuition 151n; mockery of 87n; his system of idealism 87
Das System der Sittenlehre 151n; *Ueber den Begriff der Wissenschafts-lehre...* 14n, 87 and n
Ficino, Marsilio (1433-99) 236*
fiction 39
fig-tree 190 and n
figurability
representations of 94; of space 94
"figure", senses of 118
figure(s) 44*, 159, 224, 293*, 306
active power of 94; in beholder's mind 164; coincidence of 222; contemplation of 73; four-sided 298; geometrical 73, 226, 245; indistinctness of particular 160; as perception in space 34; perfect equality of 222; plane 161; product of acts 73; production of 73; question which is true f. 117; sciences of 23; space not representable without 46; of speech 241; spherical 161; spiral 75; *see also* syllogism(s)
finding wrong thing 92
fingers 201, 234
finis finium 68
finite, the 229
fire 187 and n
living 213; sacred 241*; seeming to burn 218 and n; spark of 174n, 175
firefly 213, 240
first, absolute 135
fish
motion of 14; whale not 301
"fix" 21*
fixation 233
"fixture" 21*
flambeau, light of 74
flats 223
Fleet Street *see* London
flint, of gun 175
flitting
of attention 199; discontent with the 137
flock 264, 266*
flour 65

understanding(s) (*cont.*)

pure 214, 263, 267, conception of 227, 228, products of 213; purposes of 165, 255; reality cognisable by 134; reason *see* reason, and understanding; and reflection 89, 197, 204; reflects objects 40; reflexes of 40; relation of principles of reason to 237; relation of "tall" to "short" and 83; rendering u. unsubstantial 204; repetition of synthetic act in 77; results of 242; rules grounded on 204; rule(s) of 34, 44*, 64, 112, 240, 293*; science of rational 76; sense distinguished from 34, 68, 154, 248, 282, 327; source, of 70, of truth higher than 203; sphere of 235; student's 243; submits to a position 135; substantiation and 61, 239; syllogism and 64; synonym for 89; synthesis of phenomena and 263; term supplied by 235; a thing defined 215; things in 227n; tree of pure 267; truth that passeth 235; twofold character of 70, 239; of words 150; *see also* mind(s)

understood 98 and n

unicity, indistinguishable 250

union

propositions by 209; subject matter of 77

unitas collectiva 253–4

units 266*

by aggregation 93

"unity, productive" 231*, 253

unity 229, 233, 262, 269

of act 254; of action 251, 253, 332; ambiguity of 251; analytic 90, 94, function of 81; antecedent 250 and n, 251, 253, 254, 332; of apperception 76, 78; of attraction 250*; attribute contemplated as 251; bearing witness to 79; common 138; communication of mind 80; completed in percipient 94; conceived through abstraction 251; of conception 62; of consciousness 71, 239; consequent 250 and n, 251; contained in conceptions 68*; contrary to subjective wholes 93; derived 70; of differential powers 250; distinct 251; essence of consciousness 71; in which form consists 134; function(s) of 68–9, 68–9*, 70, 73, 255, 333, of synthetic 78, 90, of u. twofold 70; generality contem-

plated as 69*; of given intuition 228; individual 253; intrinsic 94; making and receiving 78; and mind 78–80; in mind of geometrician 73; of object 321; occasion of 94; operative 254; in organ of sense 93; of perception 73, 93; personal 253; plurality involves no breach of 46; positive 94, 250; of primary perception 70, 320; principle of 77; productive or producible 250; real 253, 254; of repulsion 250*; resulting 250, 253; and sameness 250–1 and n, 250–1*; several 251; supplied by poet 28; synthetic 76, 90, 94, 321, "is" grounded in 76–7, 90, products of 78; synthetic function of 81; of totality 249–50, 332; twofold 250; what is opposite to 77; of whole 73

"universal" 234

universal(s) 40, 287

logical sign of 99; opposed to individual 43*; particular and 95, 111, 166, 306

universality 173

absolute 247; given by reason 97; in reason 212; strict 167; of syllogistic form 95

universe 199

change of place of 119; grains of sand in 231n; motion of 115, 116; *see also* heaven(s)

universities lx

unlearning, effort of 148*

"unreal" 129

unthinking, the most 134

Uranus 195n

Urteil 79

Urteilskraft 79 and n

usage, criteria of 112–13

v, letter 25

vacuum, infinite 116

vain, the 124

validity

a priori 145; of distinctions subjective and logical 93; independent of experience 193*; objective 227; practical 191; real 227; of synthetic judgments 186

vanity of vanities 131

vapours 135

variation, in optical instruments 140

Veal, Mrs (Defoe) 172, 173n

INDEX
OF GREEK WORDS AND PHRASES

The English equivalents of Coleridge's Greek words and phrases are included in the main Index.